68-70 Red
London W
libraryholbo...
020 7430 7099

DISCLOSURE IN CRIMIN
PROCEEDINGS

To Sparky

DISCLOSURE IN CRIMINAL PROCEEDINGS

John Niblett, O.B.E

BLACKSTONE
PRESS LIMITED

First published in Great Britain 1997 by Blackstone Press Limited,
9–15 Aldine Street, London W12 8AW.   Telephone 0181-740 2277

© John Niblett, 1997

ISBN: 1 85431 598 6

British Library Cataloguing in Publication Data
A CIP catalogue record for this book is available from the British Library.

Typeset by Style Photosetting Limited, Mayfield, East Sussex
Printed by Livesey Limited, Shrewsbury, Shropshire

Contents

Preface

In 1981, I was promoted to take charge of the prosecution office at Knightsbridge Crown Court. My career with the Metropolitan Police Solicitor's Department had taken me, in the previous 16 years, to offices at most of the London Crown Courts but my move to Knightsbridge coincided with significant changes to prosecution practices and procedures. In addition to a heavy and varied case load emanating from the court's catchment area of central and west London, prosecutors soon had to get used to the requirements of the newly published Attorney-General's Guidelines on Disclosure which took effect from the beginning of 1982.

If prosecutors thought they had a lot to contend with then in relation to disclosure, they would have blanched at the duties which would be imposed on the prosecution a decade or so later as the disclosure rules were subjected to frequent scrutiny and change by the higher courts. By 1991, the prosecuting solicitor's division of the Metropolitan Police had been well and truly absorbed by the Crown Prosecution Service and my own career path had taken me out of the courts to head one of the branches in the DPP's Policy Group, where I was given responsibility for issues of disclosure and public interest immunity.

This book is, therefore, born out of many years' practical experience of not only implementing the disclosure rules of the day but also advising prosecutors on how the developing law should be followed. The views expressed in the pages that follow, however, are my own and not those of the Metropolitan Police or the Crown Prosecution Service. Indeed, by the time the disclosure provisions of the Criminal Procedure and Investigations Act 1996 came into operation, at about the time that this book was completed, I had been retired from the CPS for nearly two years and had taken no part in any discussions leading to whatever prosecution policy may now be in operation in relation to the disclosure of material to the accused.

Just because a career is spent entirely in the prosecution service does not mean that one is myopic to the hardships and unfairness that are sometimes encountered by the defence as a result of the disclosure rules. In tracing, and commenting on, the history and development of the law relating to disclosure, I have tried to be objective and to set out as fully and fairly as possible the difficulties and obstacles encountered by both sides.

As this book was written before the 1997 General Election, any references to the Government should be taken to mean the former Conservative Government.

I owe a debt of gratitude to many persons who have, either directly or indirectly, influenced this book. Former colleagues in the MPSD, notably Walter Ball and Bill McCrory, were major influences on my early career and Chris Newell and Ken Ashken, then Directors of CPS Casework and Policy respectively, provided me with help and the opportunity to tackle the ever-increasing demands of the changing law. I am particularly grateful for the library facilities offered by Robert Brall at CPS Headquarters, Bob Chronnell, the Chief Crown Prosecutor at St Albans, the University of Hertfordshire Law Library at St Albans and the Central Resources Library, Hatfield. My thanks also to Sue Ross for helping to keep me up to date with new case law and to Martin Niblett for his assistance with the research and checking of key documents and reports.

A number of persons were good enough to provide either information or comments on my drafts of the disclosure position in other jurisdictions. My thanks to W. Gilchrist of the Crown Office in Scotland; Michael Liddy from the DPP's Office in Dublin; J. Pike from the New Zealand Crown Law Office; Elizabeth Kelly from the Commonwealth Director of Public Prosecutions Office in Australia; and I. Greville Cross, QC, the Deputy Director of Public Prosecutions in Hong Kong.

My thanks also to Heather Saward and Alistair MacQueen from Blackstone Press for their help and encouragement during the book's long gestation period. But above all, thanks are due to my wife, Ann. Early retirement by husbands is often greeted with mixed enthusiasm by their wives. In this case, however, my demands for attention, opinions and general advice were met with encouragement and assistance beyond the call of duty, which was greatly appreciated.

John Niblett
May 1997

Table of Cases

Table of Statutes

Table of Statutory Instruments

1 Introduction

In the early hours of St Valentine's Day 1974, a police constable detained a woman standing in a doorway in the centre of Liverpool. She told him she had just arrived from London but her luggage had been stolen there and she was now going to Newry in Northern Ireland by the night boat for Belfast. No one could possibly have anticipated that from such an ordinary and commonplace occurrence, the law on the disclosure of material in criminal cases would be so significantly and dramatically changed nearly 20 years later. The woman's name was Judith Ward and the outcome of her appeal in the summer of 1992 was to signal one of the most important developments in criminal proceedings this century.

Following her detention, Ward was interviewed over a period of several days by a number of police officers. She was eventually charged with causing explosions at three separate locations. The first was at Euston station on 10 September 1973 where a number of people were injured and over £5,000 worth of damage was caused. The second explosion was on a motorcoach travelling on the M62 motorway on 4 February 1974. Twelve of the passengers, including two children, were killed and many more were injured. Ward was also charged with the murder of those killed in the explosion. Lastly, she was alleged to have taken part in an explosion eight days later at the National Defence College at Latimer in Buckinghamshire. On this occasion no one was killed but many were injured and damage in excess of £6,000 resulted.

On 3 October 1974 Judith Ward pleaded 'not guilty' to each of these allegations at Wakefield Crown Court. The prosecution case was based largely upon confessions and admissions made to the police. Scientific evidence was also adduced to link the accused with each offence. At the conclusion of a four-week trial, she was convicted on all counts and sentenced to a total of 30 years' imprisonment. She did not appeal and remained in prison for some 18 years. Then, on 17 September 1991, in the wake of successful appeals by other alleged IRA terrorists, the Home Secretary referred Ward's case to the Court of Appeal in exercise of his powers under s. 17(1)(a), Criminal Appeal Act 1968.

At the appeal hearing, it was argued that the confessions and admissions could not be relied upon as true. It was also claimed that the scientific evidence was unreliable. At the heart of these twin arguments were allegations of non-disclosure of material evidence by the prosecution. In allowing the appeal, the Court strongly criticised all those individuals and organisations comprising the prosecution that had failed in their duty of disclosure. In delivering the judgment of the Court in *R* v *Ward* (1993) 96 Cr App R 1, Glidewell LJ stated (at p. 22):

> Non-disclosure is a potent source of injustice and even with the benefit of hindsight, it will often be difficult to say whether or not an undisclosed item of evidence might have shifted the balance or opened up a new line of defence . . . we are satisfied that the failures to disclose on the part of the prosecution which we have found to exist were of such an order that collectively, and in some cases individually, they constituted material irregularities in the course of the trial.

Responsibility for the most substantial failures was shared by the West Yorkshire Police Force and the office of the Director of Public Prosecutions (the DPP). While the Thames Valley and Metropolitan Police Forces submitted all their statements to the DPP, West Yorkshire Police revealed only 225 of the 1,700 statements they had taken. Some of the material not submitted to the DPP contained police interviews and notes of conversations with Ward. Had those statements been revealed to the DPP and disclosed to the defence, Ward's tendencies to fantasise and to make and withdraw false confessions would have been apparent. Furthermore, one police officer had made a witness statement saying that he found the defendant's protestations of innocence, made at one stage of her detention, convincing.

The DPP could not, of course, be criticised for failing to disclose what he did not know existed, but there were statements that had been submitted to his office which were not disclosed on the grounds that they were not considered to be relevant. The decision not to disclose was taken on the advice of prosecuting counsel, and the collective judgments of those responsible for the case in the office of the DPP and counsel were condemned by the Court although it was made clear that there was no suggestion of relevant material being withheld deliberately.

Not only were the investigating and prosecuting authorities censured, so too were experts who had been instructed by the prosecution. Psychiatrists who prepared medical reports on Ward were accused of putting the interests of secrecy and security before the interests of Judith Ward. Had certain information been made available to the defence, those preparing Ward's defence would undoubtedly have realised that they required the assistance of psychiatric advice.

Perhaps the severest criticism of all, however, was reserved for forensic scientists who gave evidence at the trial. They were accused of making misleading and exaggerated statements calculated to discourage investigation by scientists instructed on behalf of the defence. For example, in relation to the Euston bombing, a 'faint trace' of nitroglycerine on a hand swab taken from Ward was described in the scientist's statement simply as 'positive', while analysis sheets and laboratory notes in respect of samples taken from a caravan where Ward had stayed, which revealed only 'faint' and 'very faint' traces, were not disclosed. In addition, it was further stated that prosecuting counsel had been misled by the answers given to certain questions that he had raised with the forensic scientists.

The outcome, according to Glidewell LJ, was a grave miscarriage of justice as a result of the prosecution's failure to carry out a basic duty of disclosing material evidence. He then went on to summarise the principles of law and practice which, at the time of the judgment, governed the disclosure of evidence by the prosecution before trial. These principles are discussed in detail in chapter 7, but so radical were at least two of the propositions that it was axiomatic that prosecutors would have to revise substantially procedures they were adopting in respect of the disclosure of information. It was made clear that the Court had not overlooked the *Attorney-General's Guidelines for the Disclosure of 'Unused Material' to the Defence* but the inference was that the *Guidelines*, which prosecutors had been following for the past ten years, did not truly reflect current law.

Ward is undoubtedly a watershed in relation to the law on disclosure. While the *Attorney-General's Guidelines* had, on occasion, been considered by the Court of Appeal and had been subjected to close scrutiny by (the then) Henry J in *R v Saunders*) (unreported, Central Criminal Court, 29 September 1989, transcript T881630), *Ward* was the first time that the Court of Appeal had suggested that they may at the very least be incomplete and, at most, unlawful. Since 1992 the law in relation to disclosure in criminal proceedings has developed rapidly and its progress has been far from smooth and free of confusion. At the same time, the expansion of the doctrine of public interest immunity in criminal proceedings has caused major practical difficulties for all participants in the criminal justice system.

Disclosure is at the very heart of the criminal process in England and Wales. The law on the subject is relevant to the way police officers and other investigators conduct and record the various steps of an investigation; the manner in which prosecutors prepare a case for trial; and the practices adopted by counsel for the Crown when discharging their responsibilities. Disclosure is also central to the way in which defence practitioners prepare and present the defence of their clients. It is surprising, therefore, that until the Criminal Procedure and Investigations Act 1996 (hereafter referred to as the CPIA 1996) entered the statute books on 4 July 1996, there had been no formal system of discovery in criminal proceedings.

In contrast, civil proceedings have been characterised by comprehensive procedures for discovery. Over a century ago, it was held in *Compagnie Financìere du Pacifique* v *Peruvian Guano Company* (1882) 11 QBD 55, that not only documents relevant to the issues in the case should be disclosed but also any information which would enable a party to advance its own case or damage that of the adversary. Today, Rules of the Supreme Court (RSC) enable the parties to discover from one another (and exceptionally from a non-party) documents and other information relevant to the proceedings in advance of the trial itself. If information is not disclosed voluntarily, compulsory procedures exist to obtain the material. The test for ordering a party to produce documents for inspection by the other party under RSC Ord. 24, r. 13 was the subject of recent scrutiny in *Wallace Smith Trust Co. Ltd (in Liquidation)* v *Deloitte Haskins & Sells* (1996) *The Times*, 12 July 1996, when guidance was issued by the Court of Appeal on the approach to be followed.

Until the arrival of the CPIA 1996, criminal courts never had the benefit of a comprehensive set rules to enable accused persons to discover what the prosecution might have which might assist their defence. A criminal court could hear defence applications for further information or the release of material in the hands of the prosecution and was able to exercise statutory powers to decide whether to issue witness summonses against third parties. In more recent years it has also been able to receive representations on behalf of the Crown to withhold material on public interest grounds. To assist them in this process, however, judges and magistrates have had to rely on case law, much of it uncertain, incomplete and confusing, and an innate sense of fairness.

What then is the explanation for the absence, until the CPIA 1996, of a clear set of rules on the subject, especially as deficiencies in the law have been apparent and debated for the last 30 years? Why have investigators and prosecutors ignored or misunderstood their duties? Could any of the recent miscarriages of justice have been avoided? Is the CPIA 1996 and accompanying disclosure code of practice, which built upon the recommendations of the 1993 Royal Commission on Criminal Justice, the answer; and are its provisions sufficient to clarify the obligations of the prosecution and safeguard the interests of the accused? This book attempts to answer such questions as well as examining critically the origins, background and development of the law in relation to disclosure.

The starting point is the general duty of the prosecution to act fairly, and in chapters 2 and 3 we will examine this obligation together with failures in the system which led to a number of miscarriages of justice. Chapter 4 looks at the disclosure of the prosecution case and chapter 5 analyses the law in relation to the disclosure of matters affecting the character and credibility of witnesses who are called in support of the case for the Crown.

Most of the difficulties affecting disclosure have arisen in connection with matters which the prosecution decide not to adduce as part of their case, either because they do not advance the prosecution or they are considered to be neutral or of no help to the defence, or because the disclosure of the information to the defence is considered not to be in the public interest. Chapters 6 and 7 trace the development of the law concerning such 'unused material' and chapter 8 explores the key disclosure issues and gauges whether they are provided for in the CPIA 1996. The Act provides that the rules of common law which were in operation prior to its coming into effect do not apply to criminal investigations commenced before 1 April 1997. It is nevertheless important that the extent of the prosecution's duty under the common law rules is clarified as not only do those rules still apply to a large number of investigations already underway when the provisions of the CPIA 1996 and the Code of Practice ('the disclosure code') issued under Part II of the Act take effect, but, when issues of law under the new legislation fall to be considered, it is inevitable that some regard will be had to the earlier case law. It is also essential to the understanding of the complicated provisions of the CPIA 1996 and disclosure code to take cognisance of the background which gave rise to the need for legislation.

In contrast to the general rules of disclosure, the rules of common law as to whether disclosure is in the public interest are not affected by the CPIA 1996. Thus the development of public interest immunity (PII) in criminal proceedings, which is pursued in chapter 9, and the manner in which PII is asserted, which is analysed in chapter 10, remain of prime importance. This involves a critical look at the findings and recommendations of the *Report of the Inquiry into the Export of Defence Equipment and Dual-Use Goods to Iraq and Related Prosecutions* (HC Paper 115, London: HMSO 1996) (the Scott Report) and the Government's response thereto.

Chapter 11 looks at how concepts such as confidentiality and legal professional privilege are affected by the disclosure rules as well as the major statutory exception to the rules provided by the Interception of Communications Act 1985. Chapter 12 explores the remedies for disclosure irregularities; and because of the frequent misapprehension that disclosure problems are confined to the Crown Court, chapter 13 considers how disclosure has affected proceedings in the magistrates' court.

While no other common law jurisdiction appears to have had a case as sensational as that of Judith Ward, and has nothing to compare with the detailed provisions of the CPIA 1996 and disclosure code, the higher courts in many countries have had to wrestle with disclosure problems. In chapter 14 the position in other common law jurisdictions is discussed. Regard is also had to how disclosure is effected in some of the inquisitorial judicial systems in Europe as well as the influence of the European Court of Human Rights, which has already been felt in *Edwards* v *United Kingdom* (1993) 15 EHRR 417. We will also look briefly at the position in one or two other countries, notably the USA and Japan.

The remaining chapters concentrate on the new disclosure provisions. A number of recommendations affecting disclosure were made by the Royal Commission on Criminal Justice (Cm 2263, London HMSO, 1993) (the Runciman Commission Report) and many of these were adopted by the Government in the Consultation Paper issued by the Home Office in 1995 which contained their proposals on the reform of the disclosure rules. Despite opposition and concern from some quarters, most of the the proposals have now been given statutory effect in the CPIA 1996. The provisions of the Act are critically examined in an attempt to ascertain whether the common law defects have been remedied, or whether the new law will bring with it new problems.

'Disclosure' is a very commonplace expression, not just in the context of legal proceedings but also in connection with matters such as parliamentary declarations of interest, data protection legislation, etc. It must be made clear from the outset that this book is confined to the law of disclosure in criminal proceedings. In effect, it covers the duties of the prosecution in relation to disclosure of material to the defence (whether that material forms part of the prosecution case or is material not to be used by the prosecution) together with information affecting the credibility of witnesses called by the Crown. The law and practice in relation to prosecution disclosure to third parties (for example, disclosure of prosecution material to social services for the purpose of family proceedings, or disclosure of prosecution information for the purpose of civil proceedings) are outside the scope of this book.

The nineteenth-century British writer Samuel Smiles, in his book *Self Help*, wrote: 'We often discover what will do, by finding out what will not do; and probably he who never made a mistake never made a discovery.' The prosecution have made plenty of mistakes in relation to discovery; but they are not alone. Until the arrival of the CPIA 1996, the disclosure rules, together with the law in relation to PII, was judge-made. Whether it was well made is open to argument. Many investigators and prosecutors claimed that the law was unclear, contradictory and incapable of being effectively carried out. Many accused allege that the rules were simply unfair. There was much opposition to some of the provisions of the CPIA 1996, notably those relating to defence disclosure, but, it is argued, defence practitioners have brought such requirements upon themselves by making unreasonable and unnecessary demands upon the prosecution. These are all issues to be faced in the coming pages.

The evolution of the law on disclosure and PII is undoubtedly among the most fascinating topics for students of criminal practice and procedure. The object of this book, however, is not simply to chart the development of the law but to consider whether the new statutory rules and guidelines are likely to result in greater clarity and effectiveness. It is intended for practitioners and those who have to observe the law and play by the rules.

The duty of fairness, which rests on the prosecution, and the right to a fair trial of persons accused of crime are vital components of any judicial system. Yet no other jurisdiction has anything quite as comprehensive as the CPIA 1996 and disclosure code in order to deal with criminal discovery. Disclosure rules must have regard to reality in a world where criminal investigations are often lengthy and generate mountains of paperwork; where prosecutors have heavy caseloads and time limits with which to comply; and where defence practitioners have limited time to inspect and digest everything which emerges from an investigation. Disclosure rules must be capable of effective observance and they must be fair — to the investigator, the prosecutor and the defence practitioner; but principally, to the accused. Only when the history and development of the law on disclosure is examined will we be in a position to evaluate fully whether England and Wales has now devised such a system.

2   General Duties of the Prosecution

A GENERAL DUTY OF FAIRNESS

The adversarial system of criminal justice in England and Wales is characterised by the presumption of innocence. An accused person does not have to prove his or her innocence; the burden of proof is on the prosecution to prove guilt beyond reasonable doubt. In the inquisitorial judicial systems which prevail in Europe, the accused is subjected to a detailed independent inquiry by a judicial officer. In an adversarial system, it is the responsibility of the prosecutor to acquaint the court with the facts, elicit evidence from the witnesses in support of the case for the prosecution and cross-examine the accused and witnesses called for the defence. How then should the prosecutor go about the task of proving guilt?

It is not difficult to imagine the public outcry that would inevitably follow if the prosecution acted dishonestly or unethically; for example, if relevant evidence was deliberately withheld or produced at the last moment, or if inadequate steps were taken to trace witnesses. There would be similar censure if the advocate primed witnesses or bullied the accused in cross-examination. It is likely, however, that complete disinterest by the prosecutor would provoke similar criticism. The failure to call admissible evidence which would establish guilt and incompetent questioning of an accused would not serve the public interest. The system obviously requires a balance which ensures that both the prosecutor and the accused are seen to participate in a fair trial. The role of the judge and magistrates is to act as umpires to ensure equity.

Nearly two centuries ago, the obligations upon the prosecutor were stated as follows (see Chitty, *A Practical Treatise on the Criminal Law*, 1816, vol. 1, p. 3):

The persons thus legally entitled to prefer an accusation against a party suspected of a crime, are in general bound by the strongest obligations, both of reason and law, to exert the power with which they are invested. It must indeed be admitted that revenge ought not to become the motive of their actions, or occasion any unnecessary harshness in their proceedings. . . . The object of criminal provisions is not vengeance for the past, but safety for the future; and to the furtherance of this design every man is bound to contribute.

Such sentiments hold good today and may be summarised quite simply as an obligation on the prosecutor to be fair. If there is unfairness in the commencement of proceedings so that an accused person cannot be assured of a fair trial, a stay of the proceedings as an abuse of process will undoubtedly result. Unfairness by the prosecution in their presentation of the case will be censured by the court.

The disclosure of information to the defence is just one example of the general obligation upon the prosecution to act fairly and must, therefore, be viewed against the wider background of the duty to act in an even-handed and impartial manner. This was made clear by Glidewell LJ when concluding his judgment in *Ward*. He stated (((1993) 96 Cr App R 1, at p. 67): '. . . it is essential that those who are responsible for a prosecution and for the provision of evidence upon which the prosecution is based should comply with their basic duty to seek to ensure a trial which is fair both to the prosecution, representing the Crown, and to the accused'. In summarising the common law duty of disclosure in *R* v *Brown (Winston)* [1995] 1 Cr App R 191, Steyn LJ (as he then was) made the same point (at p. 198):

> . . . the right of every accused to a fair trial is a basic or fundamental right. That means that under our unwritten constitution those rights are deserving of special protection by the courts. However, in our adversarial system, in which the police and prosecution control the investigatory process, an accused's right to fair disclosure is an inseparable part of his right to a fair trial. That is the framework in which the development of common law rules about disclosure by the Crown must be seen.

The duty of fairness must, however, be examined in the context of arrangements that exist in England and Wales for investigating and prosecuting crime.

THE PROSECUTION PROCESS

In England and Wales the functions of the investigator and the prosecutor are quite distinct. Most allegations of crime are investigated by the police, and until comparatively recently the police were also responsible for prosecuting such allegations. This was more as a result of gradual historical development than any specific decision by Parliament to give them that duty. There was indeed no mention of the prosecutorial role of the police in any of the statutes which were responsible for the creation of police forces in England and Wales.

The Prosecution of Offences Act 1879 established the office of the Director of Public Prosecutions (DPP) whose powers to institute, undertake or carry on criminal proceedings, or to give advice and assistance to chief constables, were defined broadly in the Act and more specifically in Regulations made under the Act. In reality, the DPP's office was involved in relatively few cases, and then only in the more serious types of offence. The vast majority of offences were investigated by the police and prosecuted by solicitors either employed or instructed on an *ad hoc* basis by the chief constable. The less serious offences, such as road traffic matters, were prosecuted by police officers themselves.

Since 1986, the responsibility for the majority of prosecutions in England and Wales has rested with the Crown Prosecution Service (CPS). Although some agencies, such as the Serious Fraud Office, Her Majesty's Customs and Excise and the Department of Trade Industry, have prosecutorial powers, and the rights of private prosecutors have been specifically preserved (by s. 6, Prosecution of Offences Act 1985), the CPS is responsible for the vast majority of prosecutions (nearly 1.4 million defendants according to the CPS Annual Report for the period 1995/6).

The duties of the DPP, as head of the CPS, are set out in s. 3, Prosecution of Offences Act 1985, and include the duty to take over the conduct of all criminal proceedings, other than specified proceedings, instituted on behalf of the police and to institute and conduct criminal proceedings in cases where it is considered appropriate to do so. The separation of the investigative and prosecutorial functions is, therefore, strictly preserved. The result of this is that although the duty of disclosure rests with the prosecutor, in most instances any documents or information to be disclosed will physically be in the hands of the investigator. It will be seen in later chapters how this division of functions is at the root of many of the difficulties which have faced 'the prosecution' in discharging their disclosure obligations.

Irrespective of the demands imposed by law, the expectation that the prosecution will act fairly in relation to disclosure requires:

- the investigator to reveal fully and honestly to the prosecutor what information exists (including the results of any findings by experts, whether they assist the prosecution case or not);
- the prosecuting agency to act equitably in the preparation and presentation of the case; and
- prosecuting counsel (in those cases where counsel is instructed) to act impartially and in accordance with the recognised traditions and standards of the Bar.

Deficiencies in any of these three stages may result in unfairness to the accused. Before examining the law in any detail, it is necessary to review briefly what is expected of those involved in the prosecution process in relation to a general duty to act fairly.

Fairness and the investigator

The police have a duty, *inter alia*, to detect and investigate allegations of crime. The manner in which they conduct such investigations is critically important. The Runciman Commission Report (at p. 10) summarised the position as follows:

Not only will serious miscarriages of justice result if the collection of evidence is vitiated by error or malpractice, but the successful prosecution of the guilty depends on a thorough and careful search for evidence which is both admissible and probative. In undertaking this search, it is the duty of the police to investigate fairly and thoroughly all the relevant evidence, including that which exonerates the suspect.

Many police powers in relation to the investigation of crime are set out in the Police and Criminal Evidence Act (PACE) 1984, which is supplemented by a series of Codes of Practice. In addition to the requirements of PACE 1984, there must exist within police forces a culture of fairness so that if information comes to light which helps an accused, justice requires that such information be made available. The police have a long-standing tradition in this respect, as can be seen from the following extract from an address to constables in the 1882 preface to *Vincent's Police Code* (see further Jerrard, Rob R., 'The Police Officer's Notebook' (1993) 157 JP 6):

In detailing any conversation with an accused person, be sure to state the whole conversation from the commencement to the end in the very words used; and, in narrating facts, state every fact whether you think it material or not, for you are not the judge of materiality. Tell, in short, everything as well that which is in favour of the accused, as that which is against him, for your desire and anxiety must be fair, and assist the innocent; and not convict any man by unfair means, such as by suppressing something which may tell in his favour, even though you feel certain of his guilt . . .

More than a hundred years later, these views are reflected in the disclosure code of practice where investigators are instructed to pursue all reasonable lines of inquiry whether they point towards or away from the suspect. These are laudable sentiments, but in an adversarial system of criminal justice they are easier to state than put into practice. The police will inevitably form suspicions as to guilt and pursue those beliefs. What they must not do is close their minds to reasonable alternative lines of inquiry, although what amounts to a reasonable line of inquiry pointing away from the suspect will often be difficult to define. Advocates of an inquisitorial system of justice argue that it is only under such a system, where the investigation is directed and supervised by someone such as an examining magistrate, that there can be a truly fair and independent investigation. With such a prospect being rejected by the Runciman Commission Report, there is no alternative but to rely on the police and others with investigatorial powers to carry out a thorough and fair investigation.

Fairness and the expert

Expert scientific and medical evidence is in common use in modern criminal proceedings. Indeed, with police evidence commonly contested, expert evidence is often the crucial factor which determines guilt or innocence. The Forensic Science Service is available to police forces outside London and the Metropolitan Police Forensic Science Laboratory is the largest forensic science laboratory in Europe. The police also have forensic medical examiners or police surgeons who they are able to call upon to carry out examinations and give opinions on causes of injury, fitness to detain, etc.

The role of expert witnesses was concisely stated by Lord President Cooper in the Scots case of *Davie* v *Edinburgh Magistrates* 1953 SLT 54: 'Their duty is to furnish the judge or jury with the necessary scientific criteria for testing the accuracy of their conclusions, so as to enable the judge or jury to form their own independent judgment by the application of these criteria to the facts in evidence.' The expert is objective and impartial and must give an opinion based on facts which are admitted or have been proved. The role does not easily lend itself to the adversarial system where the expert is called either by the prosecution or by the defence; consequently, the witness is often associated with one side or the other rather than regarded as in a position of neutrality, which is how most experts view themselves.

For many years, though, the justice in the prosecution providing the defence with a copy of an expert's report has been recognised. In *R* v *Casey* (1947) 32 Cr App R 91 where a defence of insanity had been relied on at the trial, the Court of Appeal said that it was 'clearly right and proper' that the defence had been supplied by the prosecution with a copy of the Prison Medical Officer's report as to the mental condition of the accused. The duty to supply copies of forensic science reports to the defence was acknowledged in Home Office Circular No. 158/1947. This put an end to uncertainty about whether the accused had a right to information obtained as a result of examinations made in a forensic science laboratory.

The concept of fairness is part and parcel of the role of an expert who is giving an opinion on known facts. There have been important developments, however, in the law on disclosure in relation to experts, and these are discussed in greater detail in chapter 8.

Fairness and the prosecuting authority

By virtue of s. 10, Prosecution of Offences Act 1985, the DPP issued a Code for Crown Prosecutors ('the Code') which gives guidance on general principles in relation to such matters as the review of cases and the evidential and public interest tests to be applied. The introduction to the current edition of the Code makes it abundantly clear to Crown Prosecutors how they must approach their task, namely: 'The decision to prosecute an individual is a serious step. Fair and effective prosecution is essential to the maintenance of law and order.' Later, in para. 2.3. Crown Prosecutors are reminded that they 'must be fair, independent and objective'.

Although there is no specific reference to disclosure in the Code, it is implicit that decisions must be taken equitably in addition to the requirements of current law. In the current explanatory guidance issued to Crown Prosecutors for use in connection with the Code, prosecutors are instructed that when assessing the evidence they should have regard to any lines of defence which are clearly available to, or have been indicated by, the accused. Furthermore, they must consider whether there are any further reasonable lines of inquiry which should be pursued which may strengthen or weaken either the prosecution or defence case. This guidance echoes requirements of the disclosure provisions of the CPIA 1996, whereby material undermining the case for the prosecution must be disclosed. Although not bound by the CPS Code, other prosecuting agencies acknowledge the principles contained therein.

Fairness and prosecuting counsel

The role of prosecuting counsel has often been likened to a minister of justice: see early comparisons in *R* v *Puddick* (1865) 4 F & F 497; *R* v *Rutland* (1865) 4 F & F 495. In *R* v *Banks* [1916] 2 KB 621, a case of unlawful sexual intercourse where the defence complained about prosecuting counsel's closing address to the jury in which he appealed to them to protect young girls from offences of this sort, Avory J stated (at p. 623): 'It is true that prosecuting counsel ought not to press for a conviction. In the words of Crompton J in *R* v *Puddick* they should 'regard themselves' rather as 'ministers of justice' assisting in its administration than as advocates.' This certainly reflected the views of Sir J. Holker, the then Attorney-General, who in *The Times*, 25 February 1880, said of prosecuting counsel: 'It is not his duty to obtain a conviction by all means; but simply to lay before the jury the whole of the facts which compose his case, and to make these perfectly intelligible, and to see that the jury are instructed with regard to the law and are able to apply the law to the facts.'

It would appear that the assumption of the 'minister of justice' role was not always so regarded by those who prosecuted. In 1956, Sir Patrick Devlin wrote 'The last half-century has seen a welcome transition in the role of prosecuting counsel from a persecuting advocate into a ''minister of justice''' (see Devlin, *Trial by Jury*, London: Stevens, 1956, p. 122). Fairness as a quality in prosecuting counsel would, therefore, appear to be a comparatively recent phenomenon!

An interesting insight into the role of prosecuting counsel was provided by Christmas Humphreys, Senior Prosecuting Counsel at the Central Criminal Court, in his address to the Inns of Court Students Union on 5 July 1955, a shortened version of which appears in [1955] Crim LR 739. After having described counsel's role in conceiving, familiarising and building up the case to the point of acceptance by the committing magistrate, he stated that counsel should, even at this early stage, consider how he can help his colleague for the defence. He continued, 'Crown Counsel is concerned with justice first, justice second, and a conviction a very bad third'. On disclosure, he interpreted prosecuting counsel's duty as 'Generally speaking, any information which the prosecution does not intend to use, but which might, if believed, assist the defence should be made available'. The 'if believed', however, left much scope for argument.

In many ways, Christmas Humphreys's view of the role of Crown counsel echoed the words of Lord Denning in *The Road to Justice* (London: Stevens, 1955, pp. 36–7):

In England today, every counsel who is instructed for the prosecution knows how essential it is to be fair. The country expects it. The judge requires it. If he knows a point in favour of the prisoner, he must bring it out. He must state the facts quite dispassionately, whether they tell in favour of a severe sentence or otherwise. No counsel would dream of doing otherwise. Likewise with the rights of cross-examination, counsel for the prosecution must exercise it in a moderate and restrained manner, not in any way browbeating the man who is on trial.

Fairness and impartiality are qualities that were also prominent in the report of a Committee chaired by Farquharson J in 1986 on the role of prosecuting counsel (set out in full in *Archbold*, 1993 edn, para. 4–71). In its introduction, the report states that prosecuting counsel has a greater independence than those instructing him and that he should conduct his case moderately, albeit firmly. This is reflected in the current Code of Conduct of the Bar of England and Wales where, in relation to the section on 'Standards Applicable to Criminal Cases', specific reference is made to the duty to ensure that all relevant evidence is either presented by the prosecution or made available to the defence.

It is clear from the above summary that the role of prosecuting counsel is not only to prosecute the case firmly and fairly, but also to act as a minister of justice and assist the court wherever possible, and furthermore, to help defence counsel by providing information which may damage the case for the Crown. This is quite a tall order in an adversarial system of justice, a matter that did not escape the notice of Lord Mustill in his leading judgment in *R v Preston* (1994) 98 Cr App R 405, when he observed (at p. 415):

The heavy responsibilities now placed on prosecuting counsel have blurred the edges [of the adversarial system], not only because he is required to perform tasks which may benefit his opponent (although they are designed to benefit the administration of justice) but also because when he decides what ought to be disclosed his acts are administrative and also in a sense judicial in character.

His Lordship went on to say how this diffusion of function was multiplied in cases which featured telephone intercepts (which are dealt with in chapter 11).

A DUTY OF ABSOLUTE FAIRNESS

It will be seen, therefore, that obtaining a conviction at all costs has never been a characteristic of the criminal process. All those with any responsibility for the prosecution must act in a fair and impartial manner and the disclosure of relevant information and documents to the defence is only one (albeit a very important one) aspect of that responsibility.

Difficulties arise, though, when the extent of what is fair is unclear or questionable. An early example in relation to disclosure arose in *R v Nicholson* [1936] JP 553. In a case at Nottingham Assizes, the accused was charged with incest with his eight-year-old daughter. The prosecution called medical evidence to the effect that spermatozoa were found on the girl's private parts, her vest and the accused's shirt. The material was examined on glass slides under a microscope, but the slides were not specially preserved and were later submitted for further expert examination with negative results. The expert who carried out the second examination was not called by the prosecution but a copy of his report was supplied to the defence. Defence counsel argued that the witness should be called by the prosecution. Hawke J refused to force the prosecution to call the witness. He ruled that the Crown had a duty to give to the defence all the information they had which they decided not to put before the court. Commenting that prosecutions in this country are not to be conducted as if they were a struggle between parties, he emphasised that they must be conducted on principles of absolute fairness.

In *R v McIlkenny* (1991) 93 Cr App R 287, the Court of Appeal highlighted the fact that a disadvantage of the adversarial system may be that the parties are not evenly matched in resources. Even with the availablity of legal aid to a large percentage of those accused of crime, it cannot be doubted that the resources of the Crown are greater than those of the accused. The point had been made in the Report to the Home Secretary on *Evidence of Identification in Criminal Cases* (HC 338, London: HMSO, 1976), para. 1.17:

> The theory [of the adversary system] is based on the presumption that the resources of the parties are sufficiently near to equality to ensure a fair fight. The presumption may be sound enough in criminal proceedings when they come to trial, now that legal aid is available. But in the preparation of the criminal case it is manifestly unsound. For in criminal cases the state has in the police an agency for the discovery of evidence superior to anything which even the wealthiest defendant could employ.

One way of ensuring that the defence are not placed at a disadvantage is by the proper disclosure of relevant material. As was said in *McIlkenny* (at p. 312): 'But the inequality of resources is ameliorated by the obligation on the part of the prosecution to make available all material which may prove helpful to the defence. The later history of the present appeal shows how well the prosecution can perform that obligation.'

That the prosecution have resources in excess of the defence is indisputable; that the prosecution have a duty to be fair in all their dealings is undeniable; that they have a duty to disclose relevant information and documents to the defence is incontrovertible. The difficulty is how to define as precisely as possible the extent of the duty in relation to disclosure and how that duty can properly and effectively be carried out. Failure to describe and explain the duty will inevitably result in confusion and, in extreme circumstances, miscarriages of justice. Before tracing the devlopment of the law on disclosure, it is, therefore, instructive to look at cases in which there have been miscarriages of justice. These provide illustrations, not just of failures on the part of the prosecution, but also of failings in a judicial system revered for justice, fairness and impartiality.

3 Miscarriages of Justice

ROLE OF THE COURT OF APPEAL

The catalyst for the movement to reform the rules governing the disclosure of information in criminal proceedings, culminating in the passing of the CPIA 1996, has been the number of so-called miscarriages of justice in recent years. The term 'miscarriage of justice' is by no means new, but it is applied with increasing regularity in commentaries on the decisions of the beleagured courts of England and Wales. Arguably, any appeal allowed under s. 2, Criminal Appeal Act 1968 amounted to a miscarriage of justice because the court was saying either that the conviction was unsafe or unsatisfactory, or that it must be set aside as a result of a wrong decision on a question of law or because of a material irregularity in the trial. In any of these eventualities, justice has not been done and the conviction cannot be allowed to stand. The proviso to s. 2, Criminal Appeal Act 1968 allowed the Court of Appeal, where they decided the point of an appeal in favour of the appellant, nevertheless to dismiss the appeal 'if they consider that no miscarriage of justice has actually occurred'. It follows, therefore, that if they did not apply the proviso the Court were satisfied that there had been such a miscarriage.

The system of appeals from the Crown Court to the Court of Appeal has long been the subject of debate, disapproval and criticism. The Runciman Commission Report recommended that s. 2(1), Criminal Appeal Act 1968 should be redrafted in view of the overlap between the grounds of appeal and the confusion over the scope of the proviso. It further proposed that a new body should be set up to consider allegations of miscarriages of justice. These recommendations have now been given effect in the Criminal Appeal Act 1995, which abolishes the power of the Home Secretary to refer cases to the Court of Appeal under s. 17, Criminal Appeal Act 1968 and establishes a Criminal Cases Review Commission with powers to look into miscarriages of justice. Section 2 of the 1968 Act is replaced by a new provision in the 1995 Act, which came into force on 1 January 1996. It gives a simplified description of the function of the Court of Appeal which shall allow an appeal against conviction if they think that the conviction is unsafe, and dismiss the appeal in any other case.

The provisions of the 1995 Act are thought by many to create as much confusion as existed hitherto (see Smith, J. C. (1995) 145 NLJ 533 and 572, and Spencer, J. R., in a feature in (1995) 9 *Archbold News* 3) and it is perhaps surprising that the Act does not define 'unsafe'. The Court of Appeal stated in *R* v *Graham* (1996) *The Times*, 28 October 1996 that their role is to consider one question: whether, in the light of any argument raised or evidence adduced on appeal, the conviction is unsafe. If satisfied, despite any misdirection of the law or any irregularity in the conduct of the trial or any fresh evidence, that the conviction is safe, the Court would dismiss the appeal. A failure to disclose information should not, in the future, lead automatically to an appeal being allowed, but it is likely that a prosecution failure to observe the provisions of the CPIA 1996 will result in an 'unsafe' conviction. Whether all unsafe convictions will continue to be cast as miscarriages of justice, or whether the term will be restricted to the more notorious examples remains to be seen. It is likely, however, that incidents of non-disclosure, whether deliberate or inadvertant, or whether caused by negligence, naivety, oversight or incompetence will continue to invite opprobium as miscarriages of justice.

MISCARRIAGES CAUSED BY DISCLOSURE IRREGULARITIES

Miscarriages of justice may be brought about for any number of reasons, of which non-disclosure is just one. This chapter considers illustrations of such cases where the failures on the part of the prosecution or the general mismanagement of their disclosure obligations justify the label of a 'miscarriage of justice'. Some of the judgments in the cases are now leading authorities in the field of disclosure where the legal points will be discussed later; others offer no new insight into the law on the topic but simply demonstrate the unfortunate consequences of a failure to disclose relevant information to the defence.

The bombing offences of the 1970s

The IRA bombing campaign of the middle years of the 1970s brought death, destruction and enormous upheaval to mainland Britain. The trials of some of the alleged perpetrators wrought similar havoc to the English judicial system as several years later a host of convictions were overturned by the Court of Appeal. The results of these cases, and the surrounding publicity, had a devastating effect on the reputation of the legal establishment and severely dented the confidence of the general public in the police and prosecuting authorities. Non-disclosure of relevant information was not the sole cause of wrongful convictions but it played a significant part in the reasoning of the Court of Appeal.

We have seen from chapter 1 that in September 1973 and February 1974, bombs exploded at Euston station, on a coach travelling on the M62 in Yorkshire, and at the National Defence College in Buckinghamshire. Judith Ward was arrested in connection with these matters. On the night of 5 October 1974 more bombs exploded in two public houses in Guildford, Surrey which were frequented by members of the armed forces. Five young persons were killed and many others injured. A month later, on 7 November, a bomb was thrown through the window of another public house in Woolwich, South London. Two people were killed by the resulting explosion (a third died shortly afterwards although he had been ill for some time and the post mortem showed that he had, in fact, died of natural causes). The bombing in Woolwich was the fourth in a series of incidents of bombs being thrown at or inside buildings since the Guildford bombing.

The incidents gave rise to intensive police activity to apprehend those responsible. Many persons were arrested and eventually 11 were charged and later stood trial. Patrick Armstrong, Gerard Conlon, Paul Hill and Carole Richardson (known as the Guildford Four) stood trial for the Guildford and Woolwich explosions in the autumn of 1975. In October they were convicted and each was sentenced to life imprisonment with recommendations that Armstrong serve not less than 35 years' imprisonment and Conlon 30 years. Donaldson J (now Lord Donaldson) ordered that Hill should be released only 'on grounds of old age or infirmity'. Their appeals against conviction, heard in October 1977, were dismissed.

In the meantime, five members of the Maguire family, together with Patrick O'Neill and Patrick Conlon (known collectively as the Maguire Seven), stood trial at the Central Criminal Court and were convicted on 4 March 1976 of separate counts of possessing an explosive substance, namely nitroglycerine. Sentences ranged from 14 years' imprisonment for Anne and Patrick Maguire to four years' detention for Patrick Maguire junior. Patrick Conlon (the father of Gerard Conlon of the Guildford Four) was sentenced to 12 years' imprisonment, but in January 1980 he died while in custody. On 30 July 1977, the Maguire Seven had their applications for leave to appeal against conviction dismissed by the Court of Appeal.

The case against the Guildford Four rested primarily on evidence of their confessions. In 1989 their case was referred to the Court of Appeal by the Home Secretary in exercise of his powers under s. 17(1)(a), Criminal Appeal Act 1968, as a result of fresh evidence concerning the physical condition of Carole Richardson at the time of her alleged confessions and fresh evidence about alibi witnesses. As a result of the reference, certain documents were re-examined by the police and forensic scientists and the results cast doubt on the authenticity of some of the interview notes.

After careful consideration by the Attorney-General and the DPP, the Crown decided not to resist the appeals of Armstrong and Hill on the ground that the police officers' evidence at the original trial could not be relied upon. Because the truthfulness and reliability of the police evidence was crucial to the convictions of all the accused, it was further decided not to resist the appeals of Conlon and Richardson.

On 19 October 1989, the appeals of the Guildford Four were allowed by the Court of Appeal. On the same day in the House of Commons, the Home Secretary announced that he was appointing Sir John May to hold a judicial inquiry into the circumstances surrounding the convictions arising out of the bomb attacks in Guildford and Woolwich. It should be borne in mind that the prosecution's reason for deciding not to resist the appeals was primarily the unreliability of the evidence of its principal witnesses. In the course of the police and judicial inquiries, however, instances of non-disclosure had come to light.

The first concerned the alibi of Gerard Conlon. The police had taken a statement from an occupant of the room in which Conlon had lodged, the contents of which, if true, would have provided Conlon with an alibi. This had not been disclosed to Conlon's solicitors. In his book *Proved Innocent* (Penguin Books, 1990), Conlon describes his excitement when told of the discovery of the statement by the solicitor acting for him in his appeal: 'The really important thing was a legal point: the prosecution had withheld evidence from the defence. They had found Charles Burke, they had got his statement before my trial, and it was their duty then to tell us. They hadn't done so. End of story. Conviction quashed. Conlon walks. The Guildford Four walk.'

In the final report of his judicial inquiry (see *Report on the Bomb Attacks in Guildford and Woolwich*, HC 449, London: HMSO, 1994, p. 302), Sir John May stated:

> I am quite satisfied that the omission to provide Conlon's legal team with the last known address of Burke or to provide them with a copy of the statement he had made to the police was not a deliberate suppression of evidence which might have assisted Conlon. Nonetheless, in my view Burke's whereabouts so far as they were known to the Crown, and at least an indication of what he could say, should have been disclosed. Although there was nothing sinister in the non-disclosure it ought not to have occurred.

Sir John also found another instance of non-disclosure in relation to a scientific correlation statement. While this statement had been in the possession of prosecuting counsel at the outset, its significance had been overlooked.

The Court of Appeal were not required to decide whether the non-disclosure of these documents, in themselves, would have been sufficient to make the convictions unsafe, but there is no disputing that the prosecution failures contributed to the miscarriage of justice in relation to the Guildford Four.

In July 1990, Sir John May reviewed in detail the scientific evidence upon which the convictions of the Maguire Seven had been based (see May, Sir John, *Interim Report on the Bomb Attacks in Guildford and Woolwich*, HC 556, London: HMSO, 1990). He concluded that there were a number of grounds for regarding the convictions unsound. The Home Secretary, therefore, referred their cases to the Court of Appeal (including that of the now deceased Patrick Conlon), with the result that on 26 June 1991 the convictions were quashed.

The case against the Maguire Seven was that although no explosives were found at the Maguires' address, traces of what was said to be nitroglycerine were found on the hands of the male appellants and on plastic gloves used by Anne Maguire. The principal grounds of appeal were that the scientists called by the prosecution failed to reveal relevant facts and were selective about experimental data which they produced, and that the prosecution had failed to disclose note books showing the results of scientific tests that had been carried out. The significance of these failures was that a defence of innocent contamination would have been open to the appellants had they known the true state of affairs.

In a judgment which was of considerable importance in relation to the role of the forensic scientist in disclosure (see *R* v *Maguire* (1992) 94 Cr App R 133, discussed more fully in chapter 8), Stuart-Smith LJ held that there could be a material irregularity in the course of a trial when a forensic scientist advising the prosecution had not disclosed relevant material. On the ground that the possibility of innocent contamination could not be excluded, the convictions of each of the Maguire Seven were held to be unsatisfactory.

The Guildford Four and the Maguire Seven had been the subject of two of the most spectacular miscarriages of justice this century. When their cases are discussed they are usually mentioned in the same breath as those of the 'Birmingham Six'. That the Birmingham Six were also the subjects of a similar miscarriage of justice is indisputable, but it is important to keep in mind that their successful appeals had very little to do with non-disclosure.

In November 1974, the bombing campaign which had caused terror, death and destruction in the south of England moved to the midlands. On 14 November, an active member of the Birmingham IRA, James McDade, was killed when a bomb he was planting at the Coventry telephone exchange exploded prematurely. A week later two explosions in public houses in the centre of Birmingham caused the deaths of 21 people and injured a further 162. The police quickly arrested six men — Richard McIlkenny, Patrick Hill, William Power, John Walker, Robert Hunter, and Hugh Callaghan — and charged them with the murders.

On 15 August 1975, each was convicted, and in March of the following year their applications for leave to appeal on the ground of the trial judge's excessive hostility towards them, were dismissed. In the years that followed many people campaigned on behalf of the Six and television programmes and books proclaimed their innocence. In January 1987, their case was referred by the Home Secretary to the Court of Appeal. Fresh scientific evidence had come to light and there had been a new inquiry by Devon and Cornwall police as a result of an allegation made by a former police officer that the men had been ill-treated while in police custody. The appeal was held over many days in the autumn of 1987 but was dismissed in January 1988.

Notwithstanding this setback, the campaign on behalf of the Birmingham Six continued unabated, and in August 1990 the case was once more referred by the Home Secretary as more fresh evidence had emerged. On this occasion, counsel for the Crown informed the Court of Appeal that he had been instructed not to resist the appeals. Much of the subsequent judgment in *R* v *McIlkenny* (1991) 93 Cr App R 287 is devoted to the powers and duties of the Court of Appeal, but in the final analysis the appeals of the Birmingham Six were allowed. Lloyd LJ stated (at p. 318):

> In the light of the fresh scientific evidence which at least throws grave doubt on Dr Skuse's evidence, if it does not destroy it altogether, these convictions are both unsafe and unsatisfactory. If we put the scientific evidence to one side, the fresh investigation carried out by the Devon and Cornwall Constabulary renders the police evidence at the trial so unreliable, that again we would say that the convictions are both unsafe and unsatisfactory. Adding the two together, our conclusions are inevitable. It was for these reasons that we allowed the appeals.

On the same day that Lloyd LJ was uttering these words and the Birmingham Six walked free, the Home Secretary announced in the House of Commons that a Royal Commission on Criminal Justice would be established. The English legal system had been rocked to its foundations and the Royal Commission, under the Chairmanship of Viscount Runciman of Doxford, CBE, had wide-ranging terms of reference. The Commission was to examine the criminal justice system, from the stage at which the police began investigating an allegation of crime right through to the stage at which accused persons who had been found guilty had exhausted their rights of appeal. This, of course, included an examination of pre-trial procedures, such as disclosure, and, as we shall see in chapter 15, the Runciman Commission was to make a number of important recommendations.

In so far as non-disclosure of vital information is concerned, however, the greatest miscarriage of justice was still to emerge. In the wake of the successful appeals of the Guildford Four, Birmingham Six and the Maguires, the case of Judith Ward was referred back to the Court of Appeal in September 1991. The facts and history of this case have already been adumbrated in chapter 1. The common law rules on disclosure; the *Attorney-General's Guidelines for the Disclosure of 'Unused Material' to the Defence*; statutory rules in the form of the Crown Court (Advance Notice of Expert Evidence) Rules 1987; and the general practices and procedures of prosecutors throughout England and Wales were discredited and confusion reigned. It is hardly surprising, therefore, against this bewildering recognition of weaknesses and failures in relation to disclosure, that more miscarriages of justice were to surface.

Stefan Kiszko case

Although the cases arising out of the IRA bombing campaign of the 1970s resulted in sympathy, from most quarters, for those wrongfully accused and convicted, they aroused nothing like the universal compassion felt for Stefan Kiszko. Kiszko was convicted on 21 July 1976 of the murder of 11-year-old Lesley Molseed who had been found stabbed to death on moorland near Rochdale the previous October. Kiszko, who was said to have a mental age of 12, was alleged to have confessed to the murder during interviews with the police. Leave to appeal against the conviction had been refused by the full Court of Appeal in 1978.

After he had served 16 years of a life sentence, Kiszko successfully appealed against his conviction in 1991. Unfortunately, he did not enjoy much of his new freedom for he died just before Christmas in 1993. His mother, who had campaigned for his freedom, died six months later. The reason for Kiszko's belatedly successful appeal was that tests on semen stains on Lesley's clothing showed that they could not have been made by him. The stains on the clothing contained spermatozoa, but Kiszko had a rare condition which meant that he was unable to produce spermatozoa. Crucially, this fact had not been disclosed at his trial and had come to light only in 1991 when the evidence was reviewed by the police.

As a result of the further police inquiry, the Detective Superintendent who was second-in-command of the original investigation and a former senior forensic scientist were charged with perverting the course of justice. It was alleged that they deliberately suppressed the scientific evidence and thus prevented the defence from considering the discrepancies in the stains on the clothing and the sample of semen produced by Kiszko. In May 1995, the proceedings against the former police officer and former scientist were stayed by a magistrate on the ground that they would be denied a fair trial because the Detective Chief Superintendent in charge of the case had died. If the case proceeded, there was a danger that the defendants would be tried on the basis of the acts or omissions of the deceased officer.

The outcome of this unsatisfactory matter means that it will proably never be known whether vital evidence was deliberately suppressed. If it was, it is fair to say that whatever disclosure regime was being operated at the time by the police and the DPP would have been circumvented. If the non-disclosure was as a result of a mistake or oversight, then it is possible that procedures for the revelation of relevant information were inadequate. Whatever the reasons, the case of Stefan Kiszko will be remembered as a major miscarriage of justice caused by non-disclosure of vital information, and if any further momentum for change in the law and procedures was still required this case undoubtedly provided it.

Laszlo Virag case

On 8 April 1974, the Home Secretary announced in the House of Commons that he was recommending a free pardon to Laszlo Virag who, in July 1969, had been convicted at the Gloucestershire Assizes of offences of theft, using a firearm to resist arrest and wounding a police officer with intent to cause grievous bodily harm or resist arrest. He had been sentenced to a total of 10 years' imprisonment. At the same time, the Home Secretary drew attention to the case of Luke Dougherty whose conviction for shoplifting had been quashed by the Court of Appeal the previous month. Honest but mistaken identification by prosecution witnesses was the prime cause of the miscarriages of justice in each case and the Home Secretary appointed a Committee, to be chaired by Lord Devlin, to look generally into the law and procedures relating to identification evidence.

At the outset of the Committee's Report (HC 338, London: HMSO,1976) (the Devlin Report) the following question was posed (at para. 1.20): 'In Virag's case the police at an early stage of the investigation discovered that certain fingerprints, evidently made by a thief on the stolen property (Mr Virag was charged with theft as well as with the wounding of a police officer in the subsequent pursuit) were not the prints of Mr Virag. Ought this evidence, if it was not to be made part of the prosecution's case, to have been communicated to the defence?' Later in the report (at chapter 5), the Committee commented on the state of the law on disclosure which existed at that time. The answer to the question posed though was undoubtedly 'Yes', especially as the fingerprint evidence was later to incrimate another man who, the Committee concluded, had committed the offences. A search of the National Fingerprint Collection had not been made by the police. Had the defence been informed that the fingerprints on the stolen cash containers and on a hand lamp were not Virag's, it might have thrown sufficient doubt on the identification evidence to secure an acquittal. Had the defence known the identity of the person whose fingerprints were found, an acquittal would have been even more likely.

The death of Maxwell Confait

The circumstances leading to the trial and conviction in 1972 of 15-year-old Ronald Leighton, 18-year-old Colin Lattimore and Ahmet Salih, aged 14 years, were the subject of a detailed report of an inquiry conducted by the Hon Sir Henry Fisher (HC 90, London: HMSO, 1977) (the Fisher Report). The boys had been convicted of arson at an address in Catford, south London; and Leighton had been convicted of the murder, and Lattimore of manslaughter on the grounds of diminished responsibility, of a man named Maxwell Confait whose body was found in a room on the first floor.

In June 1975, the cases of the three boys were referred by the Home Secretary to the Court of Appeal and in October the convictions were quashed. The Court held that 'The admissions, in whatever circumstances they came to be made, if they were made as alleged, must then be unreliable and the convictions, accordingly, must be unsafe and unsatisfactory.' Part VI of the Fisher Report, however, focused on issues of disclosure, particularly in relation to the non-disclosure of fuller statements made by two key persons who featured in the inquiry. As in the Devlin Report on identification the previous year, there was much comment on the unsatisfactory state of the law and guidance on disclosure, culminating in a recommendation that where there is a large number of witnesses the prosecution should provide a summary of the evidence which the witnesses can give rather than just their names and addresses.

Michelle and Lisa Taylor

On 24 July 1992, at the Central Criminal Court, the two sisters were convicted of murder. The prosecution had alleged that because Michelle had been having a sexual relationship with the deceased's husband and was consumed with jealousy, the pair had stabbed the victim to death. The principal ground of appeal was that material had come to light since the trial which cast doubt on the veracity of a witness who had provided the main evidence of identification. The witness had first stated that one of the girls he had seen leaving the scene of the crime may have been black, but he later said that both girls were blonde.

The existence of this crucial information was unknown to the CPS and prosecuting counsel, but the Court concluded that the officer in charge of the case had been aware of the document in question and its significance and had failed to reveal it to those responsible for the prosecution as they would have to disclose it. In addition, the same witness had written to the deceased's employers claiming a reward that they were offering for information about the murder. This information too had not been disclosed. Counsel for the Crown conceded on the appeal that a failure to disclose a previous inconsistent description must be a matter of significance and, therefore, there had been a material irregularity. Because of media treatment of the appellants (described by the single judge giving leave to appeal as 'unremitting, extensive, sensational, inaccurate and misleading'), a retrial was not ordered and the appeals were allowed.

Other miscarriages of justice

No summary of post-war miscarriages of justice, however brief, would be complete without reference to two criminal trials which have generated enormous controversy. Post-mortems on the conviction of Timothy Evans for the murder of his wife and child in 1949 and the conviction of Derek Bentley for the murder of a police officer in 1952 both included allegations of non-disclosure.

As a result of points raised in a debate in the House of Commons on 29 July 1953 on the Inquiry Report into the conviction of Evans, J. Scott Henderson QC submitted a supplementary report to the Home Secretary of the day, Sir David Maxwell Fyfe. In it he dealt with the suggestion that 32 statements had been suppressed by saying that he was satisfied that there was no reason why prosecuting counsel should have made the statements available to the defence. In his opinion, none of the statements in any way raised doubt about the truth of Evans's confession. Today, of course, there is no question that the statements would be disclosable and fully available to the defence.

In his book 'Let Him Have It, Chris' (1992), M. J. Trow highlighted the failure of the prosecution to disclose crucial statements in the trial of Bentley and Craig. He also drew attention to the debate in the House of Lords in 1972 when there were differences of opinion about the duty of disclosure among speakers at the debate.

There can only be speculation as to whether the disclosure of further statements would have made any difference to the outcome of the trials of Evans and Bentley and Craig. There can be little doubt, however, that under current disclosure procedures, the statements would have been available to the defence.

In 1989, JUSTICE published a report entitled *Miscarriages of Justice*, which dealt fully with alleged miscarriages and made recommendations to prevent recurrences. It instanced (at para. 2.27) the case of Paul Ngan who was convicted in February 1983 of wounding with intent and causing an affray following a serious fight between Singapore Chinese and Hong Kong Chinese. One of the alleged perpetrators, named Chong, fled abroad but Ngan was arrested, principally as a result of identification evidence, and upon conviction was sentenced to four years' imprisonment. Chong was later arrested in Malaysia and admitted the wounding for which Ngan had been convicted. Ngan's appeal out of time was allowed.

After the appeal it came to light that Chong had made his confession to English police officers sent to Malaysia to interview him, some five months before Ngan's trial. The confession had not been disclosed to Ngan's legal representatives, and JUSTICE presumed that the reason for this was because the police had not disclosed it to the prosecuting authority. This caused JUSTICE to recommend that it should be a breach of professional duty for the police or breach of professional conduct for the prosecution to fail to observe the *Attorney-General's Guidelines for Disclosure* which had been in operation since 1982.

Baksh v R [1958] AC 167, was an appeal to the Privy Council from the Court of Appeal of British Guiana which had dismissed an appeal against conviction for murder. It was alleged that the appellant and another had been involved in the shooting of the deceased. The case rested largely on the identification evidence of three witnesses and the defence was one of alibi. The basis of the appeal was that the statements of the witnesses showed material discrepancies and contradictions when compared with the evidence given at trial. A new trial had been ordered for the co-accused on this basis, but the Court of Appeal had decided that there was nothing favourable in the statements to this appellant. The Privy Council disagreed and ordered a new trial. The judgment, however, throws no light on the prosecution decision not to reveal information in the statements. It does emphasise the importance of disclosing matters affecting the credibility of witnesses to each accused, even though the importance of the evidence of the witness may not necessarily touch upon each accused.

In *R v Hassan and Kotaish* (1968) 52 Cr App R 291, the two appellants had been convicted of wounding with intent. The case rested almost entirely on the evidence of the complainant who said that the appellants attacked him with bottles and then stabbed him. The complainant admitted at trial to a conviction for threatening behaviour, but in fact he had many other convictions for offences of violence and had served terms of imprisonment. These had not been revealed to prosecuting counsel as the convictions had been recorded in variations of the complainant's name. There was no question that the convictions should have been revealed and, had they been so notified, prosecuting counsel would have informed the defence. It is to be hoped that with the more sophisticated forms of recording criminal convictions that exist today, such failings have been eradicated.

On 12 December 1991, Chris Mullin, MP for Sunderland South and a vociferous campaigner against miscarriages of justice, secured a debate in the House of Commons on the case of *PC Tony Salt* (see Hansard HC, 12 December 1991, col. 1221). A case against three men charged with the murder of this officer from the West Midlands Police Force had been dropped amidst allegations of false confessions and non-disclosure.

The officer and a colleague had been keeping watch on an alleged illegal drinking club when PC Salt was beaten to death. One of those charged with his murder had supposedly confessed to stealing the officer's wallet and a cubiton, a martial arts weapon. Mr Mullin launched an all-out attack on officers from the West Midlands force, who had been involved in the arrest and charging of the three suspects, and the matter was later fully investigated by an independent police officer and the DPP. Of particular concern was the non-disclosure of a statement from PC Salt's widow which, among other things, stated that she had found the missing cubiton. The results of the independent investigation and a further investigation by the CPS did not bear out some of Mr Mullin's criticisms, but the evidence against the three men charged was later considered to be insufficient to proceed with the case and charges were withdrawn nearly a year after they had been brought. Had the case proceeded to trial, there is little doubt that not only the contents, Mrs Salt's statement but also the circumstances of its non-disclosure by the CPS, would have been the subject of examination and comment.

At the time of writing, the Court of Appeal is considering one of the most notorious cases of the last 30 years, concerning the murder of 13-year-old Carl Bridgewater in September 1978 when he was delivering newspapers to Yew Tree Farm in Staffordshire. On 9 November 1979, four men were convicted of the murder. Less than two years later, one of the men, Patrick Molloy, died in prison, but the campaign to prove the innocence of Michael Hickey, Vincent Hickey and James Robinson (the so-called Bridgewater Three) has been ceaseless. In 1987 the case was referred to the Court of Appeal by Douglas Hurd, the then Home Secretary, but on 17 March 1989 the appeal was dismissed. Two years later a new police inquiry was announced, but in 1993 Kenneth Clarke, who was then Home Secretary, rejected a fresh referral. More recently, in December 1995, another Home Secretary, Michael Howard, refused a referral, but on 26 July 1996 he announced that the matter would be referred back to the Court of Appeal. On 21 February 1997, the prosecution informed the Court of Appeal that they would not contest the appeals and the Bridgewater Three were released on bail pending a full hearing. The main plank of the defence case in the unsuccessful appeal in 1981 surrounded the alleged confession of the now deceased Molloy which dominated the trial. The new hearing in April 1997 (which is underway at the time of writing), is likely to involve allegations of non-disclosure of fingerprints found on Carl's bicycle which could not be linked to the convicted men. If such information was withheld, the case of the Bridgewater Three will unquestionably be added to the depressing list of cases where non-disclosure has been instrumental in bringing about a miscarriage of justice.

THE 'ARMS TO IRAQ' CASES AND PUBLIC INTEREST IMMUNITY

Between the period 1989–92, investigators from Her Majesty's Customs and Excise were involved in a number of inquiries into allegations of the illegal export to Iraq of machine tools, components, parts and similar equipment. Some investigations (such as those into Wickman Bennett Limited, the Contractors 600 Group and Microwave Modules Limited) concluded with sums of money being compounded. Other prosecutions either were not commenced because of the absence of a realistic prospect of conviction (the so-called 'Supergun' case), or were discontinued before trial (BSA Tools Limited). The convictions of defendants employed by Euromac (London) Limited were overturned by the Court of Appeal because of misdirections to the jury by the trial judge, and defendants connected with a firm known as Atlantic Commerical who had pleaded guilty to being knowingly concerned in the attempted exportation of arms to Iraq with intent to avoid the prohibition on their export also had their appeals allowed on the extraordinary grounds that the prosecution had been responsible for preventing witnesses for the defence being available for the trial (see *R* v *Dunk* (unreported), Court of Appeal 28 July 1994). Each of these cases was examined with great thoroughness by Sir Richard Scott's *Inquiry into the Export of Defence Equipment to Iraq* (which is considered in relation to public interest immunity (PII) in chapters 9 and 10). The two prosecutions which captured most attention, both in the Scott Report and the media headlines, were those of employees of the companies Matrix Churchill and Ordtec. Both would amply justify the label 'miscarriage of justice'.

The investigation into Matrix Churchill Limited commenced in 1990 as a result of information supplied by West German Customs. Later that year officers of the company, Paul Henderson, Peter Allen and Trevor Abraham were, arrested on the allegation that they were knowingly concerned in the export of engineering equipment to Iraq without having a valid Department of Trade licence. The equipment was to be used for military purposes, such as the making of artillery shells and missiles. The three men were subsequently charged with offences contrary to s. 68(2), Customs and Excise Management Act 1979.

In September 1992, the prosecution made an application to the trial judge, His Honour Judge Smedley QC, in respect of a large number of documents in their possession. It was contended that PII attached to the documents, and although prosecuting counsel had taken the view that the documents would not assist the defence in relation to any forseeable issue, he regarded it as essential that the court should consider the position. PII certificates, signed by a number of Government ministers, were produced to the court. In the event, Judge Smedley, after reading the documents and having been told that the general defence was that there was no intention to deceive the Government in the application for export licences and, in fact, the Government were never misled, ruled that many of the documents should be disclosed (see *R* v *Henderson* (unreported), Central Criminal Court, 5 October 1992, transcript T920175 at p. 17):

> If they are documents which deal with the applications by Matrix Churchill, or which shows departure from the stated policy in relation to applications by others wishing to export to Iraq, which can be used for the purpose of undermining the prosecution case as to the Department's policy in respect of the applications for export of dual purpose machinery then access to those documents, it seems to me, may well assist the case for the defence. And to prevent access to those documents may well result in a miscarriage of justice in an important criminal case. If that is the position then the documents must be disclosed.

The prosecution's decision to withhold the documents on the grounds of materiality and PII was scrutinised during the Scott Inquiry and the relevant law is examined later. Suffice it to say, disclosure was made and the trial commenced only for the prosecution to collapse in the face of evidence given by Alan Clark, a minister at the DTI at the relevant time. Sir Richard Scott's post-mortem on the case concludes that, with the benefit of hindsight, this was a trial that ought never to have commenced. His report of nearly 2,000 pages examines events in minute detail and explains why he arrives at that conclusion. He does not subscribe to the simplistic view that all that went wrong was that Mr Clark gave evidence which was in certain respects inconsistent with his witness statement. Other factors which undermined the prosecution included investigation inadequacies, the Government's grudging attitude towards disclosure to the defence and the prosecution's approach to PII claims.

The defendants in the Ordtec prosecution were convicted; indeed Stuart Blackledge, Paul Grecian, Bryan Mason and Colin Phillips had pleaded guilty in February 1992 at Reading Crown Court to conspiracy to export goods with intent to evade the prohibition on their exportation and, with the exception of Phillips who was fined, were sentenced to suspended terms of imprisonment. The goods in question were assembly parts and components which were destined for Iraq, and the case for the Crown was that the appellants had to resort to various deceptions in order to obtain export licences for the goods as they knew that licences would not be granted to export the goods in question to Iraq. Applications had been made for licences to export 'equipments and machines' to Jordan. The defence case was that the authorities were well aware that Jordan was being used as a conduit for exports to Iraq and were, in effect, turning a blind eye to exports reaching Iraq in that way. Before the trial, a number of unsuccessful requests had been made to the Solicitor for the Customs and Excise, for the disclosure of documents concerning the policy and guidelines governing the grant of export licences.

The appeal was based on the non-disclosure of relevant material by the Crown, it being argued that documents ought to have been disclosed and that if they had been available at the trial the case would have been terminated or the appellants would not have felt constrained to have pleaded guilty. A number of documents were shown to the Court of Appeal and they were satisfied that the documents ought to have been made available before the trial. Although a jury may not necessarily have acquitted, it was considered that the documents would have enabled the appellants to present an arguable case along the lines that they had illustrated when requesting the documents. PII certificates were produced at the appeal hearing and, with minor amendments, the disclosure of documents as proposed in the certificates was approved by the Court.

Public interest immunity is judge-made law and, as will be seen when it is examined more closely later, an extremely complicated area of the law. The *Matrix Churchill* case can be distinguished from the other cases summarised above as reliance was being placed on an understanding of the law which, some would say, was misplaced. No matter what the reasons were for withholding documents, however, the fact remains that there was a danger of persons being convicted of crimes they had not committed and, as a result, a miscarriage of justice occurring.

MISCARRIAGES BY FAILING TO PROSECUTE THOSE SUSPECTED OF COMMITTING CRIME

It will be concluded from this brief summary of some well-known cases that while non-disclosure has featured in a number of celebrated so-called miscarriages of justice, the circumstances surrounding the non-disclosure are varied and sometimes complicated. The starting point has to be the honesty and integrity of those involved in the prosecution. However, it is also vital that the police and prosecutors know precisely what their duties are and that they are not unfairly hampered by a disclosure regime which prevents or inhibits the successful prosecution of those who may be guilty of crime.

In *R* v *Livingstone* [1993] Crim LR 597 (a case where prosecuting counsel failed to show the contents of a manual to defence counsel, even though the document itself was in court), Rougier J commented (transcript 91/1212/XZ, Court of Appeal, 8 March 1993, p. 4):

It is the duty of the prosecution in all cases where material, whether documentary or otherwise, which is of relevance to the defence comes into their hands to make the defence a present of such material. . . . The question of discovery in criminal cases is not the sort of tactical tit for tat or a game of Happy Families played according to technical rules such as if you do not say thank you for the card you lose your turn. It is a serious matter conducted in a court of law and, one piously hopes, in a court of justice as well.

While levity in the courtroom is always to be welcomed, comments such as this do nothing to clarify the law and the responsibilities of a prosecutor. Disclosure should never be a question of making 'presents' to one side or the other. It requires a carefully defined regime which, as far as is possible, prevents miscarriages of justice to either side. If disclosure obligations are too wide and ill-defined then there is the inevitability of miscarriages of justice whereby the guilty are acquitted. This was an important consideration in the Government's reasons for introducing the CPIA 1996. It was also part of the theme of the speech of the DPP, Barbara Mills QC, which she delivered the Tom Sargeant Memorial Lecture on 28 November 1994 and said:

> To protect an innocent person being wrongfully accused, it is essential that he or she should have access to material which can cast doubt on the prosecution case, or even go so far as to establish innocence. At the same time, it is necessary that the duties on the prosecution are clear, certain and capable of being fulfilled. If the balance is wrong, meritorious prosecutions collapse under voluminous paperwork, or relentless requests for material which may be of no real value to the defence. In some extreme cases, such requests lead to important criminal trials being abandoned to protect an informant's personal safety.

An example of this last point is provided by Charles Pollard, the Chief Constable of Thames Valley Police, in 'A case for disclosure' [1994] LR Crim 42. He cites the case of police officers searching a van in the early hours of the morning and finding a radio scanner, regularly used by criminals to monitor police radio frequencies, together with six bottles containing petrol. Each bottle had been adapted to make it an incendiary bomb. The three occupants of the van were arrested and it was later established that they were active members of the Animal Liberation Front. The subsequent prosecution of the defendants was, however, abandoned following an order by the trial judge to disclose intelligence documents relating to the Animal Liberation Front organisation. Following their acquittal, the three issued a statement to the media saying that it had been their intention to remove animals from a vehicle and damage it. The statement continued: 'The only reason the trial collapsed was because the prosecution refused to reveal to our defence lawyers material about us held on computer by the police'. Can there be any doubt that this too is a miscarriage of justice?

According to the police, this was not an isolated occurrence. Speaking at a conference in London following the publication of the Runciman's Commission's findings, Paul Condon, the Metropolitan Police Commissioner, stated that 'disclosure is being caught up in a tactical game where more and more professional criminals are able to exploit the rules and walk free' ('Today', 28 July 1993). He said that 60 major trials had been shelved rather than risk the lives of informants and undercover officers. He was supported by other police chiefs including David Shattock, Chief Constable of Avon and Somerset, who said that in a six-month period his force had withdrawn at least ten cases because it was felt that the disclosure rules being evolved by the courts would have put informants and witnesses at risk (*Daily Telegraph*, 23 March 1994). Police concerns are repeated by David Rose in his book *In the Name of the Law* (Jonathan Cape: London, 1996) which suggests the collapse of criminal justice in England and Wales. He cites a Regional Crime Squad officer as saying that in 1994 and 1995, a tenth of the output of his unit was being withdrawn because of the disclosure rules.

It was not just the police who were complaining of miscarriages where criminals were not being prosecuted and convicted owing to the increasingly complex disclosure rules. Delivering the annual James Smart Lecture under the title 'Intelligence, Security and the Law', the Director General of the Security Service, Stella Rimington, claimed that the rules sometimes acted as a constraint on investigations which involved sensitive techniques which had to be protected (*Daily Telegraph*, 5 November 1994). Those concerned with the detection and prosecution of alleged offenders were not happy that they were participating on a level playing field.

CONCLUSIONS

There can be no argument that a judicial system which has seen so many convictions overturned because of disclosure irregularities is seriously defective. If, in trying to shore up inadequacies, the effective detection and prosecution of crime is frustrated, the system only falls further into disrepute. The dangers of an inadequate system of disclosure in both criminal and civil proceedings were summed up by Lord Templeman in *R* v *Chief Constable of the West Midlands Police, ex parte Wiley* [1994] 3 WLR 433, when he stated (at p. 436): 'The indiscriminate and undisciplined preparation and presentation of documents for trial increase the length and cost of trials and sometimes enable a litigant to snatch an undeserved victory under a cloak of confusion and obscurity which baffles judge and jury.'

By the middle years of the 1990s, condemnation of the disclosure rules was universal. The prosecution stood indicted of acting unfairly and causing the wrongful conviction and imprisonment of a number of innocent persons. Defence solicitors were accused of manipulating the rules to allow the acquittal of the guilty, and the courts were denounced as impotent in their attempts to define the law and preserve the integrity of the criminal trial process. How had such a situation come to pass?

It is now necessary to trace the history and development of the law on disclosure in criminal proceedings in order to try to understand how and why the deficiencies illustrated by *Ward* and other cases arose.

4 Disclosure of the Prosecution Case

GENERAL PRINCIPLES

It is highly improbable that prosecuting counsel in the Crown Court would endeavour to introduce, as part of the case for the prosecution, evidence which had not been disclosed to the defence. In reality, it would be a waste of time even to try as the judge would accede to the inevitable defence application for an adjournment in order that the fresh evidence could be considered. It is surprising, therefore, that there is no statute or legal authority which states, in terms, that the prosecution must disclose their case to the defence. Indeed, it is one of the anomalies in the law relating to disclosure that there is far more legal authority on the disclosure of material which the Crown proposes not to adduce than on the disclosure of the prosecution case itself. There are, of course, statutory provisions for the service of statements prior to a committal or transfer, but nothing which strictly prohibits the prosecution calling evidence which they have not disclosed to the defence. Many text books describe this practice as a duty, but it is more a requirement born out of a general desire to see natural justice done than an obligation in law.

It is a general principle of the common law that an accused should know the details of the allegation against him or her. Thus, a charge or summons sets out the date and brief particulars of the alleged offence together with the relevant statute that has been contravened. With regard to an offence tried at the Crown Court, an indictment is preferred which provides brief particulars of the statement and particulars of the offence alleged. The purpose of these formal documents is to inform an accused of the proceedings against him or her and invoke the jurisdiction of the court. They are not intended to supply more detailed information about the evidence which the prosecution will call in support of the allegation.

During the nineteenth century there was a definite presumption against providing an accused with a copy of any depositions taken by the court. The principal reason for this was the fear that if accused persons knew the nature of the evidence against them, they would be tempted to tamper with, or falsify, such evidence or intimidate those who would be called to give the evidence. Such fears are understandable and the dangers of witnesses being intimidated and evidence interfered with are as real today as they have ever been. Against this, however, there has to be balanced the accused's right to a fair trial. While the onus is on the prosecution to prove the case against an accused, it seems only right that the nature of the case should be disclosed in order that a defence can be prepared. If an accused is taken too much by surprise, the prospects of convicting the innocent are increased.

An early recognition of the principle of giving reasonable notice to the defence may be found in *R* v *Spry and Dore* (1848) 3 Cox CC 221. The accused were charged with the murder of an infant by poisoning and an application was made on their behalf in advance of the trial for a doctor to be allowed to inspect the stomach of the deceased child and its contents, and a medicine that the prosecution intended to produce. The Recorder of London sitting at the Central Criminal Court doubted whether he had jurisdiction to entertain the application, but continued: 'I have less difficulty in granting this application, because the judge would no doubt at the trial stop the case until such examination had been made.'

An interesting insight into the state of the law during this period is provided by a report of an application in a case of arson at the Cambridgeshire Summer Assizes in March 1845 (see *R* v *O'Connor* (1845) 1 Cox CC 233). It is reported that copies of the depositions had been supplied 'in the usual manner', but the application on behalf of the defendants was for them to be supplied with 'a great body of additional evidence' against them. Prosecuting counsel opposed the application on the ground that the court had no power in the matter, and further objected to furnishing his opponent with a list of the witnesses as they might be tampered with before the case came on. Patterson J remarked that while it was desirable that the whole evidence be shown to the prisoners, he had no authority to interfere and could not order the prosecutor to furnish the prisoners with all the evidence. In other words, judges did not have the power to compel the prosecution to disclose their evidence in advance, but the general view of the judiciary was that it was a practice that should be followed.

STATUTORY REFORMS

Statutory reforms were nevertheless encouraging a wind of change in respect of the rights of accused persons. Whereas in the early part of the nineteenth century the balance in favour of non-disclosure predominated over the entitlement of the accused to be informed of the evidence against them, changes in the nature of preliminary inquiries brought about a shift in the balance. The accused became entitled to legal representation at committal proceedings by virtue of the Prisoner's Counsel Act 1836, while the Trials for Felony Act 1836 allowed all persons tried for felony to make their defence by counsel or attorney. The provision of legal assistance was supported in s. 4 of the latter statute by an entitlement, at the time of trial, to inspect all depositions or copies thereof.

The Indictable Offences Act 1848 empowered justices to examine witnesses and record their evidence in writing in the case of an accused charged with any indictable offence. Section 17 of the Act allowed cross-examination in the presence of accused persons who would thereby know the case against them. Section 27 provided that an accused was entitled to copies of the depositions, after the preliminary examination had been completed and before the first day of the assizes to which the accused had been committed, but only on payment of a reasonable sum, not exceeding the rate of three halfpence for each folio of 90 words!

By s. 3, Administration of the Criminal Law Act 1867, an accused was able to call witnesses and present a defence; and by s. 1, Criminal Evidence Act 1898, the accused was made a competent witness for the defence. These developments allowed the accused to know the nature of the prosecution case so that the allegations could be answered. Towards the end of the century, the practice of providing not only copies of the depositions but also details of further evidence was becoming established. In *R v Pietro Stiginani* (1867) 10 Cox CC 552, Willes J observed that 'I never let evidence of which notice has not been given, pass without strong observation'. Such sentiments were echoed by Brett J in *R v Greenslade* (1884) 15 Cox CC 412, when he allowed a witness, who had not been before the magistrates, to give evidence at the trial, 'but, however, notice of its production ought to be given to the prisoner, or his attorney, and if such notice was not given, it was a subject for strong comment'.

If strong comment was not enough, the court would usually be prepared to grant an adjournment to ensure that the accused was not placed at a disadvantage as a result of the prosecution calling evidence at the last minute. In *R v Flannagan and Higgins* (1884) 15 Cox CC 403, the co-accused who were sisters, were charged with the murder of Higgins's husband. The prosecution wished to introduce expert evidence concerning the alleged poisoning which had been obtained only on the morning in question. Butt J ruled that he could not exclude the evidence, but he was prepared to postpone the trial in order that the defence could conduct an analysis of their own in order to rebut the evidence.

Although the practice of disclosing the evidence for the prosecution was established by the turn of the century, it could still not accurately be described as a positive duty. This is illustrated in *R v Wright* (1934) 25 Cr App R 35, where one of the grounds of appeal was that the appellant had had no notice that the prosecution proposed to put in evidence the specimens of his handwriting which had been taken while he was in custody. The judgment of Avory J on this point (at p. 39) was as follows:

> It is quite true that there was an omission to give specific notice of these two specimens of the appellant's handwriting. At most this is a grievance and cannot affect the admissibility of the evidence put before the jury, and, if the appellant or his counsel thought that he was being prejudiced by having no notice and really desired to call expert evidence to deal with the question of handwriting, he could have applied for an adjournment, but he did not do so.

An adjournment is the proper course for the late service of details of the prosecution case. In *R v Johnson* [1996] Crim LR 504, the prosecution had not served fingerprint evidence connecting the accused with a robbery until the day of the trial. Prosecuting counsel had decided only the night before the trial that the evidence should be used in addition to the accused's admission that she had been present at the scene. Objection had been taken by defence counsel on the ground that the accused was prejudiced. The judge had invited the defence to have an adjournment but they had refused, and the Court of Appeal held that there was no reason to interfere with the way the judge had handled the matter.

COMMITTAL PROCEEDINGS AND TRANSFERS

Today, well over 90 per cent of allegations of crime are heard at the magistrates' courts, but this was not always the case. Following the consolidation of the law relating to the functions of magistrates in the Administration of Justice (No. 1) Act 1848, it became the function of magistrates to conduct a preliminary examination of allegations of crime before the offences were eventually tried at quarter sessions or assizes. The purpose of the preliminary judicial hearing was to ensure the existence of a prima facie case against the accused. The prosecution did not have to call all their evidence, neither was there any requirement to disclose their case to the accused prior to the hearing. Committal proceedings were not, therefore, a means whereby the accused could obtain discovery of the evidence in its entirety.

The procedures for committal proceedings have undergone considerable statutory change. Part II of the Criminal Justice Act 1925 provided a basis for the taking of depositions and their being read over to the witness in the presence and hearing of the accused. The Magistrates' Courts Act 1952 further explained the role of examining justices, but it was not until the introduction of major reforms in committal proceedings brought about by the Criminal Justice Act (CJA) 1967 that prosecution disclosure requirements were affected. Before the CJA 1967, magistrates could receive and consider evidence in deposition form only with the accused being present and having an opportunity to hear the evidence and cross-examine the witness. The 1967 Act introduced committal by the tendering of written statements, and provided that the statements were in prescribed form and had been served on the accused in accordance with requirements of the Act, the case could be committed without consideration of the evidence.

For the first time, therefore, the prosecution had a statutory duty, by virtue of s. 2, CJA 1967, to serve statements on the accused which were sufficient to show a prima facie case on each of the charges brought. In committals where the evidence was to be considered and where witnesses were still to be called, provision for the taking and supply of depositions was made in the Magistrates' Courts Rules 1968. Further reform of the magistrates' procedure was made by the Magistrates' Courts Act (MCA) 1980, which required the service of statements under s. 102, MCA 1980 for a committal under s. 6, without consideration of the evidence.

There is still no requirement, however, for the prosecution to serve all its statements or call all witnesses at the committal stage (see *R* v *Epping and Harlow Justices, ex parte Massaro* (1973) 57 Cr App R 499). In addition, other witnesses may not come to the notice of the prosecution until after committal. The prosecution are not precluded from calling such persons. It is the practice in both circumstances, however, for the Crown to serve a Notice of Additional Evidence. The practice was stated succinctly by Scarman LJ in *R* v *Kane* (1977) 65 Cr App R 270 (at p. 274): 'In general, evidence which is capable of forming part of the affirmative case for the prosecution should be tendered and led in the course of that case. If it did not form part of the evidence upon which an accused was committed for trial the practice is to give notice of the additional evidence to the defence before it is tendered.' The notice invariably takes the form of service of the statement of the witness, but it is sufficient (albeit unusual) to serve a proof of the evidence (where, for example, the statement contains irrelevant or inadmissible material).

Following a recommendation in the Runciman Commission Report, committal proceedings were to be replaced by transfer provisions introduced by s. 44 and sch. 4, Criminal Justice and Public Order Act 1994. These affected cases where the defendant was charged with an indictable only offence, or where the mode of trial decision had resulted in the Crown Court being deemed the appropriate venue of trial. However, those drafting the proposed measures encountered considerable opposition and insuperable difficulties with the result that s. 44 was abolished by s. 47, CPIA 1996. Transfer provisions are not new, having been introduced for cases of serious fraud and child abuse by virtue of s. 5, Criminal Justice Act 1987 and s. 53, Criminal Justice Act 1991 respectively (transfer procedures for war crimes have been abolished by s. 46, CPIA 1996). In cases where transfer provisions are still applicable, details of the prosecution case are disclosed by service of a notice of transfer giving details of the charges and copies of documents containing the evidence. The majority of cases for trial at the Crown Court will continue to be subject to the committal provisions which are now contained in sch. 1, CPIA 1996.

ADVANCE DISCLOSURE AT THE MAGISTRATES' COURT

Background

While there has been some element of disclosure of the prosecution case in relation to cases destined for the higher courts since the middle of the last century, it is quite a different picture in the magistrates' court. Until 40 years ago, there was no form of statutory requirement at all. This eventually came with the provisions of ss. 1 and 2, Magistrates' Courts Act 1957 in connection with pleas of guilty invited by post. The provisions have since been re-enacted as s. 12, Magistrates' Courts Act 1980, whereby a plea of guilty in writing may be received provided that the prosecutor has served on the accused a concise statement of the facts relating to the charge.

Such a requirement for the least serious offences hardly provided a satisfactory solution to those who were pressing for a more formal system of disclosure in proceedings which would, or might, be heard summarily. It would be wrong, however, to conclude that there was no disclosure at all in such cases. Despite the absence of a formal legal requirement, many prosecuting authorities adopted informal procedures, usually in the hope that disclosure would encourage a plea of guilty. Informal disclosure of statements or a summary of the evidence prior to the day of the hearing, or even at court on an advocate to advocate basis, was very much an *ad hoc* system and varied from one prosecuting authority to another.

The position clearly needed to be addressed. There was no good reason in principle why a defendant who was contemplating trial summarily should be placed at a disadvantage when compared with an accused who was to be tried at the Crown Court. There were, however, a number of practical obstacles and these were considered fully in 1975 by an Interdepartmental Committee, chaired by Lord Justice James — the *Report on the Distribution of Criminal Business between the Crown Court and Magistrates' Courts*, Cmnd 6323, London: HMSO, 1975 (the James Report), paras 213 *et seq*. There were four main concerns why copies of witness statements should not be disclosed to a defendant before election as to mode of trial.

The first was the old chestnut of the danger of witnesses being intimidated or persuaded to change their evidence. However, as the service of such statements for a committal under s. 1, CJA 1967, where the offence would usually be more serious, was by this time accepted legal practice, the objection was hardly sustainable. Secondly, concerns were expressed that the statement might contain defamatory, prejudicial or confidential information. While such anxieties were recognised, there was nothing that editing of the statement could not circumvent. The third cause of disquiet was the belief that the defence would be able to make capital out of minor or immaterial discrepancies between the oral evidence of the witness and the written statement. The Committee believed that this would happen only rarely (although, as shall be seen, when the effects of the enlarged disclosure rules of the 1990s came into play, this point may have deserved greater consideration). The main objection, however, was the practical one of the work involved for the police and prosecuting authority in having to copy and serve statements in a vast number of cases, or alternatively to prepare a summary of the offence(s). At the end of the day, though, the validity of the principle of fairness triumphed over the more pragmatic considerations and the Committee recommended that before consenting to summary trial, an accused should have a statutory right to copies of the statements of those witnesses on whom the prosecution proposed to rely. If the prosecution called a witness whose statement had not been served, the defence were entitled to an adjournment. The Committee also recognised that there might be some circumstances where a summary of the facts, as distinct from the statements themselves, would suffice.

The recommendations of the James Report in this regard were broadly accepted and the power to make rules as to the furnishing of information by the prosecutor in criminal proceedings was provided in s. 48, Criminal Law Act 1977. But while the Government hestitated to make rules under s. 48, principally on the grounds of cost, the *Report of the Royal Commission on Criminal Procedure* (Cmnd 8092–1, HMSO: London, 1981) endorsed the James recommendations. It was not until 20 May 1985, however, that the Magistrates' Courts (Advance Information) Rules 1985 (SI 1985 No. 601) (referred to hereafter as 'the Rules') came into force.

Magistrates' Courts (Advance Information) Rules 1985

The Rules apply to proceedings for an offence triable either way. Before mode of trial is decided, the prosecutor provides advance disclosure upon request by accused persons or their representatives (r. 4). The scheme of advance disclosure encountered a number of teething problems. The timing of its introduction was particularly unfortunate as it coincided with the emergence of the CPS, to which advance disclosure was another, not inconsiderable, burden. There had to be a standardisation of disclosure as some police forces were providing statements while most had opted for summaries. In its early days advance disclosure was often blamed for delays in hearings, but gradually procedures became established and it is now acknowledged as a fair way of informing defendants of the evidence in support of the allegation so that they may exercise the right of election. Whether it has achieved the secondary objective of increasing guilty pleas is questionable, but at least there is some degree of parity with the disclosure of the more serious offences tried at the Crown Court.

The prosecutor has a discretion whether to furnish the accused with statements of witnesses or with a summary of the facts. The prosecutor is also entitled, by virtue of r. 5, to withhold any fact or matter if it is considered that an attempt might be made to intimidate a witness or otherwise interfere with the course of justice. If the court considers that r. 4 has not been complied with, it has power under r. 7 to adjourn the matter. The application of the Rules was considered by the Divisional Court in *King* v *Kucharz* (1989) 153 JP 336, where in proceedings for an offence of criminal damage, the prosecutor at first refused to provide advance information under r. 4 on the ground that disclosure would result in further damage and intimidation, reliance being placed on the provisions of r. 5. At an adjourned hearing he agreed to provide information and furnished the accused with a limited summary. The justices found that the summary was inadequate, and concluded that the prosecutor's conduct amounted to an abuse of process and dismissed the case. The Divisional Court held that it was not open to the justices on the basis of the Rules alone to find that the conduct of the prosecutor amounted to an abuse of process. The proper course was to adjourn the matter in accordance with r. 7 pending compliance with the request for further information, or to proceed to hear the case if they were satisfied that the defendant would not be substantially prejudiced by the non-compliance.

It is, of course, open to justices to refuse to hear an information on grounds of the more recognised circumstances which would lead to an abuse of process, such as delay. In *Daventry District Council* v *Olins* (1990) 154 JP 478, it was held that the magistrates were entitled to conclude that delay, and in particular the delay in informing the defendant of the identity of the complainant, was prejudicial and amounted to an abuse of the process of the court.

The Privy Council considered in *Vincent* v *The Queen*; *Franklyn* v *The Queen* [1993] 1 WLR 862, whether the refusal of the prosecution to supply copies of statements of its witnesses in a trial at the magistrates' court caused a denial of a fair hearing. In two trials heard before a resident magistrate in Jamaica, no statements of the prosecution witnesses had been served on the accused, in accordance with the usual practice which then obtained. The judgment of Lord Woolf made the obvious point that an accused will be assisted in the preparation of his defence by the provision of the statements and commented that it would, therefore, be desirable for copies to be provided. In Jamaica, a resident magistrate has jurisdiction to try serious offences and their Lordships were of the opinion that the practice of refusing to provide statements of proposed witnesses, as a matter of course, was inappropriate. The DPP was invited to give further guidance on the subject.

The Privy Council had, of course, been informed that there was no requirement in England and Wales to provide copies of statements in relation to offences which were triable summarily only, and Lord Woolf remarked on this by saying that when the court is concerned with 'petty offences' it is not normally practical or necessary in order to obtain a fair trial for the defendant to be served in advance with copies of the statements of witnesses. The Divisional Court has consistently refused to extend such an obligation to the prosecution, although it is the practice of the CPS to volunteer such disclosure in the more serious summary offences which are punishable by imprisonment.

In *R* v *Kingston-upon-Hull Justices, ex parte McCann* (1991) 155 JP 569, it was held that there was no general obligation to disclose statements in advance of a summary trial, and if it was thought that there ought to be such an obligation it was a matter for the legislature and not the courts. Bingham LJ did remark that:

Ordinarily, I have no doubt that Crown Prosecutors are well advised to adopt a policy of disclosing to the defence the material upon which they rely. That, as we are told, is the general policy of the Crown Prosecution Service in Humberside and I have no doubt it is a beneficial policy. In some circumstances it may even be that disclosure is necessary in the interests of fairness.

An attempt to persuade the Divisional Court to enforce r. 4 by an order of mandamus failed in *R* v *Director of the Serious Fraud Office, ex parte Kevin Maxwell* (unreported), Divisional Court CO/2312/92, 6 October 1992. In his judgment, Mann LJ entertained grave doubts as to whether r. 4 is enforceable by mandamus, but even if it did lie, he said that the Court would not order the performance of a statutory duty in order to achieve a purpose which is plainly not for the achievement of which that the duty is imposed. It was common ground among the parties that the purpose of the Rules is to enable an accused to make an informed choice as to mode of trial. The applicant was charged with theft, an either-way offence, and also with conspiracy which is triable only on indictment. The Court would not enforce compliance by the Serious Fraud Office with a request under r. 4 to provide advance disclosure of interviews held with the applicant under the provisions of s. 2, Criminal Justice Act 1987.

It is clear, therefore, that although the Rules impose a duty of disclosure on the prosecution in respect of either-way offences only in order to assist the defendant in the choice of mode of trial, the courts look favourably upon the voluntary disclosure of information in connection with offences triable summarily only. The practice was described in *R v Haringey Justices, ex parte DPP* [1996] Crim LR 327 as sensible, since in all but the relatively simple cases the defence may otherwise need an adjournment to prepare their case properly. To this extent, the practice of prosecutors to provide disclosure in the more serious summary offences is commendable and ensures fairness to an accused by identifying the evidence which will be adduced in support of the allegation.

Calling witnesses disclosed by way of advance information

As in cases heard in the Crown Court, the prosecution have a discretion over which witnesses they will call in support of their case. The statements of witnesses not to be called (or the names and addresses of the makers of the statements) will normally be supplied to the defence. The discretion is not entirely unfettered, however, and the general principles governing circumstances when witnesses should be called or made available in the Crown Court were summarised in *R v Russell-Jones* [1995] 1 Cr App R 538 and re-stated in *R v Brown and Brown* [1996] Crim LR 659. In relation to cases heard at the magistrates' court, the principles were adopted in *R v Haringey Justices, ex parte DPP* (above), although the Divisional Court recognised that the point, equivalent to serving statements for a committal, was more difficult to determine when cases were being heard summarily. In the judgment of Stuart-Smith LJ, in cases triable either way where the prosecution have provided advance information under r. 4, the discretion to call witnesses becomes fettered. In other words, if a witness's statement is served as advance information, the prosecution should call that witness on the trial. The *Haringey Justices* case specifically considered the position of a suspended police officer whose statement had been served but whom the prosecution refused to call. It is to be hoped that this decision does not encourage prosecutors to serve less than full advance information in fear that they may later be compelled to call a witness that they did not wish to present as part of the prosecution case. It should have the effect of concentrating attention at advance information stage on what evidence should be adduced and what can be 'given away' to the defence as unused material.

In relation to offences into which no criminal investigation has begun before 1 April 1997, no witness will be called to give evidence or be cross-examined in committals under s. 6(1), Magistrates' Courts Act 1980. This is as a result of the modifications introduced by s. 47 and sch. 1, CPIA 1996.

ADVANCE NOTICE OF EXPERT EVIDENCE

In concluding this résumé of the law and practice in relation to the disclosure of the prosecution case, mention must be made of the Crown Court (Advance Notice of Expert Evidence) Rules 1987 (SI 1987 No. 716), although these will be dealt with in more detail in chapter 7. Section 81, Police and Criminal Evidence Act 1984, provided for the making of rules requiring parties to proceedings before the Crown Court to give advance notice of any expert they proposed to call. Irrespective of these Rules, we have already seen that the prosecution will have served the expert's statement as part of the committal or transfer arrangements, or as notice of additional evidence. The 1987 Rules do, however, permit the other party to have a reasonable opportunity to inspect the record of any observation, test or calculation on which the expert's opinion is based and, since the decision in *R* v *Ward* (1993) 96 Cr App R 1, provide for the defence to be informed of the results of any other test which do not support the opinion being given by the expert called on behalf of the Crown. In so far as cases to be tried in the Crown Court are concerned, the rules therefore provide an additional duty of disclosure concerning an expert witness. Section 20(3), CPIA 1996 provides power to make similar rules in relation to hearings at the magistrates' court, and this was given effect by the Magistrates' Courts (Advance Notice of Expert Evidence) Rules 1997 (SI 1997 No. 705) in relation to criminal investigations commenced on or after 1 April 1997.

DISCLOSURE OF REBUTTAL EVIDENCE

When the Crown is in possession of documents which are not introduced as part of the prosecution case, should they be disclosed before they are used in cross-examination of the defendant in order to rebut a defence? The duty of disclosure in such circumstances was at the heart of the appeal in *R* v *Phillipson* (1990) 91 Cr App R 226, where it was alleged that the failure by the prosecution to disclose certain letters and a photograph, which were then used in cross-examination of the defendant to rebut her defence of duress, amounted to an irregularity in the course of the trial. The Court of Appeal ruled that there had been such an irregularity.

It is a general rule of practice that all evidentiary matter on which the prosecution propose to rely as probative of the guilt of an accused, should be adduced as part of the prosecution case (see *R* v *Rice* (1963) 47 Cr App R 79 and *R* v *Kane* (1977) 65 Cr App R 270). This means that the Crown cannot hold back material which it knows to be of potential help to the prosecution, in order to surprise the defendant in cross-examination. In the judgment of the Court in *Phillipson*, Gibson LJ stated (at p. 233):

Where the material in question, on the facts known to the prosecution, could only be damaging to the defence and of assistance to the prosecution, the obligation to disclose, if any, must, we think, be sought primarily in the principles governing the obligation of the prosecution to include within its case all probative material upon which it intends to rely, having regard to the facts and circumstances known to the prosecution when the case is presented.

The fact that a defendant would be able to prepare an answer to the incriminating evidence in advance was not sufficiently good reason for refusing to disclose. The principle of fairness to the defendant in knowing the full extent of prosecution case, which would better equip the defendant to decide whether or not to give evidence, was paramount. *Phillipson* was followed in *R* v *Sansom* (1991) 92 Cr App R 115, where it was contended that certain documents used in cross-examination should have formed part of the prosecution case. The Court of Appeal ruled that they should and in their judgment urged the prosecution to take scrupulous care in seeing that material which should form part of the prosecution case is so presented.

Part of the argument of the Crown in *Phillipson* was based on the fact that the material in question was not 'unused material' within the definition of the *Attorney-General's Guidelines for the Disclosure of 'Unused Material' to the Defence* (1982) 74 Cr App R 302. There is no doubt that the material would be disclosable under the CPIA 1996. Even if the material had not been disclosed at the primary stage on the grounds that it would not undermine the prosecution case, once the nature of the defence was known, the material could not be held back for cross-examination purposes but would have to be served as secondary disclosure. The combined effect of the principle enunciated by Gibson LJ and the provisions of the CPIA 1996 is to ensure that evidence probative of the accused's guilt is either led as part of the prosecution case or disclosed. It is highly unlikely in the future that the courts will sanction the keeping back of probative evidence in order that the prosecution gain a tactical advantage by surprising the accused in cross-examination.

5 Disclosure of Matters Affecting Character and Credibility of Prosecution Witnesses

The previous chapter considered the law and practice relating to the disclosure of the prosecution case. This chapter examines the duty of the prosecution in relation to the disclosure of matters affecting the character and credibility of the witnesses who are called on behalf of the prosecution.

CROSS-EXAMINATION AS TO CHARACTER AND CREDIBILITY

The object of cross-examination of a prosecution witness is to test the evidence given by the witness-in-chief and, possibly, to provide evidence which may assist the defence. The questioning is not limited to the scope of the examination-in-chief, but it must be directly relevant to the matters in issue. To this end, cross-examination as to credit is often a crucial weapon in the defence armoury in undermining the reliability of a prosecution witness and the strength of the evidence given. Witnesses may be cross-examined about prior inconsistent statements; previous convictions, cautions or disciplinary findings; a reputation for untruthfulness; bias or partiality; or any physical or mental instability which may affect reliability. The prosecution have a duty at common law to disclose information which has a bearing on the credibility of the witness. The information may relate to any of the matters listed above. Whether the court allows the defence to pursue a line of cross-examination as to credit is immaterial; there is a duty on the prosecution to make disclosure, although, as with so many aspects of the law on the subject, the extent of the prosecution's duty is less clear.

DISCLOSURE OF PREVIOUS INCONSISTENT STATEMENTS

Sections 4 and 5, Criminal Procedure Act 1865 (sometimes referred to as Denman's Act) permit cross-examination of a witness about previous inconsistent oral or written statements provided that the witness is given an opportunity to comment on the alleged statements and state whether he or she did, in fact, make them. In many instances, the defence will know of the prior statements only if the prosecution have so informed them. Where the prosecution have in their possession an earlier statement from a witness which conflicts substantially with the evidence given by the witness during the trial, the defence *must* be so informed: see *R* v *Howes* (unreported), Court of Appeal, 27 March 1950. In other cases, the judge has acceded to defence applications to see the statements, as in *R* v *Hall* (1958) 43 Cr App R 29, and *R* v *Xinaris* (1955) 43 Cr App R 30. In these days of more open disclosure, it is highly unlikely that the defence would need to make the application, unless the prosecution were objecting to disclosure on public interest grounds; but even then communication of the inconsistent statement could be made by means other than showing or copying the statement itself.

If further authority is needed in relation to the prosecution's duty to disclose previous inconsistent statements, it may be found in the decision of the Privy Council in *Berry* v *The Queen* (1993) 96 Cr App R 77 where Lord Lowry stated (at p. 82): 'There is also a rule of practice under which Crown counsel owes a duty to inform the defence of any material discrepancy between the contents of a witness's statement and the evidence given by that witness on the trial.' *Berry* was an appeal from the Court of Appeal of Jamaica where the Privy Council held that where the prosecution knew that the statement of a witness which had been made to the police departed significantly from his deposition, there was a duty to supply a copy of that statement to the defence before the trial.

The principle is exactly the same where a witness has given evidence in summary proceedings and is to give evidence again in an appeal at the Crown Court. In *R* v *Halton Justices, ex parte Hughes* (1991) 155 JPN 348, there were discrepancies in the original statements of the main witnesses and the evidence they had given at the magistrates' court hearing. It was held that where there was a summary trial (and statements had not been disclosed in advance of the hearing) the prosecution should ensure that the defence were made aware of any material differences, whether of addition, substitution or outright contradiction, which appeared between a witness's evidence and any earlier statement and which could afford the defence an opportunity for potentially effective cross-examination.

Of course, many instances of prior inconsistent statements will not come to light until the witness actually gives evidence. In such circumstances, the prosecutor is under a duty to inform the defence immediately. If, however, the inconsistency is known before the hearing, the duty to disclose without waiting for a request is established. Whether the inconsistency is of significance may be less clear, but this is a matter for the discretion of the prosecutor and will depend entirely on the facts and circumstances of the case.

The duty is not confined to discrepancies which may occur in witness statements made to the police, but also exists in relation to any document on which the defence may wish to rely to assist their case. In *R* v *Clarke* (1930) 22 Cr App R 58, a police officer had been cross-examined at the trial about differences in the description of the defendant which he had given at the committal proceedings and that which he had provided in a report to his senior officer. Although the Court of Appeal applied the proviso to s. 4(1), Criminal Appeal Act 1907 in dismissing the appeal, it was held that a defendant is entitled to see a written description of himself given by a police officer to his superior. Defence counsel had been quite entitled to make the request of the prosecution.

In *R* v *Taylor* (1994) 98 Cr App R 361, the failure to disclose an inconsistent prior description made by a witness was held to be a material irregularity; and it is likely that non-disclosure of any inconsistency in relation to descriptions, whether they are in statements, police note books, identification forms or any other document, will result in a successful appeal. There is, therefore, a duty upon the police to draw such inconsistencies to the attention of the prosecutor and for the latter to ensure that proper disclosure is made to the defence.

Furthermore, the information should be disclosed to any other co-defendant against whom the witness also gives evidence. This is because any prior inconsistent statement goes to the credibility of the witness and not the factual evidence which he or she may give: see *Baksh* v *R* [1958] AC 167. The same applies to details of antecedents and previous convictions of a witness.

DISCLOSURE OF MATTERS OF BIAS OR PARTIALITY

Witnesses may be cross-examined to show that bias, partiality or prejudice against the accused is the reason for giving incriminating evidence against him or her. If the prosecution have any information which affects credibility in this way, they are under a duty to disclose it to the defence. Illustrations of this are provided by a number of recent cases featuring the non-disclosure of the fact that a witness has sought a reward. In *R* v *Taylor* (above), the defence had been told that the fiancée of the principal prosecution witness had written to the deceased's employers, Barclays Bank, claiming a reward. The witness had duly been cross-examined on this point. However, what was unknown to both prosecuting counsel and the defence, although it was known to the police, was that the witness himself had also written claiming a reward. At the appeal hearing, the Crown conceded that this fact should also have been disclosed.

A similar point arose in *R* v *Rasheed (Abdul)* (1994) *The Times*, 20 May 1994, where the accused had been convicted of manslaughter, assault with intent to rob, wounding with intent and doing an act with intent to pervert the course of justice. Much of the evidence against him was provided by a former girlfriend who, it later transpired, had asked to be considered for a reward about five weeks after the robbery and ten months before the trial. After the trial she received an award of £2,000. Counsel for the appellant submitted that the prosecution were under an obligation to disclose the information as it was relevant to the witness's credibility. Steyn LJ agreed, stating (at transcript 89/4043/W3, Court of Appeal, 17 May 1994, p. 14):

As a matter of common sense a request for a reward by a witness may have a bearing on his motives for coming forward to give evidence. It must, therefore, always be disclosed by the police to the Crown Prosecution Service, and the prosecution must disclose it to the defence. That duty is a continuing one, and a failure to disclose such a document is, therefore, an irregularity in the trial within the meaning of s. 2(1)(c) of the Criminal Appeal Act 1968.

In *Law Officers of the Crown* v *Renouf* (unreported), Guernsey Court of Appeal, 9 December 1995, the decisions in *Taylor* and *Rasheed* were followed. The Procureur considered whether he had a duty to disclose to the defence a conversation between witnesses about a reward, but decided that there was no such obligation. At the appeal, the Crown did not contest that the duty of disclosure in Guernsey is the same as in England. The Court held that the Procureur's decision was mistaken and the appeal against conviction for a bank robbery was allowed.

    R v *Brown (Winston)* [1995] 1 Cr App R 191 and *R* v *Browning (Edward)* [1995] Crim LR 227 also make reference to the fact that a request for a reward by a prosecution witness is a matter affecting credibility which must be disclosed. In *Browning*, the non-disclosure of the fact that a witness had undergone a hypnosis session in order to recall more of the registration number of a car, was also held to be a material irregularity. Clearly, knowledge of the fact would have given the defence the opportunity to test his credibility in cross-examination.

    The mere fact that the husbands of prosecution witnesses had previous convictions could not, however, properly go to the credit of their wives. Thus, in *R* v *Black (Catriona)* (unreported), Court of Appeal, 24 July 1994, the non-disclosure of the bad character of the husbands of two key prosecution witnesses was not fatal to a conviction on counts of obtaining property by deception. The case against the appellant was that she had pretended that there had been two burglaries at her home and had made false insurance claims in respect of the alleged losses. The defence claimed that the husbands of the witnesses may have been responsible for the burglaries reported by the appellant. The judgment commented that there must be some practical limit to the obligation of disclosure in such a case when the issues are unformulated or formulated only at the last minute by the defence and when, even then, the defence give no clear or precise indication of the material sought.

DISCLOSURE OF PREVIOUS CONVICTIONS

Previous convictions of accused

The disclosure of the previous convictions of accused persons is governed by *Practice Direction (Crime: Antecedents)* (1966) 50 Cr App R 271, the first paragraph of which states:

Details of previous convictions must always be supplied by the police to the defending solicitor, or if no solicitor is instructed to defending counsel, on request. The judges are of the opinion that there is no obligation on a police officer to satisfy himself that the prisoner has authorised a statement of previous convictions to be given as it is clearly within the ordinary authority of solicitor and counsel to obtain this information. In order that the defence may be properly conducted, the prisoner's advisers must know whether they can safely put the defendant's character in issue.

The reason for the disclosure is to enable the defence to decide whether to make any issue of character. It is the long-established practice of prosecuting authorities to provide, upon request, copies of previous convictions of any co-accused. This is because s. 1(f)(iii), Criminal Evidence Act 1898, allows for bad character to be admitted in evidence when one co-accused has given evidence against another co-accused. The final sentence in para. 1 of the *Practice Direction* is of equal force for solicitors for one co-accused deciding whether to make character an issue.

Previous convictions of witnesses

Where a witness for the prosecution has a criminal record, the prosecution have a duty to disclose details to the defence. Behind that simple statement of principle, which appears in most leading text books on criminal procedure and evidence, are, however, a number of ancillary questions, the answers to which are neither easy nor covered by legal authority. Do the police have a duty to check the criminal records of all prosecution witnesses? Do they need to go further and, for example, make inquiries to see if there is anything known about the witness in intelligence records, or anything known in other jurisdictions? Does the prosecutor have to disclose all convictions known against a witness, no matter how trivial or remote in time or similarity from the type of offence with which the accused is charged; or does the prosecutor have a discretion? Does the duty extend to all proceedings, even those tried summarily? When should such disclosure take place; at the outset or when it is known that the evidence of the witness is to be challenged? Is there any need to disclose on a known plea of guilty?

These are the sort of questions which daily face the police and prosecutors in the magistrates' courts and Crown Court. Not only is there a duty to be fair to the defendant, but there is a corresponding obligation of fairness to the witnesses. It is often difficult to encourage witnesses to give evidence, and the task is not made any easier if the witnesses realise that they may be cross-examined about past misdemeanours which they have tried to put behind them. Section 6 of the Criminal Procedure Act 1865, provides that a witness may be questioned as to whether he has a previous conviction, so no one can deny the right of defendants to test the credibility of those who may testify at the trial; but there is also a responsibility on those who prosecute not to embarrass further witnesses who make themselves available to assist in the administration of justice. They may have done something in the past which casts doubt on their general reputation and good character, but it may not be of the slightest relevance to the current proceedings.

For example, is it relevant that a witness to an armed robbery had a conviction for gross indecency ten years ago?

The authority most often cited in support of the prosecution's duty to disclose previous convictions against prosecution witnesses is *R v Collister and Warhurst* (1955) 39 Cr App R 100. It is important, however, to emphasise exactly what Hilbery J said in his judgment, namely:

> The police are not to be expected to examine the records or see whether possibly there exists anywhere in the country any matter which might affect the character of a witness. It is their duty to disclose to the defence . . . actual convictions of crime standing on the record of the prosecutor. (p. 104)

The *ratio* of the decision in *Collister and Warhurst* is that if the police are aware of convictions recorded against the 'prosecutor', i.e. the complainant or principal prosecution witness, they are under a duty to reveal them to the prosecuting authority which must inform the defence. Thus, the convictions in that case were not to be overturned simply because the defence were unaware that the 'prosecutor', in the course of his public examination in bankruptcy, had admitted that on occasions he told lies in order to obtain sums of money. The prosecution did not know of the matter themselves and could not, therefore, disclose that of which they were unaware.

The duty on the police to reveal details of convictions has since been extended to all prosecution witnesses. In *R v Chambers and Wilson* [1960] Crim LR 436, a decision of first instance at the Sheffield Winter Assize, Edmund Davies J ordered the Crown to supply a list of convictions against a prosecution witness on the ground that otherwise the defence might be placed in the dilemma of putting character in issue without any precise knowledge of the value of such a course.

At common law, prior to the CPIA 1996, there is little doubt that the prosecution should inform the defence if they are aware of any convictions recorded against a prosecution witness. In *R v Harrow Crown Court, ex parte Dave* [1994] 1 WLR 98, the Crown conceded that the defence were entitled to information about previous convictions, whether or not they had asked for it, and the Divisional Court concurred with that concession. *R v Brown (Winston)* [1995] 1 Cr App R 191, is an authority of some importance generally in relation to disclosure in criminal proceedings, but in his judgment Steyn LJ specifically referred (at p. 199) to the rule that the prosecution is obliged to disclose previous convictions of a prosecution witness as the most important illustration of the Crown's duty to give disclosure of significant material which may affect the credibility of a prosecution witness.

The grounds of appeal in *Brown* included issues of non-disclosure concerning defence witnesses, and the Court rejected the defence contention that the Crown was under a duty to disclose convictions against defence witnesses stating (at p. 201) that: 'We are satisfied that it would impose an unnecessary and excessive burden on the Crown to impose a legal duty to disclose material which is only relevant to the credibility of defence witnesses.' Here, the Court is having some regard to the extent of the duty of disclosure on the prosecution. It is a theme that was taken up in *R v Cannon* (unreported), Court of Appeal, 30 January 1995, where the grounds of appeal were that the prosecution should have made more full disclosure relating to the background information on two of their witnesses, principally the fact that they were informants. The judgment of Lord Taylor CJ recognises the difficulties facing the prosecution and states (at transcript 94/2354/Z2, p. 8):

> Onerous though the duty on the prosecution is to disclose material to the defence which may be of assistance . . . it is not, and cannot be, the duty of the prosecution to disclose that of which they are unaware. They are not expected to be omniscient. To require the prosecution in every case which they undertake to carry out exhaustive inquiries as to the possibility of some previous history which might affect a witness's credibility would be to put too heavy a burden upon them.

Helpful though these judgments are to the police, who have to check criminal records, and prosecutors, whose responsibility it is to effect disclosure, they still beg the fundamental question, is there a duty to check the criminal record of all prosecution witnesses in every prosecution? It is accepted that the prosecution cannot disclose what they do not know exists about their witnesses, but are they under a legal duty to try to find out in every case? The authority which comes closest to appreciating the practical difficulties involved, and which attempts to solve them, is *Wilson v Police* [1992] 2 NZLR 533, from the Court of Appeal of New Zealand.

Wilson was charged in the District Court with damaging a motor vehicle, assault with intent to injure and using threatening words. Upon a request from the defence, the police stated that none of the witnesses for the prosecution had previous convictions affecting credibility. Counsel for the defendant then applied to the District Court for an order to the police to provide details of any convictions recorded against prosecution witnesses. Leaving aside jurisdictional issues, the judge rejected the contention that all convictions must be disclosed, holding that the duty is confined to convictions which can reasonably be regarded as relevant to credibility.

The Court of Appeal held that it was a common law principle that the prosecution must disclose convictions of witnesses relevant to credibility. It was too sweeping, however, to impose a duty on the police to disclose any convictions against a prosecution witness, as such a duty would require a computer check of all witnesses in every prosecution, whether on indictment or summary. Prospective witnesses were entitled to privacy from exposure of any conviction they might have, unless it was truly necessary for the disposal of criminal proceedings.

The Court then went further and gave assistance on how the police and the prosecuting authority should approach their responsibility. Before all defended trials, whether on indictment or summary, the prosecution should as a general rule notify the defence of any conviction known to the prosecution of a proposed witness whose credibility was likely to be in issue, if that conviction could reasonably be seen to affect credibility. For this purpose knowledge must extend to every such conviction of which the prosecution are, in fact, aware as the result of a computer check or otherwise. For trials on indictment, computer checks should be made as a matter of course. For summary trials, such a check should be made only if requested by the defence, or if the prosecuting authority sees fit. In cases of doubt the advice of counsel should be sought. In the event of a decision not to disclose, on grounds either that credibility is unlikely to be in issue or that interference with the witness is feared, the defence should be notified in general terms so that they can apply to the court for information where they wish to challenge the decision of the prosecution.

This decision goes much further than any English authority in indicating that the prosecution have a discretion to disclose only that which is considered relevant to credibility in the particular case. As shall be seen when the question of 'unused' material is explored, the English courts have moved positively towards a general duty of disclosure in relation to matter affecting the potential issues in the case (see *R* v *Ward* (1993) 96 Cr App R 1 and *R* v *Keane* (1994) 99 Cr App R 1). There seems to be no reason why the same tests should not be applied when assessing credibility, particularly in circumstances where the issues in the case are either known or are clear-cut.

It is submitted, therefore, that at common law the prosecutor has a limited discretion in relation to the disclosure of previous convictions. On the authorities considered above, there is no obligation upon the police to check whether all witnesses have a record in every summary trial. They should check whether any witness whose evidence is known or believed to be the subject of challenge, has a record and they should reveal that information to the prosecuting authority. They should also make any checks that the prosecutor deems necessary. Upon the receipt of the information, the prosecutor should normally provide the information to the defence irrespective of whether a request has been received. That practice should be departed from only if the prosecutor is satisfied that the conviction has no relevance to the known issues, and in coming to such a decision regard should be had to the materiality test in *Keane*. In proceedings on indictment, the police should check all witnesses, but, unless exceptional circumances exist, there should be no duty upon the prosecutor to provide details of convictions against a witness who is the subject of a conditional witness order or where the defence have signified agreement with the witness's evidence.

Disclosure of convictions under the CPIA 1996

In the future, disclosure of previous convictions and other matters affecting credibility will be made by applying the tests set out in the CPIA 1996. Where the conviction affects credibility to the extent that the prosecution case is undermined, disclosure must be made. In some cases, however, the previous conviction may be considered to be so remote from the issues in the case that disclosure is unnecessary, and in such circumstances the prosecution have no obligation to disclose. Matters may become clearer when the accused provides a statement of his or her defence, and the prosecution will then have to consider whether disclosure of the conviction might reasonably be expected to assist the defence. In the example given above of a witness to an armed robbery with an old conviction for gross indecency, the defence case may be that his evidence is not only crucial but that the witness is untruthful and has an ulterior motive for giving evidence against the accused. In these circumstances, the prosecution may wish to find out more about the conviction, such as whether the accused pleaded guilty or was disbelieved in court, before deciding whether disclosure is appropriate. It will nevertheless be surprising if the CPIA 1996 brings about a significant alteration in existing prosecution policy on the disclosure of the convictions of witnesses.

It is important, though, not to confuse the duty of disclosure of matters affecting credibility with arguments as to the admissibility of such cross-examination during the trial. It is not the function of the police or prosecuting authority to anticipate the court's ruling in cases where it is clear that the evidence of the witness is to be challenged. The duty is to make disclosure and leave the question of admissibility to the court. The court's approach was set out by Lawton J in *R* v *Sweet-Escott* (1971) 55 Cr App R 316, in considering the question 'How far back is it permissible for advocates when cross-examining as to credit to delve into a man's past and to drag up such dirt as they can find there?' Lawton J considered the relevant principle to be (at p. 320): 'Since the purpose of cross-examination as to credit is to show that the witness might not be believed on oath, the matters about which he is questioned must relate to his likely standing after cross-examination with the tribunal which is trying him or listening to his evidence.' It should be the task of the police to see whether any dirt exists, and for the prosecutor to disclose any impurities to the defence in cases where the evidence of the witness is to be challenged in relation to the issues in the case. It is the court's role to decide how much delving by the defence is appropriate.

The courts will sometimes have difficulty in deciding the relevance of credibility. In *R* v *Murray (Peter)* [1995] RTR 239, for example, the knowledge of the convictions of the other driver in a two car incident, was held to be something which could have assisted the jury. The driver had in fact left the country, and although the trial judge had properly applied himself to the correct issue, which was relevance, he had erred in not allowing cross-examination of the police officer in the case about the character of the absent driver.

Effect of failure to disclose previous convictions

Not all instances of a failure to disclose previous convictions have led to a conviction being quashed, despite the fact that it amounted to an irregularity in the trial. In *R* v *Paraskeva* (1982) 76 Cr App R 162, where the defendant was charged with assault occasioning actual bodily harm, the defence were not informed that the complainant had a spent conviction some seven years earlier for theft. It was held that as there was a head-on collision between the complainant and the defendant where one or the other was not telling the truth, the trial judge would have given his consent for questions on the record being put. The non-disclosure was a material irregularity and the proviso to s. 2(1), Criminal Appeal Act 1968 could not be applied. A similar conclusion was reached in *R* v *Brook and Sheffield* (unreported), Court of Appeal, 14 July 1995, where the defendants had been convicted of obtaining property by deception. The non-disclosure by the police of a previous conviction for dishonesty against a prosecution witness was held to be a material irregularity. The evidence of credibility was not merely collateral but went to the main issue in the case and the jury might have reached a different conclusion about the evidence of the witness had they known of the conviction. The Court declined to apply the proviso (to s. 2(1), Criminal Appeal Act 1968).

In *R* v *Matthews* (1975) 60 Cr App R 292, however, the conviction was allowed to stand even though the defence had not been informed of the long criminal record of the victim of an unlawful wounding, which included a conviction for grievous bodily harm where he was sentenced to 12 months' imprisonment. This is because the defence raised was that the victim must have been stabbed by one of his own party and not by the defendant who did not have a knife. The Court indicated that it would have been different if the defendant had admitted having a knife but had claimed self-defence. A similar conclusion was reached in *R* v *Thornton (Brian)* [1995] 1 Cr App R 578. Although the failure to disclose convictions of the victim of a serious attack was an irregularity, it was not material in a case where there was no dispute that the victim had been attacked and where he gave no evidence which substantially implicated the appellant. The appeal against conviction was allowed on other grounds.

In *R* v *Knightsbridge Crown Court, ex parte Goonatilleke* [1985] 2 All ER 498, the Divisional Court ruled that the non-disclosure of the bad character of a witness was a breach of the rules of natural justice and quashed the summary conviction of the applicant and also the subsequent dismissal of his appeal by the Crown Court. The main witness, a store detective, had a previous conviction for wasting police time and had concealed during cross-examination the real reason why he had left the Metropolitan Police. The true character of the witness came to light only later when he was prosecuted for theft.

DISCLOSURE OF DISCIPLINARY FINDINGS AGAINST POLICE OFFICERS

Complaints against the police

Many defences to allegations of crime involve an attack against the police. Despite the provisions of the Police and Criminal Evidence Act (PACE) 1984 — which was intended, *inter alia*, to safeguard persons in police detention — and the introduction of tape-recorded interviews, the police remain the frequent targets of claims of impropriety. Section 83, PACE 1984, established the Police Complaints Authority, the constitution, membership and proceedings of which are now set out in sch. 5, Police Act 1996. The procedures for the handling of complaints against the police are detailed in Part IV of the Police Act 1996. The investigation of complaints sometimes results in officers appearing before disciplinary tribunals which decide their guilt and, in the case of those officers where the charge is proved, determine any punishment to be imposed. Of course, other officers may be subjected to disciplinary proceedings not as the result of a complaint, but by reason of internal measures taken by chief officers. Some allegations against police officers amount to more than breaches of discipline and those officers are prosecuted for a criminal offence in the same way as any other alleged offender. Conviction of a criminal offence will usually lead to dismissal from the police force, but some officers found guilty of a disciplinary offence only may be allowed to continue in the force after a suitable punishment. This means that there are a number of serving police officers with findings of guilt in relation to disciplinary matters of varying degrees of seriousness.

The decision in *R* v *Edwards*

In addition to proved disciplinary matters, there will be many occasions when a police officer has not been believed by a court hearing his or her evidence. This is difficult to prove conclusively, but in cases where it is the defendant's word against that of the officer(s), the inference is reasonably clear. What, then, is the duty of disclosure in relation to disciplinary matters and occasions where police officers have plainly been disbelieved? In *R* v *Edwards (John)* (1991) 93 Cr App R 48, the Court of Appeal was not specifically considering the duty of disclosure in such matters, but its finding in relation to what evidence about the police officers in the case could have been put before the jury had a considerable impact on the obligation to disclose such information.

The defendant was charged with a robbery at a post office and it was alleged that he was one of the three robbers. The case against him consisted of the evidence of one of the other robbers and police officers to whom he had allegedly confessed. The defendant claimed that he been 'fitted up' by the police. Before the trial, the prosecution were asked to supply the names of any officers who were subject to investigation for fabricating evidence. One name was given, but another officer's name was not supplied as the evidence of that officer was to be read and, the prosecution contended, whatever he may have done wrongly in another case was immaterial. At the appeal hearing, counsel for the appellant addressed the court on matters of credibility affecting not only police officers who featured in the case against Edwards but also others in the West Midlands Crime Squad where, it was suggested, there had been a strikingly similar pattern over a period of about three years of tampering with and fabricating evidence against persons arrested by the Squad. If the appellant had known of the full position concerning allegations against officers in the Squad, he would have been entitled to pursue such a line of cross-examination and call evidence to establish the way in which the Squad was operating.

The judgment of the Court of Appeal, handed down by Lord Lane CJ, considered the law relating to questioning as to credibility, notably the decisions in *Hobbs* v *Tinling* [1929] 2 KB 1; *R* v *Funderburk* [1990] 1 WLR 587; and *R* v *Busby* (1981) 75 Cr App R 79. The conclusions reached were of significance and Lord Lane's judgment held (at p. 56) that '. . . the police officers could certainly be cross-examined as to relevant criminal offences or disciplinary charges found proved against them'. Later, the Lord Chief Justice stated (at p. 56):

We do not consider that it would have been proper to suggest to the officer in the present case that he had committed perjury or any other criminal offence by putting to him that he had been charged but not yet tried. Nor do we think that complaints to the Police Complaints Authority which have not been adjudicated upon would properly be the subject of cross-examination. It would not be proper to direct questions to an officer about allegedly discreditable conduct of other officers, whether or not they happened to be serving in the same Squad.

Finally, the Court ruled on the problem of other cases in which the officer had, so to speak, unsuccessfully given evidence. Following earlier decisions in *R* v *Thorne* (1977) 66 Cr App R 6 and *R* v *Cooke (Gary)* (1987) 84 Cr App R 286, the Court came to this conclusion (at p. 57):

The result of those two decisions seems to be this. The acquittal of a defendant in case A, where the prosecution case depended largely or entirely upon the evidence of a police officer, does not normally render that officer liable to cross-examination as to credit in case B. But where a police officer who has allegedly fabricated an admission in case B, has also given evidence of an admission in case A, where there was an acquittal by virtue of which his evidence is demonstrated to have been disbelieved, it is proper that the jury in case B should be made aware of the fact. However, where the acquittal in case A does not necessarily indicate that the jury disbelieved the officer, such cross-examination should not be allowed. In such a case the verdict of not guilty may mean no more than the jury entertained some doubt about the prosecution case, not necesarily that they believed any witness was lying.

The consequences of the decision in *Edwards* were, in so far as the prosecution's duty of disclosure was concerned, pervasive. The Runciman Commission Report said of the second limb of the judgment in *Edwards* (at p. 97): 'We think that this goes too far'. From a pragmatic point of view, compliance by the police and prosecuting authorities is virtually impossible unless some sort of data base could be created into which information could be fed every time a police officer gave evidence, together with an assessment as to whether he or she had been believed or not believed.

Prosecution reaction to *R* v *Edwards*

Despite the far-reaching consequences of the judgment in *R* v *Edwards*, the CPS, the Home Office and the Association of Chief Police Officers reacted swiftly and the following year were able to issue comprehensive guidance to Crown Prosecutors and police officers. Normally, advice given by the DPP to the police is treated as confidential, but in a Written Answer to Brian Sedgemore MP, the Attorney-General was able to say that copies of the advice given following *Edwards* (together with the advice given by the DPP following the *'Guinness Ruling'*, which is discussed in chapter 7) had been placed in the Library of the House: see Hansard HC, 13 June 1995, written answers, col. 451.

The character and credibility of a police officer is affected if he or she has been disciplined, and for this reason the prosecution have a general duty to inform the defence of a disciplinary finding of guilt. As with the duty concerning previous convictions, however, a number of other points arise which erode the general duty. Does the ruling, for example, apply to expunged as well as current disciplinary findings; does it apply to all breaches of the Discipline Code set out in sch. 1, Police (Discipline) Regulations 1985 (SI 1985 No. 518) no matter how serious the breach or the punishment imposed; how much detail should be provided; what about disciplinary matters still in progress or where an officer is suspended without charge, etc.? The DPP advice sought to provide practical guidance on these and other matters arising out of the judgment in *Edwards*.

It is, of course, necessary in the first instance for the police to bring such matters to the notice of the prosecutor, but it is submitted that the prosecutor should have a greater element of discretion than with the disclosure of previous convictions. With convictions against prosecution witnesses, disclosure normally follows, whereas in relation to disciplinary findings regard should be had to the nature of the finding and its likely relevance to the matters in issue. Findings which involve some element of dishonesty should invariably be disclosed, while matters such as disobedience to orders, neglect of duty and discreditable conduct will often have no relevance to the officer's veracity or the guilt or otherwise of a defendant. Certainly, there should be no duty on the prosecution to disclose details of unsubstantiated complaints even though this is a popular type of inquiry from some defence representatives. The imposition of such a duty would only encourage the making of false complaints in the hope that they might be used to discredit an officer in the future.

Extent of disciplinary information to be disclosed

The question of how much information should be disclosed was considered in *R* v *McCarthy* (1994) 158 JPN 108, where the arresting officer in a drugs case was later charged with possessing drugs and resigned from the police force. The defendant's solicitors were informed of those facts and, further, that the prosecution did not intend to call the officer. The Court stated that there will clearly be cases where a disclosure of the general outline of the case will be sufficient to put the defence on inquiry as to possible lines of defence, so that if they want more information they can ask for it. In this instance, however, the defence had not been told of certain salient points in both the prosecution of the officer and the case against the defendant, and had they known the full extent of those matters, they would have been able to mount an attack on the officer's credibility. The non-disclosure amounted to a material irregularity and the appeal was allowed. Although the facts were somewhat unusual, the judgment in *McCarthy* does mean that where criminal proceedings have been instituted against an officer, and as a result of those proceedings it has been decided not to call him as a witness in another case, there is a duty to disclose in that other case not simply the fact and substance of the proceeedings but also the nature of the case against the officer.

Effective compliance with the second limb of the *Edwards'* judgment raises many difficult issues. There will undoubtedly be some cases where an officer's behaviour in one case is so linked to his evidence in a second case that a court's view of credibility is bound to be affected by knowledge of details of the first case. In such instances disclosure would be appropriate on grounds of general fairness as well as the decision in *Edwards*. In some cases where an officer has been censured by the court, a disciplinary hearing will follow and a finding of guilt should be disclosed in accordance with the first part of the judgment. There will, however, be many occasions where the reason for an acquittal does not fall conveniently into Lord Lane's analysis, and even more cases where the prosecutor simply will not know whether the officer has been disbelieved on an earlier occasion. To impose a duty of disclosure in such circumstances is not only unrealistic, but also hardly in keeping with the concept of fairness which the common law on disclosure is intended to achieve.

The duty of post-conviction disclosure is dealt with in detail in chapter 8, but it should be asked at this point whether, if there is a duty on the Crown to inform defendants in current cases of other instances where officers have plainly been disbelieved, there is a duty to inform defendants who have been convicted on the evidence of those same officers in the past? There have been attempts in some recent Crown Court trials to extract an undertaking from the prosecution that they should keep under review officers whose credibility has been attacked so that if they are found, at a later stage, to have acted improperly, the convicted defendant should be informed. The courts have yet to impose any specific duty in this regard.

The decision in *Edwards* has been criticised by some commentators as being too generous to the police in limiting cross-examination to cases of proved misconduct. It is also argued that it ought to be open to a defendant to raise the issue of the officer's conduct in previous acquittals. There are others who say while the decision is relevant to a situation where the conduct of an entire squad is under scrutiny, it is too wide in relation to disciplinary matters affecting officers generally. Whatever view is held of the judgment, it has created an onerous duty of disclosure which is neither clearly defined nor capable of effective compliance. In the future, however, as in the case of previous convictions, disclosure will fall to be made in accordance with the CPIA 1996 tests. The disclosure code makes it clear that any material casting doubt on the reliability of a witness must be revealed to the prosecutor. A disciplinary finding comes into this category and it then falls to the prosecutor to decide whether the finding undermines the case or assists the accused's defence. In so far as *Edwards* 'second limb' disclosure is concerned, decisions should be easier when the nature of the defence is clarified.

DISCLOSURE OF FINDINGS IN CIVIL PROCEEDINGS

There is little authority on the duty of disclosure where a witness has been impugned in civil proceedings. In *R* v *Steadman Thompson* (unreported), Court of Appeal, 11 May 1986, the defendant had been convicted of possessing a controlled drug with intent to supply. Before the trial, one of the officers in the case had been the subject of an allegation of assault in unrelated proceedings in the county court which found for the plaintiff and where the judge expressed the view that the officer had not told the truth. In the appeal of Thompson, counsel for the respondent conceded that it would have been better not to have called the officer. The Court agreed and stated that it did not welcome as witnesses police officers who have been adjudged in another court to have given false evidence and where they have been adjudged to have committed a serious assault justifying exemplary damages.

The Court did not expressly confer on the prosecution a duty of disclosure, but there is little doubt that where the prosecutor is made aware of a relevant finding in civil proceedings, this information should be revealed under the disclosure code and considered for disclosure in the same way as a conviction. Of course, if the officer is disciplined, the defence would be informed in accordance with *Edwards*.

DISCLOSURE OF OTHER PRE-TRIAL INFORMATION

Meetings of witnesses

The credibility of witnesses will be affected if it is known that they have discussed their evidence or agreed their testimony in advance of the trial. Sometimes such discussions are quite innocent, for when persons have been involved in an investigation it is natural that they should want to talk about their experiences. The temptation is greater for police officers who are regularly in one another's company and often have to attend case conferences to discuss aspects of the case with senior officers, the prosecuting authority and counsel. The dangers of rehearsal, coaching and fabrication during, or in preparation for, case conferences were highlighted in two cases before the Court of Appeal, namely *R* v *Arif* (1993) *The Times*, 17 June 1993 and *R* v *Skinner (Gary)* (1994) 99 Cr App R 212. It is essential that witnesses do not discuss the evidence that they will be giving, for their credibility will undoubtedly be undermined if it is believed that they have been influenced by others. More blatant attempts to change or fabricate evidence may, in themselves, lead to criminal proceedings for perverting the course of justice. If there has been any unusual type of pre-trial meeting of witnesses, consideration will have to be given to disclosing the fact to the defence.

An unusual pre-trial situation arose in *R* v *Dye, Williamson and Davies* [1992] Crim LR 449, where there was not a meeting, as such, between witnesses, but a television film had been made in advance of the trial which involved the most important witnesses being filmed almost as though they were giving evidence. This had not been disclosed to the defence and, on appeal, counsel for the appellants (who were charged with a variety of drug offences) argued that had the television testimony been known, the witnesses could have been cross-examined about any differences between what they had said on camera and the evidence they had given in court. The Court of Appeal held that the decision to co-operate in the filming had been wrong and the failure to tell the defence about it was a material irregularity. However, the differences in testimony were such as to allow the application of the proviso to s. 2(1), Criminal Appeal Act 1968.

Therapy and counselling sessions

Special care needs to be taken when witnesses take part in therapy sessions. These are often a vital part of the rehabilitation process for children or mentally disordered victims of abuse. It is important, however, that the evidence which such persons will give is not influenced by suggestions or propositions made during the sessions. When therapy sessions have been held, the fact should be disclosed.

Counselling is now an accepted part of helping victims of crime to cope and readjust following the traumas experienced. It is also used by many police forces when officers have been involved in traumatic situations, for example, when firearms have been used or even after road, rail or air disasters. Counselling raises difficult issues of confidentiality, for unless those being subjected to therapy are given assurances of confidentiality, they are unlikely to participate fully in, or gain the necessary benefit from, the sessions. At the same time, if anything emerges during the sessions which undermines the prosecution case by casting doubt on the evidence of a potential witness or indicating a previous inconsitent statement, disclosure of such facts (or, in exceptional circumstances, the abandonment of the case) would have to be considered.

6 The Path to the Attorney-General's Guidelines

The previous two chapters examined the duty of disclosure in relation to the prosecution case, and the character and credibility of the witnesses to be called by the prosecution. It is now time to look at the more controversial subject of the disclosure of information which the prosecution do not intend to use. This chapter traces the development of the law and practice culminating in the introduction of the *Attorney-General's Guidelines for the Disclosure of 'Unused Material' to the Defence* (1982) 74 Cr App R 302 (the *A-G's Guidelines*). The chapters that follow examine the operation of the *A-G's Guidelines* and the case law which eventually led to their demise.

EARLY CASE LAW

Although the question of disclosing statements and information which the prosecution did not propose to use, was raised from time to time in the course of criminal proceedings (see, for example *R v Nicholson* [1936] JP 553 in chapter 2), the point did not receive any authoritative ruling by the courts until 1946. The position was considered by the Court of Appeal in *R v Bryant and Dickson* (1946) 31 Cr App R 146, where the appellants appealed against a conviction at the Central Criminal Court for conspiracy to defraud and obtaining money by deception. They were charged with an extensive fraud on the London County Council whereby the Council sent vehicles to the appellants' garage for repairs where they were charged for thousands of pounds' worth more work than was actually carried out.

The garage employed a supervising mechanic named Campbell whose sanction was required for the work, and the prosecution case was that Campbell, either consciously or unconsciously, facilitated the frauds. A statement had been taken from Campbell but the prosecution decided not to call him and told the defence of the decision, raising no objection to their taking a statement from him if they so desired. At no time was Campbell's statement disclosed to the defence and this was one of the grounds of appeal, i.e. that having taken a statement from Campbell and having decided not to call him, the Crown was under a duty to furnish the defence with a copy to enable the defence to decide whether they should call him.

The judgment of Lord Goddard CJ on the point was quite unequivocal:

> It is said that it was the duty of the prosecution to have supplied the defence with a statement which Campbell had admittedly made to the prosecution. The prosecution, for reasons which one can well understand, did not call Campbell. Is there a duty in such circumstances on the prosecution to supply a copy of the statement which they have taken to the defence? In the opinion of the Court there is no such duty, nor has there ever been. . . . In the opinion of the Court, the duty of the prosecution in such a case is to make available to the defence a witness whom the prosecution know can, if he is called, give material evidence. (at p. 151)

The appeals of Bryant and Dickson were dismissed and the practice, which was to be followed by most prosecutors for the next 30 years, was established. It is not difficult to see why, on the facts of the case, the Court adopted such a clear line. The defence had been aware of the prosecution's decision not to call Campbell since the committal hearing, and Campbell himself was actually present at the Old Bailey during the trial, so there was no reason why the defence could not approach him to obtain a statement upon which basis they could decide whether he should be called. Consequently, it was not the strongest of cases on which to challenge the prosecution's decision not to disclose!

The next occasion when the duty came under scrutiny from the Court of Appeal appears to be in the context of a civil appeal, *Dallison* v *Caffery* [1965] 1 QB 348. Dallison brought an action against a detective constable for false imprisonment and malicious prosecution. He had been arrested for breaking and entering into an office and stealing £173, but the prosecution had later offered no evidence against him as there were doubts surrounding the identification evidence and there existed some evidence to support an alibi. The civil action failed as the judge held there was no case to go before the jury since there was no want of reasonable cause for the arrest and the prosecution of the accused. The appeal was largely on the basis that there was evidence fit to be left to the jury because the constable did not honestly believe that the credible evidence known to him raised a case against Dallison. In this context, the judgment of Diplock LJ continued (at p. 375):

> This contention seems to me to be based on the erroneous proposition that it is the duty of the prosecutor to place before the court all the evidence known to him, whether or not it is probative of the guilt of the accused person. A prosecutor is under no such duty. His duty is to prosecute, not to defend. If he happens to have information from a credible witness which is inconsistent with the guilt of the accused, or, although not inconsistent with his guilt, is helpful to

the accused, the prosecutor should make such witness available to the defence
(see *Rex* v *Bryant and Dickson*).

Had the matter remained there, the decisions in *Bryant and Dickson* and *Dallison* v
Caffery would have been entirely consistent and the duty of the prosecution
unambiguous. Unfortunately, however, another member of the Court, Lord
Denning MR, expressed the duty somewhat differently by saying that if a
prosecuting counsel or solicitor knows of a credible witness who can speak to
material facts which tend to show the arrested person to be innocent, he should
either call the witness himself or make his statement available to the defence. The
early seeds of confusion had been sown and, not for the last time in connection
with the prosecution's duty of disclosure, eminent judges were not *ad idem*.

PROPOSALS FOR REFORM

Prosecution policy

As a general rule, the *Bryant and Dickson* approach was the one favoured by
prosecuting authorities. The office of the DPP had no formal policy in relation to
disclosure, but it was the usual practice to supply to the defence the names and
addresses of persons from whom statements had been taken but who were not to be
called by the prosecution. Any defence request to see statements would usually be
acceded to, but on a counsel to counsel basis and often only shortly before the trial.
The largest prosecuting authority, the Solicitor's Department of the Metropolitan
Police, introduced a policy in 1974 which incorporated some of Lord Denning's
approach in *Dallison* v *Caffery* as it allowed the disclosure of a statement which of
itself would tend to show the defendant to be innocent. The general practice,
though, was to supply names and addresses; although if the defence requested a
copy of the statement it would be provided unless there was a compelling reason
not to do so. Other police prosecuting authorities had variations on the same theme,
but generally the supply of names and addresses was regarded as sufficient for
making the witness available to the defence as stated in *Bryant and Dickson*.

In the open disclosure days of the 1990s, when it is the practice of a number of
defence practitioners to inspect every document and scrap of paper in the
possession of the prosecution, it is inevitable that there is speculation as to the
fairness of trials in the less enlightened earlier years. The answer seems to be that
as a general rule trials were heard in a climate of trust that the prosecution would
do what was fair and just and make proper disclosure. Such trust is now markedly
absent, partly because of the miscarriages of justice in the 1970s, coupled with the
belief of many practitioners that the concept of fairness is one that is totally alien to
the police. Whether one subscribes to those views or not, the absence of clear
statutory direction or judicial guidance on disclosure issues, coupled with the
fragmented prosecutorial system with each force at liberty to formulate its own
disclosure practices, did not make the task any easier.

JUSTICE proposals

In 1966, the JUSTICE Committee on the Laws of Evidence produced a report
entitled *The Availability of Prosecution Evidence for the Defence* in which they
considered arguments for and against disclosure not only of material which would
form the basis of the prosecution case but also of statements which were not to be
used. They found the case for disclosure made out and their recommendations for
legislative proposals included the following:

> (2)   Where the prosecutor has in his possession statements relevant to the
> case, taken from persons whom it is not proposed to call or to tender to give
> evidence, copies of such statements shall, as soon as reasonably practicable, be
> supplied to the defence.

A further recommendation was that 'A police officer or other person in charge of a
case shall supply to the prosecutor a copy of all the statements taken by him in the
course of the investigation into the alleged offence which are relevant to the case'.

Proposed legislative amendments

Seven years after the JUSTICE Committee Report, in 1973, recommendation (2)
above was included verbatim in a new clause 3 on 'Provision of Statements in
Criminal Cases' proposed by a private Member of Parliament, Mr Stanley Clinton
Davis, for inclusion in the Administration of Justice Bill. The proposed clause
enjoyed healthy debate in the House of Commons (see Hansard vol. 854, HC Deb,
5th ser., coll. 365–385) but it was withdrawn after the Solicitor-General gave an
undertaking to invite comments from interested bodies. The scepticism of the
Government on the subject may be inferred from the Solicitor-General's comment
on the future of the clause: '. . . I should prefer to see it become a matter of practice
rather than of law. I am not sure that it is necessary that the actual statements of the
witnesses for the prosecution should be handed over, literally, to the defence.'

A year earlier, on 11 April 1972, during the committee stage of the Criminal
Justice Bill, there had been a debate on an even more detailed proposed new clause
29 concerning the 'Provision of Information to the Defence' (see Hansard HC
Standing Committee G Reports, 11 June 1972, coll. 1159–1172). The clause had
been tabled by Sir Elwyn Jones, Mr Samuel Silkin and others, and read:

> (1)   Upon any trial by indictment it shall be the duty of the prosecution to
> make available to any defendant—
>   (a)   the name and last known address of any person who is not called by
> the prosecution as a witness and who appears to be able to give material
> evidence;
>   (b)   any material written statement made by any such person as is referred
> to in paragraph (a) above and which the prosecution is able to make available;

(c)   in the case of a person who is called by the prosecution any material written statement made by him which the prosecution is able to make available and which either—

(i)   materially conflicts with his deposition or with any written statement made by him and used in evidence in the committal proceedings or with any additional evidence to be given by him, of which notice is given to the defendant, or

(ii)   appears likely to support the case, so far as is known to the prosecution, of the defendant; . . .

The clause also called for disclosure of matters affecting the character and credibility of prosecution witnesses and dealt with the timing and extent of the proposed duty. The proposed clause was defeated by seven votes to five; and subsequently, in a letter to the Home Office, the Lord Chief Justice said that judges he had consulted were unanimously of the opinion that the topics referred to in the clause were not appropriate either for legislation or a practice direction.

While the legislature hesitated and the judiciary expressed satisfaction with the current situation, the police were about to embark on some of the largest investigations the country had ever seen, namely the hunt for those responsible for the bombings in mainland Britain. They did so not knowing what specific duty they had in relation to the hundreds of statements that would be taken and the thousands of messages and actions that their inquiries would generate. The judiciary's confidence that prosecuting counsel would act fairly and do what was right and proper was based on the assumption that counsel would be fully aware of everything that had emerged during the course of the investigation of those who were to be prosecuted. Such confidence was mispaced and the problem was not to go away.

The James Report

The 1975 *Report on the Distribution of Criminal Business between the Crown Court and Magistrates' Courts*, chaired by Lord Justice James, focused, as we have seen in chapter 4, on advance disclosure in summary proceedings. It made no recommendations in connection with statements not to be used by the prosecution, although the recommendation that persons should have a statutory right to receive, upon request, statements of the prosecution case was indicative of the trend towards a more open framework for disclosure.

The Devlin Report

The *Report on Evidence of Identification in Criminal Cases* (HC 338, London: HMSO 1976) (the Devlin Report) made some pertinent comments on the disclosure of statements not to be used by the prosecution and concluded that the current practice did not give universal satisfaction. The protagonists of the JUSTICE recommendations of 1966 found support for their cause in the case of Laszlo Virag (referred to in chapter 3) and the Home Secretary had appointed the Committee, chaired by Lord Devlin, to investigate the question of identification evidence following that case. The Devlin Report recognised that the prosecution and defence may have different perspectives on what is relevant and also acknowledged the absence of machinery for ensuring that the disclosure of information was given in sufficient time, 'as well as sufficient width', to enable the defence to give it full consideration. The Report made a number of recommendations concerning the recording and disclosure of descriptions of persons accused of crime and the communication of information to the defence when alibi statements had been taken. The Report made no broader recommendations in relation to disclosure as Lord Devlin had been informed by the Home Office that they were engaged in consultations on the subject and that 'the Home Secretary has not yet formed any final view on the matter'.

The Fisher Report

The Report of Sir Henry Fisher in 1977 into the circumstances leading to the trial of persons arising out of the death of Maxwell Confait (HC 90, London: HMSO, 1977) (the Fisher Report) showed no such constraints as were imposed on the Devlin Report. Non-disclosure and the practices and procedures adopted by the prosecution had featured prominently in Fisher's inquiry (see chapter 3) and he was not slow to criticise those who had been involved in the prosecution of the boys allegedly responsible for Confait's death. For example, Sir Henry Fisher had been informed by the then DPP, Sir Norman Skelhorn, that the practice of disclosure had become more liberal under his regime. The Report observed (at para. 29.24): 'He [the DPP] said that he had a policy that statements should be disclosed unless there were special reasons to the contrary, and that he thought Treasury Counsel were aware of it. Unfortunately the history of the present case suggests that this may not be so, or that the policy is not always followed.' It was certainly the case that the 39th edition of *Archbold* published in 1976 contained a comment (in para. 443) that did not appear in the 38th edition in 1973. Referring to *Bryant and Dickson*, it stated:

> Certain prosecuting authorities not infrequently use this authority as a justification for never supplying the defence with the statement in such circumstances. It should be borne in mind, however, that an inflexible approach to these circumstances can work an injustice. For example the witness's memory may have faded when the defence eventually seek to interview him, or he may refuse to make any further statement. It is submitted that the better practice is to allow the defence to see such statements unless there is a good reason for not doing so.

The Fisher Report concluded with a recommendation for a change in the rules affecting disclosure to the effect that all statements taken by the police should be disclosed by prosecuting counsel to defence counsel in the absence of any special reason to the contrary, such as national security, safety of the witnesses or the interests of justice. The prosecution might also withhold the statement of a witness whom the defence might call. The Report further recommended that time limits for disclosure should be laid down and that disclosure should be made whether or not the defence asked for it. Unless and until rules along these lines were introduced, the Report suggested that the rule in *Bryant and Dickson* be modified so that where there was a large number of witnesses, the prosecuting solicitor effecting disclosure should give a summary of the evidence that each was able to give.

WORKING PARTY ON DISCLOSURE OF INFORMATION TO THE DEFENCE

The Government could delay no longer. It had the recommendations of judicial inquiries and the representations of a number of interested bodies who had submitted suggestions at the request of the Solicitor-General in 1973. Further evidence of how seriously the courts considered non-disclosure by the prosecution was provided by the decision in *R* v *Leyland Magistrates, ex parte Hawthorn* [1979] 1 All ER 209, where the Divisional Court concluded that the non-disclosure of the names of two witnesses to a case of driving without due care and attention, amounted to a denial of natural justice whereby an order of certiorari could be granted and the conviction quashed.

At the end of 1977 the Home Secretary and the Attorney-General set up a working party to consider the matter. The terms of reference of the working party were:

To consider in relation to cases committed for trial what statements, documents and information in the possession of the prosecution should be disclosed to the defence, the means whereby such disclosure should be made and any grounds upon which it would be proper not to make disclosure. Also to consider in what circumstances it is proper to edit witness statements and by what means this should be done.

The group had little difficulty in identifying a number of matters for discussion. They included:

- In what circumstances could the name and address of a person from whom a statement had been taken, be withheld?
- In what circumstances could the contents of the statement be withheld?
- How should disclosure be made?
- Should disclosure be made automatically or on request?
- Should there be time limits on disclosure?
- How should the unedited versions of statements be dealt with?
- What disclosure should be made of documents other than statements?

The working party looked into a number of ancillary questions, including the disclosure of previous convictions and forensic reports, and it took account of all the reports and recommendations summarised above. In November 1979, the group produced a detailed report with a number of recommendations. The report was referred to the Royal Commission on Criminal Procedure, chaired by Sir Cyril Philips, which was looking into the law and procedure relating to the investigation and prosecution of criminal offences in England and Wales. The Royal Commission's report (the Philips Report) endorsed the proposals of the working party, the main thrust of which was that disclosure of material beyond that made at present should be at the discretion of the prosecutor (see Cmnd 8092-1, London: HMSO, 1981, para. 8.19). The Philips Report was also of the view that the proposals should apply equally to magistrates' courts.

In December 1981, adopting the majority of the proposals of the working party, the Attorney-General issued *Guidelines for the Disclosure of 'Unused Material' to the Defence* in cases to be tried on indictment (see Appendix 1). Thirty-five years after *Bryant and Dickson*, and 15 years after JUSTICE had highlighted difficulties, prosecutors had guidance on how to deal with material which they did not intend to adduce as part of their case. The *A-G's Guidelines* would serve prosecutors well for almost a decade until judicial opinion against the fact and the exercise of the prosecutor's discretion would once again propel disclosure to the forefront of the debate on criminal procedure.

7 The Attorney-General's Guidelines and their Demise

STATUS OF THE ATTORNEY-GENERAL'S GUIDELINES

The *Attorney-General's Guidelines for the Disclosure of 'Unused Material' to the Defence* (1982) 74 Cr App R 302 (the *A-G's Guidelines*) came into operation at the beginning of 1982. Their status was advisory only. When they were considered by Henry J (as he then was) in *R v Saunders* (unreported), Central Criminal Court, 29 September 1989, transcript T881630 (the *Guinness Ruling*), however, he was of the opinion that they had attained the force of law. The Runciman Commission Report concurred with that view when it stated (at p. 91, n. 20): 'The guidelines, although non-statutory, to all intents and purposes have the force of law.' Millet J was, however, of a different opinion when, in the course of the judgment in *Re Barlow Clowes Gilt Managers Ltd* [1991] 4 All ER 385, he stated (at p. 393): 'The Attorney-General's guidelines provide guidance to the prosecution in the perform-ance of its duties. They do not have the force of law. They are independent of the rules of evidence or the substantive law.' A year later, when the *A-G's Guidelines* were scrutinsed by the Court of Appeal in *R v Ward* (1993) 96 Cr App R 1, they were said not to represent the law in so far as the disclosure of sensitive material was concerned; and by 1994, Steyn LJ concluded in *R v Brown (Winston)* [1995] 1 Cr App R 191, that they no longer conformed to the requirements of the law of disclosure in a number of critically important respects. Indeed, he went further and stated (at p. 197): '. . . if the guidelines, judged by the standards of today, reduce the common law duties of the Crown and thus abridge the common law rights of a defendant, they must be *pro tanto* unlawful.'

This chapter examines the turbulent history and ultimate demise of the *A-G's Guidelines*, and the chapter that follows considers the state of the common law prior to the coming into force of the CPIA 1996. The new legislation and the supporting code of practice, which are analysed in chapters 16 and 17, will eventually give rise to a new body of law on disclosure, but the earlier common law rules cannot totally be ignored. Some of the salient points from the judgments discussed below provide the basis for provisions in the CPIA 1996, but the contradictions and eccentricities of some of the views expressed in the judgments provide illustrations of the inability of the courts effectively to control the position and, as a result, indicate why legislation became inevitable.

THE ATTORNEY-GENERAL'S GUIDELINES

Whatever criticisms they may have attracted in recent years, the introduction of the *A-G's Guidelines* in 1982 provided much needed assistance to prosecutors in clarifying their responsibilities and providing advice on how they should exercise their discretion. The *Guidelines* (which are reproduced in full at Appendix 1) introduced the term 'unused material' which included:

- witness statements and documents not included in the committal bundles;
- the statements of any witnesses who are to be called at committal, and any documents referred to therein; and
- the unedited version of edited statements included in the committal bundle (para. 1).

(Nearly all the debate on disclosure (summarised in the previous chapter) had centred on the disclosure of statements made by persons who would not be called by the prosecution. It was not until the *Guinness Ruling* (see page 70) that serious consideration was given to documents other than statements that came within the definition of 'unused material'.)

Paragraph 2 of the *A-G's Guidelines* explained that the unused material should normally be made available to the defence solicitor 'if it has some bearing on the offence(s) charged and the surrounding circumstances of the case'. This phrase (which would return to haunt police officers and prosecutors in the years to come) was drawn from the recommendations of the working party (see above). Interestingly, the Philips Report, while endorsing the working party's proposals, adapted the phrase to read 'offences charged *or* surrounding circumstances etc' but the conjunctive 'and' was restored in the *Guidelines* themselves. Whether anything can be read into this is a matter for conjecture. What is clear beyond any doubt is that the duty of disclosure could not have been described more widely. Is it possible that the police investigation file would contain anything which did not have a bearing on the offence(s) or surrounding circumstances? If not, the result was that everything gathered, created or generated by the police was potentially disclosable (subject to the later paragraphs concerning sensitive material).

The *A-G's Guidelines* also provided advice on the timing and manner of disclosure. The duty of the prosecutor was to make the material available as soon as possible and by means of photocopies, provided the documents did not amount to more than 50 pages. Thus, the *Bryant and Dickson* rule had, effectively, been replaced by the requirement to disclose statements unless there were reasons why the statements should not be copied to the defence.

It was the circumstances where the prosecutor should exercise a discretion not to make disclosure which had presented the working party with their most difficult task, and their proposals, which were accepted by the Royal Commission of 1981, were reproduced in para. 6 of the *A-G's Guidelines*. It is important to note that the *Guidelines* permitted the exercise of discretion without reference to the Court or the defence. The working party had reported that: 'The discretionary power to withhold statements by "suspect" witnesses has been exercised by Counsel for as long as any of us can remember and this practice was endorsed by the Lord Chief Justice when he was invited by the Home Office to comment on the new clause 29 of the Criminal Justice Bill 1972.' The message in the *Guidelines* was clear — prosecuting counsel could be trusted to do what was right and proper. Furthermore, there was no mention of any principle, such as the doctrine of PII in civil proceedings, which required the intervention of the court.

Paragraph 6(i) to (iv) described circumstances when the prosecutor might withhold statements. Paragraphs 6(ii) to (iv) required the prosecutor to assess whether the witness was likely to be believed and whether the statement was favourable to the prosecution or defence, or was neutral or negative. If there were fears for the safety of the witness or a danger that the witness might change his or her story, the statement might be withheld. If the witness was likely to give evidence for the defence, it might be kept for cross-examination purposes. In any of these circumstances, the name and address of the witness should normally be supplied.

Paragraph 6(v) allowed a statement to be withheld if it was, to a greater or lesser extent, 'sensitive' and therefore not in the public interest to disclose it. A number of examples were given: national security and the protection of informants at one end of the scale; and matters of private delicacy and which might cause domestic strife at the other. It is to be noted that throughout para. 6, reference was made to statements and the *Guidelines* gave little consideration to documents other than statements that the prosecution might wish to withhold.

Having given the prosecutor the discretion not to make disclosure, the *A-G's Guidelines* made it clear that fairness to the defendant was essential and doubts should be resolved in favour of disclosure (paras 8 and 9). Prosecuting counsel had the ultimate responsibility and must be told if any material had been withheld (paras 7, 9 and 11). The *Guidelines* also provided assistance on how to overcome the difficulty of disclosure when parts of the statement might be 'sensitive'. Editing or redacting was permissible and the long-established practice of disclosure on a counsel to counsel basis was a further option.

In relation to editing, four years later a *Practice Direction* [1986] 2 All ER 511 was issued which provided guidance and advice on editing single statements and the making of composite statements. Paragraph 8 of that *Practice Direction* drew attention to the *A-G's Guidelines* and stated that the earlier unedited statement(s) should be given to the defence unless grounds existed to withhold disclosure.

At the end of the day, however, it was made clear in para. 15 of the *A-G's Guidelines* that if the information was so sensitive that disclosure thereof would not be in the public interest, it would probably be necessary to offer no evidence. This provided confirmation that the defendant's right to a fair trial was paramount, and it is worth recalling that in accordance with the terms of the *Guidelines*, cases have always had to be abandoned, or individual charges dropped, when no alternative form of disclosure could be made. The discontinuance of proceedings following changes in the common law disclosure rules were treated by some, particularly the police, as if the procedure was something new. While such abandonments may not have been made with the same frequency, and certainly not in the glare of publicity that often accompanied later cases, prosecutors have always had that option open to them and as a last resort would have followed the guidance in para. 15.

Between 1982 and 1989, the *A-G's Guidelines* received little attention from the courts as they were, in the main, recognised as a genuine attempt to provide a consistent framework for disclosure where none had existed before. In *R v Lawson* (1989) 90 Cr App R 107, the Court of Appeal concluded that prosecuting counsel had made an error of judgment in exercising his discretion under the *Guidelines*, but there was no critisicm of the *Guidelines* themselves. Counsel had relied on para. 6(ii) to withhold the statement of a vital witness of whose existence the defence were aware, although they did not know her current whereabouts and they did not know that her statement contained information which would have been helpful to the defendant. Because an injustice had occurred, the defendant's appeal was allowed. Within a matter of months, however, the *A-G's Guidelines* were to become the focus of judicial attention to an extent that they could never again be regarded as comprehensive guidance on how disclosure in criminal proceedings was to be effected.

THE 'GUINNESS RULING'

On 27 November 1995, the Court of Appeal dismissed the appeals of Ernest Saunders, Anthony Parnes, Gerald Ronson and Jack Lyons against their conviction in 1990 for conspiracy to contravene sections of the Prevention of Fraud Investments Act 1985, theft and false accounting. This brought to an end one of the longest and most expensive sagas in legal history which had begun in 1986 when the Guinness company sought to take control of Distillers. The Court of Appeal held in *R v Saunders (No. 2)* (1995) *The Times*, 28 November 1995, that there had been no unfairness in the trial of the defendants in allowing the use of evidence arising out of interviews with the defendants by inspectors from the Department of Trade and Industry.

Six years earlier Henry J (as he then was) had been concerned with a defence application that the Serious Fraud Office (SFO) should disclose what was described as preparatory material, namely notes made by the police or other investigators in interviewing witnesses or potential witnesses, tape recordings of interviews, transcripts of such recordings, and drafts of statements made by witnesses or potential witnesses. The SFO accepted that they had a duty to disclose preparatory material where it indicated an inconsistency in the evidence of a witness or where it affected the credibility of the witness, but, in refusing to disclose a large amount of other preparatory material, they took the view that such disclosure would not help the defence and would not assist justice. In a judgment of considerable importance, Henry J disagreed: see the *Guinness Ruling* (at page 9).

The *Guinness Ruling* contained three main points of significance. First, 'unused material' in the *A-G's Guidelines* was given a wide meaning and the definition contained in para. 1 was held to be inclusive and not exclusive. Secondly, relevance was a matter for the defence and not the prosecution. Thirdly, Henry J was not impressed with the suggestion that the *A-G's Guidelines* did not have the force of law. At the end of the hearing, disclosure of all the material was ordered. The floodgates had opened.

With regard to the first point, Henry J conducted a full examination of the terms of the *A-G's Guidelines*, commenting that evolutionary process had been towards fuller disclosure in recent years. The meaning of 'unused material' was expressed in very wide terms ('it is hard to imagine wider words' was the way in which Henry J put it) and the definition in para. 1 was inclusive and not exclusive. The general scheme of the *Guidelines* was a presumption in favour of disclosing all unused material that had some bearing on the offences charged and the surrounding circumstances. As long as the material was capable of having some impact on the evidence in the case, it was disclosable, and this included oral statements and preliminary thoughts and expressions which might, in certain circumstances, have an evidential value. Henry J conceded that:

there might be some sort of material, using the word broadly, which would be too preliminary really to count; material that would not, in itself, be capable of having some impact on the evidence of this case, that is to say, material that was at once discarded or abandoned, thrown into the waste paper basket or something of that kind, but that does not apply to any of the categories before me. (transcript T881630, p. 9)

It was plain therefore that, in his judgment, the *Guidelines* were not confined to statements but included any document or information conveyed orally which had a bearing on the offence charged or surrounding circumstances. In short, virtually everything gathered or created by the investigator was prima facie disclosable.

If that part of the judgment came as a disappointment to prosecutors, it was nothing compared to their astonishment that relevance was not a matter for them to have any part in deciding. In a short sentence, the discretion to decide what was relevant, which prosecutors had been exercising for years, if not centuries, had been swept away. Not only was all the material in the possession of the prosecution potentially disclosable, the prosecution no longer had the right to determine what was relevant and what was not. Sensitive material was not an issue in this hearing, but Henry J stated *obiter* (at p. 7): 'It should be noted that it is only in the case of such sensitive materials that the prosecution are required under the guidelines to make any assessment of the utility of the disclosure to the defence's legitimate case. Otherwise this is not an exercise that the guidelines call on the prosecution to use at all. . . .'

Lastly, arguments about the status of the *A-G's Guidelines* were summed up in this passage from the *Guinness Ruling* (at p. 7):

> Now, it was initially suggested to me — though I think that finally there was some retreat from this position — that the Attorney-General's Guidelines do not have the force of law. I found a certain unreality in that submission because it seems to me that any defendant must be entitled to approach his trial on the basis that the prosecution will have complied with the Attorney-General's Guidelines and those, accordingly, are the ground rules which govern his trial.

The *Guinness Ruling* (as it became known) was of crucial importance to all investigators and prosecutors. Although a judgment at first instance, it had been given by a highly respected and experienced High Court Judge in the context of a high profile prosecution. Whether his opinion on the *A-G's Guidelines* having the force of law was accepted or not, it was beyond dispute that they contained advice and information upon which a defendant was entitled to rely in order to have a fair trial (see also judicial consideration of the status of other guidelines: *R* v *Home Secretary, ex parte Hosenball* [1977] 1 WLR 766 in relation to immigration, and *R* v *Mason* (1980) 71 Cr App R 157 concerning jury vetting). In the light of the *Ruling*, prosecuting and investigating authorities had to look closely at existing practices and procedures.

There was speculation that the Attorney-General would issue fresh guidelines to replace those of his predecessor, but he made the position abundantly clear in a Parliamentary Answer to Chris Mullin MP who asked if he had any such plans. The written reply (see Hansard, vol. 202, HC, 20 January 1992, written answers, col. 39) was: 'No. The question of disclosure has ceased to be one of good practice — as under the guidelines issued by my predecessor in 1981 — and is now a matter of rights and obligations. Further guidelines would not be a suitable means of effecting any modification deemed necessary.'

Prosecution response to the *Guinness Ruling*

In order that a prosecutor may comply with the duty of disclosure, as explained by the *Guinness Ruling*, it is essential that the prosecuting authority is made fully aware of all the material which falls to be disclosed. For those prosecuting authorities that have a role in the investigation, such as the SFO, the task should not be too difficult, although the the nature of SFO cases means that there will usually be a considerable volume of documents to gather, list, and ultimately disclose. Those prosecuting authorities which have an investigation branch, such as the Customs and Excise and Department of Trade and Industry, face greater problems in the revelation of disclosable material to their prosecutors, although the existence of a common departmental head is obviously an aid to the introduction of operational procedures. The logistical difficulties facing the CPS and 43 autonomous police forces are enormous, but as the CPS is responsible for the vast number of prosecutions in England and Wales, the DPP was expected to take a lead in implementing the requirements of the *Guinness Ruling.*

The CPS response to the ruling was to set up a working group which comprised senior CPS lawyers and police officers nominated by the Association of Chief Police Officers. The fundamental tasks for the group were to identify categories of material commonly handled or created by the police as part of an investigation and to determine how such material should be preserved and then revealed to the CPS. There were a number of options, which included 'unused material' being categorised and listed; the material being deposited with, or copied to, the CPS in each case; or prosecutors could visit police stations to inspect such material in order to advise on disclosure. Whichever option was decided upon, the manpower and financial resources were huge, but suitable arrangements for the revelation of unused material had to be found in order that the newly defined duty of disclosure could be complied with.

In 1992, the working party reported to the DPP, and in August of that year Barbara Mills QC issued advice to chief constables on the disclosure of unused material. The advice (commonly referred to as the *Guinness Advice*) was given pursuant to the DPP's statutory obligations and as such was initially confidential and not made public. The *Guinness Advice* provided a framework for disclosure and was later supplemented by Operational Instructions agreed by the CPS, Home Office and police which came into force at the beginning of 1993. Such was the importance of the *Guinness Advice*, the DPP decided to disseminate the document more widely and a copy was provided to those affected by it, namely defendants and their solicitors. In 1995, the Attorney-General confirmed that a copy was available in the House of Commons library: see Hansard vol. 261, HC, 13 June 1995, written answers, col. 451. The Operational Instructions made pursuant to the *Advice* remained confidential, although a summary of them was endorsed by the Divisional Court in *R v Bromley Magistrates' Court, ex parte Smith and Wilkins*; *R v Wells Street Magistrate's Court, ex parte King* [1995] 2 Cr App R 285, at p. 291 as 'perfectly satisfactory'.

The thrust of the DPP's advice was that police officers should preserve material which comes into existence during an investigation and reveal such material to the CPS, which then has the responsibility of deciding what information should be disclosed to the defence and whether public interest grounds exist to justify the withholding of any information. It was recommended that officers should maintain a schedule of the material preserved and, as the duty of disclosure is a continuing one, the schedule should be kept up to date when additional documents come into the possession of the police. In order to provide as much assistance to the police as possible, examples were provided of documents commonly held by the police which should be retained and scheduled. Those examples were to be used and developed in the disclosure code issued under the CPIA 1996. Although the *A-G's Guidelines* were confined to cases heard in the Crown Court, the police were further advised that the common law authorities and best practice required the prosecution to observe a similar duty of disclosure in cases to be tried at the magistrates' court.

The practical effect of the *Guinness Advice* was that from the early part of 1993, case papers submitted to the CPS were accompanied by a schedule of unused material which was then vetted by the Crown Prosecutor with responsibility for the case. Provided that there were no items of sensitive material, a copy of the schedule was sent to the defence who were then at liberty to inspect any of the material listed therein at the police station. Statements of persons not to be called by the prosecution would be copied to the CPS and, in turn, would normally be sent to the defence. The schedule of documents and the availability of the schedule to the defence was to be one of the most important points at issue in the Government's proposals which culminated in the CPIA 1996 (see chapters 15 and 17).

The *Guinness Advice* was the first step in establishing a new climate of disclosure for police officers and prosecutors. Before the *A-G's Guidelines*, prosecuting authorities and prosecuting counsel had invariably disclosed statements in accordance with the established traditions of fairness and impartiality. The *Guidelines* had refined the duty of disclosure and provided advice to prosecutors on how discretion should be exercised. But there was no guarantee that the existence of all potentially relevant information had been drawn to their attention by the police. The *Guinness Advice* now made it clear that investigation material must be retained and its existence revealed to the prosecutor.

The scheduling and photocopying requirements were, for the police, time-consuming, expensive and, generally, onerous. Chief constables had justifiable concerns over the protection of sensitive information despite reassurances offered in the *Guinness Advice*. The amount of time spent by Crown Prosecutors reviewing cases would increase dramatically as they were to spend more time assessing disclosure issues; while, in some cases, prosecuting counsel would spend as much time in police stations satisfying themselves that disclosure had been effected properly, as they would spend in court. The rights of defendants had, however, been safeguarded. No longer would they be in the dark about what non-sensitive information the prosecution possessed. However, following the next judicial torpedo to hole the beleaguered prosecution — the judgment following the successful appeal of Judith Ward — defendants were to learn more about the nature of sensitive information held by the Crown.

R v *JUDITH WARD*

Two months before the DPP issued her Advice to Chief Officers of Police following the *Guinness Ruling*, the Court of Appeal concluded the lengthy hearing of the appeal of Judith Ward ((1993) 96 Cr App R 1). The facts appear in chapter 1 and Ward's case is one of the more notorious miscarriages of justice commented on in chapter 3. The judgment records a catalogue of instances of non-disclosure and then provides a summary of the principles of law and practice which (at the time of the judgment) governed the disclosure of evidence by the prosecution before trial. The six principles set out by Glidewell LJ in the judgment of the Court require careful scrutiny.

The Court cited with approval a passage from *Archbold* (1992), 44th edn at para. 4-276, that 'where the prosecution have taken a statement from a person they know can give material evidence but decide not to call that person as a witness, they are under a duty to make that person available as a witness for the defence'. Few would disagree with that statement of principle, but the Court then went on to define 'material evidence' as 'evidence which tends either to weaken the prosecution case or to strengthen the defence case'. Unfortunately, this was not entirely consistent with what had been said earlier in the judgment when Glidewell LJ had adopted the words of Lawton LJ in *R* v *Hennessey* (1979) 68 Cr App R 419, at p. 426, where he said that the courts must 'keep in mind that those who prepare and conduct prosecutions owe a duty to the courts to ensure that relevant evidence of help to an accused is either led by them or made available to the accused'. Observing that that statement reflected the position in 1974 (the time of Ward's arrest) as well as today, Glidewell LJ went on to emphasise (at p. 25) that:

all 'relevant evidence of help to the accused' is not limited to evidence which will obviously advance the accused's case. It is of help to the accused to have the opportunity of considering all the material evidence which the prosecution have gathered, and from which the prosecution have made their own selection of evidence to be led.

Did this mean (i) that the defence were entitled to see all the material evidence that the prosecution had gathered; or (ii) only that which might strengthen the defence case or weaken the prosecution case? And where did it leave the exhortation to prosecutors in the *A-G's Guidelines*, approved by Henry J in the *Guinness Ruling*, to disclose material which had a bearing on the offences charged and surrounding circumstances of the case — a quite different criterion from that now being stated in *Ward*. As Henry J had stressed the wide definition in the *Guinness Ruling*, there is an apparent conflict with the narrower definition(s) of the Court of Appeal! If you were an accused wanting to inspect all that you are entitled to see, or a prosecutor trying to comply with the law, these were more than mere academic musings.

The second and third principles in the judgment confirmed that unless there were good reasons for not doing so, statements and records of interview should be copied or made available to the defence. Where there were good reasons for not supplying copies of statements, the name and address of the witness should be provided. Although this had not been done in *Ward*, these two principles were little more than re-statements of advice given in the *A-G's Guidelines*. The only practical difficulty was that witnesses were afforded the protection of the exclusion of their addresses from statements as a result of the Magistrates' Courts (Witnesses' Addresses) Rules 1990. Care had to be exercised in disclosing addresses of persons not to be called by the prosecution, and in certain circumstances this resulted in arranging interviews with the defence solicitor on 'neutral territory', usually a police station.

The most glaring examples of non-disclosure in *Ward* had been in relation to scientific evidence, and the Court addressed this in the fourth principle which acknowledged the requirements of the Crown Court (Advance Notice of Expert Evidence) Rules 1987. The judgment continued (at p. 56):

What the rules do not say in terms is that if an expert witness has carried out experiments or tests which tend to disprove or cast doubt upon the opinion he is expressing, or if such experiments or tests have been carried out in his laboratory and are known to him, the party calling him must also disclose the record of such experiments or tests. In our view the rules do not state this in terms because they can only be read as requiring the record of all relevant experiments and tests to be disclosed. It follows that an expert witness who has carried out or knows of experiments or tests which tend to cast doubt on the opinion he is expressing is in our view under a clear obligation to bring the records of such experiments and tests to the attention of the solicitor who is instructing him so that it may be disclosed to the other party.

The Court was imposing a clear duty on an expert witness called by the prosecution to reveal all findings to the prosecuting authority so that they might be disclosed. For example, if 20 tests were carried out and 19 supported the opinion which the expert would give in evidence, there was a duty to disclose the results of the 20th, together with any relevant working papers, to the expert advising the other side. This was reinforcing the judgment of the Court of Appeal in the earlier case of *R v Maguire* (1992) 94 Cr App R 133, when it had been stated that what should have been disclosed were notes and results of all tests carried out on the actual samples; and notes of any experimental tests or trials carried out for the purpose of the trial and with a view to supporting an opinion to be expressed at trial. *Maguire* held that what did not need to be disclosed were tests relating to other cases.

In practice, expert witnesses are nearly always formally instructed by the police who submit items for examination as part of the investigation long before the prosecutor enters the picture. As the police would not necessarily know what tests had been carried out by the scientist and what documentation existed, this principle imposed a legal duty of revelation of information on a member of the prosecution team who was neither the investigator nor the prosecutor. It is equally clear that the duty was not confined to scientists in police laboratories or the Forensic Science Service but extended to all experts called by the prosecution, from pathologists to accountants.

The fifth, and undoubtedly the most far-reaching, principle stated by the Court in *Ward* concerned the means by which the prosecution were able to withhold sensitive material from the defence. The history and development of public interest immunity (PII) in criminal proceedings is summarised in chapter 9, but suffice it to say for the present that PII was completely unknown in criminal proceedings at the time of Ward's trial in 1974 and was a relative newcomer to criminal proceedings at the time of the appeal in 1992. Nevertheless, the Court adopted the principles of PII with alacrity and held that it would be wrong for the prosecution to withhold material documents without giving any notice of that fact to the defence. If, in a wholly exceptional case, the prosecution were not prepared to have the issue of PII determined by a court, the inevitable result would be that the prosecution must be abandoned.

The *Guinness Ruling* had removed the prosecutor's discretion in relation to non-sensitive material; *Ward* had now done so in relation to sensitive material, which was to be handled in accordance with the civil doctrine of PII. The *A-G's Guidelines*, while providing comprehensive advice on the steps to be taken by the prosecuting authority and prosecuting counsel when considering sensitive material, had never suggested making an application to the court, let alone any form of notice to the defence. The impact on the prosecution of this part of the decision in *Ward* was devastating. For example, if there was an informant in the case, an application had to be made to the court to withhold material relating to the informant and the defence must be notified. In many cases, the defendant would be only too aware of the existence (albeit not the identity) of an informant; but in others, the fact that an informant existed would not be known and, in many such cases, would not be of the slightest relevance. In its attempts to redress the non-disclosure of relevant information in Ward's case, the Court of Appeal had concluded that the prosecution could not be trusted in dealing with sensitive information and arguments to the contrary were dismissed as 'opaque'. The Court had revolutionised the approach to the way sensitive material would be dealt with in the future. Unquestionably, the new procedures would go far in protecting the innocent, but had they also provided a means of escape for the guilty?

Glidewell LJ concluded his summary of the law and practice on disclosure by making it clear that the *A-G's Guidelines* had not been overlooked, 'but nothing in those Guidelines can derogate in any way from the legal rules which we have stated'. It was therefore unnecessary for the Court to consider whether that part of the *Guidelines* relating to sensitive material was in conformity with the law expressed in the judgment. In other words, the *A-G's Guidelines* did not represent the law on disclosure and probably never had!

R v DAVIS, JOHNSON AND ROWE

The identity of those who provide information in confidence to the police has been protected by the courts for over a century in a succession of well-known authorities (which are discussed more fully in chapter 10). In the majority of cases where the prosecution hold sensitive material, it is possible to give some information to the defence without revealing the identity of the informant or the exact nature of the sensitive material. There are some cases, however, where to inform the defence of the fact that an application will be made to the court gives the defendant the very knowledge of information that the Crown is seeking to protect on public interest grounds. The Court of Appeal had made it plain in *Ward* that they did not approve of the prosecution acting as judges in their own cause and unilaterally deciding not to disclose information to the defence on public interest grounds. But had they considered the possibility of circumstances existing where it would be damaging to the public interest, and fatal to a prosecution, to provide any information at all to the defence? Whether they had considered it or not in the context of *Ward*, they soon had to in a case which came before them shortly afterwards: *R v Davis, Johnson and Rowe* (1993) 97 Cr App R 110.

In February 1990, three men, named Michael Davis, Randolph Johnson and Raphael Rowe, were convicted at the Central Criminal Court of a number of offences, including murder. They appealed, and at an interlocutory hearing counsel for the Crown handed to the Court a document which was not shown to defence counsel. Because of the sensitivity of the contents of the document, he invited the Court either to hear his application *ex parte*, or for defence counsel to undertake not to inform the appellants or their solicitors what had taken place. The Court agreed with defence counsel's submission that the latter course would be wrong, but they then set out what they considered should be the proper approach to applications by the Crown on grounds of PII or sensitivity.

In general, it was held, the prosecution should give notice to the defence that they are applying for a ruling by the court and indicate to the defence at least the category of the material held. The defence must then have the opportunity to make representations to the court. The judgment of Lord Taylor CJ continued (at p. 114):

> (3)   Where, however, to disclose even the category of the material in question would in effect be to reveal that which the Crown contends should not in the public interest be revealed, a different procedure will apply. The Crown should still notify the defence that an application to the Court is to be made, but the category of the material need not be specified and the application will be *ex parte*. If the Court, on hearing the application, considers that the normal procedure under (2) above ought to have been followed, it will so order. If not, it will rule on the *ex parte* application.
>
> (4)   It may be that, in a highly exceptional case, to reveal even the fact that an *ex parte* application is to be made, could 'let the cat out of the bag' so as to stultify the application. Such a case would be rare indeed, but we accept Mr Bevan's contention that it could occur. In that event, the prosecution should apply to the Court, *ex parte* without notice to the defence. Again, if the Court, on hearing the application, considered that at least notice of the application should have been given to the defence or even that the normal *inter partes* procedure should have been adopted, it will so order.

Thus, a new phenomenon entered criminal proceedings — the *ex parte* application. Furthermore, the Court recognised that in rare circumstances, an *ex parte* application could be made without the knowledge of the defence. The Court saw no alternative to the rules set out above and conceded that *Ward* had gone too far. The fears of the prosecution had thus been assuaged, but those of the defence intensified at the thought of information being conveyed to the trial judge without the knowledge of defendants or their representatives. 'Secret justice' became the cry of many defence practitioners, but they had to concede that even that was better than the pre-*Ward* days of the withholding of information by the prosecution without the knowledge and consent of the court.

Confusion over the prosecution role in deciding materiality

We saw at the beginning of this chapter how the prosecution's role in deciding materiality had effectively been removed as a result of the *Guinness Ruling*. It will be recalled that Henry J had stated that relevance was a matter for the defence to judge; and it was only in the case of sensitive material that the prosecution were required, under the *A-G's Guidelines*, to make any assessment of the utility of the disclosure to the defence case. As a result of the decision in *Ward*, that assessment of utility had been devolved to the court, for once the prosecution came into possession of any material which it was desired to withhold on public interest grounds, they could not do so without the approval of the court and without notifying the defence that they were seeking the court's consent (apart from the very rare *ex parte* without notice cases). It soon became clear, however, that the courts were not altogether comfortable with their new role. It is doubtful whether the Court of Appeal had anticipated the number of applications which the Crown would be compelled to make, or indeed, the volume of documents that would often be involved. Removing the prosecutor's discretion was one thing, but monitoring the disclosure of information and hearing an increasing number of defence applications to inspect and/or have copies of material which they considered might be relevant to their case, was something which had not been foreseen. In addition, not all judges took quite the same view of the matter as Henry J.

On 2 November 1993, Tuckey J heard an application where the defence asked him to rule that the prosecution were obliged to disclose four memoranda because they fell within the definition of 'unused material' in the *A-G's Guidelines*: see *R v Wallace Smith* (unreported), Central Criminal Court, 2 November 1993. The indictment included a count of fraudulent trading and the memoranda recorded meetings between the liquidator, a witness for the prosecution, and representatives of the SFO. While quantities of other unused material had been provided, prosecuting counsel had advised that the memos should not be disclosed.

Tuckey J sought to distinguish the *Guinness Ruling* on the basis that Henry J was referring to the question of whether the preparatory material contained any inconsistency when he said that it was a matter for the defence to judge. Consequently, his ruling in *Smith* included the following passage (at p. 84 of the transcript of submissions and ruling):

I am quite unable to accept that it is for the Defence to decide what is relevant and what is not. To hold otherwise would mean that the Defence could demand unfettered access to all material in the Prosecution's possession with a view to deciding whether any of it fell within the guidelines. This cannot be right. In my judgment, provided it can be shown that proper consideration has been given to the question of relevance, then the Prosecution's view of the matter is conclusive.

A month later, Jowitt J gave his views on the subject in the context of 'the burden which is created and the demand made on scarce judicial resources when there is a claim for public interest immunity': see *R* v *Melvin and Dingle* (unreported), Central Criminal Court, 20 December 1993. He had been asked to consider the contents of about 12,000 pages of documents which the prosecution considered were covered by PII and which, on the basis of the judgment in *Ward*, it was a matter for the court to rule upon. Jowitt J disagreed:

> It is quite clear that the prosecution have no discretion to withhold from disclosure evidence which is material, subject to any claim to PII, where again they have no discretion but must disclose the evidence to the Court and submit to its judgment. It is equally clear though that the prosecution is called upon to make a judgment as to what evidence is material and must therefore be disclosed. The evidence is in the possession of or available to the prosecution. It has a duty to disclose material evidence. Who else, therefore, is to decide what is material except in the first place the prosecution?

Later in his ruling, he went further:

> In my judgment, for the prosecution to abandon the proper and may I say the confident performance of its duty to make a decision as to materiality and so place upon the Court a burden of quite unnecessary magnitude is capable of amounting to an abuse of process of the court.

It would have been very rare indeed at the end of 1993 for any prosecuting authority or prosecuting counsel to approach the duty of disclosure with absolute confidence that they were doing all that was required of them. After all, if eminent judges had such widely differing views on a subject as important as 'who decides relevance', how could prosecutors be expected to have a clear idea of what was necessary? If the dilemma lay with the prosecution, though, the situation was hardly a satisfactory one for the defence. Were they entitled to trawl through all the material gathered by the prosecution, or were they bound by the decision of the prosecution which, according to Tuckey J, was conclusive? And if the Crown's decision on the relevance of PII documents was final, then the Court would not have an opportunity of ruling thereon. The position was confusing to all participants in the criminal justice process and needed an early resolution. The opportunity presented itself in *R* v *Keane* (1994) 99 Cr App R 1.

R v *KEANE*

Stephen Keane had been convicted at the Central Criminal Court in October 1992 of offences contrary to the Forgery and Counterfeiting Act 1981, and was sentenced to a total of six years' imprisonment. The grounds of his appeal ((1994) 99 Cr App R 1) were based on the trial judge's rulings as to disclosure and the scope of the cross-examination that he permitted. It was common ground that the prosecution had not dealt with the sources of information which led to the appellant's arrest in accordance with the recently stated procedures laid down by the Court of Appeal. *Davis, Johnson and Rowe* had not yet been decided and *Ward* had not been fully reported, although part of the judgment had been quoted to the trial judge during the course of submissions. Nevertheless, the Court saw no grounds for regarding the jury's verdict as unsafe or unsatisfactory and the appeal was dismissed.

The judgment of the Court, delivered by Lord Taylor CJ, contained a number of points of importance which went some to way to resolving some of the unsatisfactory aspects of disclosure canvassed above. First, it was decided that it is for the prosecution to put before the court only those documents which it regards as material. As to what documents are 'material', the Court of Appeal adopted the test of materiality which had been used by Jowitt J in *Melvin and Dingle* when he had stated (at p. 5 of the transcript):

I would judge to be material in the realm of disclosure that which can be seen on a sensible appraisal by the prosecution: (1) to be relevant or possibly relevant to an issue in the case; (2) to raise or possibly raise a new issue whose existence is not apparent from the evidence the prosecution proposes to use; (3) to hold out a real (as opposed to a fanciful) prospect of providing a lead on evidence which goes to (1) or (2).

The application of this will be discussed in the following chapter when the common law is analysed, but at least the prosecution had a definition of 'materiality' to assist them now that their role in deciding relevance had been restored. It will be recalled that *Hennessey* had indicated that relevant evidence was material which was helpful to the accused (see page 75); *Ward* had given differering interpretations, on the one hand saying that material evidence meant evidence which tended to weaken the prosecution case or strengthen the defence case; but on the other saying that relevant evidence was not limited to evidence which would obviously advance the accused's case. These were different from the all-embracing definition of material which has a 'bearing on the offence charged and the surrounding circumstances of the case' given in the *A-G's Guidelines*. Jowitt J's definition had the benefit of concentrating on the issues or likely issues in the case, and the Court of Appeal in *Keane* clearly welcomed a test which was more focused than some of the wider tests which had been propounded in the past.

What was not altogether clear from the judgment was whether the assessment of materiality by the prosecution of materiality was confined to PII documents or included non-sensitive documents as well. The Court endorsed (at p. 6) the observations of Jowitt J in *Melvin and Dingle*, that 'it would be an abdication of that duty for the prosecution, out of an over-abundance of caution, simply to dump all its unused material into the court's lap and leave it to the judge to sort through it all regardless of its materiality to the issues present or potential'. Yet this had never been the practice of the prosecution in relation to non-sensitive material or documents not covered by PII. The general practice with regard to such documents was to schedule them and to make them all available to the defence for inspection. If there was an over-abundance of caution it was in offering too much irrelevant information to the defence as a result of the *Guinness Ruling*. The prevailing view appeared to be, however, that the Lord Chief Justice was saying that the test of materiality should be applied to all documents, and only in the case of those documents considered to be both material and attracting PII should they be placed before the court.

Secondly, the judgment provided much needed help for judges on how they should conduct the balancing exercise when weighing the public interest against non-disclosure against the public interest in the defendant having a fair trial. In *R v Agar* (1990) 90 Cr App R 318, Mustill LJ had commented (at p. 324) that: 'There was a strong and, absent to any contrary indication, overwhelming public interest in keeping secret the source of information; but as the authorities show, there was an even stronger public interest in allowing a defendant to put forward a tenable case in its best light.' Was this then the proper test for judges to apply?

It was indisputable that the number of cases in which the trial judge had ordered the disclosure of PII material, thus causing the prosecution to abandon the case, had grown. Some would say that this was because the prosecution had been improperly withholding material in the past. The police response, however, was that judges were being misled into believing that the nature of the confidential information they held was essential for the defence and judges were bending over backwards to be fair to defendants. Whatever the reasons, it was apparent that judges had no clear guidance on how they were to approach the discharge of the balancing exercise. The judgment in *Keane* stated that on the one hand the judge had to consider the weight of the public interest in non-disclosure, and on the other the importance of the documents 'to the issues of interest to the defence, present and potential so far as they have been disclosed to him or he can forsee them'. Lord Taylor CJ continued (at p. 7): 'Accordingly, the more full and specific the indication the defendant's lawyers give of the defence or the issues they are likely to raise, the more accurately both prosecution and judge will be able to assess the value to the defence of the material.'

As with the test of materiality, the balancing exercise was to be determined following an examination of the issues. The Court did not make it clear whether 'issues' should be construed narrowly or widely, but at least the emphasis was on what will be, or is likely to be, in dispute as distinct from a remote possibility of what might be raised. The suggestion that defence lawyers should assist the prosecution and the court in defining the issues is probably the closest that the judiciary had come to encouraging some form of defence disclosure in order that the judge could make a proper assessment of where the public interest lay in a particular case.

The disclosure wheel had almost turned full circle. Under the *A-G's Guidelines* the prosecution could decide relevance and could withhold sensitive material which it considered would not be helpful to the accused. The *Guinness Ruling* had deprived them of their role in determining relevance and *Ward* had passed the role of sanctioning the withholding of PII documents to the court. *Keane* had now made it clear that the prosecution must assess materiality and had provided a test for the Crown to apply; PII must similarly be assessed for materiality, but documents must not be withheld without the prior consent of the court in accordance with the procedures laid down in *Davis, Johnson and Rowe*. The doctrine of PII would be developed further in later judgments (which are considered in chapter 9).

Needless to say, *Keane* was welcomed by prosecutors although it was to result in more preparatory work and created a further challenge in ensuring that the test of materiality would be carried out in at least those cases where there existed vast quantities of unused material and/or PII documents. The CPS introduced a series of standard letters, commonly known as '*Keane* letters' which would accompany the disclosure schedule and identify the issues as known or perceived, upon which basis disclosure had been made. In accordance with the Lord Chief Justice's advice, defence representatives were invited to provide more full or specific details if they disputed the prosecution appraisal of the issues. The iniative was to receive a lukewarm response as few defence solicitors were prepared to show their hand unless it became absolutely necessary; but at least the prosecution could not be accused of ignoring the changing law in their efforts to focus on the issues

R v *WINSTON BROWN*

Before concluding this summary of the key decisions in the development of the common law on disclosure, reference must be made to the decision of the Court of Appeal in *R* v *Brown (Winston)* [1995] 1 Cr App R 191. It has been a feature of the evolution of the disclosure rules that judgments in many of the cases which have come before the Court of Appeal have gone much further than was necessary to decide the issues raised in the appeal. It is, of course, part of the function of the higher courts to provide assistance and guidance on the interpretation of the law, but it is essential that the directions given are both clear and consistent. Some of the *obiter* comments in the leading authorities on disclosure have failed to satisfy that criterion and, although intended to be helpful, have often had the opposite effect. *Winston Brown* may be considered a case in point.

The question for the Court of Appeal was comparatively straightforward and asked whether the Crown owed a legal duty to disclose information tending to reflect unfavourably on the credibility of a defence witness. The Court answered in the negative as they were satisfied that it would place an unnecessary and excessive burden on the prosecution to impose such a duty. However, as the position of the

A-G's Guidelines had been raised during argument, the judgment of Steyn LJ dealt with their status in some detail. In fairness to the Court, counsel at the hearing had asked for general guidance on the *A-G's Guidelines* and PII, although why such an invitation was made is unclear as the grounds of appeal had little to do with PII. Steyn LJ (as he then was) said that the Court were unable to satisfy counsel's expectations but, despite the fact that many points had been clarified by the judgment in *Keane* a few months earlier, he nevertheless felt it necessary to state (and re-state) a few points of legal principle. For example, it was said that 'an issue in the case' must not be construed narrowly but must be given a broad interpretation. There was also further advice for judges on their balancing exercise, with a reminder to keep disclosure under review as the trial develops.

The judgment is of particular significance, however, as it finally rings the death knell of the *A-G's Guidelines* (at p. 197): 'But today the Guidelines do not conform to the requirements of the law of disclosure in a number of critically important respects.' Steyn LJ opined 'that while the Guidelines had served a useful purpose in the past, they had been eroded by other legal advancements, particularly the developments in the field of PII.' The judgment continued (at p. 198): 'The concept of sensitivity *simpliciter* surely has no place in this particular corner of the law.' Thus, unless there was an objection to disclosure on public interest grounds or under a statutory exception, such as s. 9 of the Interception of Communications Act 1985, mere sensitivity (such as in matters of private delicacy or which might create domestic strife — as shown in the *A-G's Guidelines*) would found no legal objection to disclosure.

The judgment concludes with a suggestion of a statutory statement of the duties of the Crown regarding disclosure which should be preceded by a paper on the topic by the Law Commission. Although this suggestion found favour in some quarters, the fact that the Runciman Commission had already looked at the problem, and the amount of time which such a paper might take to prepare, made such an undertaking by the Law Commission unlikely.

CONCLUSIONS

It is perhaps unfortunate that the issues covered by the authorities summarised above were never directly considered by the House of Lords. Their Lordships might have helped to put the Court of Appeal out of their misery in trying to distinguish their own judgments and the differing opinions of High Court Judges sitting at first instance in order to settle on a regime of disclosure which was not only fair to both the defence and the prosecution but which was capable of being observed effectively. The evolving law on disclosure has received only two *obiter* references by the House of Lords in *R v Preston* (1994) 98 Cr App R 405 (in the context of telephone intercepts — see chapter 11) and *R v Chief Constable of the West Midlands Police, ex parte Wiley* [1994] 3 WLR 433 (in a review of PII — see chapter 9).

In his leading judgment in *Preston*, Lord Mustill stated that the law and practice were in the course of evolution, and in some instances surrounded by controversy, so it was important not to pre-empt future development by unguarded comment without the benefit of argument. For that reason their Lordships did not consider the formal status of the *A-G's Guidelines* or whether the duty of disclosure had been enlarged by the judgment in *Ward*. In *ex parte Wiley*, Lord Templeman made some general observations on disclosure to the effect that if a document is relevant and material then it must be disclosed unless it is confidential and a breach of the confidentiality will cause harm to the public interest. He offered no further guidance on how relevance was to be determined and by whom, and the status of the *A-G's Guidelines* was not a matter that had any bearing on the issues of PII with which their Lordships were concerned.

The *A-G's Guidelines* are now finally dead and buried, although some of the advice in relation to how disclosure is to be effected still remains sound and has been embraced by the new legislative provisions. Although the *Guidelines* served a useful purpose in the 1980s by improving the consistency in prosecutors' decision-making and by setting minimum standards of fairness at a time when there was a lack of clarity in the common law duty of disclosure, there was to be no place for them in the 1990s. They have now been replaced by the CPIA 1996 and disclosure code, but it remains to be seen whether this detailed set of rules to be followed by investigators and prosecutors provides defendants with greater safeguards than they had before. There is no doubt that the disclosure rules and the roles and duties of those who form part of the prosecution process are more clearly defined; but has all of the uncertainty and ambiguity of the common law been removed by the CPIA 1996? The next chapter will look at some key disclosure issues and see how the common law endeavoured to resolve them. We will then be in a position to assess, in later chapters, whether the 1996 Act has provided the required solution.

8 Key Disclosure Issues

FUNDAMENTAL QUESTIONS TO BE ANSWERED

Having traced the history and rapid development of the law on disclosure in the previous chapters, it is now time to look at some key disclosure issues that have given rise to difficulty for practitioners and the courts alike. The questions posed below are by no means exhaustive, but only if they can be answered satisfactorily can the basis for fair and equitable disclosure be established:

- Who is 'the prosecution' for the purposes of disclosure?
- What is the position with regard to the disclosure of material in the hands of third parties?
- What sort of information should be disclosed?
- How should relevance or materiality be assessed?
- How should disclosure be effected?
- At what stage of the proceedings should disclosure take place, and where does the duty end?
- What are the duties of the prosecution in relation to disclosure post-conviction?

The common law confronted these issues with varying degrees of success, but we are now looking to the CPIA 1996 and disclosure code to provide greater certainty and clarity in order that disclosure may be conducted fairly. The analysis below takes the form of a consideration of the common law followed by a brief commentary on how the position is affected by the new legislation. A more detailed examination of the relevant CPIA 1996 and disclosure code provisions is contained in chapters 16 and 17.

This chapter is concerned primarily with the disclosure of non-sensitive material (a term that will be used to deal with material where there is no objection to disclosure on public interest grounds). Developments in the law on PII, and how PII is asserted in criminal proceedings, are considered in chapters 9 and 10. The rules of common law as to whether disclosure is in the public interest are unaffected by the CPIA 1996.

WHO IS 'THE PROSECUTION' FOR THE PURPOSE OF DISCLOSURE?

The prosecution process

The early authorities and the *A-G's Guidelines* refer to a duty on 'the prosecution' to make disclosure in particular circumstances, but they did not take account of the fact that the term embraces more than just a single entity which has responsibility for instituting and undertaking criminal proceedings. Invariably, proceedings are instigated by the police and are then taken over by the CPS in exercise of powers given to the DPP in s. 3, Prosecution of Offences Act 1985. In addition, other organisations have statutory powers to investigate and prosecute breaches of the law, while in all cases conducted at the Crown Court, and some at the magistrates' court, independent counsel are instructed to act on behalf of the prosecution. Before any disclosure can take place, there is, by implication, a duty on those involved in the prosecution to preserve and retain material which is potentially disclosable. The determination of who comprises the 'prosecution team' (for want of a better expression) is, therefore, important in order that the legal requirements and duties can be defined and discharged effectively.

Those involved in the prosecution process were considered for the purposes of jurisdiction and costs in *R* v *Bolton Justices, ex parte Scally* [1991] 1 QB 537, where the Divisional Court granted an application for judicial review of a number of convictions for driving with excess alcohol. It was subsequently discovered that at the time of taking the specimens of blood, the medical cleansing swabs in some of the blood sampling kits then in use in the Greater Manchester area contained alcohol. The CPS decided not to prosecute in cases where the specimen may have been contaminated by the use of such swabs. On the question of jurisdiction, the Divisional Court agreed with the view expressed by Farquharson J in *R* v *Birmingham Crown Court, ex parte Ricketts* (unreported), Divisional Court, 8 June 1990, when he stated that 'the prosecution' did not mean any particular individual or body. The term included those responsible for the conduct of the prosecution, which may vary with, at one stage, the responsibility being in the hands of the police, and at another, in the hands of the CPS. Both were collectively part of the prosecution process.

It will be recalled from the previous chapter that in the *Guinness* case the prosecution accepted that they had a duty to disclose preparatory material in certain circumstances and no attempt was made to distinguish between the obligations of the prosecuting authority and the police. Notwithstanding the separate functions of the investigator and prosecutor, it was considered that it would be quite unacceptable for one to hide behind the other and for the prosecuting authority to claim that there was no duty to consider material which was in the physical possession of the police. Although the revelation and communication of information by the investigator to the prosecutor may present difficulties in practice, that in itself is not sufficient good reason for advocating separate disclosure responsibilities for the investigator and prosecutor.

Experts instructed by the investigator or prosecutor

Other members of the prosecution team are not quite so straightforward and their position was considered by the Court of Appeal in *R* v *Maguire* (1992) 94 Cr App R 133. The facts of the case against the Maguire Seven are set out in chapter 3. The principal reason for allowing the appeals against conviction was on the ground of non-disclosure of important scientific tests. Neither prosecuting counsel, nor those instructing them were aware of all the tests and experiments carried out by scientists, but the Court held that there had nevertheless been an irregularity in the trial. The judgment of Stuart-Smith LJ considered the question of who is embraced by the word 'prosecution', and he stated (at p. 147):

> We are of the opinion that a forensic scientist who is an adviser to the prosecuting authority is under a duty to disclose material of which he knows and which may have 'some bearing on the offence charged and the surrounding circumstances of the case'. The disclosure will be to the authority which retains him which must in turn (subject to sensitivity) disclose the information to the defence. We hold that there is such a duty because we can see no cause to distinguish between members of the prosecuting authority and those advising it in the capacity of a forensic scientist.

The Court was saying in clear terms that forensic scientists are joined with the investigator and prosecutor on the prosecution team and their responsibility is to reveal information to the authority which retains them, which in most instances will be the police.

The theme was developed further by Glidewell LJ in *Ward*, and when commenting on the failures to disclose by the prosecution he said (at p. 23):

> We have spoken of 'the prosecution'. In this term we include four categories of individuals and organisations, namely (1) the three police forces . . . ; (2) the staff of the Director of Public Prosecutions and counsel who advised them; (3) the psychiatrists who prepared medical reports on Miss Ward at the request of the prosecution; and (4) the forensic scientists who gave evidence for the prosecution at the trial.

There seems little doubt, therefore, that at common law the prosecution team comprised the investigator, the prosecuting authority, prosecuting counsel and any expert who had actively been involved in assisting the prosecution, such as a forensic scientist, pathologist, psychiatrist or accountant. The duty of disclosure rested with the prosecutor and it was the responsibility of the investigator and expert to reveal to the prosecutor the existence of potentially disclosable material.

The position of social services

There are certain individuals and organisations whose status as part of 'the prosecution' is less clear. The social services departments of local authorities feature in many cases of physical or sexual abuse. Some inquiries are undertaken jointly by the police and social services. Where there are allegations of child abuse it is usually in the best interests of the child for social services to co-operate fully with the police in their investigations. Likewise, there is a responsibility on the police to work together with social services in such cases, as was made clear in the *Report of the Inquiry into Child Abuse in Cleveland 1987* (Cm 412, 1988). At p. 247 of the Report it is stated that 'The police should recognise and develop their responsibility for the protection of the child as extending beyond the collection of evidence for court procedures. This should include their attendance at case conferences and assistance to the other child protection agencies'. In this spirit of mutual co-operation, therefore, are social services to be regarded as part of the prosecution team so that the prosecuting authority has a duty of disclosure in respect of material held by them?

Many social workers would be surprised to learn of the suggestion that they may be considered part of the prosecution. Co-operating with the prosecuting agencies is one thing, but allowing those agencies to trawl through their confidential files in order to discover whether there is anything which should be disclosed to the defence is another matter. The view of most local authorities is that they are no more than a third party with an interest, sometimes an active interest, in the case and its outcome. There appears to be no legal authority which suggests anything different. The police have a duty to investigate allegations of crime, whereas the statutory duty of social services is to protect the welfare of the child. Section 47 of the Children Act 1989 provides that the local authority shall investigate cases of suffering or harm and make such inquiries to enable them to decide whether to take any action to safeguard or promote the child's welfare. In many cases, the objectives of a joint investigation with the police coincide when the best interests of the child are served by the arrest and prosecution of the perpetrator of the abuse. But in certain family or domestic circumstances this will not always be the case. Furthermore, much material in the possession of social services will attract PII, and while this need not prevent any disclosure to the prosecuting agencies, it will preclude production of documents in court without an order of the judge.

Many local authorities and police forces have introduced arrangements for the sharing of information, whereby the police notify social services when they commence an investigation and the social services may provide copies of documents relevant to the criminal investigation. When such material comes into the possession of the police, they have no alternative but to consider whether disclosure is necessary and proper, but the third party status of the social services means that defence requests for information held by those agencies must be pursued with them and not with the prosecuting authority.

There is no denying that, on occasions, the result has been less than satisfactory. Prosecutions have collapsed and accused persons have been freed because relevant documents held by social services have been revealed shortly before, or even during, the trial. The displeasure of the judge and the frustration of the accused are readily understandable, but to impose a general duty of disclosure on the prosecution in circumstances where the existence of material may not even be known to the police or the prosecuting authority would be bad law. Communication and co-operation between social services and prosecuting agencies is essential and defence requests for specific information must be dealt with, but the common law imposed no specific duty of disclosure in relation to third party material (*cf* comments below in *Blackledge* and *Saunders* in relation to inter-departmental obligations).

When an accused makes application for material held by a local authority, the courts will balance the interests of justice in the accused having a fair trial against those statutory provisions designed to protect the interests of children. For example, in *Kent County Council* v *K* [1994] 1 WLR 912, a father charged with the rape of his young daughters was successful in an application under r. 4.23, Family Proceedings Rules 1991, in obtaining statements taken in connection with proceedings under the Children Act 1989 which would be of help to his defence to the criminal charges.

The Attorney-General did have a role to play in questions of disclosure of documents held in connection with adoption cases as a result of an order made by Ewbank J in *Re Adoption Application* [1990] 1 All ER 639. The Attorney-General subsequently agreed to assist the court in cases where the disclosure of confidential adoption information arose. However, the decision of Ewbank J has since been overruled by a judgment of the Family Court in *Re H (A Minor) (Originating Application in Adoption Proceedings)* [1995] 2 FCR 711, where a local authority successfully applied for the setting aside of a witness summons obtained by the accused in a rape trial. It was held that such disclosure issues were a matter for the judge with conduct of the criminal proceedings and the decision of the Attorney-General could not bind the judge.

Not only do complicated disclosure issues arise in relation to the accused having available all material held by third parties which may be relevant to a defence, but also similar matters of complexity occur in the context of disclosure of care evidence to the police to assist them with their inquiries and disclosure of material held by the prosecuting authority to others in connection with care proceedings. These matters are outside the scope of this book, which is concerned with the prosecution's duty of disclosure to those charged with criminal offences, but it is pertinent to record that the paramountcy of the welfare of children often results in disclosure being made to the detriment of criminal proceedings. The CPS has acknowledged that it may be necessary to disclose information for use in care proceedings before the criminal trial, thus jeopardising a successful prosecution. When the prosecution consider that disclosure cannot be made, the court may derive assistance from the tests explained by Johnson J in *Nottinghamshire County Council* v *H (Minors)* [1995] 1 FLR 115. Similarly, genuine concerns held by local authorities on the disclosure of information to the police may sometimes be overriden by the need for a full and proper criminal investigation into allegations of abuse to children (as shown in the facts of *Re C (A Minor) (Care Proceedings: Disclosure)* (1996) *The Times*, 22 October 1996).

It is no exaggeration to say that disclosure issues arising between the accused, the prosecution and the local authority are something of a nightmare which is unlikely to be totally relieved by the provisions of the CPIA 1996.

Government departments, agencies and financial institutions

Equally indeterminate is the position of the many and varied agencies who provide information in connection with the regulation and supervision of financial services. Some organisations are part of the machinery of government, such as the Department of Trade and Industry, with its responsibility for regulating the insurance industry and supervising a variety of matters affecting companies, and the Treasury, which regulates overseas investment exchanges. Other bodies include the Bank of England, the Stock Exchange, the Securities and Investments Board and self-regulating organisations such as the Securities and Futures Authority, the Personal Investment Authority and the Investment Management Regulatory Organisation. Any of these organisations may have material relevant to a criminal prosecution. If they participated in the criminal investigation there is a strong argument for saying that they are, for disclosure purposes, part of the prosecution. If, on the other hand, they have simply given assistance, they are in no different a position from anyone else who provides information to the investigating or prosecuting authorities and are, therefore, no more than a third party. If it were otherwise, there would undoubtedly be a severe risk of lack of co-operation for fear that information held by the body in question would be potentially disclosable.

Recent cases have, however, provided vivid illustrations of the fact that one government department may hold documents and files which are highly material to a prosecution being conducted by another department. The facts of *R v Blackledge (William Stuart) (No. 2)* (1995) *The Times*, 8 November 1995 (the Ordtec appeal) are given in chapter 3. The appellants had pleaded guilty to conspiracy to export goods with intent to evade the prohibition on their exportation, but their appeals were allowed on the basis that certain documents ought to have been available to the defence before the trial. Importantly, the Court also held that documents in the possession of one or other government department which was involved in the inter-departmental consideration of licences, were to be regarded for the purposes of the case as in the possession of the Crown as an indivisible entity. If this decision is not to be confined to the special facts of the case, a prosecuting authority has a duty to make inquiries of other government departments to ensure that those other departments have has no documents which might be material to the issues or likely issues in a current prosecution.

The Court of Appeal, comprising two of the same members as in *Blackledge*, made similar observations a few days later in *R v Saunders (No. 2)* (1995) *The Times*, 28 November 1995. Non-disclosure was one of the grounds of appeal where it was contended that the prosecution should have made available documents which may have assisted the appellants to the extent that they revealed similar activity to that involved in the Guinness takeover by others in the City. Once again the Court held that such documents should have been disclosed, but they had some observations to make on the general duty of disclosure by the prosecution in fraud cases.

It had been submitted by the Crown that there had to be practical limitations on the duty of the prosecution in fraud trials where dishonesty was in issue, in relation to the disclosure of documents in the possession of the prosecuting agency and other departments. It was held that the common law did not extend to a duty to disclose similar transactions by other suspects simply because defendants in the current prosecution wished to demonstrate that others had been doing the same thing as they had. However, as the undisclosed documents in question were either in the possession of the prosecution or were known and available to them on request from another department, the documents in the instant case were treated as having been in the possession of the prosecuting authority.

It will be seen, therefore, that 'the prosecution' has an elasticity which will often depend on the circumstances of the individual case. Because of the failure of Customs and Excise in the Matrix Churchill and Ordtec cases to take into account, or to disclose to the defence, a number of highly relevant documents held by other government departments or agencies, the Scott Report made a number of recommendations (at para. K5.1) as to future procedures. They involve a consideration by the prosecuting solicitor and counsel of any documents which may be relevant, either to the way the prosecution puts their case or the way in which the defence propose to put their case, and which may be held by another government department or agency. Written requests should then be made to the department or agency concerned, which in turn should complete a report setting out what inquiries have been made. The defence should be kept informed of what steps are being taken.

The position of prosecution witnesses

A person is not part of the prosecution team simply by virtue of the fact that he or she is a witness for the prosecution. It is assumed that in the majority of cases, a witness will make available to the investigator any document relevant to the inquiry. Those documents which are retained will either be exhibited as part of the case for the prosecution, or made available to the defence if they do not form part of the case. If further material is sought by the defence, there is nothing to prevent them taking their own steps to procure it. The status of certain prosecution witnesses has, however, from time to time caused difficulty. For example, is a doctor an expert, thus enforcing the prosecution's disclosure obligations? This may depend on the role of the doctor in the instant case. If the doctor is no more than a witness of fact who examines a victim at the surgery or at hospital, he or she is probably in no different position from any other witness. If any doctor is employed as a Divisional Surgeon or Forensic Medical Examiner, or has been instructed to give an opinion on injuries, he or she comes closer to the position of an expert and under the common law rules would probably be part of the prosecution for disclosure purposes.

These are not just academic points. Not only is it essential that those who might be considered part of the prosecution team are aware of their responsibility to preserve relevant documents and to reveal them to the investigator, but the defence must also know whether they can expect information from the prosecution or whether they must take their own steps to approach the individual or organisation concerned. If persons are unsure what material they ought to be retaining, or to whom they should be relating pertinent facts and information, there is a danger that relevant matters may not become known to the accused, thus increasing the potential for a miscarriage of justice.

There are no disclosure requirements on experts in the CPIA 1996 and disclosure code. The onus is very much on the investigator. Paragraph 3.4 of the code makes it clear that the investigator should pursue all reasonable lines of inquiry, whether these point towards or away from the suspect. As a matter of practice, however, it will still be necessary for there to be arrangements for the revelation of information which is potentially disclosable by those experts with whom the police deal on a regular basis, such as forensic scientists and police surgeons.

Agencies in other jurisdictions

The inspection of material in a foreign jurisdiction can often be a frustrating experience for solicitors acting for an accused. The prosecution have no duty of disclosure in relation to material held by agencies in other jurisdictions. Even where there has been a joint investigation with, for example, law enforcement agencies in another jurisdiction, material held by those agencies is not deemed to be in the possession of the prosecution (unless copies have been provided). Requests to inspect the material or for copies can be channelled through the prosecution, but there is no means by which a foreign agency can be compelled to allow facilities to inspect or produce documents. From time to time difficulties have even been experienced in relation to material in Scotland where the disclosure rules are quite different from those in England and Wales.

The position under the CPIA 1996

The CPIA 1996 does not directly address the question 'Who comprises the prosecution?'. The prosecutor is defined in s. 2 and the status and duties of the investigator and prosecutor are set out in the disclosure code. 'Prosecution material', for the purposes of primary and secondary disclosure, is material which is in the prosecutor's possession or which has been inspected in connection with the case for the prosecution which has been retained by the investigator. Paragraph 3.5 of the code requires that in a criminal investigation, the officer in charge or the disclosure officer should inform other persons of the existence of an investigation, if it is believed that those other persons may be in possession of material that may be relevant to the investigation. However, the investigator is not required to make speculative inquiries of other persons; there must be some reason to believe that they may have relevant material. Thus, if the police are investigating a suspected drug trafficker and have reason to be believe that Customs investigators have also had the suspect under investigation, there is a duty on the police to check with Customs for the existence of any relevant information.

DISCLOSURE OF MATERIAL IN THE POSSESSION OF THIRD PARTIES

Use of witness summons

As the prosecution's duty of disclosure was enlarged by the fast-developing common law rules, defence expectations increased that the Crown had a role in obtaining material from third parties on their behalf. As we have seen above, there is no such duty either at common law or under the CPIA 1996; and in those cases where the prosecution are unable or unwilling to volunteer to try and obtain the documents, the defence must fall back on the only alternative means of inspecting such material, namely an application for a witness summons. In the Crown Court this entails an application under s. 2, Criminal Procedure (Attendance of Witnesses) Act 1965, as was emphasised in *R* v *Seeleg* (unreported), Central Criminal Court, 28 November 1990. When setting aside a witness summons on the ground that it represented a fishing expedition, Henry J observed (at p. 18, transcript T881630) that: 'While the obligation of disclosure on prosecuting authorities has changed dramatically, the extent to which third parties may be compelled by the defendant to assist the defendant has not changed at all. The statutory basis remains the 1965 Act.' The statutory basis is still the 1965 Act but, as will be observed below, s. 2 has now been substantially amended by s. 66, CPIA 1996. The equivalent jurisdiction in the magistrates' court is provided by s. 97, Magistrates' Courts Act 1980.

There are, however, a number of obstacles for an accused to overcome before s. 2 or s. 97 may be utilised to procure the production of material held by third parties. The two principal barriers facing the defence are that they must satisfy the court that the documents are both (i) relevant and (ii) admissible. The relevance point is illustrated by *R* v *Skegness Justices, ex parte Cardy* [1985] RTR 49, where witness summonses for the production of documents concerning intoximeter devices were set aside because it was impossible to say that the documents would be material. On the question of admissibility, *R* v *Cheltenham Justices, ex parte Secretary of State for Trade* [1977] 1 WLR 95 decided that a witness summons may not be issued to obtain documents which could not be admitted in evidence in the case. Attempts have been made from time to time to distinguish the harsh effects of *Cheltenham Justices*, which are inconsistent with general disclosure obligations where materiality and not admissibility is the decisive factor. In applying for a witness summons, however, admissibility remains an essential criterion, unless the amendments introduced by the CPIA 1996 will herald a change in approach to the issue of a summons.

The pre-CPIA 1996 state of the law in relation to the granting of a witness summons was conveniently summarised in a judgment at first instance given by the Common Serjeant of London in *R* v *Baqi* (unreported), Central Criminal Court, 14 December 1993, (at p. 6, transcript S/1374):

> (1) Although there is an obligation on the prosecution to disclose all unused material, the position of third parties is still covered by the 1965 Act.
>
> (2) That Act allows a witness summons to be issued for a document which contains material which is both relevant and admissible.
>
> (3) A witness summons may not be issued to obtain documents where the only purpose is the hope that the material which can be used in cross-examination will emerge.
>
> (4) There is no doctrine of discovery applicable to third parties, and fishing expeditions are not permitted.

The distinction between the disclosure duties of the prosecution and those of a third party was made in the Chancery Division by Millet J in *Re Barlow Clowes Gilt Managers Ltd* [1991] 4 All ER 385, when holding that the liquidators of a company were under no duty to assist directors of the company in defending criminal charges brought against them. The disclosure of information given in confidence in the course of winding up the company would be contrary to public policy as it would jeopardise the proper and efficient functioning of the liquidation. After remarking that the prosecution had a duty to be objective and balanced in their presentation of the case and must not withhold from the defence matters which might prove helpful, Millet J continued (at p. 393):

> But all this has nothing to do with the third party who is not himself involved except possibly as a witness. He is under no obligation to provide voluntary assistance whether to the prosecution or the defence. He is not bound to disclose his private documents except to the extent that statute has laid such an obligation upon him.

Further confirmation of the position may be found from the judgment in *R* v *Maxwell* (unreported), Court of Appeal, 9 February 1995, which decided that even though documents were made available to the SFO when exercising its powers under ss. 1 and 2, Criminal Justice Act 1987, this did not result in them coming into the possession of the SFO. The Director had no duty of disclosure in relation to the documents which remained in the possession of the third party.

The position in relation to a witness summons at the magistrates' court received detailed consideration in *R* v *Reading Justices, ex parte Berkshire County Council*

(1995) *The Times*, 5 May 1995, an application for judicial review to quash the Justices' decision to issue a witness summons directed to the Director of Social Services of the County Council. The summons had been granted on the application of two police officers who were due to face trial for common assault on a child who was resident in a children's home under a care order. The judgment contains an examination of the conditions necessary for the granting of a witness summons, but its significance in the current context arises out of the submission of counsel for one of the defendants to invoke the developing law of disclosure of documents by the prosecution. Simon Brown LJ's response (at p. 16, transcript CO 426/95) was quite succint: 'That is not a submission that I can accept. It seems to me that quite different considerations arise with regard to the production of documents by third parties.' He confirmed that the principles established under s. 97, Magistrates' Courts Act 1980 were untouched by other developments in the criminal law.

Although the distinction between the composition of the prosecution team and third parties may sometimes be blurred, there is little doubt that once the separation has been made, the prosecution have no obligation in relation to material held by the third party. The dilemma for the defence under the original provisions of s. 2 of the 1965 Act and the common law rules was that they could not apply for a witness summons unless they could demonstrate that the witness was able to give material and admissible evidence or produce material and admissible documents. They could not go on a fishing expedition and must not use the witness summons procedure as a camouflage for discovery. Suspicion that a third party may hold relevant material was not enough and the defence had to rely on the third party and/or the prosecution volunteering that information existed which might assist them. It appears as though they were, however, entitled to seek a witness summons with a view both to discovering the contents of documents and adducing them in evidence. In *R v Clowes* [1992] BCLC 1158, in upholding the issue of a witness summons despite the objections of the liquidators, Phillips J stated (at p. 1167):

> The use of a witness summons simply to obtain discovery is an abuse of process, but where a document is likely to contain material evidence, the precise nature of which is not known to a party, the issue of a witness summons by that party is likely to be motivated by a desire to see the contents of that document and a desire to adduce the evidence before the jury. . . . It does not seem to me to offend against section 2 of the 1965 Act to issue a witness summons seeking production of documents which are admissible in evidence with the motive both of discovering the precise nature of the contents of the documents, and, if these are helpful, adducing them in evidence.

A practical difficulty facing the defence, prosecution, third party and court alike is the question of who actually examines third-party documents in order to determine their relevance; and in some cases, whether the documents may be covered by PII. In fraud cases and child abuse allegations, the documents and files in question could entail, and sometimes have entailed, many hours of reading thousands of pages. This point was answered by the Court of Appeal in *R* v *W (G)*; *R* v *W (E)* (1996) *The Times*, 12 July 1996, when it was held that the judge was entitled to accept an assurance from an independent and competent member of the Bar who had inspected the documents in the possession of a third party, that they were irrelevant to an issue in the case. If the claim was implausible or suspect, the judge might look at the documents himself or herself.

Witness summonses under the CPIA 1996

Section 66 of the CPIA 1996 amends the Criminal Procedure (Attendance of Witnesses) Act 1965 by substituting new provisions for s. 2. At the time of writing, s. 66 has not been implemented. Section 66 was introduced at the eleventh hour in the Bill's passage through Parliament and one of its intentions presumably is to ameliorate the inconsistency in prosecution material being readily disclosed yet third-party documents, which may be relevant, not being freely available.

Under s. 2(1) of the 1965 Act the Crown Court may issue a witness summons where it is satisfied that 'a person is likely to be able to give evidence likely to be material evidence, or produce any document or thing likely to be material evidence', and where the person will not voluntarily attend as a witness or produce the document or thing. The wording of s. 2(1) closely resembles that in s. 97, Magistrates' Courts Act 1980, and the decision of the Divisional Court in the *Reading Justices* case (above) indicates that admissibility remains a condition in the magistrates' court. Under the new provisions, however, the Crown Court has only to be satisfied that the person is likely to be able to give evidence, *which evidence is likely to be material* (whereas s. 97 states that the person *is likely to be able to give material evidence*). It remains to be seen whether admissibility is still essential under the new provision.

Importantly, s. 2A of the 1965 Act now allows prior inspection of documents by advance production at a place and time stated in the summons. Section 2B enables the court to direct that the summons shall be of no further effect if the inspecting party concludes that it is no longer required. This is in line with the inspection of prosecution material in the possession of the prosecutor which may be inspected prior to the trial and not produced if it is of no relevance or help to the defence. Applications to set summonses aside or make them ineffective are preserved by new s. 2C if any party satisfies the court that they were not served with a notice of the application and given an opportunity to be heard, or satisfies the court that they cannot give any evidence or produce a document or thing likely to be material evidence. The Crown Court may issue a summons of its own motion by virtue of s. 2D and the person's right to apply to make such a summons ineffective is preserved by s. 2E. Crown Court rules will deal with the requirements and procedures for applications, which may be supported by an affidavit giving particulars of the document to be produced and grounds for its production.

It is, of course, essential that third parties are protected from speculative, unnecessary, inconvenient and, sometimes, expensive requests from the defence.

This is why the authorities discussed above, culminating in *Reading Justices*, require as central principles that the documents requested must be relevant and admissible and not merely desired for possible cross-examination purposes. If documents exist which undermine the case for the prosecution, however, it is unfair that the defence should be denied them simply because they are in the possession of a third party and not the prosecution. The investigator has a duty under the disclosure code to pursue all reasonable lines of inquiry, but it is still possible that material documents may escape notice and remain in the possession of another person. It will be interesting to see whether the conditions for the issue of a witness summons under the new s. 2(1) will be interpreted as strictly as the old s. 2 and s. 97 of the 1980 Act.

THE TYPE OF INFORMATION TO BE DISCLOSED

Broad categories of disclosable information

At common law, following the adoption of Jowitt J's materiality test in *Keane* (see chapter 7, page 81), documents which are relevant or possibly relevant to a likely issue in the case are disclosable. Such documents include:

- statements not included in the committal or transfer bundles and unedited statements (by virtue of *A-G's Guidelines*);
- preparatory material such as tape recordings, transcripts, notes and first drafts of statements (see *Guinness Ruling* of Henry J);
- relevant interviews with the accused (see *Ward*);
- the results of tests and experiments that disprove or cast doubt on the opinion expressed by an expert (see *Ward* and *Maguire*).

In the *Guinness Advice* (see chapter 7, page 73), the DPP gave examples of other documents which should normally be preserved by the police with a view to disclosure. They included documents commonly held or created by the police during an inquiry, such as crime reports, custody records, material casting doubt upon the reliability of a confession, etc. The examples have been enlarged in para. 5.4 of the disclosure code. In the last five years the courts have been asked to consider the nature of certain documents in the context of allegations of non-disclosure of relevant material, but before examining the cases the criterion for disclosability must be emphasised.

Criterion of materiality and not admissibility

It matters not that the information or document itself may be inadmissible in evidence. For example, one of the documents not disclosed in *Ward* was a statement made by a Detective Inspector which included the comment, 'Despite being further interviewed with regard to this aspect of her confession, she continued to profess her innocence and I must concede that I found her to be convincing'. Although this comment was inadmissible, it was information which was helpful to the defence and counsel for the Crown conceded that failure to disclose was a material irregularity.

Confirmation of this point is provided by the judgment of Lord Mustill in *R* v *Preston (Stephen)* (1994) 98 Cr App R 405, when he states (at p. 429):

> In the first place, the fact that an item of information cannot be put in evidence by a party does not mean that it is worthless. Often, the train of inquiry which leads to the discovery of evidence which is admissible at a trial may include an item which is not admissible, and this may apply, although less frequently, to the defence as well as the prosecution. As the Court of Appeal pointed out in *Ward* (supra) (1993) 96 Cr App R 1, 25, [1993] 1 WLR 619, 645, it is of help to the accused to have the opportunity of considering all the material evidence which the prosecution have gathered and from which the prosecution have made their own selection. In my opinion the test is materiality, not admissibility.

The Court of Appeal have recently reinforced the position in *R* v *Law (Anthony)* (1996) *The Times*, 15 August 1996, in the context of the disclosure of information concerning informants and undercover police officers. It was held that the judge is not restricted to considering evidence that would be admissible in a court of law. Material which amounted to no more than hearsay could also be looked at.

Identification material

The courts have frequently had to examine documents in cases involving disputed identification. In 1976, the Devlin Report had recommended (at para. 8.10) that the police should record in writing descriptions of the alleged criminal and then disclose such descriptions to the defence. Nearly 20 years later a similar recommendation was made by the Court of Appeal in *R* v *Fergus* (1994) 98 Cr App R 313, where the case against the appellant, a 13-year-old schoolboy, was based solely on the identification evidence of the victim. Steyn LJ concluded his judgment by urging the police, in all identification cases and as a matter of routine, to forward photographs and crime reports to the CPS. In the instant case, the photograph and crime report were material in that they would have alerted the defence solicitor (who also came in for criticism for the preparation of the defence case) as to weaknesses in the identification evidence.

In *R* v *Wright* [1994] Crim LR 131, an identikit of the alleged assailant in a wages robbery was not disclosed, as a result of an oversight. It was not disputed that it was a relevant document that should have been disclosed although as it bore such a striking resemblance to the defendant, its admission before the jury would have damaged his case rather than helped it. The appeal, the main grounds of which were in connection with the Identification Codes of Practice, was dismissed. Non-disclosure of messages received by the police concerning first descriptions was at the heart of the appeal of the Taylor sisters (see chapter 3, page 23). Identification was crucial to the prosecution case and counsel for the Crown conceded that he could not possibly argue that a failure to disclose a previous inconsistent description was not a matter of real significance and, therefore, a material irregularity.

There was little doubt under the common law rules that any document containing a description of an alleged offender must be preserved and disclosed. The point has now been reinforced in the new disclosure code where the investigator has a duty to retain, *inter alia*, telephone messages containing descriptions of an alleged offender. There is also a duty to reveal to the prosecutor a copy of records of the first description of a suspect given to the police by a potential witness, whether or not the description differs from that of the alleged offender (para. 7.3).

Police messages

As the criterion for disclosure is materiality and not admissibility, any relevant document held or made by the police is potentially disclosable. A good example of inadmissible but potentially relevant documents are police messages, and these received the attention of the Court of Appeal in *R* v *Browning (Edward)* [1995] Crim LR 227. The appellant had been convicted of the murder of a heavily pregnant woman whose car had broken down on the M50 motorway. The Court of Appeal was informed that the incident room received a total of 2,987 messages during the course of the investigation, four of which were of particular significance in the case. The judgment comments that in the normal course of events, a message to the effect that someone may be able to give relevant information will contain nothing falling within the duty of disclosure, but there will be instances when such information is disclosable; for example, an inconsistency between the message and the subsequent witness statement, or where there has been an omission of something of particular significance going to identification or timing. It goes without saying that this places a considerable onus on the police to ensure that relevant messages are retained, and this is especially difficult when messages may be received at different locations and by different means. The commentary to *Browning* at p. 229 of the report is particularly apposite: 'The police received some 2,987 messages during the course of the investigation into the killing, which received much national coverage. Ensuring that nothing has been omitted from the duty to disclose which might benefit the defence in any of the ways described by the court looks to be a Herculean labour, possibly of the Poirot variety.'

Video recordings

Video recordings are a common feature of modern day life with cameras in public areas such as shopping centres, factory estates, public houses, clubs and football stadia. These may be inspected by the police during an investigation, and if nothing of significance is revealed they are likely to be handed back to the owners and ultimately destroyed or the tapes re-used. It would be unrealistic to expect the police to retain a video recording simply on the basis that it exists and might possibly be of interest to a potential suspect. In many instances an arrest may never be made following an investigation. The consequences of failing to disclose a relevant video recording can, however, be severe, as in *R* v *Birmingham* [1992] Crim LR 117 where a Crown Court Judge stayed the prosecution on the somewhat questionable grounds of an abuse of process.

The disclosure code provides (in para. 5.6) that all material which may be relevant to the investigation must be retained until a decision is taken whether to institute proceedings. Police officers and other investigators will, therefore, have to make a decision on whether third-party video tapes should be retained or returned. A practical problem for the police has arisen in the case of those police stations where experiments in video recording custody suites have been introduced. The length of time that the tapes should be retained and their availablity to any person charged as a matter of routine, are just two questions of disclosure that arise.

Information received orally

It was made clear by Henry J in the *Guinness Ruling* (see chapter 7) that it is not just written statements and documents that are disclosable but oral statements as well. This caused the DPP to include in the *Guinness Advice* that 'Where information is received orally rather than in written form, then the police officer should make a written record of that information and include the record in the schedule to the CPS'. This advice was endorsed by the Court of Appeal in *R* v *Brown (Winston)* (see chapter 7, page 83) and it had also been stated in *R* v *Livingstone* [1993] Crim LR 597, that the duty of disclosure arose where material, 'whether documentary or otherwise' was of relevance. This caused a certain amount of apprehension among police officers as to exactly what information they should be recording. Paragraphs 4.1 and 5.5 of the disclosure code now give some help, but at the end of the day each officer concerned must make a sensible appraisal of the information received orally which, in the normal course of events, is likely to be relevant to the investigation.

The duty of disclosure of relevant information received orally is not confined to the police. In *R* v *Birmingham Magistrates' Court, ex parte Shields* (unreported), Divisional Court, 7 July 1994, the wife of the applicant filed an affidavit saying that she had been spoken to by the Crown Prosecutor at court and that she had informed him that she did not wish to give evidence against her husband and that the statement she had made was not entirely accurate as she had been upset and confused. Kay J was of the opinion that if such information is in the possession of the prosecutor, there is a duty to disclose it to the defending solicitor.

Some of the points canvassed above are now dealt with in the CPIA 1996 and the disclosure code. Section 2 of the 1996 Act interprets references to material as material of all kinds and, in particular, information and objects of all descriptions.

Thus, information received orally remains disclosable. Furthermore, references to recording information are to putting it in durable or retrievable form (such as writing or tape). The duty to retain material includes, in particular, the duty to retain material falling into a number of defined categories set out in para. 5.4 of the code, and these essentially embrace the categories which have emerged from the *A-G's Guidelines*, case law and the DPP's *Guinness Advice* (see chapter 7).

Miscellaneous investigation, arrest and detention records

Defence requests to the prosecution for access to police notebooks, incident records, surveillance logs and a host of other routine investigation, arrest and detention material are commonplace. There is no denying the defence entitlement to access to such information provided that it is relevant. This is a far cry from attitudes prevailing in the pre-PACE 1984 days when, for example, in *R* v *Hackney* (1982) 74 Cr App R 194, Watkins LJ condemned the use made of custody forms which 'are called for at a moment's notice by the defence during a trial and when produced invariably used to assail the police, often with a total lack of responsibility and no acknowledgement of the rules of evidence'. The use of computer systems, such as 'HOLMES', for major inquiries presents the police with further disclosure challenges as each step of the investigation is recorded. Many of the actions logged will be irrelevant, some will be of doubtful relevance and others will be confidential or sensitive. In order to effect disclosure at a later stage, it seems essential that some sort of sifting or categorisation is carried out at the input stage.

It is, of course, quite impossible to provide a comprehensive list of what should be retained; and notwithstanding the attempts at categorisation in the disclosure code, issues are bound to arise as to whether certain documents should have been retained or whether certain information should have been reduced to a durable or retrievable form. Much will depend on the nature of the information, the type of offence and the circumstances of the case, and disclosability will ultimately be determined by the question of relevance.

THE ASSESSMENT OF RELEVANCE

Relevance or materiality?

The assessment of relevance or materiality is probably the most important aspect of the disclosure process and it is the feature which has changed more than any other as the prosecution's common law duty was developed and refined. The *A-G's Guidelines* test of material having a bearing on the offence(s) charged and the surrounding circumstances of the case made way to a new test in *Ward*, only to be replaced by another in *Keane*; and now there are the statutory tests provided by the CPIA 1996.

The courts have tended to use the words 'relevant' and 'material' interchangeably. *R* v *Hennessey* (1978) 68 Cr App R 419, spoke of a duty to make available all relevant evidence of help to an accused. *R v Lawson* (1990) 90 Cr App R 107 and *Ward* defined 'material evidence' as evidence which tends either to weaken the prosecution case or strengthen the defence case. A test of 'materiality' rather than 'relevance' was used by the Court of Appeal in *Keane*. Is there any significance in the choice of words? 'Relevance' is described in the *Oxford English Dictionary* as 'bearing on or having reference to the matter in hand', while 'material' is defined as 'important, essential, relevant (at the material time)'. It might be said, therefore, that a test of materiality is narrower in that it relates to documents which are important and essential to the case, rather than to documents which have a bearing on the case. The reality is that it is more likely there is no significance in choice of words and common law assessments of materiality and relevance are one and the same.

The *Keane* test of materiality

It was made clear in *R v Keane* (1994) 99 Cr App R 1 (see chapter 7) that, whatever had been the perceptions before, the prosecution were under a duty to assess the materiality of documents in their possession. They should do this by applying the Jowitt test of a sensible appraisal of documents which are considered:

(a)   to be relevant or possibly relevant to an issue in the case;

(b)   to raise or possibly raise a new issue the existence of which is not apparent from the evidence the prosecution propose to use; and

(c)   to hold out a real (as opposed to fanciful) prospect of providing a lead on evidence which goes to the criteria above (see page 81).

The Court of Appeal did not elaborate on what was meant by 'an issue in the case' and how it was to be construed. Steyn LJ proffered his view in *R v Brown (Winston)* [1995] 1 Cr App R 191, when he stated at (p. 199) that 'an issue in the case must not be construed in the fairly narrow way in which it is used in a civil case. It must be given a broad interpretation'. He then went on to illustrate the difference by citing examples affecting the credibility of witnesses, the discovery of which is not permitted in civil proceedings (see *Ballantine and Son Ltd v FER Dixons and Sons Ltd* [1974] 1 WLR 1125).

It was still unclear, however, whether the broad interpretation extended to anything more than a contested or disputed issue. For example, in a case of handling stolen goods where the defence is an absence of guilty knowledge, should disclosure be limited to that defence; or, because it is essential for the prosecution to prove that the goods are stolen, does disclosure attach to any unused documents which relate to proof of the theft? More importantly, if there was an informant in the case who led the police to the defendant but who could clearly add nothing to the question of the defendant's belief or knowledge of the origins of the goods, can that safely be ignored for disclosure purposes? It is one of the broad issues in the case to explain why the police arrived at the defendant's door, but it is not a matter that need trouble the jury who are really concerned only with the issue of guilty knowledge. Early post-*Keane* signs were that the courts were interpreting 'an issue in the case' as a contested or disputed issue.

Although the Jowitt test of materiality adopted in *Keane* was welcomed by prosecutors as a more focused approach to disclosure responsibilities, it is often not easy to apply in practice. Any test of materiality is entirely dependent on the facts of the case and the issues as known or perceived from the statements or from information provided by the defence. Where the issues are unclear, advantage can be taken of Lord Taylor's statement in *Keane* to the effect that the more information that the defence are able to provide, the greater assistance the prosecution and the court are able to give. Clarification from the defence may be sought to enable a more acccurate assessment to be made. In the absence of clarification, the prosecutor must make an assessment of what the issues are, or are likely to be, and act accordingly.

The second limb of the Jowitt test is less straightforward. Assessing materiality in relation to a new issue whose existence is not apparent from the evidence requires a degree of crystal-ball gazing. The type of scenario which was probably in mind is where there is scientific evidence to connect the defendant with the crime but the tests and experiments carried out were not all conclusive. If the defence were aware of that fact, a new issue would arise which they must be given an opportunity to explore. The third limb of the test, regarding a prospect of providing a lead on evidence, is best illustrated by the point made already that materiality and not admissibility is the acid test. The fact that the document is inadmissible in evidence does not prevent the defence from using it as a lead or introduction to find something which may be both helpful and admissible.

Keane clearly anticipated that, in most cases, prosecutors would be able to assess materiality on the information at their disposal, because Lord Taylor's judgment stated that the court should be asked to rule only in exceptional cases. However, applications for the assistance of the court are not as exceptional as envisaged; but practitioners have had comparatively little time to settle into the application of the *Keane* approach in view of the new procedures envisaged by the CPIA 1996.

The disclosure tests under the CPIA 1996

The Jowitt test of materiality is now replaced by a two-stage process: first, of disclosing material which in the prosecutor's opinion might undermine the case for the prosecution; and, secondly, where the defence have set out their case in a written statement, by the prosecution then disclosing any material which might reasonably be expected to assist the defence as shown in the defence statement. The application of these tests is examined in chapter 16, but the introduction of yet another criterion for disclosure presents more problems for the parties. In some cases, it will always be obvious what information should be disclosed, whether the test is the all-embracing one in the *A-G's Guidelines*, the carefully defined one given by Jowitt J or the supposedly narrower CPIA standard of undermining the prosecution case. If an accused says he was not at the scene of the crime and information exists which may support that, disclosure must follow. There will be many cases, though, where the application of the test of materiality needs careful appraisal. It is easy, with the benefit of hindsight and when the matters in dispute are clear, to say that this should have been disclosed and that should not. The Government's expectations are that the volume of material falling to be disclosed will be reduced as a result of applying the new test, while the dangers of justice miscarrying will not increase. Whether those expectations are fulfilled will depend very much on how the courts interpret the new tests.

THE WAY IN WHICH DISCLOSURE IS EFFECTED

Practices under the *A-G's Guidelines*

The *A-G's Guidelines* stated that if the unused material to be made available to the defence did not exceed about 50 pages, disclosure should be by way of provision of a copy. If the material exceeded 50 pages, the defence solicitor should be given an opportunity to inspect it at a convenient police station or at the office of the prosecuting solicitor. Although the *Guidelines* are to all intents and purposes redundant, there was never any suggestion that this means of disclosure should not remain best practice. The procedure adopted by the CPS in most cases is to provide copies of statements and records of interview together with a schedule which lists the documents held by the police. If the defence wish to examine the documents, they may do so at the police station; and if they require copies of certain documents then, provided the request is reasonable, it will be complied with in accordance with para. 5 of the *Guidelines*. A major complaint of the police has been the drain on resources caused by photocopying demands, but this is an inevitable consequence of the development of the law. Illustrations of the scale of the problem were highlighted in an article in the *Daily Telegraph*, 23 March 1994, which reported that six police officers had worked full-time for two years preparing and copying 20 tons of documents for delivery to lawyers representing the accused in a pending child murder case. It further reported that in relation to the prosecution of Asil Nadir (who later absconded), 11 separate agencies demanded full copies of the unused material in the case. With each copy running to more than a million documents, the cost of copying, ultimately to be borne by the SFO, came close to £2 million.

   While some defence solicitors have unreasonable expectations of what they should be provided with, most are content to carry out an inspection at the police station and be provided with copies of anything they consider relevant. In order to defray photocopying costs, the police and some prosecuting authorities began to charge solicitors, who then claimed payment from the Legal Aid Fund. The police then had the embarrassment of having to reimburse many firms of solicitors following advice received from Treasury Counsel that the making of a charge for carrying out what was plainly a duty under the *A-G's Guidelines* and current law, was illegal in the absence of specific statutory authority (see Attorney-General's written reply to Mr Bates MP, Hansard vol. 240, HC, 31 March 1994, written answers, col. 949).

Advances in technology since the issue of the *A-G's Guidelines* have meant that in major inquiries much information is now stored on computer. Hard copies of relevant information can be provided, but in other cases it has been more convenient for both sides for the police to allow supervised access to a terminal screen. It may be that in the future, defence representatives can be provided with a disk containing non-sensitive information. Provided that security can be assured, this may prove to be the most efficient and economical way of supplying such information.

Effecting disclosure under the CPIA 1996

The CPIA 1996 provides for the manner of disclosure by allowing the prosecutor either to give a copy of the material to the accused, or, if in the opinion of the prosecutor copying is not practicable or desirable, to provide facilities for an inspection of the material. Paragraph 10.3 of the disclosure code of practice further provides that if an accused person asks for a copy of any material inspected, a copy should be provided unless that is not practicable or desirable. In practice, the new provisions for effecting disclosure do not appear to differ in any significant respect from practices adopted under the common law. The somewhat artificial threshhold of 50 pages has been removed and there is an onus on the prosecution to supply copies of material documents unless the items cannot physically be copied or copying is not desirable on sensitivity or security grounds. As under the common law rules, sensitive documents may be edited or redacted in order to facilitate disclosure.

Confidentiality of disclosed information

A major source of disquiet for the police and prosecuting authorities has been how material is dealt with once it has been disclosed. Unlike the position in civil proceedings, there was no express restriction at common law on the use to which material could be put after it had been disclosed. In civil proceedings, any documents discovered can be used by the party only for the purpose of proving its case and there is an implied undertaking that the documents will not be used in collateral proceedings. If the documents are misused, contempt proceedings or an injunction to restrain misuse may be appropriate. In criminal proceedings, however, once statements or other documents left the prosecution, they had limited control over their use. It had been the practice with some prosecuting authorities to seek an undertaking that the documents would not be used for purposes other than the criminal prosecution, but it was an undertaking which was in practice difficult to enforce.

Whether an implied undertaking also exists in relation to documents served for the purpose of criminal proceedings was considered in *McGrath* v *Chief Constable of Lancashire* (unreported), Divisional Court, 3 April 1996, in the context of an application with regard to the proposed use in civil proceedings of certain documents served on the applicant for the purpose of a criminal prosecution. It was conceded by both parties that the unused material served by the Crown was the subject of an implied undertaking not to use the material for purposes other than the criminal proceedings. The rationale for such an implied undertaking had been explained by Browne-Wilkinson VC in *Derby and Co.* v *Weldon* (1988) *The Times*, 20 October 1988. Discovery in the course of an action is an interference with the privacy that individuals enjoy in relation to their own documents and any invasion of such privacy should be for the sole purpose of enabling a proper trial of the action in which the discovery is given. In *Ex parte Coventry Newspapers* [1993] QB 278, it was held that that there was a public interest underlying the undertaking not to disclose further, which was based on the confidence and co-operation required by the police from those whose information and evidence is sought in the course of investigating crime. *McGrath* decided that the implied undertaking recognised in *Ex parte Coventry Newspapers* attaches to all documents disclosed by the prosecution, whether they are served as part of the prosecution case or as unused material. For the court to release or vary the implied undertaking required the application of exacting standards, but those standards were met in the circumstances of the instant case where a variation was granted.

In *Cunningham* v *Essex County Council* (1997) *The Times*, 31 March 1997, the plaintiff was not allowed to use a letter which had been disclosed to him for the purposes of criminal proceedings for theft, in order to pursue an action for libel and malicious falsehood against the defendant council. It was held that the plaintiff could not use the letter without an order from the Crown Court varying the implied undertaking not to disclose for purposes other than the criminal trial.

It has therefore been recognised that persons who provide statements and assist in criminal prosecutions should be able to do so in the confidence that their statements are not misused. While most solicitors would no doubt be content to provide an undertaking of confidentiality, there is little that they can do once copies are released to their clients, some of whom may be on remand in prison. Police and Home Office concerns over the absence of express provisions relating to the confidentiality of disclosed material, particularly in relation to statements of a sexual nature sometimes circulating in prison and falling into the wrong hands, have now been addressed by ss. 17 and 18, CPIA 1996. These are dealt with more fully in chapter 16, but broadly speaking, an accused can use the information disclosed only for the purpose of the criminal proceedings and may be dealt with for contempt if the disclosure is knowingly made in contravention of s. 17.

TIMING AND LIMITS FOR DISCLOSURE

Timing under the *A-G's Guidelines*

Paragraph 3 of the *A-G's Guidelines* recommended that in relation to cases being committed for trial, disclosure should take place as soon as possible before the date of committal. This was especially important if the material might have some influence upon the course of the committal proceedings or the charges upon which the justices might commit. In other words, if the prosecution had material which would weaken their case to the extent that the magistrates might conclude that there was no prima facie case, disclosure should not be delayed. Paragraph 3 contained the caveat that if disclosure might cause delay and was unlikely to influence the committal, it should be made as soon as possible after committal. Thus, in a prolonged inquiry which involved a considerable amount of unused material, matters should not be held up simply in order to disclose material which did not have a bearing on whether there was a prima facie case.

In so far as non-sensitive material is concerned, this guidance has attracted little judicial attention. In the majority of cases destined for the Crown Court there is no reason why disclosure should not be made at the same time as, or shortly after, service of the committal statements or transfer documents. In the more substantial cases, there may be a practical difficulty in the police compiling a schedule of all the unused material in time for the service of committal documents, but there should be no other reason in law for delaying disclosure. The *A-G's Guidelines* did not, of course, apply in summary proceedings, although, as we have seen in the previous chapter, it was the practice of prosecuting authorities to make disclosure in the more serious offences to be tried summarily. The higher courts have never had to consider whether disclosure should be made prior to election or, in the case of summary offences, before a plea is taken. The practice has generally been not to make disclosure until after plea. Disclosure should then be effected as soon as possible since the longer it is delayed, the greater the potential for an adjournment and delay.

Applications involving sensitive material

The position is less straightforward in cases involving material which the prosecution intend to place before the court on public interest grounds. The means of asserting PII are considered in chapter 10 and there is litle doubt that a Crown Court judge is better placed to understand the complexities of PII than are lay justices. The Divisional Court had to consider the position in *R v Crown Prosecution Service, ex parte Warby* [1994] Crim LR 281. The applicant sought judicial review of the CPS refusal to disclose unused material to him on the ground that they had failed to comply with the *A-G's Guidelines*. The CPS had refused disclosure on the basis that the material in question was sensitive and it was proposed to place it before the Crown Court in accordance with the procedures laid down in *Davis, Johnson and Rowe* (see chapter 7, page 77). The Divisional Court held that there was no jurisdiction to review a refusal by the CPS to disclose unused material prior to committal, but Watkins LJ commented (at transcript CO/337/93, p. 10):

Nevertheless, I am in no doubt at all that, even supposing the decision of either the CPS or the Justices is reviewable, which on ample authority I do not think it is, it would be entirely inappropriate for decisions as to disclosure of unused material to be taken at a lower level of judicial activity than the Crown Court. There are, in my opinion, sound reasons for that view, including the sensitivity of the material in question as a general rule and the fact that regardless what attitude has been adopted on committal, or even before it, the issue as to whether unused material should be disclosed will inevitably have to be determined by a judge of the Crown Court.

The Crown is therefore entitled to delay PII applications until the Crown Court, but should make arrangements for a hearing as soon after committal as possible so that if the judge orders disclosure this can be effected in good time, or, in circumstances where it is considered that disclosure cannot be made, the case abandoned at the earliest opportunity.

Prosecution's continuing duty of disclosure

The duty of disclosure is a continuing one. Police inquiries may continue up until the time of trial and material may be taken possession of or created after initial disclosure has been made. Such material should be made available to the defence at the earliest opportunity. Similarly, where a judge has sanctioned the withholding of information on public interest grounds, the prosecution are under a duty to keep the matter under review as the trial develops and the issues are crystallised. This was made clear in *R* v *Brown (Winston)* where Steyn LJ added (at p. 200): 'Prosecuting counsel, as a minister of justice, must inform himself fully about the content of any disputed material so that he is in a position to invite the judge to reassess the situation if the previous denial of the material arguably becomes untenable in the light of developments in the trial. See also observations on the point in an article by Andrew Mitchell (1993) 137 SJ 854.

The continuing duty of disclosure is given statutory effect in s. 9, CPIA 1996. The prosecutor must keep under review questions of disclosure and the court must keep under review, in cases where the withholding of material has been sanctioned, the question whether at any given time it is still not in the public interest to disclose the material. For further details, see chapter 16. The Criminal Procedure and Investigations Act 1996 (Defence Disclosure Time Limits) Regulations 1997 (SI 1997 No. 684) made under s. 12 have not prescribed any periods for prosecution disclosure and are confined to time limits for defence disclosure. The relevant periods for prosecution disclosure are those set out in the transitional provisions of s. 13.

POST-CONVICTION DISCLOSURE

Prosecution duty to act fairly

Under the common law rules and by virtue of the provisions of the CPIA 1996, the duty of disclosure continues throughout the investigation and up to and during the trial. The extent of the duty and the obligations of the prosecution in relation to material which arises after conviction are, however, less certain.

As part of their overall responsibility to act fairly, the prosecution have a duty to volunteer any information to the defence which casts doubt upon the reliability of a conviction. Such a situation may arise when documents are discovered which were in existence at the time of the trial but which were overlooked or mislaid. It is more usually likely to occur when material, of which the prosecutor was previously unaware, is brought to his or her attention, or when there has been a further investigation, such as a complaint against a police officer in the case, which generates new information. The test of materiality set out in *Keane* (see page 81) included a duty to disclose documents and information which might raise a new issue, or which might hold out a real prospect of providing a lead on evidence going to an issue in the case. The proper course should, therefore, be for the prosecuting authority to make the defence aware of the position at the earliest opportunity.

Post-conviction disclosure and PII

The prosecution may be placed in a dilemma where the material in question is that for which PII is normally asserted. Until recently, such material could be disclosed only with the consent of the court. (If there is already an appeal pending, the Court of Appeal should be notified so that an application may be made in advance of the appeal hearing.) Since the decision of the House of Lords in *R v Chief Constable of the West Midlands Police, ex parte Wiley* [1994] 3 WLR 433, it is possible for the Crown to disclose PII material voluntarily which will facilitate the passing on of relevant information which may help a defendant with an appeal, or even provide grounds to seek leave to appeal. Furthermore, *ex parte Wiley* also held that police complaints material is no longer covered by PII, so there is no longer any objection on public interest grounds to the disclosure of information which has come to light since the trial as a result of an investigation into a complaint against an officer. This had been a stumbling block to disclosure in *R v Backhouse* [1993] Crim LR 69, where the accused had been convicted of murder and sought disclosure of something approaching 2,000 pages of statements and documents obtained during a subsequent Police Complaints Authority investigation. The Court of Appeal held that there was no prima facie basis for the disclosure of the material which was then covered by PII.

R v Meads (unreported), Court of Appeal, 25 February 1994, transcript 92/5886/S2, was also decided before *ex parte Wiley* removed police complaints material from a PII class covered status. The case had been referred by the Home Secretary under s. 17, Criminal Appeals Act 1968, following a complaint made to the Police Complaints Authority. The approach to post-conviction disclosure set out by the Court nevertheless still appears appropriate. The Court had to determine whether the documents were relevant and essential either to establish the innocence of the person convicted of crime, or to cast doubt on the reliability of the conviction. Those documents that were relevant should be disclosed; and if PII was to be raised, the Court should examine the documents and, if necessary, hear from the Crown in the absence of the defence before deciding whether to order disclosure.

Consequences of changing disclosure rules

The rapid development in the law on disclosure has meant that requirements on the prosecution today are considerably wider than they were a few years ago (certainly pre-*Ward*, which is widely regarded as the watershed for changes in disclosure duties of the prosecution). It is indisputable that persons convicted prior to about the beginning of 1993 would not have had disclosed to them all that the law requires today. Some of those persons are still, no doubt, serving sentences of imprisonment and may well consider that they are entitled to confirmation that proper disclosure was made in their cases.

Just because disclosure was made under different rules, that is not to say that there were necessarily irregularities in the trials or that the convictions are automatically unsafe or unsatisfactory. Disclosure was made in accordance with the common law as it was understood at the time and in accordance with the *Guidelines* laid down by the Attorney-General. There appears to be no direct legal authority dealing with post-conviction disclosure under different rules, which is unsurprising as it would probably emerge only if the prosecuting authority refused a request and the convicted person sought judical review of the refusal. The way in which the prosecution deal with any request for assistance will probably depend on the nature of the request, whether there is an appeal pending, and particularly whether the grounds of appeal relate to non-disclosure. Setting aside practical problems as to whether all the case papers are still in existence and the resources available to the prosecuting authority and the police to check through original case papers, it is likely that the prosecution's responsibility extends to no more than a duty to deal fairly with any reasonable requests. Here again, the *Keane* materiality test (or, in future, the CPIA 1996 tests) may be utilised to determine what is reasonable. A request for information which is relevant to an issue raised in the trial will be reasonable, whereas a request which is so wide that it cannot be related to the issues raised at trial would be unlikely to satisfy any criteria of reasonableness.

The Divisional Court's decision in *R* v *Secretary of State for the Home Department, ex parte Hickey* [1994] 1 All ER 794, was not concerned with the prosecution's duty of disclosure. The challenge was to the Home Secretary's policy and practice with regard to his determination of petitions under s. 17, Criminal Appeal Act 1968. His almost invariable practice of providing a summary of the information available to him and his process of reasoning while declining to disclose statements of evidence obtained during any further inquiries, were held not to satisfy the requirements of openness and disclosure that fairness requires. The decision is further evidence of the courts' desire to ensure candid disclosure in criminal proceedings, and it is therefore incumbent on the prosecution to continue to deal with disclosure issues in a fair and open manner, even after the conclusion of the trial.

The point has been further emphasised by the very late amendment to the disclosure code made as a result of the prosecution's decision not to oppose the appeals of the Bridgewater Three (see chapter 3, page 26). The full background to the amendments to retention periods in the code is dealt with in chapter 17, but the code now lays down minimum retention periods for holding case papers to ensure their availablity in cases where it is necessary to review or re-examine evidence that was called, or not called, at the trial. Making sure that the papers are retained, however, is only part of the answer to the problems posed by post-conviction disclosure. Gaining access to them and persuading the prosecuting authority and/or the police that they should be re-examined continues to be reliant on the premise that the prosecution will act fairly.

9 The Development of Public Interest Immunity in Criminal Proceedings

ORIGINS OF PUBLIC INTEREST IMMUNITY IN CRIMINAL PROCEEDINGS

Ex parte Osman

In 1987, Lorrain Osman was committed to custody pending his extradition to Hong Kong on charges of conspiracy to defraud and other offences of dishonesty. He had been in custody for two years and had periodically made applications for *habeus corpus*, at which time he sought discovery of various documents. In 1990, a motion was made on behalf of the Secretary of State for the Foreign and Commonwealth Office (the FCO) to exclude nine of those documents on grounds of public interest immunity (PII) and irrelevance. The FCO motion was allowed and in the course of his judgment, Mann LJ made the following observations on PII (see *R v Governor of Brixton Prison, ex parte Osman* (1991) 93 Cr App R 202, at p. 208):

> The seminal cases in regard to public interest immunity do not refer to criminal proceedings at all. The principles are expressed in quite general terms. Asking myself why those general expositions should not apply to criminal proceedings, I can see no answer but they do. It seems correct in principle that they should apply. The reasons for the development of the doctrine seem equally applicable to criminal as to civil proceedings.

This short *dictum* marked the somewhat diffident arrival of the doctrine of PII into criminal proceedings. Mann LJ said that he derived comfort in his view from a decision of the Supreme Court of the Northern Territory of Australia in *Robertson, ex parte McAulay* (1983) 21 NTR 11, which acknowledged that public interest privilege in criminal cases was governed by the same principles as the general law although a different balancing exercise might be required from that applied by the court in civil proceedings. Up until this time, leading text books on criminal law and practice contained no reference to a doctrine of PII. For example, the 40th edition of *Archbold*, published in 1979, said nothing about PII and devoted just ten lines to Crown Privilege (notwithstanding the fact that such terminology had been deemed 'not a happy expression' by Lord Simon in *Duncan v Cammel Laird & Co. Ltd* [1942] AC 624, at p. 641, and 'wrong and may be misleading' by Lord Reid in *R v Lewes Justices, ex parte Secretary of State for the Home Department* [1973] AC 388, at p. 400).

Five years after Mann LJ had given his views on PII in criminal proceedings, Sir Richard Scott V-C would place an interesting and novel interpretation upon them in the course of his *Report of the Inquiry into the Export of Defence Equipment and Dual-Use Goods to Iraq and Related Prosecutions* (HC Paper 115, London: HMSO, 1996 at paras G18.70 *et seq.*). Sir Richard Scott's views on PII in criminal proceedings are dealt with in greater detail below, but in the years that elapsed between *ex parte Osman* and the publication of the Scott Report, every criminal law practitioner involved in a Crown Court trial faced the distinct possibility of having to deal with an application in relation to PII. Phillips J reviewed the position of PII in the criminal sphere during the course of an application made at the Central Criminal Court to discharge a witness summons (see *R v Clowes* [1992] 3 All ER 440) and the Court of Appeal confirmed the advent of PII in the criminal trial in decisions handed down in *Ward, Davis, Johnson and Rowe, Keane* and *Winston Brown* (discussed earlier in chapter 7).

Public policy of non-disclosure

Prior to *ex parte Osman,* criminal courts had recognised the existence of a public policy whereby witnesses might not be asked to disclose facts or produce documents which were prejudicial to the state or the effective performance of the public service. Whether the correct terminology for such public policy was Crown Privilege or PII is really immaterial; as a matter of fact, exceptionally, criminal courts were asked to withhold relevant evidence from the defence on the grounds that disclosure would damage the public interest. When such matters fell to be decided, it was usually in the context of the disclosure of the identity of informants. In *R v Hallett* [1986] Crim LR 462, the trial judge refused to order the prosecution to reveal the identity of the informants. Dismissing the appeal, Lord Lane CJ said that disclosure would be necessary only in order to prevent a miscarriage of justice or to prevent the possibility of an accused being deprived of an opportunity of casting doubt on the case against him. In *R v Agar* (1990) 90 Cr App R 318, the court was called upon to rule whether the public interest in preventing a miscarriage of justice or allowing a defendant to put forward a tenable case in its best light was greater than the public interest in keeping secret the source of information. The appeal was allowed and the conviction quashed. An example of a case where the balance fell in favour of disclosure is provided by *R v Langford*

[1990] Crim LR 653, where a Crown Court judge ordered the disclosure of an informer's name and address on the basis that it could help the defendant to show why she was innocent of the offences with which she was charged. Such cases were, however, rare — that is, until the judgment of the Court of Appeal in *Ward*.

Public interest immunity in civil proceedings

Ward provided the Court of Appeal with the opportunity of stating whether the doctrine of PII, by now well-established in civil proceedings, was to become part and parcel of the criminal trial. The principle of PII operates in civil proceedings to prevent the disclosure of documents and information where such disclosure would be contrary to the public interest. It does not provide absolute immunity from disclosure but enables the public interest in confidentiality to be balanced against the public interest that the administration of justice should not be frustrated. The House of Lords had laid down in *Duncan* v *Cammell Laird & Co. Ltd* [1942] AC 624, that Crown Privilege arose in any case where relevant documents should not be produced if the public interest required that they should be withheld. The principles, as well as the practice in relation to PII applications, were re-stated by the House in *Conway* v *Rimmer* [1968] AC 910. It was held that the court had a role in deciding whether the public interest in non-disclosure was outweighed by the public interest in the proper administration of justice, and in coming to a decision the judge was entitled to go behind a ministerial certificate and inspect the documents before carrying out the balancing exercise.

The leading authorities on PII in civil proceedings, as well as the Divisional Court's judgment in *ex parte Osman*, were reviewed in *Ward*, and the Court of Appeal had no difficulty in deciding that the principles were equally applicable in the criminal trial. Thus, in delivering the judgment of the Court, Glidewell LJ confirmed that the ultimate decision as to whether evidence, which was otherwise disclosable, should be withheld on grounds of PII, was one for the court. He continued (at p. 27): 'But the rule that the court and not the litigant must be the ultimate judge of where the balance of public interest lies must have always applied to the prosecution in criminal cases, though it may not have been clearly spelt out in 1974 [the date of Ward's trial]'. As a result, one of the principles of law and practice laid down by the Court of Appeal in *Ward* was that the prosecution could not withhold material documents without giving notice to the defence and having the issue of PII determined by the court.

Public interest immunity in practice in the criminal trial

The practical effect of this part of the decision in *Ward* was that where the prosecution were in possession of any material that had a bearing on the offence charged and surrounding circumstances of the case, they were under a duty to put the material before the court. If the material consisted of documents that the prosecution wished to withhold, the court had to signify approval. Even if there was no objection to disclosure of the documents because of their contents, the fact that they belonged to a recognised class which prevented disclosure in the public interest meant that the court still had to rule. The prosecution could not judge relevance (*per* Henry J in the *Guinness Ruling*) and could no longer act as judge in their own cause in relation to sensitive material. The correctness of this interpretation has since been questioned in the Scott Report and the law has changed as a result of the decision in *ex parte Wiley* (see page 123), nevertheless this was how *Ward* was construed by criminal practitioners. The Scott Report itself acknowledges (at paras G10.4 *et seq.*) that Government lawyers, and senior counsel advising the Attorney-General, were of the opinion that the application of PII in criminal proceedings meant that class documents had to be placed before the court for a ruling.

A practical guide for criminal practititioners by an experienced barrister confirmed the court's supervisory role in matters of PII in criminal proceedings — see Mitchell, Andrew, 'Disclosure — whose responsibility? (1993) 137 SJ 854. The guidance, part of which was quoted with approval in *R* v *Brown (Winston)* [1995] 1 Cr App R 191, said that the role of the prosecutor in deciding whether or not to to disclose sensitive material appeared to have passed to the judge. Even in cases where the disclosure of PII material was considered appropriate, the proper course was thought to be to allow the court to make the final decision. It is doubtful whether Glidewell LJ appreciated that the effect of his judgment would signal a flood of applications into the Crown Courts now that the PII barriers were open. Furthermore, no thought had been given to the position in magistrates' courts and a steady stream of PII applications meandered in front of bemused justices. The combined effect of *ex parte Osman* and *Ward* was not simply to introduce PII into criminal proceedings, but to ensure that it became the most contentious, confusing and frustrating aspect of the criminal trial for years to follow.

DIFFERENCES BETWEEN CIVIL AND CRIMINAL PROCEEDINGS

It was recognised in the *Ward* judgment that considerations of PII in criminal proceedings were not quite the same as those in civil cases, when Glidewell LJ commented (at p. 27): 'We are conscious that we are applying statements made in the relatively peaceful context of an extradition case, or a civil case, to the circumstances surrounding the trial of the appellant'. The accuracy of this observation may be illustrated by highlighting three principal differences between the proceedings, namely, the balancing exercise to be performed by the court, the use of certificates and the inspection of documents.

Balancing exercise

In civil proceedings, the party seeking disclosure needs to establish that the documents in question will substantially assist its case, and this must be balanced against disclosure which might be injurious to the national interest or might prejudice the proper functioning of the public service. In criminal proceedings, however, Mann LJ acknowledged in *ex parte Osman* (at p. 208) that a different exercise was called for in that 'a judge is balancing on the one hand the desirability of preserving the public interest in the absence of disclosure against, on the other hand, the interests of justice'. In the *Osman* case, where the FCO produced a PII certificate, Mann LJ stated (at p. 209) that the balancing exercise 'may be shortly put: do the interests of justice in the particular case outweigh those considerations of public interest as spoken to in the certificate?' Later, in specific reference to the privilege in regard to information leading to the detection of crime, he made it clear that no balance would be called for if the evidence was necessary to prevent a miscarriage of justice. This was echoed by Lord Taylor CJ in *R* v *Keane* (1994) 99 Cr App R 1, when clarifying the position that if the disputed material might prove the defendant's innocence or avoid a miscarriage of justice, the balance comes down resoundingly in favour of disclosure.

The Scott Report questions whether the expression 'balancing exercise' is really applicable to PII in a criminal trial; but whether it is or not, there is no doubt that the approach to disclosure in criminal proceedings is of a different character to that in civil proceedings.

Certificates

The second major difference relates to the question of certificates. As a general rule, where questions of PII arise in civil proceedings, a certificate is produced to support the claim. As Lord Scarman made clear in *Burmah Oil Co. Ltd* v *Bank of England* [1980] AC 1090, the minister's certificate is not final and the claim's applicability to the case in question is for the court to determine and not the minister. In criminal cases too, where Government documents are involved, there is likely to be a certificate setting out details of the documents in question together with the rationale for the claim and the damage to the public interest that is likely to result in the event of disclosure. In cases where national security is likely to be endangered or the disclosure of the formation of Government policy would undermine the functioning of the public service, certificates are signed by the appropriate minister and placed before the court. Since *Ward*, however, the vast majority of applications to withhold material are made by the prosecution without a certificate. This is because the documents do not emanate from Government sources and their contents, as well as the class relied on, invariably concern the well-established public policy of protecting the of the identity of informants and the nature of the information they supply, the arguments in support of which prosecuting counsel are able to advance.

An illustration of the infrequency of the use of certificates in criminal proceedings is provided by the Home Secretary's written answer to a question by Harry Cohen MP asking about the number of certificates used by ministers from the Home Department (see Hansard HC, 20 November 1995, written answers, col. 668). The Home Secretary replied that records had been kept only since 1992, but since then only 28 certificates had been signed. As the responsibility for asserting PII falls, in the vast majority of cases, on the Home Department, 28 is but a tiny fraction of the number of applications made by the prosecution since 1992. When the Court of Appeal have been called upon to consider procedures to be adopted for PII applications, notably in *Davis, Johnson and Rowe*, they have never suggested that in circumstances where informant material is in question the production of a ministerial certificate is necessary.

This practice has, however, been thrown into doubt as a result of the decision of the House of Lords in *R* v *Chief Constable of the West Midlands Police, ex parte Wiley* [1994] 3 All ER 420. The principal issue in the appeal was whether statements made for the purposes of an investigation into a complaint against the police belonged to a class of documents which attracted PII. The House decided that they did not and overruled the decision in *Neilson* v *Laugharne* [1981] QB 736 together with a number of other authorities which had decided that police complaints statements were covered by PII. The question of whether the investigating officer's report still attracted PII on a class basis was left open (although it was later decided in *Taylor* v *Anderton (Police Complaints Authority Intervening)* [1995] 1 WLR 447 that it did).

In the leading judgment in *ex parte Wiley*, Lord Woolf made some wider observations on the subject of PII, in particular the roles that ministers and courts should play in deciding such issues. The judgment indicates a completely different approach to PII applications, whether in connection with civil or criminal proceedings. Lord Woolf stated that is open to a minister to form a judgment as to where the overall public interest lies and, if disclosure is considered proper, it may be made to the other party without advancing a claim for PII to the court. This concept of voluntary disclosure is discussed more fully below, but in the context of applications being accompanied by certificates, it seems as though their Lordships were envisaging that where disclosure is not to be volunteered, and where the prosecution still desire to withhold information on public interest grounds, some form of certification may be necessary. In most prosecutions where sensitive information exists, PII will be asserted on the informant or sensitive crime detection techniques bases, so it is possible that certificates may have to be signed by, or on behalf of, chief constables, although it will still be appropriate for prosecuting counsel to make the application. It remains to be seen how the far-reaching implications of the decision in *ex parte Wiley* are to be interpreted by prosecuting authorities, government departments and the police.

Inspection of documents

The third significant difference concerns the inspection of documents. The procedure to be adopted in PII applications was given in *Air Canada* v *Secretary of State for Trade (No. 2)* [1983] 2 AC 394, when the House of Lords endorsed many of the observations on the subject made by Bingham J at first instance. The court examines the certificate and considers whether the claim for immunity is a valid one. It will then consider whether the party seeking production of the documents can demonstrate that there is a public interest in the production of the documents to assist his or her case. Seldom will it be necessary to inspect the actual documents themselves. This approach was reinforced in *Balfour* v *Foreign and Commonwealth Office* [1994] 1 WLR 681, where it was held that although a court was obliged to be vigilant to ensure that a claim for PII was raised only in appropriate circumstances, it was not necessary to exercise the right to inspect that material. This is not the approach in criminal proceedings which was recommended by the Court of Appeal in *R* v *K (Trevor Douglas)* (1993) 97 Cr App R 342.

The appeal in *R* v *K (Trevor Douglas)* challenged a judge's ruling not to disclose a video tape made for therapeutic purposes in hospital which featured the young victims of sexual offences. On the application for disclosure, the local council and hospital were represented although the Crown was not; a fact which was criticised by the Court. The judge was not specifically invited to look at the video and did not do so. At the appeal hearing, the prosecution conceded that the judge could not properly rule on the relevance of the video without seeing it. Lord Taylor CJ agreed (at p. 346):

> In our judgment the exclusion of the evidence without an opportunity of testing its relevance and importance amounted to a material irregularity. When public interest immunity is claimed for a document, it is for the court to rule whether the claim should be upheld or not. To do that involves a balancing exercise. The exercise can only be performed by the judge himself examining or viewing the evidence, so as to have the facts of what it contains in mind. Only then can he be in a position to balance the competing interests of public interest immunity and fairness to the party claiming disclosure.

The Court of Appeal decided that it was necessary to see the video, but were satisfied that there was nothing which could have assisted the defence and applied the proviso to s. 2(1), Criminal Appeal Act 1968. The propriety of the court inspecting documents was endorsed by Phillips J in *R* v *Clowes* [1992] 3 All ER 440, where, in relation to the inspection of transcripts of interviews with investigators from the Department of Trade and Industry, he stated (at p. 455):

> There was some discussion as to whether it was appropriate that I should myself inspect the transcripts. In relation to this question I was referred to *Air Canada* v *Secretary of State for Trade (No. 2)* [1983] 1 All ER 910, [1983] 2 AC 394, but no counsel suggested that the approach to inspection there laid down was appropriate in a criminal trial. I could see no reason for refraining from looking at the transcripts if I felt this would assist in reaching my decision, particularly as they are not, in themselves, sensitive material and are in the possession of officers of the court.

In criminal proceedings, therefore, the prosecution must be prepared for the court to inspect the material in question.

VOLUNTARY DISCLOSURE

Prosecution practice following *Makanjuola*

Before the re-stating of the law by the House of Lords in *ex parte Wiley*, prosecutors were of the opinion that, as a matter of law, they were under a duty to assert PII. The authority relied on in support of this proposition was the judgment of Bingham LJ (as he then was) in *Makanjuola* v *Commissioner of Police for the Metropolis* [1992] 3 All ER 617. (The judgment had, in fact, been delivered in 1989 in an appeal by the Commissioner against an order to disclose statements and other material obtained in pursuance of a complaints inquiry on the ground that they were covered by PII.) Bingham LJ stated (at p. 623):

> Where a litigant asserts that documents are immune from production or disclosure on public interest grounds he is not (if the claim is well founded) claiming a right but observing a duty. Public interest immunity is not a trump card vouchsafed to certain privileged players to play when and as they wish. It is an exclusionary rule, imposed on parties in certain circumstances, even where it is to their disadvantage in the litigation.

The practice adopted by prosecuting authorities was explained by the Attorney-General who, when writing to the President of the Board of Trade in connection with a certificate to be used in the *Matrix Churchill* prosecution (see Scott Report, para. G13.65), cited *Makanjuola* and continued:

> In other words, once a Minister accepts that documents fall within a class which should normally be immune from production in litigation as a matter of public interest, it is the duty of that Minister to make the public interest immunity claim whatever his personal views about the desirability of disclosing the particular documents in question. I am quite sure that because of the intelligence aspect to this case and the involvement of two other departments this is not one of the 'very exceptional' cases to which Bingham refers. On the other hand it is quite proper for the Minister to make clear that he is not expressing any view as to whether, looking at the public interest as a whole, the documents should be disclosed.

Thus, the existence of PII material has been notified to the defence in some form or other by the prosecuting authority (in accordance with the *Davis, Johnson and Rowe* procedures) and placed before the court for a ruling. These procedures have been adopted in a large number of cases. A minority involve documents such as Cabinet minutes, Government policy memoranda or information affecting national security (i.e. *Matrix Churchill* type PII material), but the vast majority feature informant material, observation posts and the use of sensitive crime detection methods. When it is considered that many arrests by the police result from 'information received', whether the source is a registered informant or an ordinary member of the public who provides information to the police in confidence, it will be seen that PII becomes a relevant issue in more than just a handful of cases.

Did Bingham LJ's *dicta* permit any exceptions? His judgment continued (at p. 623):

> This does not mean that in any case where a party holds a document in a class prima facie immune he is bound to persist in an assertion of immunity even where it is held that on any weighing of the public interest, in withholding the document against the public interest in disclosure for the purpose of furthering the administration of justice, there is a clear balance in favour of the latter. But it does, I think, mean: (1) that public interest immunity cannot in any ordinary sense be waived, since, although one can waive rights, one cannot waive duties; (2) that, where a litigant holds documents in a class prima facie immune, he should (save perhaps in a very exceptional case) assert that the documents are immune and decline to disclose them, since the ultimate judge of where the balance of public interest lies is not him but the court; and (3) that, where a document is, or is held to be, in an immune class, it may not be used for any purpose whatever in the proceedings to which the immunity applies, and certainly cannot (for instance) be used for the purposes of cross-examination.

Unless documents could be brought within the '*Makanjuola* exceptions', the law was construed as giving prosecutors no option but to place them before the court, even in circumstances where disclosure was considered appropriate. This sometimes resulted in absurd situations. For example, in a case where the defendant complained against the police, made a statement in support of the complaint and was then examined by a doctor with the alleged injuries being photographed, the defendant himself was not entitled to see the material without the court's approval! This is because until the law on PII in relation to police complaints material was re-stated in *ex parte Wiley*, the Crown could not waive PII, which was a matter for the court and not the prosecution. The position was highly unsatisfactory and was exposed, first, by the House of Lords in *ex parte Wiley* and then by the caustic comments in the Scott Report. It was hardly surprising that judges became annoyed with the volume of applications being made to them, although their irritation with the parties was frequently misplaced and would have been better directed at the increasing complexities of the judge-made law. The removal of the prosecutor's discretion to decide relevance, coupled with the inability to waive PII, left both sides impotent. If Bingham LJ had really meant that a minister, head of a Government agency, chief constable etc. could disclose voluntarily, why had he not said so in terms that could be readily understood?

The whole confusing scenario was amply illustrated in the wake of the Scott Report where, in the correspondence columns of *The Times* and other broadsheets, High Court Judges, Treasury counsel and eminent practitioners in criminal law leapt to the defence of the Attorney-General's understanding of the law, only for an equally impressive array of legal talent led by Lord Scarman to conclude that he had misread the law. How were civil servants, Crown Prosecutors and members of other prosecuting authorities expected to unravel *Makanjuola* in the face of such sharp divergence of opinion about its meaning? What Bingham LJ really meant is a matter for conjecture. On the one hand he voiced the contention that a party is not bound to assert PII; on the other he stated that it cannot be waived as it is a duty and not a right. But if this contradiction is not enough, it is further confused by the qualification that there are very exceptional cases (which are not described) where disclosure would be proper. It is hardly surprising that prosecutors played safe and sought the approval of the court before sensitive information was withheld from disclosure!

Prosecution practice in relation to advancing own case

If the prosecution were constrained by the law in assisting the defence by disclosing voluntarily documents which were covered by PII, there was also an understandable reluctance by the courts to allow them to adduce PII documents which would advance their own case. This was made clear in *R v Horseferry Road Magistrates' Court, ex parte Bennett (No. 2)* [1994] 1 All ER 289. The Divisional Court had ordered the CPS to disclose a number of documents which ordinarily attracted PII and the CPS raised no objection to their production. However, the Court was asked to indicate whether the CPS themselves were entitled to take the decision to disclose PII documents without referring the matter to the court for a ruling. The CPS argued that this was a course that should be open to them in criminal proceedings whenever they concluded that the balance obviously fell in favour of disclosure, not just for the assistance of the defence but also when the public interest in the prosecution being able to present their case effectively demanded that the documents be adduced as part of the case for the Crown.

The judgment of Simon Brown LJ acknowledged that the administration of justice is not one-sided and that circumstances might arise when the Crown's case would benefit from the introduction of documents for which PII would normally be asserted, but the integrity of the public interest class extended beyond disclosure in any particular case. For this reason, he was anxious to introduce the safeguard of a responsible and independent guardian of the public interest — the Treasury Solicitor. If the CPS wished to disclose class documents voluntarily, they must seek the prior approval of the Treasury Solicitor who would consider not merely the importance of the documents in the prosecution case, but also the importance of the prosecution itself. He added (at p. 297): '. . . it may be preferable to abandon the case rather than damage the integrity of the class claim'.

While the Court's reluctance to allow the prosecution to play fast and loose with PII classes as it suited them in any particular case is understandable, this was an unsatisfactory response to the question which the Divisional Court had been asked to answer. The Treasury Solicitor would inevitably be placed in the unenviable position of interfering with prosecutorial discretion and might even be faced with an embarrassing scenario where the law officers had given consent to a prosecution — for example, where the Attorney-General consented to the prosecution of a spy

— in the knowledge that the prosecution could be brought only by introducing documents for which PII would normally be asserted. What effective role could the Treasury Solicitor play? Could he cope with all these potential referrals in any event? The Scott Report is strangely silent on *ex parte Bennett*. In that case the Divisional Court were being asked if PII could be waived for class documents, albeit by the prosecution in their own favour; but the Court were presented with a golden opportunity to clarify *Makanjuola* and the circumstances when disclosure may be made voluntarily in the public interest. The current position of the *Bennett* guidance is uncertain as it was not referred to at all in *ex parte Wiley*, which must now point the way forward for PII to be asserted in the future. It is presumed that *ex parte Bennett*, and any role perceived for the Treasury Solicitor, is now redundant.

Ex parte Wiley

While endorsing Bingham LJ's comments in *Makanjuola*, Lord Woolf stated in *ex parte Wiley* that he would be surprised if he (Bingham LJ) was intending to extend the principles of PII or to make their application more rigid. Lord Woolf continued (at p. 438):

> If a Secretary of State on behalf of his Department as opposed to any ordinary litigant concludes that any public interest in documents being withheld from production is outweighed by the public interest in the documents being available for litigation, it is difficult to conceive that unless the documents do not relate to an area for which the Secretary of State was responsible, the court would feel it appropriate to come to any different conclusion from that of the Secretary of State. The position would be the same if the Attorney-General was of the opinion that the documents should be disclosed. It should be remembered that the principle which was established in *Conway* v *Rimmer* is that it is the courts which should have the final responsibility for deciding when both a contents and a class claim to immunity should be upheld. The principle was not that it was for the courts to impose immunity where, after due consideration, no immunity was claimed by the appropriate authority. . . . As far as contents of documents are concerned, I cannot conceive that their Lordships in *Conway* v *Rimmer* would have anticipated that their decision could be used, except in the most exceptional circumstances, so that a Department of State was prevented by the courts from disclosing documents which it considered it was appropriate to disclose.

It appears, therefore, that in future ministers must make up their minds where the overall public interest lies. If they conclude that it favours disclosure, they may disclose voluntarily; if, on the other hand, they consider that the public interest in withholding the material outweighs that of the interests of the accused, then the court will be called upon to rule as the final arbiter.

Later in his judgment, Lord Woolf turned to the position of chief constables who may be called upon to make decisions in connection with disclosure. He said that where the courts have already established that a class immunity applies to the documents, provided the chief constable has consulted with other chief constables (or in particular circumstances with the Police Complaints Authority, Attorney-General or Home Secretary) he too may make disclosure. Lord Woolf continued (at p. 440): 'The court, if the matter came before it, would act on their views, this being the evidence of those best able to assess the importance of the public interest involved in making disclosure. If their views were that the documents should be disclosed the result of seeking the court's assistance would be a foregone conclusion.' In practice, this means that if in any case the chief constable concludes that the overall public interest is served by disclosing details of an informant, or of a confidential report or correspondence with the prosecuting authority, disclosure may be made provided that he has consulted with others. The importance of the consultation process is to ensure that the PII class is not irreparably weakened. It is difficult to imagine all the chief constables in England and Wales writing to one another whenever they want voluntarily to disclose material which may be necessary for a sucessful prosecution, but there appears to be a role here for a body such as the Association of Chief Police Officers, and of course, the Home Office and CPS, to ensure that the overall public interest is being taken into account before disclosure is made. If, as a result of too frequent or cavalier disclosures, the courts took the view that the immunity extending to the class had effectively been removed, the prosecution might find themselves with the additional burden of establishing a basis for contents claims. They may have to do that anyway if the recommendations in the Scott Report about class claims are implemented.

It seems as though the prosecution is already taking advantage of their newly acquired power to disclose voluntarily in relation to non-Government documents. In *R* v *Adams* [1997] Crim LR 292 the prosecution consented to the disclosure of contract sheets between Adams and his police 'handler', material which would normally be regarded as sensitive. The case is of particular interest, however, as the Crown went further and were prepared to disclose to a co-defendant of Adams. Adams objected but the trial judge ruled that since the Crown were prepared to disclose, he could not properly decline to allow them to do so. On appeal, the trial judge was held to have been in error in relation to disclosure to the co-defendant. It was not so much an issue of PII but of relevance of the documents to the co-defendant's defence. Disclosure of sensitive material to one defendant does not automatically mean that there should be disclosure to a co-defendant, and it should be noted that s. 2(2), CPIA 1996 states that where there is more than one accused in any proceedings, Part I, CPIA 1996 applies separately in relation to each of the accused.

THE SCOTT REPORT

The Report of Sir Richard Scott into the arms to Iraq affair and related prosecutions has been referred to from time to time throughout this chapter. Not only did he examine closely the law in relation to PII, but he also made a number of recommendations on the approach to PII claims in future criminal trials. His views on the law are summarised below as being relevant to the development of the law under scrutiny in this chapter. His recommendations are dealt with in chapter 10 which looks at the procedures for PII applications at the present time and how they are likely to be dealt with in the future.

Part 3 of the Scott Report is devoted to the *Matrix Churchill* case and a close examination of the PII certificates and the law which the prosecution relied on in order make the claims. Sir Richard concluded that the prosecution's view of the law on which the making of the PII class claims was based was unsound in a number of respects.

Criticisms of ministerial practices

At para. G18.54 of his Report, Sir Richard stated that the proposition that a minister is ever under a legal duty to claim PII in order to protect documents from disclosure to the defence notwithstanding that in the minister's view the public interest requires their disclosure to the defence, is based on a fundamental misconception of the principles of PII law. In *Matrix Churchill*, claims had been made even though ministers, in particular the President of the Board of Trade, Michael Heseltine, considered that disclosure to the defence should be made. Sir Richard was of the opinion that this conclusion does not offend *Makanjuola* which is interpreted as meaning that only where a minister has formed an opinion that disclosure would be contrary to the public interest, is the minister bound to claim PII. The practice hitherto adopted by Government departments and prosecuting authorities of asserting PII, and leaving the decision on disclosure to the court, in any case where class documents fell to be disclosed was based on a misreading of *Makanjuola*. Sir Richard is supported in these propositions by the decision in *ex parte Wiley*.

Secondly, in forming a view as to what the public interest requires, the minister must take into account the contents of the documents in question and, in cases where the documents are within a PII class, the class itself. The advice to the contrary given by Government lawyers and the Attorney-General, to the effect that it was not permissible for ministers to take into account any administration of justice factors, was said to have no sound legal foundation. Paragraph G18.67 of the Report was critical of the practice of ministers claiming PII without having regard to the consequences on the administration of justice of their doing so. Such criticism would have a better foundation if it could be stated with certainty that in all cases ministers had sufficient knowledge of the facts and circumstances of a prosecution to enable them to make an accurate judgment on disclosure. The circumstances of many prosecutions are complex, the issues in dispute uncertain and the information which may be helpful to the defence unclear. While there appears no good reason why ministers should not take administration of justice factors into account, however, it must be questioned whether they are in a position to weigh the competing public interests and come to a proper decision on disclosure without the intervention of the court.

Class claims

Given that *ex parte Wiley* has now effectively incorporated into the common law the proposals summarised above, the more controversial PII conclusions of the Scott Report are probably those in relation to the observations on class claims. Sir Richard puts forward that *ex parte Osman* is not an authority for allowing class claims in a criminal trial. It is authority for allowing class claims in *habeus corpus* applications, which are criminal proceedings, but a distinction has to be drawn between such applications and criminal trials. This dissection of Mann LJ's judgment is both surprising and novel, and it remains to be seen whether it will find universal favour. Certainly, the Court of Appeal did not seek to make such a distinction in *Ward*, and the House of Lords has yet to consider a point of law in relation to PII in the criminal sphere. This reading of *ex parte Osman* led Sir Richard to the conclusion (in para. G18.85) that 'the justification for PII class claims in criminal trials seems to me to be on shaky ground'.

In para. G18.86 of his Report, Sir Richard developed his views on class claims and concluded that where the potential of the documents to provide assistance to the defence is apparent, the balance must favour disclosure and no class claim should be necessary. This is, of course, consistent with his views on voluntary disclosure and accords with *ex parte Wiley*. More controversially, however, he continued that even where relevant and prima facie disclosable documents may appear to lack the potential to assist the defence, this is not a sufficient reason for a continuance of the making of PII class claims in criminal trials. In other words, if contents claims cannot be justified, PII should not be claimed. If accepted, this would be a radical departure from the way in which many claims for PII have been advanced in the past.

The Scott Inquiry was concerned, in the main, with two recognised classes, namely advice to ministers and security and intelligence information. These are only two, albeit important, classes and the next chapter will examine more closely some other important classes which commonly feature in criminal trials. It is fair to say that many PII claims, notably those falling within the police informant category, could be made on a contents basis rather than on a joint contents/class basis, but it has to be questioned whether the abandonment of class claims is justified solely on the Scott interpretation of the law and Sir Richard's reluctance to admit the accepted principle of class claims in civil cases into the criminal trial. Not only was the preponderance of legal opinion against him — including Treasury counsel, the Attorney-General and, indeed, Judge Smedley, who in the *Matrix Churchill* case ruled that class claims had been put forward properly — but the most recent authorities in civil proceedings which touch upon criminal investigations (*ex parte Wiley* and *Taylor v Anderton*) do not suggest that there is no place for a class claim in the criminal trial.

GOVERNMENT RESPONSE TO SCOTT REPORT RECOMMENDATIONS

On 18 December 1996, the Government issued their response to the Scott Report recommendations when statements on the future of PII in England and Wales were made in both Houses of Parliament by the Attorney-General and Lord Chancellor (see Hansard vol. 287 HC Deb, 6th ser., coll. 949–58 and Hansard vol. 576 HL Deb, 5th ser., coll. 1507–17). The statements followed a lengthy consultation process whereby comments had been invited from interested parties and organisations. The Government repeated their commitment to the principle of maximum disclosure consistent with protecting essential public interests, but concluded that legislation on PII was neither necessary nor desirable. Underlying this view was the fact that since the unfortunate events surrounding the *Matrix Churchill* prosecution, the law had changed markedly as a result of the decision of the House of Lords in *ex parte Wiley*.

The new approach for the future, in relation to Government documents, will see ministers focusing directly on the damage that disclosure would cause. In so doing, the division into class and contents claims is no longer be applied and ministers will claim PII only when it is believed that disclosure of a document would cause real damage to the public interest. Such damage may relate to the safety of an individual, such as an informant, or to a regulatory process or to international relations caused by the disclosure of confidential diplomatic communications. Normally, the damage would be in the form of direct and immediate harm to the nation's economic interests or relations with a foreign state; but in some cases, the harm may be indirect or long-term, such as damage to a regulatory process.

It was stated that the test for claiming PII would be rigorously applied and future certificates would be more detailed, setting out clearly the damage that would be likely if disclosure was made. The only basis for claiming PII would be a belief that disclosure would cause real harm, but in any criminal case, at the end of the day, the claim would always be subject to a review by the court.

It is to be noted that the Government's new approach is confined to Government documents. Importantly, applications in respect of police information and documents will continue to be made in acordance with the common law rules. In answer to a question by Lord McNally on what proposals the Government had for encouraging bodies not covered by the Parliamentary statement to adopt similar practices and procedures in relation to PII, the Lord Chancellor stated that it was believed that the new approach was likely to inform the approach taken by non-Government bodies (see Hansard vol. 576 HL Deb, 5th ser., col. 375). How such bodies are likely to operate in the future as a result of the combination of the Parliamentary statements and the coming into effect of the CPIA 1996 and disclosure code is considered in the next chapter.

CONCLUSIONS

The development of PII in criminal proceedings since *ex parte Osman* has been as rapid and contentious as any concept in the criminal trial. It strikes at the heart of open disclosure and the entitlement of accused persons to see material which can assist them to prove innocence. The withholding of any relevant information must, therefore, be a cause for concern and must be justified on strong public interest grounds. The reputation of the criminal justice system will be sorely undermined if there is any suggestion of unfairness, and *Matrix Churchill* provided a prime example.

It is hoped that voluntary disclosure, coupled with the Goverment's new approach, will ensure that the expression 'damage to the public interest' is given far greater attention than may have been the case in the past. In so far as advice to ministers and other Government documents are concerned, the prosecution will have to do more than point to the class or nature of the document if they wish to withhold its production. In relation to other sensitive documents (as now defined in the disclosure code), the prosecution may now disclose the information voluntarily. As in so many areas of disclosure, however, the crucial point is relevance. If information is truly relevant, it must be disclosed or the potential for a miscarriage of justice cannot be removed. There can be no doubting the correctness of this general principle, but it must follow that it is incumbent on both sides to play their part in determining relevance. Lord Taylor CJ made this abundantly clear in *Keane*, and if support is needed, the Scott Report provides it at para. G18.55: 'In many cases there will be a grey area into which will fall documents whose relevance is arguable. The less explicit the defence have been in revealing the proposed lines of defence, the wider will be the grey area.' Where documents are concerned, the disclosure of which involves potential harm to the public interest, can there be any reasonable argument against defence disclosure?

10 Asserting Public Interest Immunity in Criminal Proceedings

GENERAL APPROACH TO QUESTIONS OF PUBLIC INTEREST IMMUNITY

Chapter 9 traced the comparatively short but eventful history of the development of the law in relation to PII in criminal proceedings. This chapter looks at how the law has been applied in practice and contemplates how PII will be asserted in the future in the light of the decision of the House of Lords in *R v Chief Constable of the West Midlands Police, ex parte Wiley* [1994] 3 All ER 420, the recommendations made in the Scott Report and the Government's response thereto. The CPIA 1996 makes provision that the new statutory rules for disclosure do not affect the rules of common law as to whether disclosure is in the public interest.

As was made clear by the Court of Appeal in *R v Keane* (1994) 99 Cr App R 1, no question of asserting PII arises unless the documents or information in question satisfy the test of materiality set out in the judgment of Lord Taylor CJ. If the documents are not material, PII does not arise. Similarly, under the CPIA 1996, if the material does not undermine the prosecution case or assist the accused's defence, PII is of no consequence. If, on the other hand, in the opinion of the prosecution the tests are satisfied, then the procedures dealt with below are followed. It is more than likely, however, that while the prosecution are wrestling with tests of relevance and examining documents to ascertain whether their disclosure is contrary to the public interest, the defence will be pursuing independently what they consider to be legitimate and essential lines of inquiry. This may take the form of contacting the prosecuting authority with requests for disclosure, or may involve the service of a summons on a prosecution witness or the police to attend court and produce specified documents.

A witness summons is issued under s. 2(1), Criminal Procedure (Attendance of Witnesses) Act 1965 (which will in due course be amended by s. 66, CPIA 1996), and if the person upon whom the summons is served wishes to have it set aside, application will be made to the court in accordance with s. 2C of the 1965 Act and Crown Court Rules. Such an application may be made, *inter alia*, on the basis that the witness cannot give evidence or produce documents likely to be material evidence. In the past, it was appropriate to assert PII at such hearings. In *R* v *Hennessey* (1978) 68 Cr App R 419, Lawton LJ, in dealing with the question of applications to the court to protect informants, stated (at p. 426):

> It will be for the accused to show that there is a good reason [to protect the liberty of the subject over the need to protect informers]. This should normally be done, not in the course of a trial, but in any proceedings which may be started to set aside a subpoena or a witness summons served upon a Crown witness who is alleged to be in possession of, or to have control over, tape recordings, transcripts of such recordings and the like.

Phillips J also ruled on an issue of PII in an application to set aside a witness summons in *R* v *Clowes* [1992] 3 All ER 440. Although he said that he did not find the concept of a balancing exercise easy, he did not take any issue that it was appropriate to deal with the matter on an application under s. 2(2) of the 1965 Act. Questions of disclosure are kept under review as the trial progresses, but applications to set aside witness summonses on PII grounds should be decided at the earliest opportunity.

PROCEDURES FOR PUBLIC INTEREST IMMUNITY APPLICATONS

In a case where the prosecution are satisfied that the information, whether in oral or documentary form, is material to the potential issues in the case, the recent practice has been to place the matter before the court for a ruling. A typical example is provided by *R* v *Bower* [1994] Crim LR 281, where there was a preliminary hearing for directions in which the court made rulings concerning PII in relation to certain documents. The prosecution had given notice to the defence and served a schedule indicating categories of material to which objection to disclosure was made. The court examined documents where objections were raised and upheld the Crown's contention with regard to some, for example, police reports, inter-police memoranda and correspondence with the DPP, reg. 7 disciplinary notices, etc.

Since *ex parte Wiley*, the prosecution are at liberty to disclose the information voluntarily, but if it is still necessary to make an application to the court, the procedures first promulgated in *Davis, Johnson and Rowe* (see chapter 7) are adopted. These procedures have been given statutory effect from 1 April 1997 by virtue of the Crown Court (Criminal Procedure and Investigations Act 1996) (Disclosure) Rules 1997 (SI 1997 No. 698) and the Magistrates' Court (Criminal Procedure and Investigations Act 1996) (Disclosure) Rules 1997 (SI 1997 No. 703) (hereafter referred to as the disclosure rules). The rules confirm that the Crown has three options: an open application which is made *inter partes*, an application which is made *ex parte* and in private, or an application which is made in secret without notice to the defence.

Inter partes applications

The open application is appropriate for those cases where the prosecution have no difficulty in informing the defence of the nature of the material but they are not prepared to disclose the contents on public interest grounds. They must give notice to the defence of their intention to apply to the court for a ruling and specify the nature of the material to which the application relates. The defence then have an opportunity of attending the hearing and making representations as to why the information should be disclosed. For example, where the police have used sensitive surveillance methods or an observation post, there is usually no objection to the disclosure of these facts, but the prosecution may wish to withhold details of the techniques themselves or the identity of the post on public interest grounds. A further example is in a child abuse allegation where the prosecution may have documents dealing with the family history of the children or confidential information between the children in care and those with responsibility for them. This has normally attracted PII on a class basis, the rationale of which is the protection of the welfare of the child. The *inter partes* hearing allows both sides (and, if necessary, the local authority) to make representations as to whether the documents should be disclosed. The judge balances the competing public interests and rules accordingly.

Separate representation for third parties

The Scott Report included observations on the question of separate representation at a PII hearing (see para. K6.19). Courts have traditionally been reluctant to allow third parties to intervene on the basis that they have no real *locus standi* in a criminal trial where the only parties are the Crown and the accused. In some cases, however, the prosecution take the view that relevant PII documents should be disclosed and it is the holder of the documents, such as another Government department or local authority, which takes objection on PII grounds. Sir Richard Scott was critical of the fact that prosecuting counsel in the *Matrix Churchill* case also represented the Government departments whose documents were in issue. He concluded that such a situation was unsatisfactory and recommended that where the prosecution have assessed the documents to be relevant, it should be for the department raising objection to disclosure to make representations to the judge, not the prosecution. This sensible proposal, which removes prosecuting counsel from any position of embarrassment and allows for interested persons to develop their own PII arguments, has been embraced by the disclosure rules.

There have been cases where a chief constable has instructed counsel to argue a PII point as a third party; and although this may, at first, seem strange with the police forming part of the prosecution, it only re-inforces the independence of the prosecuting authority and counsel who is acting in the capacity of a minister of justice to ensure that disclosure issues are dealt with fairly. A case in point, where the chief constable not only intervened in the trial but then sought judicial review of the judge's order, was *R v Chelmsford Crown Court, ex parte Chief Constable of Essex Police* (1994) 99 Cr App R 59. The chief constable challenged the judge's decision to order the disclosure of statements taken by the police during the informal resolution of a complaint, on public interest grounds. The prosecution in the trial of five men for offences of violent disorder made no challenge to the order. The application was refused as the order in question was a matter relating to trial on indictment and the court had no jurisdiction to grant the declaration sought. From 1 April 1997 the prosecutor must give notice to a party claiming an interest in the material and that person is entitled to make representations at the application.

Ex parte applications

An *ex parte* application is suitable only where the prosecution have genuine concerns that to reveal to the accused the nature of the material would have the effect of disclosing that which the prosecutor contends should not, in the public interest, be disclosed. For example, in cases where the material falls within the informant category, if notification to the defence of the fact that there is an informant would leave no doubt as to the source or even the nature of the information itself. It is important, however, that the prosecution do not rely unnecessarily on the *ex parte* procedure. In the majority of 'informant' cases, the existence of an informant will be known or suspected by the defence. Confirmation of the fact by disclosing the *existence* of documents (as opposed to the actual information itself) will not necessarily create any damage; it is the identity of the informant and the nature of the information which is to be safeguarded, and this can often be argued in the context of an *inter partes* application.

If the application is to be made *ex parte*, the prosecution must notify the defence that an application is to take place but it will then be pursued in the absence of the accused and any defence legal representative. At a *Davis, Johnson and Rowe* hearing the judge had three courses available. On the basis of the representations made by the Crown, either disclosure of all or part of the information could be ordered or the non-disclosure of the information could be upheld. A third possibility was that the judge considered that the application should be made *inter partes*. The effect of such an order is that the prosecution must disclose the nature of the information to the accused or, presumably, abandon the case.

What the prosecution cannot do is go 'forum shopping'. This was made clear in *R v Sherlock; R v Wharrie* [1995] Crim LR 799, where, following an order to disclose information concerning a third person involved in the offence, the prosecution went before another judge who (wrongly) ruled that the first judge did not have jurisdiction to entertain the *ex parte* application. As a result no disclosure was made and the matter was raised yet again before the trial recorder who also refused disclosure. The Court of Appeal quashed the convictions in view of the irregularities that had taken place in the proceedings.

The disclosure rules provide for the practice and procedure to be followed in the Crown Court and magistrates' court. They allow for hearings to be heard in private (r. 9(2)) and for the recording of reasons where an order for non-disclosure is made.

Ex parte application without notice

The final option available to the Crown is a secret application which is made *ex parte* and without notice to the defence. The Court recognised in *Davis, Johnson and Rowe* ((1993) 97 Cr App R 110, at p. 114) that 'in a highly exceptional case, to reveal even the fact that an *ex parte* application is to be made, could "let the cat out of the bag" so as to stultify the application'. It was stressed that such situations would be very rare indeed, and it follows that misuse of this procedure by the Crown will inevitably heighten justifiable concerns about 'secret justice'. For obvious reasons, cases in which such a procedure has been utilised are not published, but it seems that it will seldom be appropriate in cases other than those involving terrorism, threats to national security, or where the lives of informants or their families are genuinely at risk.

The sanctioning by the courts of an *ex parte* procedure which gives the Crown an avenue to the trial judge in the absence, not just of the accused but of any representations made on their behalf, has not been universally welcomed. Although, as a general principle, the public interest requires open justice, there are precedents for hearings in closed sessions, namely s. 8(4), Official Secrets Act 1920 and s. 11(4), Official Secrets Act 1989, where evidence may be heard *in camera*. Furthermore, courts have a discretion at common law to hear evidence behind closed doors where a public hearing is not in the interests of justice. This discretion is exercised exceptionally and it is usual for the accused to be present and represented. Many practitioners, however, would agree with the conclusions reached by the Runciman Royal Commission that the *Davis, Johnson and Rowe* procedures struck a satisfactory balance between the public interest in protecting material, such as that concerning confidential information to assist in the detection of crime, and the legitimate needs of the defence to be made aware of the existence of such information. The disclosure rules provide that where the prosecutor has reason to believe that to reveal to the accused the fact that an application is being made would have the effect of disclosing that which the prosecutor contends should not, in the public interest, be disclosed, the accused need not be told of the application.

Reviewing an order for non-disclosure

The judge's ruling is final and there is no right of appeal by either side as s. 29(3), Supreme Court Act 1981 prohibits the review of a decision on a matter relating to trial on indictment. Under s. 14, CPIA 1996, the magistrates' court or youth court must review orders made not to disclose material in the public interest upon an application made by the accused. Under s. 15, judges must keep the question under review regardless of any application being made. The disclosure rules (r. 5) set out procedures to be followed when an accused applies for a review of a non-disclosure order.

The prosecution must comply with any order made by the court or discontinue either the proceedings as a whole, or, possibly, only the relevant part of the proceedings. An example of the latter might be where a judge orders the disclosure of information which is relevant to counts of possessing drugs with intent to supply. The prosecution consider that they cannot comply with the order and therefore abandon those counts while still proceeding on counts of simple possession. It is interesting, however, that while the prosecution always have the option to abandon proceedings following an order to disclose made by magistrates or a judge at the Crown Court, the result in the event of a successful appeal against conviction on grounds based on the judge's wrongful decision not to order disclosure is more speculative. If the Court of Appeal did not allow the appeal but ordered a retrial with an order to disclose, presumably it would still be open to the prosecution to decide whether to comply or abandon. More difficult, however, would be a case where the prosecution had withheld documents following a secret application prior to trial. They would have to renew the application before any appeal, and if the Court of Appeal ordered disclosure it would be difficult for the prosecution simply to abandon in the face of a conviction properly returned by the jury.

FORM OF THE APPLICATION

While the Court of Appeal gave helpful guidance in *Davis, Johnson and Rowe* on the types of application to be employed for dealing with matters of PII, they offered no assistance on the form that an application should take. This gave rise to a number of uncertainties. Did the Crown have to provide details of the substance of the application (especially if a certificate was not being produced) to the court in advance of the hearing? If so, how much information about the law was required, particularly in relation to class claims? Should copies of documents be provided prior to the application? Is the exercise simply a paper one, or should the court hear evidence from, for example, a police officer about the potential dangers to an informant if disclosure is made? As a result of the absence of direction on form, a variety of practices were adopted at Crown Courts. Some judges even countered the prosecution's entitlement to be heard *ex parte* by allowing the defence to put their arguments forward without the prosecution being present. This was clearly contrary to what had been said by Lord Taylor CJ in *R* v *Keane* (1994) 99 Cr App R 1, at p. 5:

> We wish to stress that *ex parte* applications are contrary to the general principle of open justice in criminal trials. They were sanctioned in *Davis, Johnson and Rowe* solely to enable the court to discharge its function in testing a claim that

public interest immunity or sensitivity justifies non-disclosure of material in the possession of the Crown. Accordingly, the *ex parte* procedure should not be adopted, save on the application of the Crown and only for that specific purpose.

In *R v Turner (Paul David)* [1995] 2 Cr App R 94, however, Lord Taylor had to make the point again (at p. 97): 'We wish to re-emphasise that *ex parte* applications are only to be made by the Crown, and only when seeking the court's ruling on disclosure. The defence application in the present case ought, therefore, not to have been heard *ex parte*.'

Keane and *Turner* were applied in *R v Tattenhove and Doubtfire* [1996] 1 Cr App R 408, where Lord Taylor CJ yet again stressed (at p. 413), that the practice of defending counsel going to the judge *ex parte* should stop, the only exception to open justice being an application by the Crown to obtain a ruling as to the propriety or impropriety of withholding material from disclosure:

> We hope that we will not hear any more about defence applications for disclosure which, as the transcripts in the present case show, may descend into a cross-examination of the judge as to his earlier ruling and may inform him of the intentions of counsel for the defence at that particular time, which could be embarrassing if those intentions were on instructions changed later or if counsel happened to be changed later. For all those reasons we are quite clear, and we reassert, that there ought not to be applications made *ex parte* otherwise than for the purpose we have indicated.

Under the disclosure rules, the prosecutor decides which type of application is appropriate, and serves notice on the court and the accused, unless an exceptional *ex parte* without notice application is to be made. In the case of *inter partes* applications, the defence are told of the nature of the material in question, while in the case of an *ex parte* application they are merely told that an application is being made.

The disclosure rules provide for representations to be made to the court. The role of the court is solely to test the prosecution conclusion that disclosure is not in the public interest. It is necessary for the prosecution to satisfy the court as to the sensitivity of the material, its relevance to the issues in the case, and the consequences to the public interest if disclosure is made. This last aspect may well depend on whether the material falls within a recognised PII class, or whether the disclosure of the actual contents will damage the public interest. In respect of a class-based claim regarding non-Goverment documents, the court may require additional assistance on the relevant law. It has been the practice in many courts for most of the information required by the judge to be conveyed in writing, together with copies of the documents in question for inspection; a procedure not dissimilar to that used by the prosecution when seeking leave to prefer a voluntary bill of indictment. Whether further oral representations are required will depend on the sufficiency of the information provided, or, in the case of an *inter partes* application, on the representations made on behalf of the defence. The court may also be assisted by suggestions as to editing or redacting once the documents have been inspected.

A person with an interest in the material may be represented and make representations. There appears to be no reason why a judge should not hear evidence from a police officer or other investigator, but it is clearly preferable that at *ex parte* applications the hearing of evidence should be restricted. If written submissions are properly formulated by the prosecution and supported, where necessary, by representations from counsel, accusations of secret justice whereby the court actually hears evidence in the absence of the accused, will have less substance.

The Court of Appeal were disturbed to note in *Turner* that no record of the *ex parte* application made by the Crown was available. This caused Lord Taylor CJ to state (at p. 97) that: 'it is essential that a verbatim record be kept of such *ex parte* applications so that this court knows exactly what was before the trial judge and what was his reaction and ruling'. It is also important for a trial judge to know whether any applications have been made prior to the trial, and their outcome. Furthermore, as the judge is under a duty to keep disclosure issues under review as the trial progresses, it is imperative that a record of documents inspected and ruled upon is readily available.

Whether *Turner* was available to the court and prosecution in the trial of an alleged possessor of drugs with intent to supply named Kudret Yirtici is not known, but the Court of Appeal noted with regret that once again no record had been kept of an *ex parte* application: see *R* v *Yirtici* (unreported), Court of Appeal, 12 July 1996, transcript 95/4882/Y2, p. 12). An *ex parte* application was described as unavoidable although unsatisfactory, and defendants should not be put to any additional disadvantage by being unable to invite an appellate court to discover just what had transpired at such an application. The disclosure rules provide for a record to be kept of the reasons why a non-disclosure ruling has been made and for the conveying of information to the accused unless the application is made a secret.

CLASS CLAIMS AND CONTENTS CLAIMS

Decisions to withhold material under the *A-G's Guidelines* were based on the sensitivity of the contents, which was balanced against the extent to which the information might assist the defence. After *Ward*, the non-disclosure of relevant information has been based on PII principles, and in coming to a decision whether to order disclosure, the courts considered the potential harm to the public interest that disclosure might bring. This would often involve distinguishing whether the claim was being made on a class basis or a contents basis. A class claim was made on the basis that the disclosure of any document falling within that class, irrespective of its contents, would be damaging to the public interest. A contents claim was appropriate where, regardless of whether the document belonged to a class which was prima facie immune from discovery, the disclosure of the contents would be against the public interest.

In the context of the criminal trial, there is little doubt that courts are more likely to approve non-disclosure where it can be established that disclosure of the contents will damage the public interest. Neverthless, class claims have often been made by the Crown in criminal proceedings with reliance being placed on well-established classes. A recent example is in *R v Clowes* [1992] 3 All ER 440, when, in refusing to discharge a witness summons seeking the production of transcripts of interviews conducted by liquidators, Phillips J observed (at p. 454): 'Turning to the public interest invoked, it is a class claim — it is not suggested that disclosure of the specific documents will injure the public interest.' In practice, however, PII has frequently been asserted on a joint class/contents basis.

The justification for class claims is found in *dicta* in civil authorities such as *Duncan v Cammel Laird, Conway v Rimmer* and *Burmah Oil* (see chapter 9). In so far as the functioning of law enforcement agencies involved in the prevention and detection of crime is concerned, the comments of Lord Reid in *Conway v Rimmer* [1968] AC 910 at pp. 953–4 are just as apposite today as they were almost 30 years ago: 'The police are carrying on an unending war with criminals many of whom are today highly intelligent. So it is essential that there should be no disclosure of anything which might give any useful information to those who organise criminal activities.'

The categories of public interest have always been susceptible to change, a fact acknowledged in *ex parte Wiley* when Lord Woolf agreed with the statement made by Lord Hailsham in *D v NSPCC* [1978] AC 171 (at p. 230) that 'The categories of public interest are not closed, and must alter from time to time whether by restriction or extension as social conditions and social legislation develop'. Thus their Lordships in *ex parte* Wiley removed police complaints material from the category of a class claim (although they did so on the basis that a sufficient case to justify the class of PII had never really been made out rather than because of any change in social conditions).

The future of class assertions in criminal proceedings was thrown into doubt following the strongly worded disapproval in the Scott Report of the use of such claims (see conclusions expressed in para. G18.86: 'If contents claims cannot be justified, PII should not, in my opinion, be claimed'). It is to be noted that *ex parte Wiley* and *Taylor v Anderton* made no such suggestion (albeit in the context of civil appeals), but it is germane that the Scott Inquiry was directly concerned with only two classes. The advice to ministers/formulation of Government policy class is seldom encountered in criminal proceedings; indeed the DPP told the Inquiry that, as far as could be established, no certificate used by the CPS had related in whole, or in part, to this class (see para. G18.85). The second class, that relating to security and intelligence, is used more frequently; but there are other classes which are far more commonplace in criminal proceedings.

The Government announced on 18 December 1996 (see chapter 9) that, in relation to Government documents, the division into class and contents claims would not longer be applied. Ministers would focus directly on the damage that disclosure would cause. The Attorney-General confirmed, however, that the new approach, which involved the abandonment of the class/contents distinction, would not affect non-Government cases instituted by the police. In answer to a question, the Attorney-General opined (Hansard vol. 287 HC Deb, 6th ser., col. 951) that 'the system works well. Although the courts may choose to adopt some of the practices that the Government are adopting, that will be a matter for them'.

How, then, does the system operate? Some applications to withhold non-Government material are made solely on a contents basis, but most are made on a joint contents/class basis. For example, the prosecution would argue that to disclose the name of the informant in a particular case would put him or her in danger, and the disclosure of informants in general would damage the system of detecting and prosecuting crime. The disclosure code lists examples of sensitive material, and although para. 6.12 adds the caveat that sensitivity will depend on the circumstances, the listing of types of material indicates that certain categories or classes may be looked upon as suitable to be withheld, irrespective of the actual contents.

RECOGNISED CLASSES OF PUBLIC INTEREST IMMUNITY

It is necessary to examine the classes which have in the past principally been relied on by the prosecution to justify non-disclosure in criminal proceedings. These relate to informants, sensitive investigation and surveillance techniques, and a class which may be described under the general umbrella of 'the integrity of the criminal investigation'. Although 'national security' claims have been asserted rarely, when they have arisen it has been in the higher profile cases and this class therefore merits separate attention. Other recognised classes will be dealt with more generally at the end of the chapter.

Informants

Two hundred years ago in *R v Hardy* (1794) 24 St Tr 199, a witness for the Crown was asked in cross-examination who had sent him to attend certain meetings. The question was objected to by the Attorney-General, later Lord Eldon, on the ground that the channels of information could not be inquired into. The resulting judgments of all judges in the Court of Exchequer were in agreement that the informer, in the case of a public prosecution, should not be disclosed. This decision was adopted by Pollock CB in *Attorney-General v Briant* (1846) 15 M & W 169 in a passage (at p. 185) which was repeated in the *A-G's Guidelines*:

> . . . the rule clearly established and acted on is this, that in a public prosecution a witness cannot be asked such questions as will disclose the informer, if he be a third person. This has been the settled rule for fifty years, and although it may seem hard in a particular case, private mischief must give way to public convenience . . . and we think the principle of the rule applies to the case where a witness is asked if he himself is the informer.

In criminal proceedings, the most frequent reason for asserting PII is to protect the identity of the informant. As can be seen from the two authorities above, the courts have always recognised the need for informants in police work. As Lord Parker CJ stated in *R* v *Birtles* (1969) 53 Cr App R 469, at p. 472: 'The Court of course recognises that disagreeable as it may seem to some people, the police must be able in certain cases to make use of informers, and further — and this is really a corollary — that within certain limits such informers should be protected.' Lord Parker was under no illusion, however, as to the potential difficulties that may arise, for he continued: 'At the same time, unless the use made of informers is kept within strict limits, grave injustice may result.' To prevent the unrestricted and improper use of informants, the Home Office issued guidance to chief officers of police in Home Office Circular No. 97/1969, although the guidelines concentrate on the actual use of informants rather than on the way they should be dealt with in evidential terms. (That is clearly a matter for the common law, although the *A-G's Guidelines* provided some assistance to prosecutors on how such matters should be approached.)

Notwithstanding the general principle that informants are provided with some safeguards by the law, it has always been the case that in certain circumstances the court may have to override the public interest in protecting informants in the face of a potential miscarriage of justice. The *A-G's Guidelines* made this perfectly clear by including in para. 12 a passage from *Marks* v *Beyfus* (1890) 25 QBD 494, where Lord Esher MR stated (at p. 498):

. . . if upon the trial of a prisoner the judge should be of opinion that the disclosure of the name of the informant is necessary or right in order to show the prisoner's innocence, then one public policy is in conflict with another public policy, and that which says that an innocent man is not to be condemned when his innocence can be proved is the policy that must prevail.

Nearly a century later, the position received clarification from Lord Diplock in *D* v *NSPCC* [1978] AC 171 when he stated (at p. 218):

The rationale of the rule as it applies to police informers is plain. If their identity were liable to be disclosed in a court of law, these sources of information would dry up and the police would be hindered in their duty of preventing and detecting crime. So the public interest in preserving the anonymity of police informers had to be weighed against the public interest that information which might assist a judicial tribunal to ascertain facts relevant to an issue upon which it is required to adjudicate should be withheld from that tribunal. By the uniform practice of the judges which by the time of *Marks* v *Beyfus* 25 QBD 494 had already hardened into a rule of law, the balance has fallen upon the side of non-disclosure except where upon the trial of a defendant for a criminal offence disclosure of the identity of the informer could help to show that the defendant was innocent of the offence. In that case, and in that case only, the balance falls upon the side of disclosure.

From time to time Crown Court judges have been called upon to balance the competing interests: see *R* v *Hallett* [1986] Crim LR 462; *R* v *Agar* (1990) 90 Cr App R 318; *R* v *Langford* [1990] Crim LR 653 and *R* v *Slowcombe* [1991] Crim LR 198. From 1993 onwards, however, when the full effect of the *Ward* judgment began to impact on criminal proceedings, a number of senior police officers complained publicly of cases that were being dropped (or, in some instances, not even commenced) because of the risk of informants being identified. Fingers were pointed at defence solicitors who made unreasonable demands for information, and there were suggestions that some defendants were concocting or tailoring their defences to ensure maximum embarassment to the prosecution in the hope that proceedings would be abandoned in the face of orders by judges to disclose details of informants and/or the information they provided.

That more orders have been made by judges post-*Ward* to disclose sensitive information is undeniable. The reasons, however, are disputed. The police view is that judges are being misled as to the true reasons for the need for sensitive information to be disclosed; they are over-cautious in their rulings either because of a desire to bend over backwards to be fair to defendants, or because of a fear of criticism by the Court of Appeal. Defence practitioners counter these suggestions with claims that because of the deficiencies in the law pre-*Ward*, the prosecution had been failing to disclose vital information either because of the wrongful exercise of discretion, or, more probably, because the police had not informed the prosecuting authority and counsel of the existence of crucial facts concerning their use of informants. There was no need to look any further than some of the miscarriage of justice cases highlighted in chapter 3 to support this.

There is an element of truth in the claims of both sides, but there is little doubt that a major source of post-*Ward* confusion has been the ill-defined balancing exercise that judges have been called upon to undertake. We have seen in the previous chapter how the appeal was allowed in *Agar* where Mustill LJ referred to the 'even stronger public interest [than that of keeping secret the source of information] in allowing a defendant to put forward a tenable case in its best light'. While the correctness of the outcome of the appeal in *Agar* is not disputed, the definition is a loose one when applied to the circumstances of other cases. If a defence is plausible or believable, then is it right for the court simply to order disclosure of the informant without exploring further the true issues in the case or the possible motives for seeking disclosure of the identity of the informant? The most recent common law test is that set out in *Keane*, whereby the judge must consider the importance of the documents to the issues of interest to the defence, present and potential, in so far as they have been disclosed to the judge or can be foreseen. This is a far more realistic approach and is unquestionably fairer to both sides. On the facts in *Keane* (see chapter 7) not only would the material in question not have afforded the defendant the slightest help, but on the contrary it would have assisted the prosecution. This, in reality, is often the case. The public policy of protecting informants often prevents the prosecution from adducing evidence which would assist the prosecution case. In future the courts will have the benefit of defence statements provided by the accused under ss. 5 or 6, CPIA 1996. If the prosecution consider that it is not in the public interest to provide secondary disclosure of such material, the court will be in a better position than at common law to rule on disclosure.

Lord Taylor clearly recognised that things were getting out of hand when he made the following observations in *R* v *Turner* [1995] 2 Cr App R 94, at p. 97:

> Since *Ward* there has been an increasing tendency for defendants to seek disclosure of informants' names and roles, alleging that those details are essential to the defence. Defences that the accused has been set up, and duress, which used at one time to be rare, have multiplied. We wish to alert judges to the need to scrutinise applications for disclosure of details about informants with very great care. They will need to be astute to see that assertions of a need to know such details, because they are essential to the running of the defence, are justified. If they are not so justified, then the judge will need to adopt a robust approach in declining to order disclosure. . . . Even when the informant has participated, the judge will need to consider whether his role so impinges on an issue of interest to the defence, present or potential, as to make disclosure necessary.

There is no independent evidence to say whether the warning has been heeded, as the recently reported cases were heard before *Keane* and *Turner* were either decided or reported. An example of the court refusing an order to disclose the source of information where the defence was one of a 'set-up' is provided by *R* v *Haghighat-Khou* [1995] Crim LR 337 (where both *Keane* and *ex parte Wiley* were considered). The defendant was charged with possessing opium with intent to supply, but he claimed that he did not know what was in a carrier bag found in his car. He said that he was minding it for a man who had since gone to Iran and whom he now suspected of setting him up. The Court of Appeal held that the trial judge had been correct to allow defence counsel to ask questions of the police suggesting a set-up or that the absent man was an informant, but had also been right to refuse questions designed to elicit the source of information. There was no need for the prosecution to disclose material relating to the source of information because it had not prejudiced the appellant in putting forward his defence.

On the other hand, in an appeal against conviction for importing cannabis, the trial of which took place before *Ward*, the Court of Appeal considered that the defence had been prejudiced by the non-disclosure of information. The facts in *R* v *Reilly* [1994] Crim LR 279 were complicated, with the appellant being introduced to an undercover police officer and other men, known only by their christian names, who were to drive a van containing drugs from Spain to England. On appeal, the Crown had sought to give information about the existence of any informer to the Court *ex parte*, in accordance with *Davis, Johnson and Rowe* procedures, but had made it clear that, if required to do so, they would not provide any information publicly. The Court did not accede to the Crown's application. If there was an informer in this case (and the Court did not know one way or the other), the protection which the law afforded had to give way to the need to allow the defence to present a tenable case in its best light. The Court considered *Ward* and *Agar* but not *Keane*.

A similar conclusion was reached by the Court of Appeal in *Yirtici* (above) where the trial judge considered material at an *ex parte* application and refused to allow defence counsel to examine police witnesses about persons who the appellant alleged were undercover police officers working with him. Although the defence seemed somewhat improbable, the Court held that the judge was wrong to make a value judgment that the information would not help the defence when it was an issue for the jury to decide.

In *R* v *Baker* [1996] Crim LR 55, His Honour Judge Rivlin, sitting at Southwark Crown Court, ordered the disclosure of the name of an informant in a drugs case so that the defence could test the veracity of the police officers who claimed that they had obtained a search warrant as a result of information. He ruled that it was necessary for the defence to know exactly why the defendant's premises had been raided.

Cases where it is truly necessary for the defence to have details of an informant ought to be rare, and application of the balancing act propounded in *Keane* will clearly depend on the facts and circumstances of individual cases. There is a responsibility on the prosecuting authority, and ultimately prosecuting counsel, to ensure that the police provide them with all the information concerning the use of any informant: see observations of the Court of Appeal in *R* v *Smith (Brian)* [1995] Crim LR 658. These matters can then be placed before the court in order that the competing public interests may be considered and a decision reached in the light of the issues, present and potential, that can reasonably be foreseen by the judge.

Observation posts

A comparatively recent extension of the informant PII class concerns the disclosure of police observation sites. The disclosure code of practice includes as a category of senstive material 'material revealing the location of any premises or other place used for police surveillance, or the identity of any person allowing a police officer to use them for surveillance'. In *R* v *Rankine* (1986) 83 Cr App R 18, it was held that a police officer could not be compelled to answer questions relating to the nature of an observation post if it would embarrass his source of co-operation. The Court of Appeal also decided that the rule protected not only the identity of the person who allowed the premises to be used, but also the identity of the premises themselves. *Rankine* was followed by *R* v *Johnson (Kenneth)* [1988] 1 WLR 1377, where guidance was given on the evidential requirements for excluding evidence of the identity of places of observation and occupiers of premises.

In *R* v *Hewitt and Davis* (1992) 95 Cr App R 81, counsel for the appellants argued that putting observation posts in the same category as informers was an unwarranted extension of the court's protection given to police sources of information. Watkins LJ's response was unequivocal:

> In our opinion it is not. The detection of crime as society evolves in this country calls, in our judgment, for in appropriate and carefully circumscribed ways an increase in the anonymity granted to police action. Anyhow, we in this respect see no essential difference between informers and the providers of observation posts for both in different ways provide the police with indispensable assistance in the detection of crime.

In *Blake v DPP*; *Austin v DPP* (1993) 97 Cr App R 169, the appellants submitted that the judge's ruling not to disclose the identity of an observation post from where police officers watched indecent behaviour in a churchyard, was wrong. They must have been disappointed to come before a Divisional Court which included Watkins LJ, who not only repeated his judgment in *Hewitt and Davis* but added the commentary that 'once it is accepted that it is or may be in the public interest to protect the identity of police informers, there is no logical reason to deny the same protection to those who supply not information but the facility to gather information such as an observation post may provide'.

The public interest in the protection of observation posts is, therefore, well established. In cases where the location of an observation post is clearly going to be an issue in the case, the prosecution are likely to apply to the court to withhold the relevant documents. In some circumstances a full PII application may be unnecessary and the prosecution will merely apply, at the start of the trial, for a ruling which will prevent any cross-examination of police officers which might lead to the disclosure of the whereabout of the observation post. This course was adopted in *R v Grimes* [1994] Crim LR 213, where the Court of Appeal dismissed an appeal against conviction on the ground, *inter alia*, that restrictions imposed by the trial judge were so onerous as to lead to a miscarriage of justice. As with any balancing exercise in ordinary informant cases, much will depend on the circumstances of the case, but it would appear that if identity is not in dispute or there is little challenge of what was seen from the post, any application for disclosure is likely to fail. Indeed, if there is no indication that these matters are in issue, the prosecution are entitled not to make an application following the *Keane* materiality test (or in later cases, the test of 'undermining the case' introduced by the CPIA 1996). In cases where there is a dispute over identification, there is a greater likelihood of the balance falling in favour of the defence who will need to cross-examine on the basis of distances, sight lines, aids to observation, etc.

Others providing information in confidence

The protection afforded by the law to those who assist the police by allowing their premises to be used for observation purposes is a recognition that it is not just 'police informers' who benefit from non-disclosure of their identities. The term 'informant' embraces a number of individuals, from the 'supergrass' and paid informant who are providing information for some form of personal advantage, to someone who provides information that comes to light as part of their employment (for example, a bank manager who provides information under s. 24, Drug Trafficking Offences Act 1986) or an ordinary citizen performing a public duty. All deserve anonymity unless disclosure is essential to prove innocence. How many people would agree to make up the numbers on identification parades if they thought that their names and addresses would be supplied to the defendant? Interestingly, although the current PACE Codes of Practice on Identification do not expressly prevent such disclosure, the Administrative Guidance Rules (para. 10) attached to their predecessor, Home Office Circular No. 109/1978, did contain such a prohibition, except on the authority of the court. This has now been rectified in the new disclosure code which includes 'material containing details of persons taking part in identification parades' as an example of sensitive material, so a defence request for such particulars today would no doubt be met by a claim for PII, presumably made on a class basis unless there was a real likelihood of a participant on the parade being harmed.

The disclosure code gives as an example of sensitive material 'material given in confidence'. The informant class has not been limited to those who provide information in confidence to the police, although the occasions when PII is asserted on a class basis in criminal proceedings for non-police informants are rare. Examples which have arisen in connection with other bodies having statutory investigatory functions include:

- Customs and Excise (see *Alfred Crompton Amusement Machines Ltd* v *Customs and Excise Commissioners (No. 2)* [1974] AC 405, where information obtained in confidence for tax valuation purposes was not disclosable; *cf. Norwich Pharmacal Company* v *Customs and Excise Commissioners* [1974] 1 AC 133, where the House of Lords held that the interests of justice outweighed the public interest in the non-disclosure of confidential information about the import of drugs);
- the Inland Revenue (see *Re Joseph Hargreaves Ltd* [1900] 1 Ch 347, where information provided to the Inland Revenue for tax purposes was not disclosed to the liquidator);
- the Gaming Board (in *R* v *Lewes Justices, ex parte Secretary of State for the Home Department* [1973] AC 388, where PII protected information was supplied by the police to the Gaming Board in connection with an application for a gaming licence;
- the National Society for the Prevention of Cruelty to Children (in *D* v *NSPCC* [1978] AC 171, which held that PII extended to the names of those who gave information to the NSPCC about the abuse of children).

There is further discussion of the issue of confidentiality in chapter 11.

Financial and trade regulators

There have been recent attempts to extend the informant class to those who give confidential information to regulators, on the basis that if such information is disclosable others would be deterred from passing on information necessary for the regulation of financial institutions. The claim was successful in *Continental Reinsurance Corporation (UK) Ltd* v *Pine Top Insurance Ltd* [1986] 1 Lloyd's Rep 8, where the Department of Trade and Industry claimed that the disclosure of communications between the reinsurers and the DTI would make the Department's supervisory responsibilities more difficult to perform. In *MGN Pensions Trustees* v *Invesco Asset Management Ltd* (unreported), 14 October 1993, a similar class claim was upheld on behalf of the self-regulatory organisation IMRO (the Investment Management Regulatory Organisation) which received confidential information in furtherance of its statutory duties under the Financial Services Act 1986.

Doubts have since been cast on the extent of a class of PII in relation to information provided to such bodies as a result of the ruling of Ardern J in *Kaufmann* v *Credit Lyonnais Bank* (1995) *The Times*, 1 February 1995. The Securities and Futures Authority (SFA) and the Bank of England asserted PII in respect of confidential information on the basis that disclosure of material volunteered by member firms of the SFA would impair the performance of the statutory functions of the Authority because members would be deterred from making prompt and full disclosures to it. Ardern J reviewed the relevant authorities, including *ex parte Wiley*, and concluded that the class claim as formulated was too wide. However, the disclosure code includes, as an example of sensitive material, 'material supplied to an investigator during a criminal investigation which has been generated by an official of a body concerned with the regulation or supervision of bodies corporate or of persons engaged in financial activities'.

Although attempts in the future to extend the informant class will obviously be carefully scrutinised by the courts, the existence of the class is undisputed. Many claims to withhold information can be, and are, put on a contents basis in that disclosure will threaten the safety and well-being of the informant in the case. It may be necessary, though, for the protection of all who may wish to give information in confidence in the future, that a claim on a wider class basis should not be too readily abandoned.

Sensitive investigation and surveillance techniques

The use of covert surveillance methods, listening devices and other sensitive techniques plays a prominent part in the investigation of crime. It is not in the public interest that details of such methods are known as it would enable criminals to frustrate police inquiries and avoid detection. That is not to say that PII can be justifiably claimed for all documents that come into existence as a result of covert operations. Surveillance records or logs are no more than memory refreshing documents, and once relied on in order to give evidence, they may be inspected by the defence. Often it will be necessary to edit or 'black out' entries in order to protect the identity of an informant, undercover operative, observation post etc., but this can usually be successfully carried out under the guidance, and with the approval of the court.

An illustration of the court's approach to PII in relation to this class is provided by *R v Roberts* (unreported), Court of Appeal, 28 July 1994, transcript 93/1878/S1, where the appellant had been kept under observation by the security services who had used listening devices. The trial judge had ruled, at an *ex parte* application, that some material should be disclosed but that other documents could be withheld. On appeal, the grounds of which were that the appellant was unable to present his case effectively as a result of the judge's order, the Court had two questions to consider. The first was whether the documents attracted PII and the second was, had the excluded evidence been given, would its disclosure have been detrimental to national security in the ways referred to in the certificate signed by the Secretary of State? The Court heard submissions *in camera ex parte* and answered both questions in the affirmative. They then turned to the balancing exercise and considered whether the appellant would be denied a fair trial if the material were withheld. They concluded that the defence had not been deprived of the opportunity to put their case effectively and dismissed the appeal.

The disclosure code gives as an example of sensitive material, material revealing, either directly or indirectly, techniques and methods relied upon by a police officer in the course of a criminal investigation such as covert surveillence techniques, or other methods of detecting crime. Also instanced is material received from intelligence and security agencies, as well as material relating to the use of a telephone system which is supplied to an investigator for intelligence purposes only.

Integrity of the criminal investigation

A criminal investigation generates a vast amount of paperwork. In addition to the statements taken from potential witnesses, there will be records of interviews, entries in notebooks, messages, records on tape and computer etc. If a suspect is arrested, the requirements of PACE 1984 demand the completion of custody records and a variety of other forms and documents. All this information is potentially disclosable, but there will be some documents which are not. An investigation file will generally include reports from the investigating officer to a senior officer, and sometimes the investigator may seek advice from the police or relevant prosecuting authority. When the investigation is complete, a covering report will almost certainly accompany the relevant evidence to the prosecuting authority. In a similar manner, DTI and Customs investigators submit reports to their legal departments concerning the investigation and prosecution of crime. Prosecution reports are also made by Official Receivers relating to possible offences committed by companies.

Irrespective of the contents of a report, it has been held that such communication between the police and the prosecuting authority is protected from disclosure on a class basis. Parallels have been drawn by other Government departments, such as the DTI and Customs and Excise, in relation to some of their internal reports. The rationale for this is one of candour, in that it is essential for the effective functioning of the criminal process that the seeking and giving of advice should be made fully, frankly and in confidence without fear of the communication being disclosed in the proceedings.

In *Auten* v *Rayner* [1958] 1 WLR 1300, the Court of Appeal refused to order that a detective should produce for inspection in civil proceedings for malicious prosecution and other allegations, reports made to senior officers and communications between the Metropolitan Police and other forces on the ground that they belonged to a class which it was necessary for the functioning of the public service to withhold from production. When Crown privilege was claimed later at the hearing of the action itself, the claim was upheld (in *Auten* v *Rayner (No. 2)* [1960] 1 QB 669).

Auten v *Rayner (No. 2)* was applied in *Evans* v *Chief Constable of Surrey* [1988] QB 588, where the plaintiff, who had been interviewed on a number of occasions and twice arrested in connection with a murder, brought an action for wrongful arrest and false imprisonment against the chief constable and sought discovery of a police report sent to the DPP. The Attorney-General provided a certificate to the court stating that disclosure would not be in the public interest. Paragraph 8 of the certificate read as follows:

In my view, it is essential for the proper enforcement of the criminal law and in particular for the proper fulfilment by the Director of Public Prosecutions and chief officers of police of their respective statutory and other duties that correspondence or other communication between them (or those acting on their behalf) relative to the seeking and giving of advice should be able to be made fully, frankly and in confidence and without fear that such correspondence, inquiries and communications may subsequently be disclosed in civil proceedings and used for other purposes than the enforcement of the criminal law . . .

The Court agreed with this reasoning, Wood J stating (at p. 600):

It seems to me important, and very important in the functioning of the criminal process of prosecutions, that there should be freedom of communication between police forces around the country and the Director of Public Prosecutions in seeking his legal advice, without fear that those documents will be subject to inspection, analysis and detailed investigation at some later stage.

Although the claim for PII arose in the context of civil proceedings, and the relationship between the police and DPP is now on a different statutory footing since the Prosecution of Offences Act 1985, *Evans* has consistently been relied on to deny disclosure of police reports and correspondence between the police and prosecuting authority in criminal proceedings where the subject matter relates to the decision to prosecute and the evidence in support thereof. Since the inception of the CPS, the nature of reports has changed with, in many instances, the report being no more than one which covers the formal submission of papers. Sometimes, however, there is a more detailed report giving the officer's views and opinions, and often there will be a confidential report which reveals, for the benefit of the Crown Prosecutor, information concerning the use of any informant, surveillance and intelligence details etc. These reports are immune from production on a class basis.

The status of the initial report form sent by the police to the CPS following an investigation was considered in *O'Sullivan* v *Commissioner of Police of the Metropolis* (1995) *The Times*, 3 July 1995. The Divisional Court, with the benefit of the judgments in *ex parte Wiley* and *Taylor* v *Anderton* [1995] 2 All ER 420 (in relation to police complaints reports), held that such forms belonged to a class of documents to which PII attached and their disclosure would be ordered only where the public interest in their production outweighed that in preserving their confidentiality. It was also held that where there was clear authority to support the assertion that class immunity applied, it was sufficient for the claim to be raised by a responsible official within the Commissioner's Organisation (in the instant case by a barrister employed in the Commissioner's solicitor's department).

Not unnaturally, the existence of such communications and reports from time to time excites interest from the defence who are anxious to know whether there is anything in the file which may be of assistance. In most instances, assurances made on a counsel to counsel basis to the effect that there is nothing of help will suffice; and, of course, since *ex parte Wiley*, the Crown may disclose voluntarily information which would in normal circumstances attract PII (subject to the safeguards set out in the judgment). It is possible, however, that a report may contain information which should be disclosed. Even before *ex parte Wiley*, prosecutors were alert to the possibility of injustice if such information were not disclosed, and even though they took the view that PII could not be waived in view of the status of a police report as a class protected document, it was usually possible to effect disclosure by other means, e.g., by a police officer making a statement which could then be disclosed. In view of the existence of case law surrounding the non-disclosure of police reports, it is perhaps surprising that the disclosure code of practice makes no mention of them as 'sensitive' documents.

In addition to police reports, the defence may seek production of internal police orders or manuals in order to cross-examine officers about action they had taken. For example, it may be relevant in a case where an officer has used his truncheon to know whether the police force in question has any instructions with which officers are expected to comply. In *Gill and Goodwin* v *Chief Constable of Lancashire* (1992) *The Times*, 3 November 1992, the defendant contended that a public order manual was protected from disclosure on the grounds of PII. The plaintiffs were police officers in the Lancashire Police Force who had been injured when practising shield movements during a training exercise and alleged negligence by the chief constable. In the judgment of the Court, Farquharson LJ said that the authorities showed that class documents could be divided into groups:

(a) Documents concerning the process of government whether central, local or delegated, and then only relating to the decision-making process; and (b) Documents concerning the detection or the investigation or the prosecution of criminal offences.

The instant case was concerned with the second category and Farquharson LJ continued:

For my part I would uphold the defendant's claim for immunity for this document. It is well know that in the past twenty five years there has from time to time been disorder in the streets. . . . If the organisers of demonstrations which seek to exploit the weapon of public disorder became aware of police methods of dealing with such situations the opportunity to frustrate the efforts of the police to impose control is clear and obvious.

He also made the point that it was still open for the party seeking disclosure to contend that without production of the document his case could not be properly presented. If disclosure of such a manual were sought in criminal proceedings, the accused would have to establish materiality and demonstrate that its production would assist in proving innocence, but it would seem that PII attaches to internal instructions, manuals etc. which are necessary for the effective prevention and detection of crime.

As well as reports, correspondence and manuals, other documents are created which the police are anxious not to disclose on the twin grounds of irrelevance and PII. These come within the general category of management documents which deal with the overall control of the investigation, briefings to other officers etc. It is argued that the prevention and detection of crime would be less effective if such documents were routinely disclosed, and it is noted that the disclosure code gives 'internal police communications such as management minutes' as an example of material for which sensitivity and non-disclosure can be claimed.

If class claims were to be abandoned in criminal proceedings, this class would probably affect the prosecution more than any other. Often, disclosure of the reports and communications discussed above would not damage the public interest on an individual contents basis. Apart from the fact that many reports are not material, either under the *Keane* test or under the new statutory tests, their contents are innocuous. When an investigator first puts pen to paper, however, he or she will not necessarily know this. The rationale for protection on a class basis is to encourage candour in the reporting of the investigation and the giving or seeking of advice. If every police, report, memorandum, letter, minute etc. has to be examined on a contents basis, the investigation and prosecution process will grind to a halt.

There seems to be no reason why such material cannot retain its PII class status with the new voluntary disclosure provisions allowing for the disclosure of anything of potential help to the accused. In cases where voluntary disclosure is inappropriate, the court will have to decide, and in so doing will consider the reasoning behind the class as well as the contents of the document(s) in question.

National security

Public interest immunity claims on the grounds of national security are rare in criminal proceedings, but when they do arise it is usually in the context of trials against spies or terrorists which have involved the security or intelligence services, Special Branch or other highly sensitive areas of police activity. Immunity is asserted on the basis that anonymity is essential to operational effectiveness and also to ensure the safety of those who carry out tasks in connection with the protection and security of the country. One of the certificates in the *Matrix Churchill* prosecution claimed protection for the identities of members of the security and intelligence services, details of their deployment, training equipment and techniques, location of premises, sources of intelligence information etc. Another recent assertion of national security on a PII class basis arose in the civil case of *Balfour* v *Foreign and Commonwealth Office* [1994] 1 WLR 681, an appeal from an Employment Appeal Tribunal. Three certificates signed by the Foreign Secretary and Home Secretary were issued objecting to the production of documents relating to the organisation of the security and intelligence services, their theatres of operation or their methods. Express reference was made to foreign powers and terrorist organisations and the threat to national security if disclosure were ordered. It was submitted on behalf of the appellant that the court should adopt a more open approach to such matters, but the Court of Appeal held that even if it was not constrained by authority, that would be contrary to principle and good sense.

There are a number of authorities in civil proceedings, stretching back to *Duncan* v *Cammel Laird* and *Conway* v *Rimmer*, which have considered PII claims on the basis of national security. They indicate that provided that evidence of a threat to national security is established, the balancing exercise will inevitably fall in favour of non-disclosure because the courts are not in a position to challenge the assertions in the certificate. The different type of balancing exercise in criminal proceedings means that the court is likely to take a more questioning and interventionist role, as indeed Judge Smedley QC did in the *Matrix Churchill* trial when he ruled on PII and the ministers' certificates: see *R* v *Henderson* (unreported), Central Criminal Court, 5 October 1992, transcript T920175. Judge Smedley inspected the documents and overrrode the certificates as the Government and security services were aware that there had been no deception by the defendants as to the use to be made of machine tools supplied by Matrix Churchill.

It may be significant that the then legal adviser to the security and intelligence services told the Scott Inquiry that, in his opinion, PII could have been asserted in the *Matrix Churchill* case on a contents basis and that a class claim was unnecessary and confusing (see para. G18.102). Once relevance has been established by applying the required tests, it may be that most, if not all, national security claims could be made on a contents basis despite the fact that the existence of the class is undoubted. This may have affected the Government's attitude in abandoning the class/contents division. The Attorney-General's statement made clear (see Hansard vol. 287 HC Deb, 6th ser., col. 950) that the Government's approach would take into account the types of information defined as sensitive in the Intelligence Services Act 1994. Schedule 3, para. 4 of the Act defines as sensitive for the purpose of non-disclosure to the Intelligence and Security Commission:

(a)   information which might lead to the identification of, or provide details of, sources of information, other assistance or operational methods available to the security service, intelligence service or GCHQ;

(b)   information about particular operations which have been or are proposed to be undertaken in pursuance of any of the functions of these bodies;

(c)   information provided by, or by an agency of, the Government of a territory outside the UK where that Government does not consent to the disclosure of the information.

Future claims for PII on the grounds of national security will therefore come within the above categories not simply because they are so designated as sensitive, but because real harm will result from their disclosure.

'Advice to ministers'

'Advice to ministers' is a PII class that was recognised in such cases as *Burmah Oil Co. Ltd* v *Bank of England* [1980] AC 1090 and *Air Canada* v *Secretary of State for Trade (No. 2)* [1983] 2 AC 394. It includes certain exchanges between ministers (such as Cabinet minutes) and internal correspondence between officials which relate to the formulation and development of policy. Although such documents are seldom material in criminal proceedings they were at the heart of the *Matrix Churchill* trial, and the decision to seek to withhold a number of documents on a class basis was severely criticised in the Scott Report. The new Government approach outlined on 18 December 1996 indicates that this class will no longer be claimed unless real harm would result from the disclosure of the advice or any part of it.

Conduct of diplomatic relations

The immunity from disclosure of communications between the Government and other foreign governments which is essential for the effective conduct of diplomatic relations rarely features in civil proceedings, let alone criminal prosecutions.

Such a claim was made in *ex parte Osman* in relation to correspondence passing between the Foreign Office and authorities in Hong Kong. However, with the increase in communications with the organs of the EU and the nature of crime becoming more international, it is possible that documents with a bearing on diplomatic relations may become more prominent in criminal proceedings in the future. There is an argument that letters of request to other jurisdictions issued under the Criminal Justice (International Co-operation) Act 1990, and the responses thereto, may be covered on a class basis, but the preferred view appears to be that they are immune from production only if the contents are damaging to the public interest. Significantly, damage to international relations caused by the disclosure of confidential diplomatic communications was cited in the Government statement as an illustration of the sort of situation where real harm may result from disclosure and, as a result, where PII may be asserted.

Welfare of children

The files in child care cases have been held to be confidential and immune from production in civil proceedings: see *D* v *NSPCC* (above) and *Re D (Infants)* [1970] 1 WLR 599. Even school reports were held to be covered by PII in *R* v *Higgins* (unreported), Court of Appeal, 22 February 1994, transcript 93/5625/Y4. In such cases, the welfare of the child is paramount, and few will argue against the correctness of the principle in cases where the future well-being of the child is to be determined in care or wardship proceedings. There are, however, real conflicts which arise in criminal proceedings when this public interest is balanced against the principle of the defendant having a fair trial. Judges often have the unenviable task of inspecting huge amounts of material in the possession of social services in order to decide whether any of the reports, minutes of case conferences, family details, medical and psychiatric information, etc. could be of any help to the defendant. Judges know that disclosure of information will sometimes be extremely damaging to the welfare of the child for it will allow cross-examination on delicate and intimate subjects, but that is sometimes the only way that a defence can be conducted. An order for disclosure will place a heavy responsibility on the Crown to decide whether the public interest is best served by continuing the prosecution or by abandoning the case and saving the child from an ordeal which is perhaps just as great as the abuse alleged.

Material supplied to an investigator during a criminal investigation which relates to a child or young person and which has been generated by a local authority social services department, an Area Child Protection Committee or other party contacted by an investigator during the investigation, is given as an example of sensitive material in the disclosure code.

Police complaints statements

Public interest immunity no longer attaches as a class to statements made for the purpose of a complaint against the police. This was established by *ex parte Wiley*, which overruled *Neilson* v *Laugharne* [1981] QB 736 and thus removed a frequently encountered obstacle to proper disclosure. The complaints departments of many police forces, aided and abetted by the Police Complaints Authority, jealously guarded the protection afforded to statements taken in connection with a complaint against a police officer witness in the case to the extent that material was sometimes denied to the CPS, which had the immediate responsibility for disclosure issues in the case. In most cases it was obvious that the balancing exercise conducted by the court would favour disclosure, yet because it was the general understanding that PII could not be waived, the material had to be placed before the court for the formalities to be complied with. Happily, the position is now more straightforward in that if the complaint statements are material to the issues in the case, they will fall to be disclosed, unless PII needs to be asserted because the contents are damaging to the public interest.

Complaint reports of investigating officers

Ex parte Wiley left open the position in relation to the investigating officers' report. There was no unanimity in the opinions of their Lordships and the point was left to be decided in a case where the issue was raised specifically. The matter was not left in doubt for long, because in *Taylor* v *Anderton* [1995] 2 All ER 420 it was held that PII does attach on a class basis. The judgment of Sir Thomas Bingham MR (as he then was) concluded (at p. 437):

> I am fully alive to the existence of a current opinion strongly flowing in favour of openness and disclosure. I am also, however, mindful of the fundamental public interest in ensuring that those responsible for maintaining law and order are themselves uncorrupt, law-abiding, honest and responsible. . . . I have no difficulty in accepting the need for investigating officers to feel free to report on professional colleagues or members of the public without the apprehension that their opinions may become known to such persons. I can readily accept that the prospect of disclosure in other than unusual circumstances would have an undesirably inhibiting effect on investigating officers' reports. I would, therefore, hold that the reports of investigating officers made in circumstances such as these form a class which is entitled to public interest immunity. . . .

ASSERTING PUBLIC INTEREST IMMUNITY IN THE FUTURE

The paragraphs above summarise how PII has been asserted since it became a feature of the criminal trial as a result of the *dicta* in *ex parte Osman* and *Ward*. Although the CPIA 1996 leaves the common law rules for dealing with disclosure in the public interest undisturbed, there are some relevant provisions in the disclosure code about the nature of sensitive material which it is not in the public interest to disclose. The categories described therein closely resemble some of the PII classes discussed above. Furthermore, the criterion for relevance established by

Keane has been superceded by the new test in the CPIA 1996 for those investigations commenced after 1 April 1997. In addition, it remains to be seen how prosecuting authorities will handle the newly bestowed powers of voluntary disclosure and how rigorously they will implement the new approach in relation to Government documents. While the Government are content for the class/contents division to abandoned in relation to Government documents, no such recommendation has been made for police documents. The listing of examples of sensitive documents in the disclosure code, coupled with the natural desire to protect investigator/prosecutor communications, makes it unlikely that the division will be completely discarded in the run of the mill prosecutions in the Crown Court and magistrates' courts.

It will be recalled that the general approach recommended in the Scott Report is that if PII documents are not within the criteria of relevance, they need not be disclosed. This accords with the common law. The Report continues that if they are relevant then PII needs to be asserted, but only on a contents basis. It is recommended that PII claims on a class basis should not in future be made. Contents claims should be made only after the use of redactions, if disclosure of the documents will cause substantial harm, and if the responsible minister forms an opinion that notwithstanding sensitivity, the public interest requires that the documents should not be disclosed. In cases where judges are asked to rule, it is recommended that they first confirm that the documents are relevant (according to whatever test is applicable), and if it is decided that they might be of assistance to the defence, they ought not to be withheld on PII grounds. If documents are to be withheld, the judge should make it clear whether non-disclosure is being sanctioned on the ground that they would not assist the defence or whether the weight of public interest factors precludes disclosure. If it is the latter, it is Sir Richard's view that the decision would be wrong in principle and contrary to authority. He supports defence disclosure in order to assist the determination of the requisite materiality.

The two key points in the recommendations are, therefore, first, that class claims should not be asserted in criminal trials and, secondly, if disclosure of the contents will assist the defence, disclosure must be made and the weight of public interest factors against disclosure is immaterial.

It is only possible to speculate on how matters will be dealt with in the light of the provisions of the CPIA 1996, the decision in *ex parte Wiley* and the new Government approach, but it seems that in the vast majority of cases an application to the court will arise in one of two sets of circumstances. First, although the accused has no right to challenge the exercise of the prosecutor's discretion in relation to primary disclosure, s. 8, CPIA 1996, supported by the disclosure rules, provides for an application by the accused for disclosure if it is considered that there is additional prosecution material which might reasonably be expected to assist the accused following the service of a defence statement. In the course of such an application, a dispute between the parties may arise concerning the relevance of sensitive material. If the court rules that the sensitive material will assist the accused, the prosecution will presumably then have to consider whether the information should be disclosed voluntarily. It may be decided at that stage to abandon the case, but if it is considered that the case should continue but that disclosure should not be made because of the greater public interest in withholding the information, the court will be asked to conduct the balancing exercise as to whether the interests of justice outweigh the withholding of the information in the public interest. The first test conducted by the court is basically one of relevance; the second is the common law one for deciding which of the competing public interests should prevail. According to Sir Richard Scott, there is no balance to be made and an order for disclosure will follow.

The second set of circumstances is where the prosecution concede, in the light of the indication of the nature of the defence, that the information might reasonably be expected to assist the accused's defence but the public interest is overwhelmingly in favour of withholding information. The court's role is then the traditional one of conducting the balancing exercise. It has to be asked, however, where there is a ruling or concession by the prosecution that sensitive information either undermines their case or can be expected to assist the defence case, whether there will be many applications to withhold that information. At common law, a concession of relevance or materiality did not prevent the prosecution arguing that the sensitive material could nevertheless be withheld as it would not help the defence in any way. However, now that the tests for disclosure have been narrowed by the CPIA 1996, if documents either undermine the prosecution case or assist the defence, it will difficult, if not impossible in most circumstances, for the prosecution to contend that there is nevertheless a greater public interest in keeping them from the defence. It would seem that once the tests in the CPIA 1996 have been satisfied, a ruling to that effect by the court will be followed in the vast majority of cases by disclosure or discontinuance.

11 Privilege, Confidentiality and Statutory Provisions Preventing Disclosure

We have seen in the previous chapters that the common law rules for disclosure generally were that, subject to materiality, documents in the possession of the prosecution were disclosable unless it was necessary that they be withheld from production in the public interest. Under the CPIA 1996, the prosecutor must disclose documents which undermine the case for the prosecution or assist the accused's defence as disclosed in the defence statement provided, once again subject to public interest considerations. This chapter examines whether there are any circumstances, other than public interest grounds, which either prevent disclosure of relevant documents to the defence or allow the prosecution to withhold relevant material. This calls for consideration of statutory restrictions on disclosure, in particular those imposed by the Interception of Communications Act 1985, and also a look at the doctrines of confidentiality and privilege which militate against discovery. First, however, it is necessary to reflect on whether the prosecutor still retains any discretion at common law to withhold documents which are believed to be false or untrue, or which may be potentially advantageous to the prosecution for use in cross-examination.

WITHHOLDING 'SUSPECT' STATEMENTS

The 1977 Working Party on Disclosure, whose recommendations led to the *A-G's Guidelines*, reported that the discretionary power to withhold statements made by 'suspect' witnesses had been exercised by prosecuting counsel for as long as any of the members could remember. Their recollection was confirmed not only by the Lord Chief Justice (see chapter 7), but also by a working group of the Criminal Bar Association which had submitted a memorandum to the Attorney-General in 1973 stating, *inter alia*:

We accept that there may be instances in which the prosecuting advocate is right not to give a sight of a statement. For example, a witness whom it is thought the defence are likely to call as an alibi witness has given a statement to the police which is inconsistent with his proposed alibi evidence. . . . . The prosecuting advocate must have a reason for declining and must use his discretion judicially. We feel the prosecuting advocate should take particular care that he makes the right decision in such a situation, but in our view this is a matter which must be left to the discretion of the prosecuting advocate, who must be trusted to come to the right conclusion.

As a result the *A-G's Guidelines* contained a description in para. 6(i) to (iv) of circumstances when the prosecutor had a discretion not to make disclosure. Basically, this covered situations where it was feared that witnesses might change their accounts and where the statement was believed to be untrue or neutral and might be of use in cross-examination. In such circumstances, the *Guidelines* advised that the name and address of the witness should normally be supplied. Until the decision of the Court of Appeal in *R v Brown (Winston)*, this part of the *Guidelines* remained largely unaffected by the wholesale changes in the law. Most of the attention, in cases such as *Ward* and *Keane*, was concentrated on 'sensitive' material and the examples given in para. 6(v) which dealt with the discretion to withhold material on public interest grounds. The holding back of statements for cross-examination purposes has nothing to do with the public interest apart from the fact that it gives a tactical advantage to the Crown which may render assistance in the guilty being properly convicted. While it may be argued that this is in the wider public interest, the courts have never accepted this as being a public interest ground for not disclosing relevant information.

Steyn LJ made it clear in *Winston Brown* that the *A-G's Guidelines* no longer accurately represented the law, but the judgment did not directly deal with the question of withholding a statement for cross-examination purposes after the defence had been told that the prosecution had such a statement and where the defence had been provided with the name and (usually) the address of the maker. (These details would probably be known in any event as the maker of the statement was more likely than not a friend or relative of the defendant.) The prosecution relied in *Winston Brown* on the aforementioned sub-paragraphs of para. 6 to keep information from the defence and the Crown's decision to withhold was upheld. The judgment stated (at [1995] 1 Cr App R 191, p. 201):

We consider that the public interest and fairness did not require the disclosure of Gordon's earlier statement that he had been drunk at the relevant time. . . . For the same reasons we conclude that Pinnock's oral statement that he was withdrawing his earlier statement implicating the defendant as a result of threats was not a statement which the Crown was obliged to disclose.

It appears, therefore, that although the *A-G's Guidelines* no longer conformed to the requirements of the law in a number of critically important respects, withholding statements in the general circumstances described in para. 6(i) to (iv) was not one of them and the principle on which these sub-paragraphs were based still held good. This was certainly the view of Hirst LJ in *R* v *White* (unreported), Court of Appeal, 30 July 1993, transcript 92/3524/W3. In that case, the prosecution declined to disclose statements to the defence, relying on para. 6(iii) and (iv) of the *A-G Guidelines*. It was submitted on appeal that the prosecution no longer had any discretion to withhold statements and that the judge should have scrutinised the statements himself. This was rejected by the Court. The prosecution's decision had nothing to do with PII and they retained a discretion in applying para. 6(iii) and (iv) of the *A-G's Guidelines*, which were unaffected by the decision in *Ward*.

The prosecutor's discretion not to disclose statements where there are reasonable grounds for believing that the information contained therein may be wholly or partially untrue or liable to be changed on grounds of fear, misguided loyalty etc., should not be confused with the duty to lead evidence which is capable of forming part of the prosecution case. We have already seen in chapter 4 that the prosecution cannot keep up their sleeve evidence which should be tendered or led as part of the case for the Crown (see principles in *Kane*, *Rice* and *Phillipson*). That is not the same as withholding statements believed to be untrue, or where there are grounds for suspecting that the witnesses will change their stories. This was confirmed in *R* v *Seymour* [1996] Crim LR 512, where the prosecution had a statement from the appellant's alibi witness which had not been disclosed and which was put to her in cross-examination. On appeal it was claimed that the statement should have been disclosed, but the Court of Appeal held, following *Winston Brown*, that there was no duty to disclose material which undermined the credibility of a defence witness.

It will be interesting to see how 'suspect' statements are dealt with under the CPIA 1996. Take, for example, a situation similar to that in *Seymour* where the police have taken statements from friends of the accused, each of which tends to provide some help to the accused in relation to an alibi. However, the statements are inconsistent with one another and the prosecution are satisfied that they are false and do not undermine their case. Indeed, if the defence call these witnesses, the prosecution can expect to make considerable inroads into the accused's alibi defence. In such circumstances, are the statements disclosable? Even if the defence statement discloses an alibi, the statements are unlikely to help the accused apart from giving notice that the alibi is far from watertight. At common law, the cases discussed above and *R* v *Williams* (unreported), Court of Appeal, 15 April 1994, transcript 92/6329/W5, provided authority for the fact that the prosecution need not disclose the statements. It may be argued that the proper course under the CPIA 1996, however, would be to make disclosure so that, in the words of Ralph Gibson LJ in *Philipson* (at p. 235), 'It is better in the interests of justice that an accused is not induced, by thinking that he is safe if he does so, to exaggerate, or to embroider, or to lie'. If the alibi defence is then abandoned in the light of the contents of the statements, the prosecution may seek to utilise the provisions of s. 11, CPIA 1996, where the court may make appropriate comments and the jury may draw any inferences that appear proper from the change in defence.

INTERCEPTION OF COMMUNICATIONS

Origins of power of interception

In 1957, the then Prime Minister Harold MacMillan set up a committee of Privy Councillors to consider and report generally on the power to intercept communications. The report of the Committee (Cmnd 283, London: HMSO, 1957) (known as the 'Birkett Report') concluded that the origin of the power to intercept communications could only be surmised, but the power had been exercised from very early times and had been recognised as a lawful power by a succession of statutes covering the last 20 years or more. Certainly the practice was being used by Sir Francis Walsingham to intercept letters to and from Mary Queen of Scots, and a glance at history books reveals that during periods of unrest or plots to subvert Parliament, communications were intercepted.

The reason for the power is to prevent and detect serious crime and to preserve the safety of the state. Not surprisingly, as the exercise of the power by organs of the state involves the infringement of a subject's liberty, the practice has received periodic attention from the legislature and the judiciary. The Birkett Report is of particular importance, for it reviewed not only the ancient practice of issuing warrants to intercept letters but also the more modern methods of issuing warrants to intercept telephone calls (a practice commonly known as 'telephone tapping'). The Report laid down guidelines which included the recommendation that in no circumstances should material obtained by interception be made available to any body or person whatever outside the public service. This recommendation arose in part out of an examination into the circumstances of the Marrinan case.

The Marrinan case

Neville Marrinan was a barrister who, it was alleged, had an improper association with a known criminal. The Home Secretary had issued a warrant to tap the criminal's telephone and some of the intercepted material related to Marrinan. A transcript of the relevant conversation was shown to Sir Hartley Shawcross, then Chairman of the Bar, who was later authorised by the Home Secretary to show the extract to the Bar Council, which was inquiring into Marrinan's conduct. The committee of Privy Councillors being chaired by Lord Birkett unanimously condemned the Home Secretary's decision as mistaken on the grounds that the power given to the Secretary of State to issue an interception warrant is so important that it must be rigorously confined to the purposes which convinced the Home Secretary that it was right to issue the warrant in the first place.

European Court of Human Rights

In 1984, the European Court of Human Rights decided in *Malone* v *United Kingdom* (1984) 7 EHRR 14, that there had been a violation of Article 8 of the

European Convention on Human Rights in relation to the tapping of Malone's telephone. Malone had been prosecuted in 1978 for handling stolen goods and had been acquitted on some counts and, after two disagreements by juries, the prosecution offered no evidence on the remaining counts. Malone then sued the Metropolitan Police Commissioner as a result of it emerging during the first trial that his telephone had been tapped. It was claimed on his behalf that the interception was unlawful, whether or not it occurred on the authority of the Home Secretary, because it was an invasion of privacy and everything said on his telephone was confidential. These arguments found no favour with Sir Robert Megarry VC who held that there was no right of privacy in English law and, despite the fact that telephone tapping had never been authorised by statute, the practice was not illegal because England is not a country where everything is forbidden except that which is expressly permitted.

Malone took his case to the European Court of Human Rights and argued that telephone tapping was contrary to Article 8, which provides that everyone has the right of respect for his private and family life, his home and correspondence. The case for the Government was that the interception had been in accordance with the law, but this argument failed since the UK was unable to indicate any precise legal rules which covered the exercise of the Home Secretary's discretion. The Government was left with no alternative but to introduce the Interception of Communications Act (IOCA) 1985, which legislation currently controls the practice of intercepting letters and telephone calls.

Interception of Communications Act 1985

The scheme of IOCA 1985, in so far as it is relevant to the issue of disclosure, is that under s. 2(1) the Secretary of State may issue a warrant requiring interception of communications in the course of their transmission by means of a public telecommunications system. (Where the system is private, or on the private side of a public system, a warrant is unnecessary and the disclosure and evidential position is quite different, as will be seen below.) The warrant shall not be issued unless the Secretary of State considers that it is necessary either in the interests of national security, or for the purpose of preventing or detecting serious crime, or for the purpose of safeguarding the economic well-being of the country.

Section 6 of the Act provides for the making of arrangements of the extent to which the intercepted material is disclosed, the number of persons to whom it may be disclosed, and the extent to which it may be copied. Importantly, s. 6(3) makes it clear that copies should be destroyed as soon as retention is no longer necessary. The effect of this is that once the intercepted material has been listened to and noted, it must be destroyed. In the case of intercepts in relation to serious crime, there is generally no reason why this should not take place within days of the intercept, with the possible exception of an ongoing inquiry where there may be some justification for retaining the material for a slightly longer period.

In the case of intercepts made in the interests of national security, usually by the security services, there may be a need for a longer period of retention because of the possible enduring nature of a threat to the safety of the nation, but the clear message in the IOCA 1985, and indeed in the earlier reports which have periodically been presented to Parliament, is that the product of an intercept should not be retained for longer than was necessary for the warrant to have been issued in the first place. The decision of the House of Lords in *R v Preston (Stephen)* (1994) 98 Cr App R 405, emphasised that any material generated as a result of a warrant for the prevention or detection of crime should not be kept for the purpose of a prosecution. Many interceptions take place long before a crime is committed and there is every possibility that the material will have been destroyed before the suspect is arrested let alone when the actual prosecution proceedings commence. In so far as the proceedings themselves are concerned, s. 9, IOCA 1985 prevents the use of any intercepted material in the proceedings and forbids cross-examination about the interception or the issue of a warrant.

It will immediately be apparent that the restrictions and inhibitions created by IOCA 1985 are in complete contrast to the common law rules of disclosure. The Act calls for early destruction which would make any question of disclosure impossible, while the common law (and now the CPIA 1996) encourages preservation and revelation of the information by the investigator to the prosecutor. The potential for inconsistency is obvious. If an intercept revealed a proposed meeting, for example, for the exchange of drugs, any record or transcript of the conversation should be destroyed once the information has been noted and acted upon. If arrangements for such a meeting came to the notice of the police via an informant, the police would have to record the information, retain it and (subject to the common law test of materiality or the CPIA 1996 tests being satisfied) place the information before the court. The tensions and conflicts between the evolving common law rules and the IOCA 1985 were the subject of detailed scrutiny by the House of Lords in *Preston*.

R v Preston and Others

Stephen Preston and five co-defendants were convicted at Portsmouth Crown Court of conspiracy to import drugs and were sentenced to terms of imprisonment. The facts of the case were complicated, but the allegation basically was that Preston had been exporting substantial quantities of cannabis from Holland over a period of time and that in 1989 he had organised a 500 kg load. Something went wrong with the arrangements when the load was hi-jacked and he came to London from Amsterdam to put matters right. As the plot developed there were a large number of telephone calls between the defendants which were intercepted. On arrest the defendants did not deny that there had been a conspiracy to import cannabis, but their defence was that they were not part of it. Following conviction, five of the six defendants appealed against conviction and sentence, and their appeals against conviction were dismissed by the Court of Appeal.

The certified questions for the House of Lords ranged over a variety of points of law covering the retention and use of material and information derived from intercepts, the extent to which the fact of an intercept and the results may be disclosed and put in evidence, and the duty of the prosecution in relation to such disclosure. The leading judgment of Lord Mustill deals with a number of important aspects of telephone intercepts made under the IOCA 1985 provisions, and although parts of the judgment are open to more than one interpretation, his observations in relation to disclosure were unequivocal. In answer to suggestions that disclosure should be on the same footing as the developing common law rules laid down in *Ward*, he stated (at p. 433):

> In the end, however, I consider that the very real apprehensions voiced by counsel for the appellants cannot prevail over the plain intent and wording of the Act. The need for surveillance and the need to keep it secret are undeniable. So also is the need to protect to the feasible maximum the privacy of those whose conversations are overheard without their consent. Hence sections 2 and 6. These policies are in flat contradiction to current opinions on the 'transparency' of the trial process. Something has to give way, and the history, structure and terms of the statute leave me in little doubt that this must be the duty to give complete disclosure of unused materials. The result is a vulnerable compromise, but it may be the best that can be achieved. At all events I conclude that it is the one which the statute does achieve. . . .

Intercept materials, therefore, comprise an exception to the general duty of disclosure, a fact which has now been given further statutory recognition by the CPIA 1996 which provides that material need not be disclosed if it has been intercepted in obedience to a warrant issued under s. 2, IOCA 1985, or if it indicates that such a warrant has been issued or that material has been intercepted in obedience to such a warrant. Lord Mustill completed his judgment in *Preston* by saying that he saw nothing in the IOCA 1985 which prevented the prosecution disclosing the fact of an intercept, as distinct from the contents. He conceded that this was unlikely and, in all probability, defence requests of the prosecution for this sort of information are almost certain to be met with a response that will neither confirm or deny that which has been asked for. This obviously leaves defendants who suspect that their telephone has been tapped and believe that some of the intercepted material will assist their defence with a feeling of helplessness.

To some extent, this was recognised in *Preston* when Lord Mustill emphasised the essential function of the investigating and prosecuting authorities, when considering material to which they alone may be privy, to make sure that there is no material which either suggests that the suspicions against the defendant are unfounded or that apparently damaging evidence should be viewed in a more favourable light. Prosecuting counsel plays an indispensable part in that function so in any exceptional case where, for whatever reason, the intercept material has not been destroyed at the time of the prosecution, s. 6, IOCA 1985 should not be interpreted as a prohibition on the surviving material being shown to the prosecuting authority and counsel so that they may satisfy themselves that the case against the defendant can be presented fairly.

In relation to material which has been destroyed, someone in the chain between telephone engineer and prosecuting authority has to satisfy themselves that the prosecution can be fairly presented without the disclosure of any intercepted material to the defence, but as Lord Mustill pointed out (at p. 433), the practical problems are great: 'The decision-maker has to decide whether what he hears may be helpful to a defendant not yet identified, not yet charged in relation to offences not yet determined, and perhaps not even committed, who may raise defences which under current practice can be concealed until the trial is well under way.' At the end of the day, this has always been an area of disclosure where the defence and the courts have had no option but to trust those with responsibility for the prosecution that in a case that goes ahead, there is nothing helpful to the defence that has been concealed or destroyed.

It is worth bearing in mind, however, that in a number cases involving the interception of mail and telephone calls, the real losers are the prosecution who are aware of incriminating evidence but are prevented by IOCA 1985 from adducing it in evidence. As a result there have been calls in recent years for lawfully obtained intercepted material to be admissible in criminal proceedings to aid the fight against organised crime. During the committee stage of the Criminal Justice and Public Order Bill, the Ulster MP, David Trimble, proposed a new clause 60 which would have enabled evidence from telephone intercepts, whether in the form of actual tapes or transcripts, to be admissible in evidence (see Hansard vol. 241 HC Deb, 6th ser., col. 141). He drew parallels between the need to combat terrorist activities and the racketeering legislation introduced in the United States where wire-tap evidence is admissible in prosecutions. After debate the motion and clause were withdrawn, but if any similar provision was introduced in the United Kingdom, or if the IOCA 1985 were to be significantly amended, the current non-disclosure rules would be difficult to justify.

Private telecommunication systems

At the outset of this discussion on the disclosure of telephone intercepts it was stressed that the IOCA 1985 is confined to a public telecommunications system. Conclusions as to where a public telephone system ends and a private system begins were given by Evans LJ in *R* v *Ahmed* (unreported), Court of Appeal, 29 March 1994, and adopted by the House of Lords in *R* v *Effik (Goodwin Eno)* [1994] 3 WLR 583. All that needs to be said here in relation to those authorities is that when interceptions are made on a system which is not public, the IOCA 1985 does not apply and disclosure issues fall to be dealt with in accordance either with the normal common law rules or with the CPIA 1996 (depending on the time the investigation was commenced).

Telephone communications to and from other jurisdictions

There are interesting, but as yet undecided, disclosure issues in relation to telephone intercepts in the 'British Islands' of calls to and from abroad, and also telephone calls made and intercepted abroad. Section 10(2) of the IOCA 1985 was briefly referred to by Lord Oliver of Aymerton in *Effik* (above) as indicating 'that a communication by means of more than one telecommunication system is statutorily, if perhaps somewhat artificially, treated as temporally split in transmission between the various systems through which it may be transmitted'. The disclosure of such intercepts therefore appeared to be covered by the provisions of the IOCA 1985; but what is the position with regard to material intercepted abroad?

Most European countries permit the interception of telephone calls in prescribed circumstances, For example, Germany, France and Italy allow interception and, provided the necessary authority has been obtained, the resulting evidence is admissible in legal proceedings. The position is the same in the USA and Canada. A prosecuting authority in England and Wales has no duty of disclosure in respect of material in the possession of investigative or judicial agencies in another jurisdiction. If, in the course of an international inquiry, transcripts of properly authorised intercepted calls in another country are supplied to the police in this country, are the prosecution obliged to disclose them in criminal proceedings or are they protected from disclosure in the same way that the IOCA 1985 prevents disclosure? Although the transcripts may be admissible evidence in another jurisdiction, the disclosure rules in that jurisdiction are certain to be very different from the common law rules in England and Wales. As a matter of courtesy, material gathered abroad ought not to be freely disclosed without the consent of the relevant authority, but if the transcripts reveal information of relevance to the issues in the criminal proceedings or of potential assistance to the defence, the duty of disclosure would appear to override judicial comity.

OTHER STATUTORY GROUNDS FOR NON-DISCLOSURE

A number of statutes preserve confidentiality by prohibiting disclosure of information, either on general grounds or in specific circumstances. It is invariably the case, however, that any restriction on disclosure does not prevent the disclosure of information for the purpose of criminal proceedings. For example, information furnished for the purpose of the Legal Aid Act 1988, the disclosure of which is generally restricted, may be disclosed for the purposes of criminal proceedings for an offence under the Act (s. 38(3)); and the general restriction on disclosure of information with respect to a particular business under the Fair Trading Act 1973 does not apply in relation to legal proceedings (s. 133(3)). The primary reason for such provisions is to enable criminal proceedings to be instituted for offences against the statutes, in which case the information supplied would probably constitute part of the evidence against the accused. In the highly unlikely situation of the information being 'unused' in the context of a prosecution, the provisions would appear to allow disclosure to the defence.

The disclosure of information normally covered by secrecy under the Taxes Management Act 1970 is specifically catered for by s. 3, Criminal Justice Act 1987. The Inland Revenue may disclose such information to the SFO for the purpose of a prosecution conducted by the SFO for an offence relating to the Inland Revenue, and the SFO may make further disclosure to the CPS or to the DPP for Northern Ireland for any prosecution they have instituted for an Inland Revenue offence. The disclosure having been made under the provisions of s. 3, any further disclosure to the defence presumably falls to be dealt with under the usual common law rules or the CPIA 1996. In view of the obligation of secrecy under the Taxes Management Act 1970, it may be necessary to involve the court in a PII application notwithstanding the prosecution's ability to disclose information voluntarily.

There are no reported cases which involve disclosure difficulties in relation to personal data held under the Data Protection Act 1984. It appears as though the exemptions to the non-disclosure provisions in ss. 27 and 34 are wide enough to permit the disclosure of data for the purpose of criminal proceedings. The police are a data user holding information which may be relevant for the prosecution of a data subject. When questions of disclosure arise in proceedings involving more than one accused, it is possible to envisage circumstances when the personal data of one accused will have to be disclosed to a co-accused, but that in itself should not provide a bar to the prosecution disclosing relevant material in accordance with the common law rules. In cases of unusual difficulty, it may be prudent for the prosecution to seek guidance from the court.

CONFIDENTIALITY

General

Public interest immunity and statutory exclusions provide legal grounds for the non-disclosure of relevant evidence. Is confidentiality *per se* sufficient reason for the prosecution refusing to disclose documents? Despite a number of earlier authorities which indicated that it is not, an argument that confidentiality may provide immunity was advanced in the House of Lords in *D* v *NSPCC* [1977] 1 All ER 589. The submission was encouraged by the dissenting judgment of Lord Denning MR in the earlier Court of Appeal hearing ([1976] 2 All ER 993) and the report of the Law Reform Committee on Privilege in Civil Proceedings (Cmnd 3472, London: HMSO, 1967, para. 1) which found 'a wide discretion [in the court] to permit a witness, whether a party to the proceedings or not, to refuse to disclose information where disclosure would be a breach of some ethical or social value and non-disclosure would be unlikely to result in serious injustice in the particular case in which it is claimed'.

The argument did not find favour with any of their Lordships in *D* v *NSPCC*, and the position was summed up by Lord Hailsham of St Marylebone (at p. 604):

Lord Denning MR, in his dissenting judgment places his own reasoning on the pledge of confidentiality given by the appellants, and seeks to found the immunity on this pledge. I do not think that confidentiality by itself gives any ground for immunity (*cf*, e.g. *per* Lord Cross of Chelsea in *Alfred Crompton*

Amusement Machines Ltd v *Customs and Excise Comrs (No. 2)* [1973] 2 All ER 1169 at page 1184). Confidentiality is not a separate head of immunity. There are, however, cases where confidentiality is itself a public interest and one of these is where information is given to an authority charged with the enforcement and administration of the law by the initiation of court proceedings. This is one of those cases, whether the recipient of the information be the police, the local authority or the appellants. Whether there be other cases, and what these may be, must fall to be decided from time to time. The categories of public interest are not closed, and must alter from time to time whether by restriction or extension as social conditions and social legislation develop.

Confidentiality is not a separate head of privilege from disclosure, neither are confidential documents, in themselves, immune from production. Nevertheless, confidentiality is significant in support of a claim for PII where the public interest to be protected is, for example, the effective functioning of the police or an authority with responsibility for the welfare of children. How then does this affect the prosecution's duty of disclosure in cases where the confidences in question are not those of an informant giving information to the public service?

Medical confidentiality

The prosecution are hardly ever faced with the disclosure of confidences made by a confessor to a priest. Banking confidences can often be circumvented by the service of a witness summons. But the most common, and perhaps the most difficult, area of confidentiality is that between doctor and patient. Medical evidence features in a large number of prosecutions. At one end on the scale of seriousness of offence is the divisional surgeon who attends the police station either to take a blood sample or to attend to minor injuries; while at the other end is the doctor who examines a rape victim or the specialist instructed to give an expert opinion.

The British Medical Association (BMA) and the Association of Police Surgeons have expressed concerns over possible conflicts between the confidentiality of the doctor/patient relationship and the prosecution's duty of disclosure which may involve allowing the defence to see working notes made by a doctor. The Hippocratic Oath forbids doctors to divulge confidences and General Medical Council guidance makes it clear that doctors have a duty not to disclose to third parties information that they have learned in their professional capacity. The tensions experienced by medical practitioners are readily apparent.

The potential problems were illustrated by a case at the Central Criminal Court in 1994, where the trial judge ordered medical notes on a rape victim to be disclosed. These allegedly revealed that she had claimed to have been raped a number of times before, sometimes in bizarre circumstances. The prosecution discontinued the case, apparently because the information raised doubts about the credibility of the witness. On the assumption that these details were accurate, the order made by the trial judge seems entirely reasonable as the information was relevant to a defence of consent. Indeed, if the prosecution had been aware of the situation, it is questionable whether a prosecution would have been brought in the first place — at least, not until they had been satisfied as to the credibility and truthfulness of the witness. Circumstances such as these show how proper disclosure lessens the possibility of a miscarriage of justice. There will be other occasions, however, where the disclosure of confidential information is unwarranted and embarrassing to patient and doctor alike, and is neither necessary nor justified in the interest of justice.

It is good clinical practice for doctors to obtain medical and personal details from a victim of crime before commencing an examination. They need to know something about the person concerned and need to build a relationship of trust and confidence before embarking on what may be an intimate and sensitive examination. The witness may reveal details of sexual experiences and physical or psychiatric disorders which are then recorded by the doctor. The doctor's notes are not covered by legal privilege and are potentially disclosable. Doctors are naturally reluctant to reveal them to anyone, including the police and CPS, so the carrying out of any sort of materiality test by the prosecution is difficult. The BMA criticises 'fishing expeditions' by the defence who hope that information may come to light which may help to discredit a witness, but the anxieties of the medical profession are in contrast with those of defence practitioners who feel that judges are often too reluctant to order the disclosure of material which may be of potential assistance to their clients. As with so many disclosure situations there is no easy solution, but what does seem clear is that if relevance of the files or notes can be established, confidentiality in itself is no justification for non-disclosure. Courts must respect confidences and must ensure that the confidential information is both relevant and admissible. Once these hurdles have been overcome, however, the interests of justice demand disclosure of the information.

The question of the disclosure of medical notes generated much debate in the report stage of the Criminal Procedure and Investigations Bill (see Hansard vol. 569 HL Deb, 5th ser., coll. 48–50). Because the CPIA 1996 narrows the range of disclosable material and also confines the duty to the investigator and prosecutor, the Government view was that doctor/patient confidential information would be protected. While it must be the case that a doctor is not charged with the duty of conducting a criminal investigation (which is restricted to police officers by the definition in s. 22, CPIA 1996), and is not, therefore, subject to the disclosure code, if information exists that undermines the credibility of a prosecution witness or assists the defence case, such information is disclosable. 'Material given in confidence' is listed in the disclosure code as an example of sensitive material and, as such, it may be necessary to involve the court in an application before disclosure is made. However, it is difficult to conceive of circumstances where information which truly undermines the prosecution case should be withheld from the accused on the grounds of medical confidentiality.

Counselling and psychotherapeutic confidentiality

The problems in relation to counselling and confidentiality have already been alluded to in chapter 5. Counselling and therapy have attracted little judicial attention in England and Wales, particularly in criminal proceedings, but in America — where analysis and psychotherapy are far more a part of everyday life — the legal system of each state includes some form of psychotherapist privilege. At the time of writing, the Supreme Court of the United States is shortly to consider in a civil action whether, when a patient consults a psychotherapist, the communications can be revealed to the court. In a major criminal trial in California, where two brothers were charged with murdering their parents, the main evidence came from a confession by one of the accused to his psychologist some months after the event. The psychologist's girlfriend overheard the admission and notified the police. In the subsequent trial, the judge ordered the production of the tape-recorded notes of the therapeutic sessions.

The USA is not the only country where courts have been called upon to weigh confidentiality against the need for disclosure in the interests of a fair trial. In Canada there is developing case law surrounding the disclosure of witnesses' psychiatric records and the records of rape crisis centres. In England and Wales, under the common law rules and the CPIA 1996, if information relevant to the issues in the case came to the notice of the prosecution, it would fall for disclosure. Whether it would be voluntarily drawn to the attention of the police is another matter.

Confidentiality of disclosed information

This is now provided for in ss. 17 and 18, CPIA 1996 and is dealt with in chapter 16.

LEGAL PROFESSIONAL PRIVILEGE

Principle

> The only profession that I know which is given a privilege from disclosing information to a court of law is the legal profession, and then it is not the privilege of the lawyer but of his client . . . (*per* Lord Denning in *Attorney-General* v *Mulholland* [1963] 1 All ER 767 (at p. 771)

Thus, confidential communications passing between clients and their legal advisers need not be given in evidence and, without the consent of the clients, may not be disclosed. The privilege is that of the client and it may be waived by the client either before the hearing, which allows for the disclosure of the communication, or by the use of the documents in court, for example during cross-examination.

In addition to waiver, the authorities indicate that legal professional privilege does not apply in three types of circumstances. First, communications to facilitate crime or fraud (see *R* v *Cox and Railton* (1884) 14 QBD 153; and s. 10(2), PACE 1984 as explained in *R* v *Central Criminal Court, ex parte Francis and Francis* [1988] 3 All ER 775); secondly, in relation to facts discovered or observed in the course of the lawyer/client relationship; and, thirdly, when the information in question tends to establish innocence.

It is beyond the scope of this book to consider the development and technicalities of the privilege in greater detail, but it is relevant to consider whether legal professional privilege has any impact on the ever-widening demands of pre-trial disclosure. Possible conflicts arise when there are solicitor/client communications held by a witness for the prosecution; privileged documents held or created by the prosecuting authority itself; similar documents held by the solicitor to a police authority (which is not the prosecuting authority as a result of the Prosecution of Offences Act 1985); and privileged documents held by the legal advisers to one defendant which are material to the defence of the co-defendant. Each of these will be considered in turn.

Privilege and a prosecution witness

If a witness for the prosecution holds privileged documents, the witness is no more than a third party to the proceedings and the prosecution have no duty of disclosure in relation to material that is not in their possession, i.e. the possession of the investigator or the prosecuting authority. If a summons is served on the witness, then he or she may raise the claim of legal professional privilege in refusing to produce the documents. This is what happened in *R* v *Barton* [1972] 2 All ER 1192, where the defendant was charged with fraudulent conversion and other offences of dishonesty alleged to have been committed in the course of his employment as a legal executive with a firm of solicitors. A partner of the firm was a witness for the prosecution, upon whom a notice to produce had been served in respect of documents which had come into existence in the solicitor's office for the purpose of the administration or winding-up of estates. Upon a claim of privilege, Caulfield J held (at p. 1194):

> If there are documents in the possession or control of a solicitor which, on production, help to further the defence of an accused man, then in my judgment no privilege attaches. I cannot conceive that our law would permit a solicitor or other person to screen from a jury information which, if disclosed to the jury, would perhaps enable a man either to establish his innocence or to resist an allegation made by the Crown.

Caulfield J's decision was not supported by authority other than his belief that natural justice demanded the production of the documents, and he was careful to make it clear that his judgment was restricted to the facts of the particular case. It has now been held to have been wrongly decided and was overruled by the House of Lords decision in *R* v *Derby Magistrates' Court, ex parte B* [1995] 3 WLR 681, which held that a defendant could not obtain a witness summons to compel production by a prosecution witness of proofs of evidence and attendance notes recording the witness's factual instructions to his solicitor where the witness had not waived legal professional privilege. The magistrates had sought to equate the prosecution's duty of disclosure with their own duty to issue a summons under s. 97, Magistrates' Courts Act 1980, and they were held to have acted wrongly. Section 97 is limited to the production of documents which are admissible *per se*. In the instant case they would be admissible for cross-examination purposes only once the witness had given evidence inconsistent with the account in the documents. There must remain, however, the possibility, albeit remote, of material in existence which may assist the defence case, yet the accused has no means of gaining access to it — something described by the House of Lords as a 'procedural impasse'. Not only is the accused faced with this technical obstacle but the difference in approach to disclosure between legal professional privilege and PII, while understandable from their historical development, is difficult to justify in practice.

If any privileged documents found their way into the possession of the prosecution and the witness indicated a waiver of the privilege, steps for disclosure would be taken in the usual way. In practice, however, such documents are unlikely to be revealed to the police or prosecutor before the trial and consequently fall outside the ambit of the prosecution's duty.

Privilege and the prosecuting authority

The CPS is not in a lawyer/client relationship with the police. The functions of the DPP are defined in s. 3, Prosecution of Offences Act 1985; and while these include a duty to give advice to police forces on all matters relating to criminal offences, the police are not the clients of the DPP. Legal professional privilege does not apply to communications between the police and CPS. This was made clear in *Evans* v *Chief Constable of Surrey* [1988] 1 QB 588, although such communications may, in some circumstances, attract PII (see chapter 10).

The relationship of the CPS (or that of any other prosecuting authority) with prosecuting counsel is such that privilege will apply to communications between them. These will include instructions to counsel; an advice or opinion received from counsel together with documents assembled for the purpose of obtaining advice; notes of conferences, etc. The privilege is that of the prosecuting authority which may waive it in appropriate circumstances, no doubt after informing counsel and seeking his or her views on the question of waiver.

What circumstances are likely to cause the prosecuting authority to waive privilege? Questions of legal professional privilege often arise in tandem with documents which attract PII. If, for example, there are communications with the police which are covered by PII on a class basis, an order for disclosure will usually result in waiver of other communications covered by legal privilege. When appeals are heard many years after the event, it is the practice of the Crown to offer as much assistance as possible in providing relevant information and it is not without precedent that prosecuting counsel's notes and opinions are made available. This involves a waiver of privilege before disclosure takes place. A more difficult decision to waive privilege may arise in the rare instance of a conference where information comes to light which could assist the defence. If an expert provided a gloss on his report or statement, or a police officer provided new information which was inconsistent with the prosecution evidence or of potential help to the defence, disclosure in some shape or form would be necessary. If this could not be effected by further statements, the waiver of privilege over conference notes may be called for. Such occurrences are exceptional, but a prosecutor must never stand on privilege in order to withhold relevant material information from the defence.

Privilege and the police authority solicitor

While the CPS is not in a lawyer/client relationship with the police, different considerations apply to the solicitor for a police authority. Most police forces have their own solicitor's department to provide them with legal advice and act on their behalf in civil claims. In these circumstances, the privilege is that of the chief constable, who may be obliged to consider waiver in certain circumstances. For example, officers may be giving evidence against a defendant in criminal proceedings while running parallel to those proceedings is a civil action being defended by the chief constable. Any statements made in connection with the civil action are covered by legal professional privilege, but if they revealed material discrepancies with the evidence to be adduced in the criminal proceedings, disclosure of the inconsistencies would be necessary. In practice, this is unlikely to arise at the criminal trial stage as the criminal proceedings will precede any civil action and the making of statements for that purpose; but disclosure may come into play at the appeal stage where the trial issues and the grounds of appeal are known and preparations for the civil action further advanced. Where there are a number of civil actions arising out of allegations of impropriety by several officers who may have given evidence in a number of criminal cases when some defendants have been convicted and others acquitted, disclosure issues in relation to privileged documents becomes more than a theoretical consideration.

It is arguable that the solicitor to the police authority, who is acting on behalf of the chief constable, is part of 'the prosecution' for the purposes of disclosure and therefore has a conflict of interests. On the one hand there is a duty to reveal relevant documents to the prosecuting authority, and on the other legal professional privilege which militates against disclosure. Such a conflict would have to be resolved on a case by case basis depending on the circumstances, but it would be quite wrong for a chief constable to use privilege as a reason for not disclosing material information which could result in the conviction of an innocent person.

Privilege and the co-accused

The disclosure of documents in the possession of a solicitor acting for an accused which may be of help to a co-accused raises difficult issues concerning legal professional privilege, but they have nothing to with the prosecution's duty of disclosure as such documents are highly unlikely to come into the possession of the prosecution. *R v Ataou* [1988] 2 All ER 32, considered the position where defendants had originally shared the same solicitor but had later changed representation because of a conflict of interests. It emerged that an attendance note of an interview with the defendant who now had new solicitors showed a different account of his evidence from that given in court. It was disclosed to counsel representing the defendant affected by it, but the judge refused to allow cross-examination on the grounds of privilege. On appeal this was held to be wrong, but the Court of Appeal went further and said that the judge must conduct a balancing exercise to decide whether the legitimate interest of the defendant seeking to breach the privilege outweighs that of the client seeking to maintain it.

There was a danger that this decision would herald the introduction of a balancing exercise into questions of legal professional privilege, in a similar way to that conducted in PII applications. This appears to have been removed as a result of *R v Derby Magistrates, ex parte B* (above) which overruled *Ataou*. Their Lordships held that the witness's right to claim privilege was not to be weighed against the public interest in securing that all relevant evidence was to be made available to the defence. Legal professional privilege was a fundamental condition on which the administration of justice as a whole rested and no exception should be allowed to its absolute nature.

There will be few occasions when legal professional privilege threatens to stand in the way of the prosecution's duty of disclosure. Some of the situations posited above are exceptional, but it is important to recognise that conflicts of duties can arise. As a general principle, though, fairness demands that where issues of legal professional privilege arise, the privilege should not be maintained if it means that relevant information is not disclosed.

12 Remedies for Disclosure Irregularities

The remedies for non-disclosure and other disclosure irregularities, such as partial or delayed disclosure, are considered in three stages: first, action open to the court of trial to ensure that disclosure is dealt with in a full and timely manner and what sanctions may be imposed on the Crown in respect of its failures, including a stay of proceedings as an abuse of process; secondly, the availability of judicial review to challenge the decisions of the prosecution and/or court in relation to disclosure issues; and, thirdly, non-disclosure or incomplete disclosure as a ground of appeal.

Most of the discussion in this chapter relates to the common law remedies for irregularities. Although the same remedies are, of course, available under the new statutory regime, the type of irregularity, i.e. failure to comply with the requirements of the CPIA 1996, will generate a new body of case law. Non-compliance with the disclosure provisions of the CPIA 1996 is dealt with in detail in chapter 16. Broadly speaking, s. 11 gives sanctions for faults in disclosure by the accused and time limits for defence disclosure have been provided in regulations made under the Act. Section 10 provides for the prosecutor's failure to observe time limits, especially in relation to grounds for an abuse of process. The relevant time limits are given in the transitional provisions of s. 13 as no period has been prescribed by the regulations for prosecution disclosure.

This chapter also looks at the role of the European Court of Human Rights in the light of a recent case on non-disclosure that was referred to it by the European Commission on Human Rights.

TRIAL REMEDIES

Pre-trial hearings

Since the enlarging of the disclosure rules prompted by the decision in *Ward*, courts have often heard applications on behalf of the defence for more full disclosure by the prosecution or for the provision of copy documents where they have not been supplied with photocopies following inspection. An order made by a trial judge will be complied with by the prosecution unless, in exceptional circumstances, it is decided to discontinue the proceedings; for example, where the prosecution feel unable to comply with an order to disclose sensitive material following a *Davis, Johnson and Rowe* hearing.

As a result of *Practice Direction (Crown Court: Plea and Directions Hearings)* (1995) *The Times*, 31 July 1995, handed down by Lord Taylor LCJ on 27 July 1995, plea and directions hearings are held in contested cases and the prosecution and defence are expected to assist the judge in relation to keys issues. Questions of disclosure often feature prominently at such hearings, and failures to comply with orders may well result in financial sanctions by way of costs orders. Preparatory hearings, already a feature of complex fraud cases, are now more widely available in circumstances prescribed by the provisions of Part III, CPIA 1996 which came into force on 15 April 1997. Section 35(1) of the Act allows an appeal to the Court of Appeal against a ruling made at a preparatory hearing by a judge on any question of admissibility of evidence or other question of law relating to the case. The appeal lies only with the leave of the judge or the Court of Appeal, and the practice and procedure for such appeals is given in the Criminal Procedure and Investigations Act 1996 (Preparatory Hearings) (Interlocutory Appeals) Rules 1997 (SI 1997 No. 1053).

Whether the new provisions will allow appeals on disclosure issues is not altogether clear. The Court of Appeal came to 'a very clear conclusion that we have no jurisdiction to entertain the appeal' in *R* v *Kevin Maxwell* (unreported), Court of Appeal, 9 February 1995, transcript 94/7352/S2. The appeal was against Philips J's refusal to order the SFO to disclose documents in the hands of others for which the SFO had obtained an order under s. 2, Criminal Justice Act 1987 but which it had not enforced. The provisions of s. 35 are very close to those in s. 7 of the Criminal Justice Act 1987, and while there was some dispute in the *Maxwell* case that the application constituted a preparatory hearing, other more straightforward disclosure matters (such as the location of an observation post or the identity of an informant) may be construed as issues which are likely to be material to the verdict of the jury.

Costs

If the court is satisfied that the defence have incurred costs as a result of an unnecessary or improper act or omission in relation to disclosure matters, it may make an order that the Crown must pay those costs under s. 19, Prosecution of Offences Act 1985; if the act or omission of a Crown Prosecutor or prosecuting counsel is held to be improper, unreasonable or negligent, a wasted costs order under s. 19A of the same Act may be made. An award of costs against the prosecution for an unnecessary adjournment caused by a failure to disclose is an effective remedy. Contrary to popular belief, prosecution costs are not limitless and public prosecutors are accountable for budgets which are eroded by orders to pay costs as a result of prosecution failings.

There do not appear to be any reported cases of a s. 19A order being made against an individual prosecutor or counsel, and this is not surprising as most delays in disclosing material are caused by the machinery of prosecution breaking down rather than by individual acts of negligence. On the other hand, there are reported instances of wasted costs orders being made against the defence in relation to disclosure. In *Re Ronald A. Prior & Co. Solicitors* (unreported), Court of Appeal, 16 June 1995, transcript 94/2537/S1, the solicitors were ordered to pay costs in favour of a local authority which attended an application after being told that a witness summons would be served in order to obtain production of files relating to the complainant in a criminal case who was in the authority's care. It was held that the application was speculative and the definition of criminal proceedings was wide enough to include proceedings relating to the issue of a witness summons. In the circumstances, the local authority was a party to criminal proceedings and was entitled to costs.

Section 78 of the Police and Criminal Evidence Act 1984

Section 78, PACE 1984 may be utilised to prevent unfairness arising out of disclosure failures by the prosecution. This important provision of PACE 1984 allows the court to refuse to admit prosecution evidence if it would have such an adverse effect on the fairness of the proceedings. A feature in *Archbold News* (see Roberts, Paul, 'Remedies for Non-disclosure after *Ward*' (1994) 9 *Archbold News* 5) argued that the prosecution could be prevented from introducing undisclosed material at the trial in exercise of the court's power under s. 78. It is difficult, however, to imagine why the prosecution would wish to introduce undisclosed material, which by its very nature is not material worthy of adduction as part of the Crown case, unless circumstances arose in which the prosecution wished to cross-examine on the basis of such documents (but see criticisms of using this method of rebuttal in *Sansom* and *Phillipson* in chapter 4). It is considered that s. 78 is more likely to come into play when the prosecution try to adduce admissible evidence, such as a confession, but the non-disclosure of material which may have put the defence on inquiry to challenge the confession has caused unfairness. For example, if there was failure to disclose that the defendant had been seen by a doctor and prescribed medication before an interview. In these circumstances, the confession and not the unused material may be ruled out under s. 78.

Abuse of process

It has been known for a trial to be stayed as an abuse of process as a result of non-disclosure by the prosecution. In *R v Birmingham* [1992] Crim LR 117, His Honour Judge Bromley QC, sitting at Wood Green Crown Court, took the extraordinary course of ordering a stay because of the absence of a video tape which might have thrown light on an incident of violent disorder outside a night club. Before the jury were sworn, the judge heard evidence that a video camera had been trained on part of the scene of the disturbance and that the tape had been viewed by police officers in the case. Despite requests from the defence solicitor to the CPS, the existence of the tape had not been revealed by the police to the CPS, and by the time of the trial it had disappeared. Judge Bromley ruled that the indictment would be stayed on the grounds that the continuation of the case would constitute a misuse of the process of the court and a fair trial would not be possible. He further ordered that two-thirds of the costs were to be paid by the CPS.

Although the law on abuse of process is almost as large a growth industry as that in disclosure, and was still in a stage of evolution in 1992, the decision does not appear to be justified on the general principles of what amounts to an abuse of process. Abuse of process was defined in *Hui Chi-ming* v *R* [1992] 1 AC 34, as something so unfair and wrong that the court should not allow a prosecutor to proceed with what is in all other respects a regular proceeding. A stay should be exercised only in a clear case where a defendant has suffered prejudice as a result of delay, or where the prosecution have manipulated or misused the process of the court so as to deprive a defendant of a protection provided by the law or to take advantage of a technicality (see judgment of Sir Roger Ormrod in *R* v *Derby Crown Court, ex parte Brooks* (1984) 80 Cr App R 164). Although defence requests in *Birmingham* for information had not been responded to promptly, there was no evidence that the trial had been substantially deferred in order to bring the matter within the category of prejudice suffered by delay.

Misuse of process is normally concerned with the institution of proceedings: for example, being prosecuted more than once (see *Connelly* v *DPP* (1964) 48 Cr App R 183); escaping statutory time limits (see *R* v *Brentford Justices, ex parte Wong* (1981) 73 Cr App R 67); improper motive (see *R* v *Horseferry Road Magistrates' Court, ex parte Stephenson* (1989) *The Times*, 25 January 1989); or improper choice of charge (see *R* v *Canterbury and St Augustine Justices, ex parte Klisiak* [1981] 2 All ER 129). According to the commentary on *Birmingham* ([1992] Crim LR 117, at p. 118), the judge's initial view was that the issue of non-disclosure was a matter for the trial but he was persuaded otherwise by defence counsel. He apparently rejected the decision in *R* v *Heston-Francois* [1984] 1 QB 278, that the matters should be considered by a jury and presumably sought to extend the principle that a police failure to disclose material of potential assistance to the defence was misconduct by the prosecution. If this was the case, it is submitted that the learned judge was wrong and that the proper approach to non-disclosure as a possible abuse of process is that given in *DPP* v *Hussain* (1994) *The Times*, 1 June 1994.

This case stated arose out of something of a storm in a tea cup, when the police were ordered by justices to disclose the telephone number of the victim which the prosecution had sought to withhold as being sensitive information. When the defence representative requested a copy of the document containing the telephone number, he was offered only supervised access at the police station and was denied a photocopy. As he could not attend the police station he applied for the case to be dismissed at the next hearing, and was probably just as surprised as the prosecutor when the application was allowed and the proceedings for common assault stayed. The DPP appealed successfully against the order, with Alliott J stating that an application for a stay should never succeed when there were other methods of achieving a fair hearing. The exceptional nature of a stay on the grounds of an abuse of process had been emphasised in *Attorney-General's Reference (No. 1 of 1990)* [1992] QB 630, and where, as in the present case, there was no evidence that the appellant had been prejudiced, such an order was not justified. The exceptional nature of justices dismissing a case as an abuse of process has also been emphasised in *R v Haringey Justices, ex parte DPP* [1996] Crim LR 327.

In *Birmingham* there was no evidence that the defendants had been prejudiced by the missing video tape; there was only the possibility that the tape might have revealed something to their advantage. This could have been explored in the course of the trial with the police officers and club management being cross-examined about the whereabouts of the tape and, with regard to those officers who had viewed it, what it contained. If the jury had considered that the police explanation was unsatisfactory or that there was a more sinister motive for the disappearance of the tape, they would surely have reflected their concerns in their verdict. It is hoped that *Birmingham* will not be followed unless the exceptional criteria stressed by Alliott J in *Hussain* are clearly established.

Section 10(2), CPIA 1996 provides that a failure by the prosecutor to observe disclosure time limits does not on its own constitute grounds for staying the proceedings as an abuse of process. Section 10(3), however, makes it clear that a stay is permissible if the prosecutor's failure involves delay to the extent that the accused is denied a fair trial (see further chapter 16).

JUDICIAL REVIEW

No power of judicial review in matters relating to trial on indictment

There is no power to seek judicial review of an order made by a Crown Court judge either to disclose information or that material should be withheld. Such an order would clearly be a matter relating to trial on indictment and s. 29(3), Supreme Court Act 1981 prevents the High Court from making orders of mandamus, prohibition or certiorari. Thus, the prosecution have no effective remedy for challenging a judge's decision (unless it falls within the circumstances prescribed by s. 35(1), CPIA 1996) and they must either comply with the judge's order or, in exceptional circumstances, abandon the proceedings. Defendants must await conviction before raising the disclosure order as a ground of appeal.

The absence of jurisdiction to seek judicial review by virtue of s. 29(3) of the 1981 Act also extends to an order for a preliminary inspection of social services' files on prosecution witnesses by legal representatives in order to assist the court on what documents should be disclosed. This was held in *R v Chester Crown Court, ex parte Cheshire County Council* [1996] Crim LR 336, where the applicant County Council sought judicial review of the judge's order but was refused on jurisdictional grounds. Its argument that s. 29(3) did not apply because the judge's order was in excess of jurisdiction, was rejected by the Divisional Court.

Power to challenge decisions of magistrates' courts

Judicial review is, of course, available in relation to decisions made by magistrates' courts where the High Court has jurisidiction by the prerogative orders to control the way justices exercise their jurisdiction and to correct fundamental irregularities in their proceedings. For example, in *R v Dunmow Justices, ex parte Nash* (1993) 157 JP 1153, the Divisional Court were asked to consider whether it was open to a magistrates' court to make an order directing the prosecution to make disclosure. It was held that it was not; where the prosecution have not dealt with disclosure fully or have been dilatory in the supply of information to the detriment of the defence case, the proper course is for the magistrates to order an adjournment.

Where a failure to disclose a potentially helpful witness statement amounted to procedural unfairness and led to a flawed conviction, the Divisional Court held in *R v Peterborough Justices, ex parte Dowler* (1996) *The Times*, 24 May 1996, that such an irregularity could be cured by following the normal appeal procedures to the Crown Court under the Magistrates' Courts Act 1980. The prosecution would rectify the irregularity by disclosing the statement before the retrial without any need for an application for judicial review.

Breaches of the rules of natural justice

Judicial review is most commonly exercised in criminal proceedings by quashing a conviction where there has been an excess of jurisdiction or a breach of the rules of natural justice. As regards the latter, it is well established that while the Divisional Court may not order a new trial merely on the ground that fresh evidence which might have affected the outcome had been discovered after the trial, where there has been a defect or irregularity at the trial which vitiated the proceedings an order of certiorari is appropriate) see *R v West Sussex Quarter Sessions, ex parte Albert and Maud Johnson Trust Ltd* [1973] 3 All ER 289). This was taken a stage further in *R v Leyland Magistrates, ex parte Hawthorn* [1979] 1 All ER 209, where the applicant was convicted by justices for driving without due care and attention but the prosecution had failed to supply the names of two further witnesses who had not been called at the trial. Hawthorn sought an order of certiorari to quash the conviction on the grounds that the failure to provide the information amounted to a breach of the rules of natural justice. The Divisional Court had little difficulty in concluding that the prosecution had been at fault in failing to notify the defence of the existence of the additional witnesses. They had more difficulty, though, in deciding whether there was jurisdiction to grant an order of certiorari; but Lord Widgery CJ eventually concluded (at p. 211):

> However, if fraud, collusion, perjury and such like matters not affecting the tribunal themselves justify an application for certiorari to quash the conviction,

if all those matters are to have effect, then we cannot say that the failure of the prosecutor which in this case has prevented the tribunal from giving the defendant a fair trial should not rank in the same category.

We have come to the conclusion that there was here a clear denial of natural justice. Fully recognising the fact that the blame falls on the prosecutor and not on the tribunal, we think that it is a matter which should result in the conviction being quashed. .

This reasoning has been followed in other cases which have featured disclosure issues. In *R* v *Knightsbridge Crown Court, ex parte Goonatilleke* [1986] QB 1, a conviction for shoplifting was quashed because the defence had not been told that the principal prosecution witness had a previous conviction for wasting police time; while in *R* v *Liverpool Crown Court, ex parte Roberts* [1986] Crim LR 622, the failure to disclose a report by a police officer which suggested that an assault may have been accidental, also led to the quashing of a conviction. In each case justice had been denied to the convicted defendant and certiorari was held to be the appropriate remedy.

At first sight it may seem strange that certiorari should be available to quash a conviction where it is not the tribunal deciding upon guilt (the magistrates' court) which has acted irregularly but the other party to the proceedings (the prosecutor) who has breached the rules of natural justice. Lord Bridge was somewhat troubled by this point in *R* v *Secretary of State for the Home Department, ex parte Al-Mehdawi* [1990] 1 AC 876, which concerned an appeal by an immigrant against the refusal of the Home Office to vary his leave to stay in this country. He explained the justificiation for the decision in *ex parte Hawthorn* in the following way, at (p. 894):

Though I do not question the correctness of the decision in *ex parte Hawthorn* . . . , I do question whether it is correctly classified as a case depending on either procedural impropriety or a breach of the rules of natural justice. Certainly there was unfairness in the conduct of the proceedings, but this was because of a failure by the prosecutor, in breach of a duty owed to the court and to the defence, to disclose the existence of witnesses who could have given evidence favourable to the defence. Although no dishonesty was suggested, it was this *suppresso veri* which had the same effect as a *suggestio falsi* in distorting and vitiating the process leading to conviction, and it was, in my opinion, the analogy which Lord Widgery CJ drew between the case before him and the cases of fraud, collusion and perjury, which had been relied on in counsel's argument, which identified the true principle on which the decision could be justified.

Judicial review of decision of prosecutor

It seems, therefore, that if a convicted defendant can demonstrate that the prosecution suppressed the truth by failing to disclose material information, which led to the vitiation of the proceedings leading to conviction, an order for certiorari resulting in the quashing of the conviction will be the outcome. However, can a defendant pursue an alternative course and challenge the prosecutor in relation to a failure to disclose? This was the jurisdictional issue facing the Divisional Court in *R v Crown Prosecution Service, ex parte Warby* [1984] Crim LR 281, where the applicant sought judicial review of the CPS refusal to disclose certain unused material. He contended that the CPS had failed to disclose the material before the date of committal proceedings and had failed to identify the category of material in the possession of the prosecution, and he sought an order of mandamus to compel the CPS to disclose the material to him. Watkins LJ was of the opinion (at p. 8, transcript CO/337/93) that '. . . this application is not only misconceived, but it is doubtful that this court has jurisdiction to determine it'. In so far as the substantive point was concerned, it was held that it was entirely inappropriate for decisions as to disclosure of unused material to be taken at the magistrates' court (see also *R v Liverpool City Magistrates, ex parte DPP* (unreported), Divisional Court, 19 July 1996), but Watkins LJ considered that there was ample authority to the effect that the CPS decision was not reviewable.

Mann LJ came to a similar conclusion in *R v Director of the Serious Fraud Office, ex parte Kevin Maxwell* (unreported), Divisional Court CO/2312/92, 6 October 1992, where the applicant sought orders of mandamus requiring the SFO to supply advance information under r. 4, Magistrates' Courts (Advance Information) Rules 1985 and to disclose unused material. Mann LJ's immediate response (at p. 8, transcript CO/2312/92) was: 'I say at once that I entertain grave doubt as to whether rule 4 is enforceable by an order of manadamus. The scheme of the rules is that if no statement is furnished then the magistrates are to adjourn the proceedings.' In relation to the provision of unused material before transfer, he drew attention to the fact that no authority had been cited for a mandatory order in advance of the procedures for a preparatory hearing at the Crown Court and was of the view that it was not arguable that mandamus could precede those procedures. The Divisional Court were prepared to assume, for the purposes of the application, however, that mandamus would lie to enforce r. 4 and then dismissed the application.

It is submitted that the reservations expressed in *ex parte Warby* and *ex parte Maxwell* are correct. There was no authority in support of the intervention of the High Court to question the exercise of the prosecutor's discretion under the *A-G's Guidelines*, let alone any authority to compel a prosecuting authority to make disclosure of material.

There have been attempts in recent years to seek judicial review of decisions taken by the CPS. For example, in *R v Chief Constable of Kent, ex parte L; R v DPP, ex parte B* (1991) 93 Cr App R 416, which concerned a decision taken with regard to the cautioning of juveniles, it was held that the discretion of a Crown Prosecutor could be subject to judicial review, but only where it could be shown that the decision was made regardless of, or clearly contrary to, the settled policy of the DPP. In relation to the general position of a decision not to discontinue a prosecution against an adult, Watkins LJ was of the opinion that judicial review was unlikely to be available; but that, even if it did exist, such review must be confined to narrow limits. This was reinforced in *R* v *DPP, ex parte C* (1994) *The Times*, 7 March 1994, where the Divisional Court held that they would act only if a decision not to prosecute was arrived at because of an unlawful policy, or because of a failure to act in accordance with established policy, or because the decision was perverse.

In the absence of bad faith, dishonesty or fraud, it is therefore highly unlikely that decisions regarding disclosure made by the police or the CPS could be challenged by judicial review. Prosecution policy on disclosure has now been superseded by the new disclosure code, so it is perhaps unnecessary to spend too much time speculating on whether the DPP could have been judicially reviewed if a Crown Prosecutor had acted in flagrant disregard of the general scheme of the Director's *Guinness Advice* which, in some respects, is analogous to the cautioning guidelines under consideration in *ex parte L and B*. Although the *Advice* was directed at chief officers of police, it set out principles of disclosure established by the developing law which ultimately had to be followed by Crown Prosecutors.

APPEAL TO THE COURT OF APPEAL

General power of appeal

The right of appeal to the Court of Appeal following conviction is now governed by the Criminal Appeal Act 1995 (the 1995 Act). The Court of Appeal shall allow an appeal against conviction if they think that the conviction is unsafe, and dismiss the appeal in any other case. Prior to the 1995 Act, appeals were heard under s. 2(1), Criminal Appeal Act 1968 (the 1968 Act), which provided that:

> . . . the Court of Appeal shall allow an appeal against conviction if they think—
> (a)   that the conviction should be set aside on the ground that under all the circumstances of the case it is unsafe or unsatisfactory;
> (b)   that the judgment of the court of trial should be set aside on the ground of a wrong decision of any question of law; or
> (c)   that there was a material irregularity in the course of the trial,
> and in any other case shall dismiss the appeal:
> Provided that the court may, notwithstanding that they are of the opinion that the point raised in the appeal might be decided in favour of the appellant, dismiss the appeal if they consider that no miscarriage of justice has actually occurred.

Non-disclosure as a material irregularity

Under the 1968 Act, it was settled law that non-disclosure was likely to amount to a material irregularity in the course of the trial within the meaning of s. 2(1)(c).

The point received detailed consideration by the Court of Appeal in *R* v *Maguire* (1992) 94 Cr App R 133, when it was debated whether the non-disclosure of material was an irregularity within ground (a) or (c) of s. 2(1). It was decided that it had no consequence as to the end result of the appeal, but in the light of the authorities the debate was resolved in favour of ground (c). The principal authorities referred to were *R* v *Phillipson* (1990) 91 Cr App R 226, where letters and a photograph should have been disclosed in advance of the trial and Ralph Gibson LJ stated (at p. 235) that 'by reason of the failure to disclose it [the evidence] and its use at the trial there was a material irregularity in the course of the trial'; and *R* v *Sansom* (1991) 92 Cr App R 115, where the then Taylor LJ stated (at p. 121) in relation to documents which had been used for cross-examination purposes but should have been disclosed in advance of the trial: 'In our view the failure to make these documents part of the prosecution case and the failure to disclose them amounted to a material irregularity.' As a result, the judgment of Stuart-Smith LJ in *Maguire* concluded (at p. 146):

> The court has now consistently taken the view that a failure to disclose what is known or possessed and which ought to have been disclosed, is an 'irregularity in the course of the trial'. Why there was no disclosure is an irrelevant question, and if it be asked how the irregularity was 'in the course of the trial' it can be answered that the duty of disclosure is a continuing one. If categorisation is necessary we are content to categorise a failure to disclose as a 'procedural' irregularity, and because that which was not disclosed ought to have been disclosed, we would expect the irregularity to be one which usually satisfied the adjective 'material'.

There was no dissent from this view in *Ward* where Glidewell LJ's judgment included the following passage ((1993) 96 Cr App R 1, at p. 22):

> The obligation to disclose only arises in relation to evidence which is or may be material in relation to the issues which are expected to arise, or which unexpectedly do arise, in the course of the trial. If the evidence is or may be material in this sense, then its non-disclosure is likely to constitute a material irregularity. The proviso makes it plain that 'material' means something less than 'crucial', because it contemplates that although there may have been a material irregularity, yet a verdict of 'guilty' can be upheld on the ground that it involves no miscarriage of justice.

Since the landmark cases of *Maguire* and *Ward*, there has been no shortage of cases where appeals have been allowed on the ground that non-disclosure amounted to a material irregularity. In *R* v *Taylor (Michelle Ann)* (1994) 98 Cr App R 361, the Crown conceded that the failure to disclose a previous inconsistent description was a material irregularity and did not seek to argue that the Court should apply the proviso in s. 2(1).

In *R* v *Rasheed (Abdul)* (1994) *The Times*, 20 May 1994, the material irregularity was the failure to disclose a request for a reward made by an important witness. Counsel for the Crown sought to persuade the Court to apply the proviso in s. 2(1), and even suggested that they should hear from counsel who acted for the appellant at the trial as to how he would have reacted if the information had been available to him. Not surprisingly, that part of the respondent's argument found no favour with the Court, which allowed the appeal.

The respondent received similar short shrift from Rougier J when counsel for the Crown sought to uphold the conviction in *R* v *Livingstone* [1993] Crim LR 597 by urging the Court to apply the s. 2(1) proviso. In a case of theft there had been a failure to disclose an internal manual dealing with payment arrangements. Rougier J declared (at p. 4, transcript 91/1212/X2): 'As an act of benevolence we will not repeat his [counsel for the respondent] arguments but merely content ourselves by saying that in the face of such grave irregularities on a highly material issue it is not a case for the application of the proviso.' The outcome was the same in *R* v *McCarthy* (1993) *The Times*, 21 October 1993, where the defence were not given full details concerning a police officer witness who had since resigned, thus reducing their ability to a mount an attack on his credibility. The non-disclosure was a material irregularity and the appeal was allowed.

Non-disclosure not amounting to a material irregularity

Were there any circumstances where non-disclosure did not amount to a material irregularity; and even if it did, when could the proviso in s. 2(1) of the 1968 Act be applied? The answers to these questions depend, of course, entirely on the particular facts of the case, but there have been examples of both.

In *R* v *Wright* [1994] Crim LR 131, the prosecution had failed to disclose an identikit of the assailant in a robbery. There was no dispute that the failure to disclose was an irregularity, although it was an oversight and there was no question of the identikit being withheld maliciously. However, as the identikit bore a remarkable resemblance to the accused, it was inconceivable that its introduction could have assisted the defence case and the irregularity in the proceedings was not material. In the same way, the information not disclosed in *R* v *Marchant* (unreported), Court of Appeal, 15 July 1994, could not possibly have given any help to the appellant, who had been convicted of conspiracy to rob. The leading witness for the prosecution was a former associate of the appellant who had provided the police with information of previous alleged wrongdoings in connection with drugs. This was not disclosed to the defence, reliance being placed on the *A-G's Guidelines*, although defence counsel were told something about the material by prosecuting counsel who had the clear impression that they 'did not want to go anywhere near it'. This is hardly suprising as the drugs matters bore no relation to the subject matter of the indictment. The trial had taken place before the procedures recommended in *Davis, Johnson and Rowe* were widely recognised; and there is no doubt that had they been in general operation at that time, the further information would have been placed before the court and not simply withheld. Despite the fact that acquiesence by the defence is not a good reason for seeking the court's consent to withhold material on public interest grounds, it was held that was inconceivable that the trial judge would have taken a different course when the defence were not inviting him to do so. In the circumstances, there was no material irregularity.

It is apparent that the irregularity must relate directly to the potential help it may afford to the accused. Just because the prosecution have erred or been responsible for an oversight, unless the non-disclosure has prejudiced the defence of the accused, the irregularity will not be fatal to the conviction. In *R* v *Birmingham Magistrates' Court, ex parte Shields* (unreported), Divisional Court, 7 July 1994, where the prosecution had failed to reveal a retraction statement made by the applicant's wife, the Divisional Court were satisfied from the justices' affidavits that they had appreciated the position and the irregularity had not been material to the outcome of the case.

In cases where the grounds of appeal are that the conviction was, in all the circumstances, unsafe or unsatisfactory, the Court will also look beyond a procedural error by the prosecution in dealing with disclosure issues. In the leading case of *R* v *Keane* (1994) 99 Cr App R 1, where public interest material had not been placed before the trial judge, the Court of Appeal examined the material in question and were satisfied not only that it could not have helped the defence but, on the contrary, that it would have assisted the prosecution. In such circumstances, there were no grounds for holding that the jury's verdict was unsafe or unsatisfactory.

Application of the proviso

Even where the irregularity was material it might still be less than crucial so the proviso in s. 2(1) of the 1968 Act could be utilised. Such a course was taken in *R* v *K (Trevor Douglas)* (1993) 97 Cr App R 342, where it was conceded on behalf of the Crown that the trial judge could not properly have ruled on the disclosure of a video tape made for therapeutic purposes in an allegation of sexual abuse (for which PII had been claimed by the local authority and hospital) without himself seeing the video. The Court of Appeal agreed with that view and held that the exclusion of the evidence without an opportunity of testing its relevance amounted to a material irregularity. After seeing the video, however, the Court concluded that it contained nothing which would have made any difference to the trial. There would have been no purpose in ordering disclosure and it was appropriate to apply the proviso. A similar approach was adopted by the Court of Appeal in *R* v *Dye, Williamson and Davies* [1992] Crim LR 449, where the Court examined alleged differences in statements made in a pre-trial television film and in the evidence given by witnesses at court. It was concluded that the defence had not been disdavantaged and it was a classic case in which to apply the proviso.

The approach to be taken to adopting the proviso was given in *R* v *Browning (Edward)* [1995] Crim LR 227, where the Court of Appeal found material irregularities in the failure to disclose details of a hypnosis session and important messages received by the police. The Court was therefore bound to allow the appeal unless the proviso could be applied, the test for which was said to be whether, had the irregularities not occurred, it was clear that the outcome would have been the same. The question in the instant case was: had the matters which were not disclosed been known to the defence and deployed before the jury, could the Court be sure that the jury would nevertheless have convicted? With the prosecution case depending entirely on circumstantial evidence, the answer was in the negative and the appeal was allowed.

Another case where the proviso was adopted was *R* v *Yates* (unreported), Court of Appeal, 13 November 1992. The appellant had been convicted on two indictments of affray and reckless driving, and did not dispute that there had been an affray or that he had been present; neither did he deny that the vehicle had been driven recklessly and that he was in it. His defence was that he had not been part of the affray and that he was not involved with others in the driving enterprise. The prosecution had failed to provide answers to a number of questions asked by the defence concerning the identity of others, and counsel for the Crown on the appeal conceded that the information should have been supplied and that there was a material irregularity in the course of the trial. The only question for the Court was whether they should apply the proviso. As the critical feature in the trials was one of identification, which was not disputed by the appellant, the Court were satisfied there had been no miscarriage of justice and it was plainly a case for the proviso to be utilised.

Cases like *Trevor Douglas K*, *Yates* and *Dye, Williamson and Davies*, where the Court of Appeal used the proviso, were, however, uncommon. In the majority of cases arising out of non-disclosure or an improper use of the established common law disclosure procedures the Court determined whether the irregularity was material, and where accused persons had been prejudiced in the presentation of their defence the appeal would be allowed. While Glidewell LJ's distinction in *Ward* between what is 'material' and what is 'crucial' is undoubtedly correct and proper, in terms of disclosure where the potential for injustice is great, the distinction is less likely to be made.

Conversely, where there had been no prejudice the appeal would be dismissed without too much attention being paid to the technicalities of the 1968 Act. In *R* v *Saunders (No. 2)* (1995) *The Times*, 28 November 1995, one of the main grounds of appeal was that undisclosed material would have shown that behaviour similar to that of the appellants during the Guinness takeover had occurred elsewhere in the City during the relevant period. This was highly material in relation to the alleged dishonesty of the appellants. It was held that while the material in question should have been disclosed, the Court were satisfied that the procedural irregularity had not resulted in prejudice. In such circumstances, whether the case was more appropriately treated as one in which the procedural irregularity was not a 'material' irregularity as required by s. 2(1)(c) of the 1968 Act, or whether it called for application of the proviso was of little consequence. On either basis, the appeal on that ground failed.

Under the provisions of the 1995 Act, the Court of Appeal should not have to wrestle with artificial complexities of whether the non-disclosure amounted to a material irregularity or whether it was simply an irregularity where the proviso could be applied. They must allow an appeal against conviction if they think the conviction is unsafe and dismiss the appeal in any other case. If the accused's defence has been prejudiced by the non-disclosure of material information to the extent that the conviction is unsafe, the appeal will be successful.

Breaches of the code of practice

Judging by the experience of the PACE 1984 codes of practice, the Court of Appeal are likely to be exercised in the future by grounds of appeal which involve allegations of breaches of the disclosure code of practice introduced by the CPIA 1996. The approach adopted by the Court was summed up in *R* v *Grannell* (1990) 90 Cr App R 149. Where a breach had occurred, it was important to determine whether unfairness had been caused by the breach. Trial judges will be constantly faced with allegations of breaches and they will exercise their discretion in deciding whether unfairness has been caused as a result of which evidence should be excluded. Individual examples of the exercise of discretion in other cases is of no assistance to the Court of Appeal as each case will depend on its own facts.

Unlike the PACE 1984 codes of practice, which are intended, *inter alia*, to ensure that evidence on behalf of the prosecution has been obtained fairly and properly, the disclosure code is designed to secure the availability of information of potential help to the accused. The ultimate sanction against a breach of PACE 1984 is to exclude the evidence under ss. 76 or 78. Breaches of the disclosure code are less likely to result in the exclusion of evidence, although this is a possibility. If, for example, there has been a failure to disclose material casting doubt on the reliability of a confession then that confession may be excluded. What is certain is that the CPIA 1996 and the disclosure code will be the source of a new body of law on disclosure irregularities and it will be for the Court of Appeal, in exercise of their new jurisdiction, to determine whether instances of non-disclosure have brought about an unsafe conviction.

EUROPEAN COURT OF HUMAN RIGHTS

After the Second World War the United Kingdom took a leading role in the establishment of the European Convention on Human Rights and Fundamental Freedoms. The Convention was signed in 1950 and ratified by the UK the following year. There was a desire by the signatories to uphold the rule of law in jurisdictions which had been debased by fascism and dictatorships. The European Court of Human Rights would then be able to validate the decisions of legal institutions in relation to basic rights and liberties.

Periodically, the UK has found itself in the dock at the European Court of Human Rights, and recent controversial decisions — such as the condemnation of the shooting of IRA terrorists in Gibraltar and the criticism of the Home Secretary's powers to determine how long juveniles convicted of murder should be detained — have caused questions to be asked about the influence of the Court on the judicial system in England and Wales. The Court has no power to prescribe remedial measures; its function is to decide whether there has been a violation of the Convention and then to leave it to the government concerned to take any necessary action.

In 1984, James Malone had a resounding triumph when he took the UK to the Court over a violation of Article 8 of the Convention in relation to the use of telephone intercepts (for a detailed account of the case, see chapter 11). In the disclosure-related case of *Edwards* v *United Kingdom* (1993) 15 EHRR 417 the applicant had less success, but the decision (and in particular the dissenting opinions of two judges) throws an interesting light on how our European neighbours view the question of disclosure and human rights.

Edwards was convicted at Sheffield Crown Court of robbery and burglary and sentenced to ten years' imprisonment. The victims in each case were elderly women and the case against Edwards was based on oral admissions made to the police. His defence was that the admissions had been concocted, and the allegations against the police continued after conviction when Edwards petitioned the Home Secretary with complaints against the officers concerned. An independent police inquiry was ordered and the report of the investigating officer (referred to as the Carmichael Report) was in due course submitted to the DPP. The DPP considered that there was insufficient evidence to prosecute any of the officers but recommended disciplinary proceedings (which were later dismissed at a disciplinary hearing). The Carmichael Report itself was never disclosed on the grounds of PII, but some of the Report's findings *were* disclosed and 16 months after the conviction the Home Secretary referred the case to the Court of Appeal under s. 17(1)(a), Criminal Appeal Act 1968. The Court of Appeal, despite concluding that there had been some slipshod police work — probably because the police took the view that in the light of the detailed admissions there was little need for them to indulge in further verification of the allegations — decided that there was nothing unsafe or unsatisfactory about the conviction and dismissed the appeal.

Edwards took his case to the European Court of Human Rights on the grounds that paras (1) and (3)(d) of Article 6 of the Convention had been violated (a further complaint of a violation of Article 13 was not considered by the Court). Article 6(1) states:

1.   In the determination of his civil rights and obligations or of any criminal charge against him, everyone is entitled to a fair and public hearing within a reasonable time by an independent and impartial tribunal established by law. . . .

Article 6(3)(d) reads as follows:

3.   Everyone charged with a criminal offence has the following minimum rights:

. . .

(d)   to examine or have examined witnesses against him and to obtain the attendance and examination of witnesses on his behalf under the same conditions as witnesses against him; . . .

The principal grounds in support of the applicant's claim comprised two instances of non-disclosure. The first concerned a statement made by the police at the trial that no fingerprints had been found at the scene of the crime, whereas two fingerprints of a neighbour had been found. Secondly, the police had failed to state at the trial that one of the prosecution witnesses had not identified Edwards's photograph in a police album although she had thought that she would be able to identify the offender. As these matters had not been disclosed, the applicant submitted that he had not been given an adequate opportunity of challenging the witnesses and, as a result, did not have a fair hearing.

The Government contended that in determining whether there had been unfairness the proceedings must be viewed as a whole; and as the Court of Appeal had considered the matter in the light of the new information, there had been no unfairness. Furthermore, it was argued that Article 6(3)(d) was not relevant to the issue of non-disclosure. The Commission (which acts as a filter through which cases must pass before they are heard by the European Court of Human Rights) found against the Government on this latter point, but by eight votes to six decided that there had been no violation of para. 1, read in conjunction with para. 3(d) of Article 6. The dissenting six, however, expressed disquiet at the fact that the Court of Appeal concluded that the evidence in question was of little significance, in effect substituting their views for those of the jury. For a more detailed analysis of the appeals and procedural aspects, see Field and Young, 'Disclosure, Appeals and Procedural Traditions: *Edwards* v *United Kingdom*' [1994] Crim LR 264.

The reference to the Court of Appeal had been heard before the landmark judgment of *Ward* in June 1992. The European Court hearing was in November 1992, so the disclosure rules in England and Wales had moved on apace by the time the Commission had given their opinion and the European Court of Human Rights finally delivered its verdict on the alleged violation. It decided by seven votes to two that there had been no violation of Article 6 and that there had been a fair trial. Does the decision have any impact on the common law rules of disclosure, and is it likely to encourage others who think that the fairness of their trial has been affected by non-disclosure to tread the human rights path to Strasbourg?

The Court considered that it was a requirement of fairness that the prosecution authorities disclose to the defence all material evidence for or against the accused, and that a failure to do so in the present case gave rise to a defect in the trial proceedings. This is now amply recognised by English law as a result of *Ward* and subsequent cases, and the overall finding of no unfairness was tantamount to the Court of Appeal finding a material irregularity in the proceedings but utilising the proviso in s. 2(1) of the 1968 Act. *Edwards*, therefore, added little to the prosecution's general duty of disclosure; and as the common law rules were as wide as, if not wider than, the general statement of principle made by the Court, the European Court of Human Rights is unlikely to be called into frequent action in non-disclosure cases. This is especially so as the Court has no remedial powers of its own. Now that England and Wales has a statutory framework for disclosure, there should be even less reason for the European Court to be called into action unless the CPIA 1996 is to be challenged as violating Article 6. This might yet happen as the the organisation *Justice* claimed that the proposals made by the Home Secretary, which preceded and have been largely embodied in the legislation, were in breach of international law on the right to a fair trial.

One of the more interesting aspects of the *Edwards* case arises out of the dissenting opinion of Judge Pettiti who grasped the opportunity to condemn recent events in high-profile investigations: 'The concealment of exonerating evidence and in other cases the fabrication of evidence have plagued police investigations (remember the Birmingham Six and the Ward case)'. But it is his sweeping statements in relation to PII that may give some indication of how European jurists are likely to view such issues in any future case. Of course, the Scott Report has already prompted extensive debate on PII and how, and in what circumstances, claims should be asserted in the future; but Judge Pettiti was dismissive of any class claim which may have protected the Carmichael Report, which in his view should not have been protected and should have been disclosed.

Edwards shows that convicted persons not only have domestic remedies for claims of non-disclosure by the prosecution, but they also have access to the European Court of Human Rights if they can substantiate the absence of a fair trial on grounds of disclosure irregularities. The case adds little to the principles derived from the common law rules of disclosure, but it does provide some insight into the European view of disclosure which is undoubtedly coloured by the experience of inquisitorial jurisdictions. A short examination of disclosure in other European jurisdictions is included in chapter 14.

13   Disclosure in Proceedings Heard Summarily

Most authorities on the disclosure of unused material arise out of cases tried on indictment. As a result, the greater part of the discussion of the topic in earlier chapters has centred on the law and practice in relation to proceedings in the Crown Court. It is inevitable that the larger and more complex investigations involve a greater number of statements and other documents, which in turn give rise to problems concerning volume of material to be disclosed as well as difficulties in relation to sensitive information. Approximately 90 per cent of persons accused of crime are tried summarily, though, and while the vast majority of them are charged with minor offences which involve a minimal amount of or no unused material, it is still necessary to ensure that those defendants are made aware of any information held by the prosecution which may help their defence. The Runciman Commission Report made no specific recommendations about disclosure in summary proceedings and made no reference to the real difficulties that face the hundreds of defendants and prosecutors who appear daily in the magistrates' courts. These are examined in this chapter; and as the disclosure provisions of the CPIA 1996 apply to contested cases at the magistrates' courts and youth courts, it is important to see how disclosure has been effected in the past and to anticipate how procedures are likely to operate in the future.

BACKGROUND

The proposals for reform of the disclosure rules in the 1960s and 1970s (dealt with in chapter 6) recognised that the prosecution's duty of disclosure was not confined to indictable offences. The new clause proposed in 1973 for the Administration of Justice Bill contained a provision that in a criminal case where, on summary conviction, the defendant was liable to imprisonment for a term exceeding three months, the prosecutor should supply to the defence copies of statements relevant to the case that had been taken from persons whom it was not proposed to call. As we have seen, the proposed clause was shelved after the Solicitor General undertook to invite comments from interested bodies.

The 1966 JUSTICE Report, which had called for the disclosure of statements taken from persons who were not to be called by the prosecution, conceded that in summary proceedings the supply of copy statements might not always be practicable. In such circumstances it recommended that the defence be given reasonable facilities to inspect the statements before the trial. However, disclosure in relation to proceedings heard summarily was excluded from the terms of reference of the working group that was eventually given the task of looking into the entire question of disclosure. They were asked to consider only cases that had been committed for trial with the result that the *A G's Guidelines*, which came into force at the beginning of 1982, were confined to cases tried on indictment.

It would be wrong to assume that there was no disclosure of relevant unused statements to the defence, either before or during the lifetime of the *A-G's Guidelines*. In 1979, the Divisional Court had made it abundantly clear in *R* v *Leyland Magistrates, ex parte Hawthorn* [1979] 1 All ER 209 (see chapter 12) that the failure to notify the defence of the existence of potential witnesses was a denial of natural justice. As a result, even in the absence of specific directions or guidelines, it was the practice of prosecuting solicitors departments to provide at least the names and addresses of persons who might be of help to the defence. It is fair to say, however, that the practice was not uniform, nor did it extend in the main to documents other than statements or pro forma accounts of road traffic incidents; and, of course, as many cases were prosecuted by the police themselves without the benefit of legal advice, there was no consistency in practice among different police forces.

The first direct recognition by the prosecution service that irrespective of where the defendant was tried the principle of disclosure was the same, was provided in the *Guinness Advice*. Paragraph 2 referred to the *A-G's Guidelines* and recent judgments and concluded: 'Common law authorities and best practice require the prosecution to observe a similar duty to disclose material in cases to be tried summarily.' The accuracy of this statement — that no distinction should be drawn between summary proceedings and proceedings on indictment — was confirmed by the Divisional Court in *R* v *Bromley Magistrates' Court, ex parte Smith and Wilkins* [1995] 2 Cr App R 285, when Simon Brown LJ stated (at p. 288):

I have no hesitation in reaching the same view. Common sense and justice alike demand that whether the proceedings are summary or on indictment the same processes with regard to the disclosure of unused material must apply i.e. those processes which a series of recent cases have now established are necessary to guard against miscarriages of justice in jury trials. An accused is as much entitled to the safeguards designed to ensure a fair trial in the Magistrates' Court as in the Crown Court.

In a number of respects the statement of principle by the DPP in the *Guinness Advice* was a courageous step, for it was made in the knowledge that the effect would create an enormous additional burden upon police officers and prosecutors alike. The preservation and revelation of documents by the police and the consideration of their ultimate disclosure by the CPS had become requirements of the law in relation to offences tried on indictment as a result of the *Guinness Ruling* and *Ward*, but there had been no specific judicial direction that offences triable summarily were to be dealt with in the same way. Nevertheless, the DPP concluded that the difficulties in practice which faced the prosecution agencies in the recording, scheduling and disclosure of documents in something of the order of a million cases a year heard by magistrates, were outweighed by the exactitude of the principle of disclosure to all accused persons, irrespective of the venue of their trial. The operational procedures agreed by the CPS and police to implement the principles set out in the *Guinness Advice* were to be tested in the first case where the higher courts had to consider directly the prosecution's duty of disclosure with regard to summary trials.

R v BROMLEY MAGISTRATES' COURT, EX PARTE SMITH AND WILKINS

A solicitor named Stephen Fidler was acting for clients charged in separate proceedings before different magistrates' courts with possessing pitbull terriers contrary to s. 1, Dangerous Dogs Act 1991. In both cases he sought from the prosecution the disclosure of unused material, in particular details of previous cases in which the expert witness called on behalf of the prosecution had given evidence. Mr Fidler's requests were denied by the CPS; and when his applications to each court to stay proceedings on the grounds of the CPS denial were refused, he commenced proceedings for judicial review of the refusal. The judgment of Simon Brown LJ in *R v Bromley Magistrates' Court, ex parte Smith and Wilkins*; *R v Wells Street Magistrates' Court, ex parte King* [1995] 2 Cr App R 285 contains a number of important points in relation to disclosure in summary trials.

First, it was confirmed that the prosecution's duty of disclosure was the same in summary trials as it was in proceedings on indictment. In so holding, the Court explained that *R v Crown Prosecution Service, ex parte Warby* [1994] Crim LR 281 was not authority for denying magistrates' courts the power to decide disputes as to the disclosure of unused material in the course of summary trials. That case concerned committal proceedings only and decided that issues concerning sensitive material should be left to the court of trial and should not be decided by magistrates at or before the committal hearing.

Secondly, the Court commented upon the practice for dealing with disclosure which had been outlined by counsel for the respondent. This followed the principles set out in the *Guinness Advice* and involved either the supply of copy documents to the defence, or the provision of a schedule inviting access to the material itself. It was pointed out that the only exception to the practice was non-imprisonable summary only traffic cases, where it was accepted that the same principles of disclosure applied but no formal procedures had been considered necessary. Simon Brown LJ indicated (at p. 291): 'I regard them to be perfectly satisfactory'. He was less than satisfied, however, with the 'absurd' stance taken by the respondent in refusing to produce the operational instructions themselves on public interest grounds. This was indeed unfortunate, but the openness of matters of prosecution policy and confidential instructions given to the police goes further than the question of placing CPS/police disclosure policy in the public domain.

The third point of importance was the emphasis given to the fact that the test of materiality set out in *Keane* was equally applicable in cases tried summarily. The prosecution must be prepared to review questions of materiality, but it would be rare for the court to become involved unless the prosecution were seeking to withhold relevant documents. Simon Brown LJ expressed the hope that those representing defendants would not too readily seek to challenge a responsible prosecutor's assertion that documents were not relevant, and the onus was on the defence to make out a clear prima facie case to the contrary. There might be occasions when the court would wish to consider its powers of making wasted costs orders.

In so far as the question falling for decision was concerned, the Court unhesitatingly rejected the request for an order requiring the prosecution to disclose statements made by their expert witness in other similar cases. In addition to noting the respondent's evidence as to the impracticability of making such disclosure, it was held that such information could not cast doubt on the credibility or reliability of the witness and there was, therefore, no advantage to the defence in making the documents available.

This decision was, therefore, of importance in placing the prosecution's common law disclosure duties in the magistrates' court on the same footing as those in the Crown Court. However, if it was thought that the judgment of Simon Brown LJ settled the more important disclosure rules affecting magistrates, it took only a matter of months for the Divisional Court to create confusion for justices and their clerks in regard to the handling of applications to withhold material.

PUBLIC INTEREST IMMUNITY IN SUMMARY PROCEEDINGS

The manner in which public interest matters were being dealt with at the lower court was a matter of concern to the defence, prosecution and justices' clerks alike. *Ward* and *Davis, Johnson and Rowe* had established the law and practice in relation to hearings before a judge, but while there was nothing to prevent magistrates dealing with public interest matters in the same way, there was much unease that lay magistrates might have to deal with such a complicated area of the law and have to consider documents of some sensitivity. Certainly they had received no help from the Court of Appeal, who showed no signs of appreciating that such matters could arise outside the Crown Court. If they did, in fact, appreciate the problem, their judgments contained no *dicta* which might assist practitioners and justices' clerks.

At the heart of the problem was the *ex parte* application, where magistrates were being asked to consider sensitive material in the absence of the accused or his legal representative (for a defence practitioner's view on the matter, see Duke-Cohan, David, 'In the Public Interest' (1994) 91 LS Gaz 17). The position was far from satisfactory from the prosecution perspective too. Informants were just as likely to feature in a case tried summarily as in one tried on indictment. While the informant was unlikely to be of the registered or participating variety, it was nevertheless just as important to afford protection to the identity of the neighbour who had told the police of suspicious activity at the house across the road, or the public spirited individual who telephoned 'Crimestoppers' with information. In small communities especially, this is not the sort of confidential information that it is desirable to place before lay justices. Before the *Keane* materiality test allowed prosecutors to decide on the relevance of such information, it was not unusual for applications concerning confidential documents to be made to lay justices. Application of the *Keane* test eased the volume of applications, but where it was still necessary to apply for material to be withheld on public interest grounds the position was far from satisfactory, and there was a marked absence of judicial authority to assist concerned defendants, prosecutors and justices' clerks.

Not surprisingly, the Magistrates' Courts Rules are silent on the question of *ex parte* hearings as the phenomenon was even more of a novelty in the lower courts than in the Crown Court. Open justice is just as important at the lower court as at the Crown Court and s. 121(4), Magistrates' Courts Act 1980 requires a magistrates' court to sit in open court. Magistrates do, however, have an inherent jurisdiction to sit *in camera*, although such a power should be rarely invoked and only for compelling reasons; for example, to safeguard the emotional state of the defendant and the nature of the evidence as in *R v Malvern Justices, ex parte Evans* (1988) 87 Cr App R 19; and in an application for a direction under s. 11, Contempt of Court Act 1981 as in *R v Tower Bridge Magistrates' Court, ex parte Osborne* (1989) 88 Cr App R 28. In *R v Ealing Justices, ex parte Weafer* (1982) 74 Cr App R 204, which arose out of an application by defence counsel for the plea in mitigation to be heard *in camera*, the judgment of Donaldson LJ drew attention to the fact that confidentiality can also be preserved by certain mitigation matters being placed before the court in writing in a sealed form. Such a practice was known in the Crown Court and it avoided the necessity of excluding press and public. While there is precedent, therefore, to support a hearing *in camera* or the use of sealed envelopes, it is obviously important that *ex parte* procedures in the lower courts are kept to an absolute minimum and that the magistrates' decision is announced in open court.

Bromley Magistrates' Court was not immediately concerned with PII applications at the magistrates' court, but in addition to advising magistrates to commit for trial wherever possible in cases where public interest issues were likely to arise, Simon Brown LJ ventured the following opinion (at p. 289) in relation to cases which had to be heard summarily:

I realise, of course, that unlike the position in the Crown Court, the Magistrates are themselves the judges of fact. That, however, presents no insuperable difficulty: there is no difference in principle between a voir dire on the admissibility of evidence and an application with regard to the disclosure of documents. Indeed, fewer mental gymnastics are likely to be required with the latter than the former. Ideally, the same constitution of the Magistrates should decide questions of disclosure — raised, as generally they should be raised, at a specially arranged pre-trial application — as will conduct the eventual trial. If, however, that proves impossible, the trial court should be apprised at the outset of the material upon any ruling in favour of which non-disclosure was originally made — see Davis 97 CAR at page 115 with regard to the analogous position in the Crown Court.

There is a strong argument that Simon Brown LJ underestimates the task of lay justices in seeing confidential material and then, once they have decided not to order disclosure, putting that information to one side when determining guilt or otherwise according to the evidence. The information in question could be highly prejudicial, possibly dealing with interviews relating to other unconnected allegations, and while stipendiary magistrates may be better qualified to distinguish between what is evidence and what is not, it is no easy task for justices. Nevertheless, the opinion of Simon Brown LJ is unambiguous and, after all, who better to keep the question of disclosure under review as the trial progresses than the tribunal which has decided the issue in the first place? Two months later, however, a differently constituted Divisional Court were not of the same view.

R v South Worcestershire Magistrates, ex parte Lilley (1995) *The Times*, 22 February 1995, was a case of handling stolen goods where the prosecution had made an *ex parte* application to justices that material in their possession should not be disclosed on public interest grounds. After a 20-minute hearing, during which the court heard evidence from a police officer and submissions from the prosecutor, the court ruled that disclosure should not be made. The justices then ruled against a defence submission that the case itself should be heard by a differently constituted bench. The application for judicial review of the refusal of the justices to disqualify themselves from adjudicating as a court of trial was granted and an order made that the case be remitted with a direction that the justices consider the application further in the light of the Divisional Court's judgment. Rose LJ held that the Court were not bound by the decision in *Bromley Magistrates* which, he considered, had not considered full argument on the particular point.

Rose LJ seemed especially concerned with the principle established by such authorities as *R v Bodmin Justices, ex parte McEwen* [1947] 1 All ER 109, *R v East Kerrier Justices, ex parte Mundy* [1952] 2 All ER 142 and *R v Barry (Glamorgan) Justices, ex parte Kashim* [1953] 1 WLR 1320, that justice in magistrates' courts should be seen to be done. In a case where the defendant and his advisers had been absent for 20 minutes during a PII application this was not apparent and left a reasonable suspicion that the justices may have been prejudiced.

In the circumstances, he held that the justices had a discretion to order a hearing before a different bench. The defendant did not have a right to a trial before a new bench, but it was open to the court to accede to such an application.

In a number of ways the decision is unsatisfactory as it is neither helpful to magistrates nor likely to ease the probability of inconsistency as different benches wrestle with the dilemma of whether a decision they have taken on disclosure is likely to be misinterpreted because it has been taken in the absence of the accused. For example, if the application in *ex parte Lilley* had taken five instead of 20 minutes, would the magistrates have looked less likely to have been prejudiced? The decision is also inconsistent with the basis of the judgment in *Davis, Johnson and Rowe* that decisions on disclosure are best taken by the tribunal hearing the facts which is best placed to keep questions of disclosure under review. If the case is heard by a different bench, there is a danger that, as the trial develops, relevant information seen in the course of the PII application may not be adduced because the new bench is in ignorance of the situation. The defendant is totally reliant on the prosecutor acting fairly and bringing such information to the attention of the court.

PROCEDURES UNDER THE 1996 ACT

The provisions of the CPIA 1996 make no distinction between the requirements of disclosure in the magistrates' court and those in the Crown Court. As soon as the defendant pleads not guilty at the magistrates' court the duty of primary disclosure arises. The prosecutor must disclose any material which undermines the prosecution case, and it matters not if the case is to be tried summarily or is to be committed or transferred to the Crown Court.

Where issues of non-disclosure in the public interest are likely to arise in either-way offences, it will be advisable for magistrates to decline jurisdiction in accordance with the Mode of Trial Guidelines (*Practice Note (QBD) (Mode of Trial: Guidelines)* (1991) 92 Cr App R 142 on the ground that PII is a circumstance which makes it more suitable for the offence to be tried on indictment. In summary trials where there is no alternative to magistrates hearing the application, *ex parte Lilley* is authority for the exercising of discretion as to whether they should then go on and conduct the trial itself. If disclosure is ordered this is unlikely to present any difficulty, but in cases where the magistrates decide not to order disclosure of information, their subsequent decision will depend on the nature of the confidential material and the prejudicial effect it may have on the defendant.

There was a lengthy debate in the committee stages of the passage of the Bill which resulted in the Government withdrawing their original proposal that magistrates should have a duty to keep non-disclosure rulings under review. It was recognised that where the bench hearing the trial itself was differently constituted from that which heard the PII application, it would be impossible to keep the matter under review. Section 14 was therefore introduced, which places the onus on the accused to make application for a review of public interest matters. Concern was expressed about the position of unrepresented defendants who neither knew nor understood what they should do in such circumstances. Undertakings were given that magistrates would look favourably on the question of legal aid in cases where public interest points were likely to arise, but where defendants decline legal aid or cannot afford private representation the courts will have to manage as best they can. Proposals that reviews should be carried out by Crown Court judges and for an avenue of appeal against non-disclosure orders to the Crown Court were rejected as too complex and duplicitous.

The Magistrates' Courts (Criminal Procedure and Investigations Act 1996) (Disclosure) Rules 1997 (SI 1997 No. 703) and the Magistrates' Courts (Criminal Procedure and Investigation Act 1996) (Confidentiality) Rules 1997 (SI 1997 No. 704) provide for the practice and procedure to be followed in applications relating to public interest material and defence time limits and contempt proceedings arising out of alleged breaches of confidentiality.

14   Disclosure in Other Jurisdictions

GENERAL

England and Wales is not the only legal jurisdiction to have been affected by changes in the law on disclosure in criminal proceedings. While no other country appears to have suffered from the same surfeit of miscarriage of justice cases, situations have arisen in other jurisdictions which have caused the courts and law reform groups (but not, as yet, the legislatures) to reconsider the law and practice in relation to the disclosure of information to the defence. This chapter examines developments in a number of jurisdictions with a view to gauging how other countries deal with the disclosure of evidence. The radical overhaul of the law on disclosure brought about by the CPIA 1996 was almost inevitable as a result of developments in England and Wales, but if similar legislation has not been considered necessary in other countries, why not? Do they have more satisfactory disclosure regimes; or are they just fortunate that a *Ward*-type case has not yet surfaced?

An examination of the law on disclosure in other jurisdictions can only be brief as a thorough analysis would, of necessity, involve a full consideration of the various legal processes and an appraisal of the investigating and prosecuting systems under which the rules operate. The law has to develop and change according to the needs of the country in question, a fact that was recognised by Lord Lowry in delivering the judgment of the Privy Council in *Berry* v *The Queen* (1993) 96 Cr App R 77, at p. 84:

Having examined the practice in different common law jurisdictions their Lordships consider that the principles endorsed by the Jamaica Court of Appeal, particularly with regard to inconsistent previous statements, represent what will normally be an acceptable way of achieving fairness to the accused and they take the opportunity of saying that in a civilised community the most suitable ways of achieving such fairness (which should not be immutable and require to be reconsidered from time to time) are best left to, and devised by, the legislature, the executive and the judiciary which serve that community and are familiar with its problems.

Nowhere is this final comment better illustrated than in Northern Ireland where, against a background of terrorism, the Diplock Courts made their controversial entrance into criminal proceedings. Our brief look at disclosure developments in other jurisdictions therefore begins in that part of the United Kingdom.

NORTHERN IRELAND

Unlike Scotland, which is discussed below, the common law in Northern Ireland has moved in a similar direction to that in England (indeed in one respect, even further). The CPIA 1996 extends to Northern Ireland, subject to the modifications set out in sch. 4 of the Act. The *A-G's Guidelines* did not apply to Northern Ireland, although prosecutors in the province generally abided by the spirit of the *Guidelines* and exercised discretion as advised therein. Until recently the general principle of disclosure was laid down by the Court of Appeal in *R* v *Foxford* [1974] NI 181, at p. 200, which stated that 'the ordinary rule' was that 'it was for the Crown to decide whether a situation had arisen which made it proper to hand (a document) to the defence'. It was recognised by Lowry LCJ that the trial judge had a discretion to direct the Crown to disclose documents, and illustrations of judicial intervention in the area of disclosure are provided by rulings in *R* v *McAllister* (1985) 10 NIJB 22 and other unreported cases.

The prosecution's independence in disclosure issues was nevertheless reinforced by Hutton LCJ in *R* v *Latimer* (1992) 1 NIJB 89, at p. 97, when, following the law in *Foxford*, he stated: 'Where the Crown brings a prosecution in the Crown Court the accused is not entitled to obtain discovery of documents in the Crown Court.' *Latimer* was decided before *Ward*, but the developments in disclosure across the Irish Sea which followed that case clearly affected judicial thinking, for when the Lord Chief Justice had to consider the question again in 1995 in *R* v *Harper and Ahty* (unreported), Crown Court of Northern Ireland, transcript HUTF1659 he concluded that:

. . . that statement should no longer be the rule in this jurisdiction. In this jurisdiction, as in England, the guiding principle should now be (and I state the principle in general terms without seeking to give a precise definition) that the prosecution, subject to public interest immunity, should disclose documents that are material and which would help the defence.

The judgment in *Harper and Ahty* arose in the context of a voir dire where the court was determining whether oral admissions made by Harper should be admitted. He claimed that they had been made as a result of threats by the police in relation to his brothers and sister. The issue of importance was whether the interviewing officers were familiar, prior to the accused's confession, with details of the crimes to which he confessed, and this brought into the picture the existence of an intelligence file. Counsel for the Crown told the court that he had disclosed to his opponent anything in the file which could assist the defence, but counsel for the accused was not satisfied with this. Hutton LCJ considered the line of English decisions from *Ward* to *Keane* and *ex parte Wiley*, and decided that it was necessary for the court to examine the file and related documents to determine whether there were entries which would be of help to the defence.

Such a course is in step with the English authorities for dealing with documents for which the Crown assert PII, but Hutton LCJ went further and indicated that the court had a role in determining materiality generally. While it is correct that there are passages in *Ward*, *Keane* and *Winston Brown* which say that where the prosecution are in any doubt about disclosure they may seek the assistance of the court, the tenor of the judgments is that such cases should be the exception and not the rule. Part of the concern of the Court of Appeal in *Keane* (prompted by Jowitt J's remarks in *Melvin and Dingle*: see chapter 7, page 82) was that judges were being overwhelmed by applications to rule on PII documents. If they were to be bombarded with applications to decide materiality in relation to non-sensitive documents as well, there would be a danger of the courts grinding to halt.

There is no provision in the CPIA 1996 for the prosecution to seek the help of the court in deciding what might undermine their case. It is a matter for the opinion of the prosecutor. The court has a role to play in circumstances where the accused believes that material has not been disclosed in accordance with the duty imposed by the Act on the prosecution. In the absence of any point being taken by the defence, the court should not have to intervene to decide questions of materiality.

There does not appear to be any authority to the effect that the law on PII in Northern Ireland should be any different from that in England and Wales, and it is presumed that the changes brought about by *ex parte Wiley*, and any that may flow from the Scott Report, will be equally applicable in Northern Ireland. The judgment of Hutton LCJ in *Harper and Ahty* concludes with the observation that when the criminal trial is being conducted by a judge without a jury and matters of PII fall to be considered which are prejudicial to the accused, it is open to the court to decide that another judge will rule on the issue of materiality or PII. This is contrary to what was said in *Davis, Johnson and Rowe*, which was not, of course, immediately concerned with Diplock Courts, but it does have a bearing on the debate at to how justices should deal with PII applications (and the conflict of authority in the *Bromley Magistrates* and *South Worcestershire Magistrates* cases discussed in chapter 13).

SCOTLAND

In 1989, Graham Higgins and Kevin Higgins were convicted of assault at Glasgow Sheriff Court. They appealed against their convictions, and one of the grounds of appeal was that they had not been given an opportunity of calling all the relevant evidence available because the prosecution had not told the defence who else was present at the scene other than those witnesses on the Crown list. Lord Cowie dismissed this ground of appeal as 'wholly without foundation, not to say impertinent', and continued:

> There is no obligation on the Crown to provide any list of witnesses other than those which are attached to an indictment, and there is no obligation on the Crown to disclose any information in their possession which would tend to exculpate the accused. (*Higgins* v *HM Advocate* 1990 SCCR 268)

Thus, at a time when, in England, Henry J in the *Guinness Ruling* was enlarging the duties of the prosecution in relation to disclosure and holding, *inter alia*, that relevance was a matter for the defence and not the prosecution, matters north of the border were very different.

Lord Cowie's judgment, although strictly an accurate statement of the law in Scotland, does not give a true reflection on how disclosure is dealt with in that jurisdiction. In *Slater* v *HM Advocate* 1928 JC 94, Lord Justice-General Clyde had stated the position (at p. 103) as:

> An accused person has no right to demand that the prosecution should — in addition to supplying him with the names and addresses of all the witnesses who may be called — communicate to him all the results, material or immaterial, of the investigations made by the procurator fiscal under direction of the Crown Office.

When *Slater* came to be considered in *Smith* v *HM Advocate* 1952 JC 66, the Lord Justice-Clerk acknowledged: 'There can be little doubt, however, that the tendency in recent years has been for the defence to expect from the Crown, and indeed for the Crown to afford, a measure of assistance beyond what would have been in the contemplation of any previous generation of Scots lawyers.' This is, no doubt, because procurators fiscal see their duty to act fairly as extending beyond the brief statement of the law given in *Higgins*. The ethical and professional duties of the procurator fiscal are set out briefly in the preface to the *Book of Regulations of the Procurator Fiscal Service* as follows:

> A Procurator Fiscal must at all times remember his professional ethics. He must never act unfairly. This will involve disclosure to the defence of any information which supports the defence, even though it may be damaging to the Crown case. Assistance will also be given to the defence to enable them to contact witnesses. It is impossible to list all the situations which may arise, but when faced with a problem for which there is no standard solution, the Procurator Fiscal should always ask himself — 'what would be fair' — and act accordingly.

In *HM Advocate* v *Ward* 1993 SLT 1202, the Crown expressly dissociated itself from Lord Cowie's statement in *Higgins*. The defence submission was to the effect that, as a matter of general principle, it was right and proper that there should be disclosed by the Crown all material which might have a bearing on the trial. The practice of prosecuting authorities in England and Wales in the light of the developing law south of the border was drawn to the attention of the High Court. Although the Court refused to make an order for the production of statements, material and precognitions, the Crown agreed to consider whether certain statements could be disclosed and subsequently undertook to lodge those statements as productions.

Public interest immunity is asserted in relation to information which may endanger life or property, or compromise the effective operation of police or other intelligence measures. Police informers are also protected from disclosure: see *Friel, Petitioner* 1981 SLT 113. A very high degree of confidentiality attaches to reports by the police to the procurator fiscal and by the procurator fiscal to the Crown Office, and this received judicial recognition in *McKie* v *Western Scottish Motor Traction Co.* 1952 SC 206.

The law in relation to the disclosure of the previous convictions of prosecution witnesses is also more restrictive than in England. The position is summed up by the judgment of the Lord Justice-Clerk in *HMA* v *Ashrif* 1988 SCCR 197, where (at p. 203) he approved the rule expressed in *Dickie* v *HMA* (1896) 24R (J) 82, that:

> The right to attack the character of a witness, and to bring evidence in support of the attack, is one which has always been carefully kept within very limited bounds. . . . It is only competent to enquire into matters directly connected with the subject of the trial then proceeding.

The duty of disclosure is therefore confined to situations where the credibility of a witness may be legitimately attacked; whereas in England the law prior to the CPIA 1996 was that if it was known that a witness had a conviction, there was a duty on the prosecution to disclose it to the defence.

The duty of disclosure — whether in relation to statements or other documents not to be introduced by the Crown, or with regard to previous convictions of witnesses — rests with the procurator fiscal. Unlike the CPS in England and Wales, the Fiscal Service is responsible for the investigation of crime. Much of the preliminary investigation is carried out by the police, but this is conducted under the general supervision of the procurator fiscal. In order that the procurator fiscal can comply with the legal and professional obligations summarised above, it follows that the police must reveal relevant material which they have gathered. As was stated in *Smith* v *HM Advocate* (above):

> . . . it is their [the police's] clear duty to put before the Procurator Fiscal everything which may be relevant and material to the issue of whether the suspected party is innocent or guilty. We repeat, it is not for the police to decide what is relevant and material but to give all the information which may be relevant and material.

Not surprisingly, the divergent disclosure practices in the jurisdictions on either side of the border can lead to difficulties, particularly in cross-border operations. The conviction in England in 1995 of the lorry driver Robert Black for the abduction and murder of young girls, had been preceded by a massive operation involving police forces in Scotland and England in which over a million 'actions' fell to be disclosed. Despite the different approaches to disclosure, inter-force co-operation meant that all material relevant to the defence was fully disclosed, much of it by allowing supervised access to a computer.

If there is no question of criminal proceedings in Scotland, it is likely that the Scottish police will release documents to England, content in the knowledge that they will probably be disclosed, even though they may not have been liable for disclosure in Scotland. Some investigations can, however, give rise to more complex disclosure problems. For example, if the police are involved in a cross-border inquiry which may lead to charges on either side of the border, there may be a reluctance to release material to another force. If documents relevant to a Scottish prosecution were released to a police force south of the border and disclosed in accordance with the wide disclosure obligations of the law in England and Wales, there might be prejudice to the pending proceedings in Scotland. It is understood that the Scottish standard of confidentiality has, on occasions, been argued successfully before English civil courts, but it is doubtful whether it would receive a sympathetic hearing in a criminal case with the threat of a miscarriage of justice if copies of relevant documents held by the police in England are not disclosed.

In practice, most problems are solved by sensible co-operation between the Crown Office and CPS, but this is not to underestimate the potential difficulty that exists where adjacent legal jurisdictions have different disclosure regimes. Scotland has never had anything similar to the *A-G's Guidelines*, and the case law which has aroused so much concern and confusion in England and Wales seems to have passed Scotland by. The prosecution approach to disclosure in Scotland is undoubtedly more robust but, despite the absence of the common law disclosure rules which have evolved south of the border, any concealment by the police or Procurator Fiscal Service of relevant material or exculpatory evidence would almost certainly lead to a conviction being quashed. There are no immediate signs of greater harmony in the disclosure regimes as the CPIA 1996 does not apply to Scotland.

CANADA

'. . . [T]he fruits of the investigation . . . are not the property of the Crown for use in securing conviction, but the property of the public to be used to ensure that justice is done.' These words were used in the judgment of the Supreme Court of Canada in *R* v *Stinchcombe* (1991) 68 CCC (3d) 1, at p. 7, a case which had a similar effect on the law and practice in relation to disclosure in Canada as did *Ward* in England. *Stinchcombe* and *R* v *O'Connor* (1994) BCCA 65, have interpreted s. 7 of the Canadian Charter of Rights and Freedoms to require the prosecution to disclose all relevant material to the defence, whether they intend to use it or not as part of the case for the Crown, in order that the accused may make full answer and defence to the charge. *Stinchcombe* recognises the importance of full disclosure by the police to the prosecutor, but acknowledges that the Crown has a discretion to withhold information on grounds of irrelevance or to delay its disclosure. This discretion is nevertheless reviewable by the court at the insistence of the defence.

The judgment in *Stinchcombe* provided the impetus for Canadian prosecuting authorities to reconsider their policies in relation to disclosure. In 1984, the Law Reform Commission of Canada had recommended that legislation be enacted to require disclosure by the Crown in criminal cases; and in 1990, the Royal Commission on the Prosecution of Donald Marshall Jr endorsed the proposal, with a further recommendation that directives on disclosure be prepared by Attorneys-General pending the enactment of legislation. The provinces of New Brunswick and Alberta had formal written disclosure policies and others, such as Ontario and Manitoba, had issued policy guidelines. The Department of Justice used these in order to develop guidelines requiring full disclosure by its prosecutors. The Advisory Committee for the Attorney-General for Ontario produced a report on *Charge Screening, Disclosure and Resolution Discussions*, which resulted in an updated policy on disclosure for Crown counsel coming into force in 1994.

All these iniatives mean that although there is no statutory formulation of disclosure requirements, prosecutors in Canada have guidelines and policy directives which are intended to guarantee the accused's common law and constitutional rights to a fair trial and to make full answer and defence. The principle of disclosure applies to all prosecutions, whether tried summarily or on indictment. Evidence in support of the prosecution's case must be disclosed and information available prior to trial should not be withheld for the purpose of cross-examination. Crown counsel have a duty to disclose relevant information to the accused, whether favourable or unfavourable, and are expected to take steps to ensure that the police have passed on all such information to the Crown. It has been recommended that failure to disclose by the police should result in a disciplinary charge of neglect of duty against the officer(s) concerned.

There is a general emphasis on the obligation to disclose relevant evidence and it seems that the decision on what is relevant is taken by the prosecutor. There does not appear to be any case law which suggests — as was once the case in England and Wales — that relevance is a matter for the defence, although there is a general exhortation to defence counsel to assist with questions of relevance, particularly in any instance where they apply to see the investigation file. There is no general duty of disclosure on the defence. Information concerning credibility of a prosecution witness is clearly of relevance and there is an obligation to disclose prior inconsistent statements, promises of immunity and relevant convictions.

The prosecution have a discretion not to disclose privileged information although the decision may be reviewed by the trial judge. The emphasis is very much on disclosure, however, unless there is a need to protect the names of informants, or to prevent the intimidation or harassment of witnesses or any interference with the administration of justice.

Canada appears to have done more than any other Commonwealth jurisdiction to provide comprehensive guidance to prosecutors on disclosure and related issues. It is not without significance that, as in England and Wales, the catalyst was provided by a case which highlighted the unfair consequences of non-disclosure. Unlike England and Wales, the courts appear to have been more consistent in their interpretation of the prosecution's duty of disclosure with fewer conflicting judgments that have been the source of much of the confusion in this country.

AUSTRALIA

Although requirements for discovery in civil proceedings have long been established in Australia, there is no formal system of disclosure in criminal proceedings. In both indictable and summary matters there is no obligation on the prosecution at common law to serve upon the defence statements and exhibits (known as the brief of evidence) which support the case for the Crown. It is nevertheless the practice of each state and territory to serve statements prior to committal. In some states, such as New South Wales and Victoria, legislation requires service by a particular time; while in others, such as Queensland and the Northern Territory, where there is no statutory requirement, the practice is nevertheless to make disclosure. In Victoria a defendant has a statutory right of access to certain information in summary proceedings, while in most of the the remaining states disclosure is made voluntarily upon request from the defence. The Commonwealth DPP and the DPPs in each state and territory have incorporated guidance in prosecution policies.

The leading authority on the prosecution's duty of disclosure is the judgment of the Full Court of the Supreme Court of South Australia in *Re Van Beelen* (1974) 9 SASR 163. As well as giving observations on the Crown's duties concerning witnesses to be called at committal and on the trial itself, the Court also provided guidance in relation to the disclosure of evidence which does not form part of the case for the prosecution. It was stated that where the prosecution decide not to call a person who can give material evidence, they are under a duty to make the witness available to the defence although there is no need to supply a copy of the statement taken. This broadly follows the *Bryant and Dickson* approach (see chapter 6) which was the general practice in England and Wales at that time; but the Court also imported the views of Lord Denning in *Dallison* v *Caffery* (see page 60 above) by holding that where the prosecution have a statement of a credible witness who can speak of material facts which tend to show that an accused is innocent, that witness must either be called or the statement made available to the defence. The Crown therefore retains considerable discretion as to how much, and in what form, information is disclosed to the defence. If the prosecution are in possession of an exculpatory statement from someone whom they do not believe to be credible, there is no need to make the witness available or any duty to supply to the defence a copy of the statement.

Prosecution guidelines issued by most states ensure that previous convictions against prosecution witnesses are disclosed, although the Northern Territory and the Australian Capital Territory guidance allow for the prosecutor's discretion as to whether the criminal history appears to be of any material significance in the trial. Some state policies also deal specifically with the disclosure of information concerning informers, indemnities and accomplices.

There have been no major developments in relation to disclosure on the scale of *Ward* in England or *Stinchcombe* in Canada, but there have been three recent appellate-level decisions concerning the general duty of disclosure by the prosecution. *R* v *Lun* (unreported), CCA (NSW) 4 December 1992, considered the decision of the trial judge that the Hong Kong police were not part of the prosecution for the purposes of disclosure; *R* v *Higgins* (unreported), CCA (Vic), 2 March 1994, endorsed the views expressed in *Clarkson* v *DPP* (1990) VR 745 to the effect that the prosecution have an obligation to disclose to the defence material which would assist the defence case; and *R* v *CPK* (unreported), CCA (NSW) 21 June 1995 held that psychiatric reports on the complainant, which were not disclosed on the trial but were made available for the purposes of sentence, should have been disclosed as they would have assisted the defence case. Some of the leading authorities in England and Wales, such as *Ward*, were considered in some of these cases.

Commensurate with the duty of fairness, the prosecuting authorities in each state are more liberal in disclosure matters than the law strictly requires. There has always been informal disclosure of relevant material, and policy initiatives have been introduced in some states to ensure that disclosure is dealt with fairly. For example, in Western Australia, where there are no rules which require the prosecution to disclose 'unused material' to the defence, the 1993/4 Annual Report of the Director of Public Prosecutions included guidance on disclosure which stated (at p. 41):

Consistent with the view that the fruits of an investigation should in general be available for all parties in a criminal action guidelines have been promulgated requiring police officers to furnish to the office all material gathered in the course of an investigation which does not form part of the Crown brief in case it should be of interest or use to the defence. Upon request, prosecutors will allow inspection of that material by defence representatives. The disclosure is subject to important qualifications as to public interest immunity as there are some matters which ought to remain confidential.

Prosecution policies have endeavoured to keep abreast of the developing law and it is of interest to compare the varying tests that have been introduced. For example, in New South Wales the criterion for disclosure is whether the information is relevant to any issue likely to arise at trial; in Queensland it is any evidence that tends to the proof of innocence; in Western Australia, the prosecutor has to consider whether the information is exculpatory; while in the Northern Territory all evidence relevant to the guilt or innocence of the accused must be disclosed. In addition, most states have professional ethical responsibilities which require a prosecutor to disclose any information which comes to notice that could be relevant to the guilt or innocence of the accused.

In summary, the position at common law in Australia is uncertain. Clearly, there is a general duty not to conceal relevant evidence or information and to reveal material which is unhelpful to the prosecution. However, there appears to be no system in operation to ensure that the duty is carried out. Furthermore, there are no formal procedures in place for the revelation of all investigation material to the prosecutor, thus leaving open the question as to whether all material information is brought to the attention of the prosecutor — a lacuna which has proved so devastating in England and Wales.

NEW ZEALAND

Although there is no formal system of disclosure in criminal proceedings in New Zealand, there has been a recognition for some time that existing judge-made law arising out of the interpretation of provisions of the Official Information Act 1982, is not comprehensive enough to safeguard an accused's rights to full disclosure of evidence by the prosecution. In 1986, the Criminal Reform Committee made a number of recommendations in their Report on *Discovery in Criminal Cases*, and this was followed by further proposals made by the Law Commission in *Criminal Procedure: Part One: Disclosure and Committal* (Report No. 14, 1990).

The courts in New Zealand have shown an awareness of the potential disadvantages to defendants in the absence of specific disclosure provisions and in the leading case of *Commissioner of Police* v *Ombudsman* [1988] 1 NZLR 385, members of the Court of Appeal made a number of observations on the subject. In relation to trials on indictment, Cooke P stated:

> It is elementary that before a trial on indictment the accused is entitled to peruse the depositions taken on his committal for trial, or the witness statements of witnesses admitted instead of depositions. In such a case, by s. 183 of the Summary Proceedings Act 1957, every party to the preliminary hearing is entitled to a copy of the depositions and certain other documents, without fee. If the Crown proposes to call an additional witness at the trial, it is the standard and proper practice to supply the defence with a copy of the brief of the proposed new evidence.

This accords broadly with the practice in England and Wales. *Commissioner of Police* v *Ombudsman* was concerned with disclosure in summary proceedings and a defendant's rights under the Official Information Act 1982. That statute requires all government departments and most government agencies to make available personal information relating to an individual. Although it was not specifically intended for the purpose of disclosure in criminal proceedings, the Court of Appeal held that it entitled persons against whom criminal proceedings have been commenced to request details of the evidence against them. Applications for the disclosure of personal information are now made under the provisions of the Privacy Act 1993, which deals with access to all personal information held by any agency. The Official Information Act continues to apply to official information that is not personal information. The material provisions of the Privacy Act do not alter the situation that existed in respect of personal information under the Official Information Act, and the prosecution therefore have a duty to supply briefs of evidence, witness statements and notes of interviews in both indictable and summary proceedings, upon request. It is still open to the police, however, to refuse to release personal information if its release could prejudice the maintenance of law or a fair trial.

In so far as statements not to be used by the Crown are concerned, New Zealand has generally followed the *Bryant and Dickson* line (see chapter 6) (with there being no general duty to make statements available to the defence but a duty to provide names and addresses of the makers of the statements. There has, however, been general approval of the views expressed in *R* v *Mason* [1976] 2 NZLR 122, that the interests of justice require the supply of statements themselves in exceptional circumstances in order to prevent a miscarriage of justice: see *R* v *Connell* [1985] 2 NZLR 233. This did not, however, extend to the disclosure of information that a former suspect in a murder case had claimed to have had a past criminal association with the deceased: see *R* v *Hall* [1987] 1 NZLR 616. The duty of disclosure in respect of material evidence not adduced by the Crown is not dependent upon a request from the defence (see *R* v *Tawhiti* [1994] 2 NZLR 697); but the information has to be relevant, and where a real possibility of a miscarriage of justice is not made out an appeal will not be allowed: see *R* v *Quinn* [1991] 3 NZLR 146. New Zealand does not appear to have been troubled, in the same way as England and Wales, with tests of relevance and materiality and whether such questions are solely for the discretion of the prosecutor.

The prosecution are under a duty to disclose inconsistent statements made by a witness: see *Commissioner of Police* v *Ombudsman*, adopting the English authorities of *Mahadeo* v *R* [1936] 2 All ER 813 and *Baksh* v *R* [1958] AC 167 and more recently followed in *R* v *Poihipi* (unreported), New Zealand Court of Appeal, 19 January 1990. As we have already seen in chapter 5, New Zealand has also adopted a practical approach to the disclosure of previous convictions following the carefully considered judgment in *Wilson* v *Police* [1992] 2 NZLR 533.

The Law Commission Report proposes a statutory code for disclosure under which the prosecution would have a duty to disclose information which 'tends to support or rebut or has a bearing upon any element of the prosecution case'. There are shades of the wide definition of disclosure in the now redundant English *A-G's Guidelines* which have now been replaced by the limiting 'undermining of the prosecution case' in the CPIA 1996. The proposed code does provide exceptions to the disclosure rule along the lines of the recognised public interest grounds of exclusion whereby there is a real risk of national security and the prevention and detection of crime being prejudiced. The Law Commission shied away from proposing defence disclosure, apart from an obligation to disclose expert evidence in addition to the existing requirement to reveal evidence of an alibi.

There has been a particularly significant advance in recent years as a result of developing jurisprudence under the New Zealand Bill of Rights Act 1990. Decisions under that Act indicate an extension of pre-trial discovery to information of potential assistance to the defence which is held by persons other than the police or the Crown. In *R* v *B* [1995] 2 NZLR 172 (CA), where the accused was charged with raping his daughter some years earlier, the defence demanded an order that would require the complainant to be medically examined by a specialist of the accused's choosing. The defence had already been supplied with a medical report from the police surgeon. The application to the Court of Appeal was made pursuant to the general entitlement to a fair trial and the need for adequate resources to prepare a defence. The Court refused to make the order ruling that it could not compel such an examination, but stated that as the defence could not exercise a right to wider access of information in pre-trial discovery, in appropriate circumstances a trial could be stayed. When the matter came before the trial judge, the application was renewed and the rape charges were stayed. There are similarities here with the fast-developing jurisprudence in England and Wales concerning abuse of process, although (as we have seen in chapter 12) there are very few reported cases where the prosecution has been stayed on disclosure grounds. This progression in New Zealand has perhaps more in common with the general constitutional rights of an accused on American lines than the development of the common law.

HONG KONG

Many Commonwealth countries take their lead from the English common law. One example is the Crown Colony of Hong Kong. The application of the English Law Ordinance provides that the common law of England shall be in force in Hong Kong in so far as it is applicable to the circumstances of the colony and its inhabitants. Hong Kong follows the English practice in matters of disclosure, and para. 29 of the Attorney-General's Prosecution Policy document provides:

> Crown Counsel must disclose to the Defence all material in his possession or material of which he becomes aware which constitutes evidence relevant to the guilt or innocence of the defendant. As regards unused materials, Crown Counsel should follow the guidelines for the disclosure of 'unused materials' to the defence in cases tried on indictment issued by the Attorney-General in England and Wales in December 1981: see *Archbold*, 44th edn, para. 4–265.

The police have also issued an order known as a Headquarters Order, which regulates the disclosure of material and specifically enjoins police not to withhold any material from prosecuting counsel in order to avoid disclosure to the defence. Hong Kong case law establishes that previous convictions of witnesses must be disclosed to the defence.

In common with other jurisdictions, Hong Kong has encountered appeals where non-disclosure has featured prominently. The most recent is *R* v *Ch'ng Poh* Cr App R 333/94, where, following conviction in a complicated fraud trial, some of the grounds of appeal alleged a material irregularity in the trial based on the failure to disclose relevant information, including a number of audio tapes recording interviews with the principal prosecution witness. The tapes had been disclosed during the trial and the prosecution conceded that disclosure should have been made earlier. However, as defence counsel chose not to raise the late disclosure with the trial judge, it was held that although the late disclosure amounted to an irregularity in the trial, it would not have made any difference to the outcome and was not a material irregularity.

On 1 July 1997, Britain's 99-year lease of the New Territories expires and Hong Kong will be restored to China under the Sino-British declaration initialled in 1984. It is believed that the colony will retain special administrative and judicial independence after restoration which should safeguard the rights enjoyed by defendants under current law. In China there is no system of disclosure. Investigations are carried out by the police and procurators, including both the taking of witness statements and interviews with the defendant before the trial commences. When the accused appear in court, the case is already proved against them and the only question for the court is the degree of culpability and the appropriate sentence. Interestingly, a new law was due take effect in China in October 1996 which would permit defence lawyers to have access to the accused in the early stages of cases, instead of the current position where the lawyer is unlikely to have any case papers (let alone any 'unused material') or even to have seen the defendant until, at most, seven days before the trial!

REPUBLIC OF IRELAND

There are similarities between the prosecutorial system in Eire and that of England and Wales. The responsibility for the investigation of crime rests with the only police force in the country, the Garda Siochana, which is completely independent of the DPP. Prosecutions in the general criminal law area are directed by the DPP, or by the Garda Siochana under delegated powers from the DPP. All cases to be tried on indictment are referred to the DPP whose office decides whether the case should commence or continue. The DPP does not have the facilities to investigate offences, although there is power to advise and to suggest the need for additional evidence. The system is accusatorial with the prosecutor placing before the court all the relevant facts and helping to ensure that the accused's constitutional right to a fair trial is upheld. This includes a duty to inform the accused of material which may be favourable to the defence.

When charged with an indictable offence, the accused has a statutory right to advance notice of the prosecution case by virtue of the Criminal Procedure Act 1967. Under the provisions of that legislation, the accused may insist on a preliminary examination by a district judge who will determine the sufficiency of the prosecution (the People's) case. Even if the accused waives the right to a preliminary examination, there is a duty of disclosure in relation to certain documents which are collectively known as the 'Book of Evidence'. Thus, accused persons have disclosed to them the charges, the statements of witnesses and a list of exhibits. Any further evidence obtained in support of the People's case must be served before the trial.

The Republic of Ireland has no specific rules for the disclosure of material which does not form part of the People's case; neither is there any system for ensuring that the Garda Siochana have revealed all relevant information to the prosecutor. Disclosure is, however, carried out on an informal basis and the deliberate withholding or concealment of relevant information would meet with the strong disapproval of the court. The prosecution are under a duty to disclose matters affecting the credibility of witnesses. In *DPP (People)* v *Kelly* [1987] IR 596, the Court of Criminal Appeal quashed a conviction because the defence had not been aware that an important prosecution witness had a number of serious convictions against him (a fact of which the prosecution themselves had been unaware).

There appear to be no instances of non-disclosure leading to a miscarriage of justice, which may be an indication that an informal system of disclosure by a prosecutor acting fairly is just as effective as the more formal or statutory regimes in other common law jurisdictions. There is no requirement on the defence to disclose their defence other than an obligation to reveal alibi evidence.

EUROPE

Criminal proceedings in most European legal jurisdictions are based on an inquisitorial system of justice where judges supervise the pre-trial preparation of evidence and examine the witnesses and the accused. This contrasts with the adversarial system in England and Wales and other common law jurisdictions where the prosecution gather and present their evidence and the defence cross-examine the witnesses and then call evidence of their own; the judge is not a participant in the proceedings but acts as a sort of referee, keeping the parties in check and ruling on the admissibility of evidence. Although each European country has its own criminal justice system which has developed to suit its own individual history, tradition and custom, there are a number of common features which are absent in the criminal justice process in England and Wales. Two factors are of particular significance when disclosure procedures are considered: first, the task and functions of the prosecutor in relation to the investigation of crime; and, secondly, the preparation of evidence gathered in what is commonly referred to as 'the dossier'.

It is no part of the function of this book to examine the comparative merits and disadvantages of the inquisitorial system of criminal justice and the adversarial system of England and Wales. Support for the continental system received the attention of the Runciman Commission, but they concluded that there would be no advantage in the introduction of wholesale changes to our system. (It is perhaps reassuring that the *juge d'instruction* attracts just as much criticism in France as do our own judicial institutions from commentators in this country!) It is relevant, however, to try to assess whether disclosure issues are dealt with effectively in inquisitorial systems. Direct comparisons are impossible because of the fundmental differences in the judicial institutions and their procedures, but the following brief examination of what occurs in some European countries may give an indication of whether the continental system of disclosure is superior to our own.

The separation of the functions of investigation and prosecution, so much a feature of the system in England and Wales and preserved by the Prosecution of Offences Act 1985, is virtually unknown in the rest of Europe. In the Netherlands the public prosecutor is usually involved from the outset in the investigation of serious offences, although the investigation of minor offences is left to the police. The prosecutor has a duty to look for exculpatory evidence as well as that which supports the case against the accused. The picture is similar in Belgium where the prosecutor's role is to look for the truth and not simply for evidence which points to the accused. In Germany, the Prosecutor's Office is part of the Ministry of Justice and its role is to investigate crime and look at facts and circumstances which not only incriminate but also exonerate. Prosecutors in France and Greece also have responsibility for investigating crime. Denmark is perhaps a little closer to the English system as the special code of criminal procedure allows for most criminal investigations to be conducted by the police, although the more serious are supervised by the public prosecutor.

In each of these jurisdictions, therefore, there is a lesser risk of material existing which the prosecutor knows nothing about. A constant theme in the development of the rules in England and Wales is the failure of the police to reveal all relevant information to the prosecutor. In a tiny number of cases the failure has been deliberate, but in others it has been brought about by inadvertence or a lack of appreciation that the material in question should be retained as being potentially relevant. If the prosecutor is involved in the investigation from an early stage, such problems are less likely to arise. Furthermore, as the duty upon prosecutors in nearly all European jurisdictions is to gather information which not only incriminates the accused but is also favourable to them, defence interests are well preserved.

A common feature of continental systems is the file of investigation or the dossier. For example, in France the dossier is usually in four parts which contain the evidence, the record of detention of the accused, the antecedents and any previous convictions recorded against the accused, and miscellaneous correspondence concerning the case. The first part (*'Pièces de fond'*) is obviously the crucial *section* of the file for it contains the police report and statements taken by the police, the record of any examination of the accused and any statements made by him or her, reports by experts, etc. While the dossier is not necessarily quite as comprehensive in other jurisdictions, its availability for inspection by the defence is the key to full and proper disclosure.

Interestingly, the timing of access to the dossier varies. In Germany, as soon as the investigation is complete the defence have a right of access to the file. Access may be denied before the completion of the investigation if the prosecutor considers that the progress of the inquiry would be endangered. There is similar access before charges have been finalised in Greece and France where the defence may view the contents at any stage of the proceedings. In Sweden the defence have a right to be kept informed of all the evidence. Denmark allows access to evidence gathered, including that which the prosecution do not intend to use; but Spain grants access only to material produced to the examining magistrate — there is no right to see material which does not form part of the prosecution case. At the pre-trial stage, the defence in the Netherlands have full access to the dossier; but this is not the case in neighbouring Belgium, where accused persons have no right to consult the file at the pre-trial stage unless they are remanded in custody. Every time the continuation of detention is considered by the court, the accused in Belgium may see the file. Once the summons to appear in court has been issued, however, the dossier is fully available for inspection. There have been recent moves in Belgium to increase access to the dossier, not only to improve the timing but also to ensure that it contains a more balanced view of the investigation and not just records made at the request of the public prosecutor. In Italy, however, there are proposals to remove the dossier altogether. Italy has traditionally had a system of full disclosure before the preliminary hearing not only of the prosecution case but also of material helpful to the defence which is contained in the file lodged with the court. There have been recent changes in the judicial system in Italy which have led to the abandonment of the inquisitorial system in favour of the adversarial system. Whether this will result in less full discovery of evidence remains to be seen.

Theoretically, disclosure of evidence by means of the dossier should provide the accused with all the information needed to prepare a full defence to any charge brought. If the police and prosecutor have done their jobs properly, all relevant material will have been gathered, including that favourable to the accused as well as that which is incriminatory. There are concessions, however, that sometimes the dossier is not quite as independent as it should be, and some criminal justice systems do not permit unlimited access until shortly before the trial. In so far as evidence to be adduced by the prosecution is concerned, the dossier appears to have no advantages over the full disclosure provisions in England and Wales. Statutory provisions for advance disclosure, service of statements in committal and transfer cases, coupled with the practice of the CPS to serve statements in imprisonable summary only cases, means that defendants are fully informed of the evidence against them.

The advantages of the dossier are in relation to the availability of exculpatory material, the timing of disclosure and a more full disclosure of the way the investigation has developed. The common law rules, and now the provisions of the CPIA 1996 and the disclosure code, have gone a long way to ensuring that information helpful to the accused is brought to notice, but disclosure does not commence until after proceedings have been instituted. This can work to the disadvantage of the defence where, for example, access to exhibits is denied until long after they have been examined and reported on by an expert instructed by the police.

Provisions for defence disclosure in the CPIA 1996 are, without doubt, the most controversial additions to the discovery rules in England and Wales. Defence disclosure is a feature of a number of continental jurisdictions, though; but it must be conceded that it is more compatible with an inquisitorial system of justice than an adversarial one where the defendant traditionally has nothing to prove. In Sweden, there are quite stringent requirements on the defence to disclose the evidence they wish to adduce and what they intend to prove by the calling of such evidence. Failure to comply with the requirements will result not only in an adjournment of the trial, but also in financial and disciplinary penalties against errant lawyers. Denmark also insists upon advance disclosure of the defence case, while the submission of the names and addresses of defence witnesses is a requirement in Denmark and Germany. The systems of Italy and France do not allow for prosecution examination of evidence which the defence intend to call, although all defence witnesses have to be designated at the start of the trial. None of the disclosure regimes appears to require the defence to inform the prosecution of any tactics or challenges of the prosecution evidence that they intend to employ. The closest to a process of discovery as in civil proceedings is reached in Spain where there is a system of pre-trial pleadings in order to clarify the issues. This involves both sides informing the court of the evidence that will be brought and the witnesses who will be called in support.

As stated at the outset, comparisons between the disclosure provisions of any European country and those of England and Wales are of limited value because of the vastly different approaches to criminal justice. It is clear from the dissenting judgments in the European Court of Human Rights case of *Edwards* (see chapter 12) that members of the Court were far from impressed with an adversarial system which allowed for the non-disclosure of evidence favourable to the defendant. Of course, disclosure provisions have changed radically since then and a continental system which guarantees no miscarriages of justice because of non-disclosure has yet to be perfected. While the introduction of a dossier in a criminal investigation in this country may have advantages to the accused, it is out of the question while the prosecutor has no role in the investigation. If, or until, that time arrives, the defence will probably have to make do with the police schedule of documents gathered or created during the investigation.

ISRAEL

The Runciman Commission looked at discovery procedures in a number of jurisdictions, including Israel, where the rules of law concerned with disclosure in criminal proceedings are more detailed and clearly defined than in many other countries. Where an indictment has been filed, the defence have a statutory right to inspect and copy the investigation material in the possession of the prosecution, which includes not just the material in the hands of the prosecutor but that retained by the investigator too. The Supreme Court of Israel has ruled that there should be a degree of flexibility in relation to the term 'investigation material' to ensure that the defence have every opportunity of inspecting material which allows a full preparation of the defence case. This includes any information which is detrimental to the prosecution's case and the results of scientific examinations.

The courts have also held that the police must inform the prosecutor of the existence of secret intelligence material and that some information concerning such documents must be conveyed to the defence. This appears to be very close to the *Davis, Johnson and Rowe* arrangements which are now an accepted part of criminal justice procedures in England and Wales. The court then conducts a balancing exercise, not unlike that encountered in PII applications, where it must decide whether the need to allow access to the information in order to do justice to the defendant prevails over the interest in not revealing the information. Non-disclosure of relevant information, whether sensitive or not, will lead to an acquittal if the court considers that the accused has been denied a fair trial.

Israeli law requires the defence to make advance disclosure of alibi and expert evidence, and the prosecution may apply to the court to inspect and copy documents such as medical certificates in order that they may make their own inquiries.

UNITED STATES OF AMERICA

The Sixth Amendment of the US Constitution requires that a defendant 'be informed of the nature and cause of the accusation against him'. This is usually taken to mean that the prosecution must inform the defendant of the charge with sufficient particularity to ensure an understanding of the allegation(s) made by the state. There is no general right under the Constitution for pre-trial discovery in criminal proceedings. States have a considerable amount of flexibility in deciding what material should be disclosed, although there is a vast amount of case law and Federal Rules of Procedure which regulate the duties of the Government in this respect. The general principle was summed up by Fortas J in *Giles* v *State of Maryland*, 386 US 66 (1967), at p. 100, as: 'A criminal trial is not a game in which the state's function is to outwit and entrap its quarry. The state's pursuit is justice, not a victim.'

Rule 16 of the Federal Rules of Criminal Procedure provides for the disclosure, upon request, of relevant written or recorded statements made by the defendant; the prior criminal record of the defendant; books, papers, documents, photographs and other tangible objects in the possession or control of the Government and which are material to the preparation of the defence; and the results or reports of physical or mental examinations or scientific tests and experiments. Disclosure is effected by giving permission to inspect and photocopy. There is no duty to provide access to internal investigation reports and memoranda. The rules also permit reciprocal disclosure of similar information in the possession of the defence.

Rule 26.2 of the Federal Rules of Criminal Procedure and 18 United States Code Section 3500 (commonly known as 'Jencks Act') govern the disclosure of witnesses' statements. Jencks Act 1957 was introduced to clarify and limit the Supreme Court's ruling in *Jencks* v *US*, 353 US 657 (1957), and allows for the production of the statements of prosecution witnesses after those witnesses have given direct evidence in a federal trial. Rule 26.2 provides for the production of the statements of defence witnesses in exactly the same manner following a ruling in *US* v *Nobles*, 422 US 225 (1975). where the Supreme Court held that the judicial power to order the production of prior statements applied equally to Government requests of the defence. Production is only upon motion by either party and the purpose of the Act and Rule 26.2 is to enable each side to cross-examine fully.

If the statement of a witness for the prosecution contains exculpatory information the Government is under a constitutional duty to disclose that material to the defence pursuant to the Supreme Court ruling in *Brady* v *Maryland*, 373 US 83 (1963) (known as the *Brady* doctrine). The duty of disclosure under the *Brady* doctrine is regarded as one of general fairness and a minimum requirement of the prosecution to conduct their case in an unbiased and unprejudiced manner. The obligation extends not only to the prosecutor's office but also to persons connected with the Government's case, such as members of investigation agencies.

Broadly speaking, there are two categories of document which are disclosable under the *Brady* rule, i.e. material which tends to be exculpatory and material which may be used to impeach Government witnesses. In a similar way to that experienced in England and Wales, the judiciary in the United States have periodically grappled with what is truly exculpatory — in other words, tests of relevance and materiality. Generally the tests seem to have been applied more narrowly; for example, there is no duty of disclosure in relation to witnesses who are already known to the accused or who are readily accessible to the defence team. The failure to reveal a confession made by another is clearly disclosable (as was the case in *Brady* itself), as is information relevant to identification and favourable reports of physical or mental examinations. There is no requirement, however, to disclose details concerning informants or arrangements with undercover operatives. The prosecution must disclose the criminal record or prior material acts of misconduct by witnesses whom they call as part of their case.

In *Brady* v *Maryland* itself, the Supreme Court held that, irrespective of good or bad faith, if the prosecution suppressed evidence which was helpful to the defence, due process had been violated. *US* v *Agurs*, 427 US 97, 107 (1976), described three situations where the court would overturn a conviction arising out of non-disclosure: first, where the prosecution knew or should have known that the case contained perjured testimony which was likely to affect the jury's judgment; secondly, where the prosecution refused to respond to specific requests for information if the material required might have affected the outcome of the trial; and, thirdly, where the defence failed to request information, if the undisclosed evidence would have cast a reasonable doubt upon the conviction. Interestingly, this analysis of the non-disclosure situation appears to require an examination of materiality which will vary depending on whether the defence asked for information or not.

Despite the plethora of case law and the Federal Rules of Criminal Procedure, no state appears to have found it necessary to legislate for disclosure in a manner which corresponds to the CPIA 1996 and disclosure code. Furthermore, there are no settled guidelines either for the preservation of documents or for the timing of disclosure. Disclosure arrangements vary; and while informal agreements exist in some states, others engage in quite open discovery procedures with statements being revealed before trial. Some states gave gone down the path of 'two way disclosure' requiring the defence to disclose details of any alibi, a defence of insanity, and the names and addresses of defence witnesses.

JAPAN

The criminal justice system in Japan is sometimes held out to be the model to which other Asian countries should aspire. The Code of Criminal Procedure 1948 is a detailed code setting out all aspects of practice and procedure. The principle of criminal investigation is explained in Article 1 as 'to clarify the true facts of cases and to apply and realise criminal laws or ordinances fairly and speedily, while thoroughly accomplishing the maintenance of public welfare and security of fundamental human rights of individuals'. There is great emphasis in Japan in eliminating from the system at the earliest possible stage those against whom there is insufficient evidence or who will not require punishment. It is an important part of the investigation process, therefore, to gather evidence which will not only help to convict but also help to exonerate suspects.

The police usually conduct a criminal investigation during its inital stages. Once the investigation is complete, the case will be referred to the public prosecutor. The prosecutor also has a role in investigating allegations of crime and may interrogate suspects, interview witnesses and examine evidence secured by the police before deciding whether the suspect should be charged. The Code of Criminal Procedure allows for the preservation of evidence and the right of the defence to inspect and, with the permission of a judge, copy relevant evidence. Defence counsel may also be present at the examination or inquiry by an expert witness.

Japan does not appear to have found it necessary to enshrine in its Code specific duties on the prosecutor to disclose material which the prosecution do not intend to use. It is nevertheless implicit in the Code and the general objectives of the criminal justice system that any information helpful to the defence will be disclosed.

15 Proposals for Reform of the Common Law Disclosure Rules

ROYAL COMMISSION ON CRIMINAL JUSTICE 1993

Recommendations relating to disclosure

As a direct result of the quashed convictions of the Maguires, the Guildford Four and the Birmingham Six, the Home Secretary announced the establishment of a Royal Commission on Criminal Justice on 14 March 1991, under the Chairmanship of Viscount Runciman of Doxford. The Government were concerned that the cases had seriously undermined public confidence in the criminal justice system. During the course of the proceedings a number of important issues had arisen, of which non-disclosure was just one; but a year into their deliberations, the Commission had a further miscarriage of justice to contend with, that of Judith Ward, where non-disclosure was the principal cause of injustice. The Commission's terms of reference were very wide and amounted to an examination of the effectiveness of the criminal justice system from the commencement of an investigation to conviction. In July 1993, the Commission reported and made 352 recommendations, 17 of which were in relation to disclosure (see The Royal Commission on Criminal Justice, Cm 2263, London: HMSO, 1993: the 'Runciman Commission Report'). Above all, the Runciman Commission Report acknowledged that all was not well in the kingdom of disclosure.

The Report reviewed the recent developments in the law which had culminated in a disclosure regime that implied a wide-ranging system for ensuring that material in the possession of the investigating authorities was revealed to the prosecutor and disclosed to the defence. As desirable and reasonable as this might appear on paper, however, it was recognised that the requirements were not capable of being met. The representations made by the police service were given a full airing in the Report and difficulties of compliance and the concerns at the inroads being made into the confidentiality of the informant system were fully appreciated. There was support for the procedures recently recommended in *Davis, Johnson and Rowe*, but disquiet was expressed that some material for which grounds could be made out for non-disclosure (for example, commercial security material) might not attract PII and consequently could not be withheld.

The unanimous view of the Runciman Commission was that:

> . . . a reasonable balance between the duties of the prosecution and the rights of the defence requires that a new regime be created with two stages of disclosure. The first stage of primary disclosure would, subject to appropriate exceptions, be automatic. The second stage, of secondary or further disclosure, would be made if the defence could establish its relevance to the case. (Report, chapter 6, para. 50)

There was not the same unanimity, however, when it came to how the defence were to establish matters which were relevant to their case. Defence disclosure, with two minor exceptions, is an alien concept in the adversarial system of criminal justice in England and Wales. The requirement that the prosecution have to prove their case beyond reasonable doubt is said to be inconsistent with any qualification that defendants should give advance particulars of their defence. The exceptions — of providing details of an alibi (under s. 11, Criminal Justice Act 1967) and advance notice of an expert to be called (by virtue of s. 81, PACE 1984 and the Crown Court (Advance Notice of Expert Evidence) Rules 1987) — are justified on the basis that they do not require complete disclosure of the defence case but merely prevent late fabrication of alibis and expert evidence which would only cause delays in the trial in order that the prosecution could investigate and, if necessary, call evidence in rebuttal. Most members of the Commission were agreed, though, that the reasons for enlarging the requirements on the defence to disclose their case outweighed the historical objections. Professor Zander was the lone dissentient, and his note of dissent was recorded at pp. 221 to 235 of the Report.

Response to Royal Commission's recommendations

There was a predictable reaction to the recommendation for a two-stage disclosure process. It was welcomed on the one hand by the police and prosecuting authorities, but viewed with considerable scepticism by those with anxieties about defence disclosure. Typical of the latter was the response of the Legal Action Group, which supported full disclosure by the prosecution and opposed the Commission's proposals for less: 'With so many miscarriages of justice arising from partial disclosure, it is necessary to have strong, even Draconian rules' (see Legal Action Group, *Preventing Miscarriages of Justice*, p. 14). Other comments from interested bodies were more constructive, but no one was pretending that the solutions would be easy. However, the Runciman Commission had identified a possible way forward, and this would be built on by the Home Secretary in his proposals for the legislation which would eventually crystallise into the CPIA 1996.

The Royal Commission had, not surprisingly, taken two years in which to report, and the ink on the Report was barely dry when the courts continued in their inexorable pursuit of change in the rules of criminal discovery. The recommendation in the Report concerning primary disclosure of material relevant to the offence or surrounding circumstances of the case was swept aside by the materiality test laid down in *Keane*; and the proposal that the prosecution should be able to apply for non-disclosure on grounds of sensitivity which fell short of a claim of PII found no support from the Court of Appeal in *Winston Brown* where the judgment concluded that there was no such concept as sensitivity *simpliciter*. The ball was now in the Government's court to decide whether to legislate, or whether to allow the courts to persevere with their attempts to regulate disclosure.

If legislation and codes of practice were to be adopted, how many of the Commission's recommendations should be embraced and, in particular, what was to be done about defence disclosure? The Runciman Commission was not the only body looking into the criminal justice system and agitating for change in the disclosure rules. In 1991, the Bar Council had considered whether there should be any extension to obligatory pre-trial disclosure; and a year later the Lord Chancellor's Department, the Home Office and the Legal Secretariat to the Law Officers issued a Consultation Paper on Long Criminal Trials. The Consultation Paper drew attention to the different requirements that a judge could impose on the prosecution and defence to state their cases under s. 9(4)(a) and (5), Criminal Justice Act 1987. The Consultation Paper identified inadequate defence disclosure as being a basic problem which added to the length of trials because the scope of the judge's powers was too restricted, orders for disclosure were often inadequately complied with, and the sanctions against non-compliance were limited (see para. 4.20 of the Consultation Paper). The Consultation Paper sought views on whether defence disclosure was likely to lead to shorter trials. Predictably, the response was mixed.

In the months following the publication of the Runciman Commission Report, there was considerable pressure on the Government to introduce changes in the disclosure rules. The courts had failed to give clear and consistent rulings on a number of disclosure issues. Practitioners, although divided on the solutions, were agreed that current arrangements were unsatisfactory. The police were complaining long and hard that the burdens placed upon them were too severe, and they were able to point to a number of examples of cases being abandoned in order to prevent their sources of intelligence being compromised. And what was the general public to make of the clamour? Having seen the convictions of a number of persons overturned because of non-disclosure by the prosecution, they were now being told in the Runciman Report that the pendulum had swung too far the other way and that the guilty were going free because the new rules of disclosure were too onerous and incapable of being met; trials were getting longer and more expensive, the technicalities of the law were clouding the real issues, and the confusion was bringing the entire criminal justice system into yet more disrepute.

HOME SECRETARY'S PROPOSALS FOR REFORM

The Government took just over two years following the publication of the Runciman Commission Report to respond, when the Home Secretary announced his proposals to the House of Commons (see Hansard vol. 260 HC Deb, 6th ser., col. 162). The measures were set out in two sets of proposals, *Disclosure: Consultation Document* (Cm 2864, London: HMSO, 1995) and *Disclosure in Criminal Cases in Northern Ireland* (which was issued by the Northern Ireland Office). They largely commanded all-party support. Michael Howard commended his proposals to the House with the words:

> There can be no doubt that the current arrangements have undermined public confidence in the criminal justice system by creating a gap between law and justice. My aim is to close that gap. The proposals should prove more effective in convicting the guilty, while continuing to protect the innocent.

The then Shadow Home Secretary, Jack Straw, welcomed the proposals and summed up the Opposition view of the current position as follows:

> There is widespread public impatience with the present trial process in England and Wales and a feeling that too much of the system may resemble a game and too little a serious examination of the truth.

On behalf of the Liberal Democrats, Simon Hughes was equally encouraging:

> They go in the right direction, and it is clearly correct that there should be a Royal Commission set of recommendations, a consultation paper, and eventually, legislation. The idea that the defence must also assist in the trial and not keep its hand secret to the last is not only right but meets the public's desire to secure a correct balance.

Response to the Government's recommendations

If the Government thought that they were in for an easy ride with their proposals, however, they were soon to be disabused of that notion. While the police and prosecuting authorities were largely content, the reaction from the Bar and Law Society was far from enthusiastic. While not necessarily opposed to the idea of a statutory framework for disclosure, the Bar Council and Law Society had deep reservations about the proposed scheme. The August editorial of *Criminal Law Review* led with 'Disclosure and Disequilibrium' [1995] Crim LR 585, which was followed by Roger Leng, 'Losing Sight of the Defendant: The Government's

Proposals on Pre-trial Disclosure' [1995] Crim LR 704, where the writer claimed that the proposals would effect a significant change in the values of the criminal process in the interests of efficiency.

Objectives of Government's disclosure scheme

The pre-conditions for the Government's proposals were set out in para. 19 of the *Consultation Document*. Any reform must:

- avoid increasing the risk that any new scheme will result in the conviction of the innocent;
- reduce the burden of current requirements on the investigating and prosecuting authorities in relation to the volume of material to be disclosed, without prejudicing the fairness of the trial;
- reduce the scope for opportunistic requests by the defence which are designed not to elicit material supporting the defendant's version of events but primarily to discover profitable lines of argument which divert from or obscure the real issues; and
- limit the scope for adverse rulings on sensitive material, at least where the material does not undermine the prosecution case, which cause the abandonment of prosecutions.

It is difficult to take issue with these objectives. There would be no support for any scheme which increased the possibility of further miscarriages of justice. There can be no doubt that current common law requirements were unnecessarily onerous for investigators and prosecutors, and if a scheme could be devised to reduce the burdens on them (and, by implication, the enormous drain on resources which are ultimately met by the public purse) it would be universally welcomed. Some would disagree that opportunistic requests for disclosure are a common feature of criminal trials or that the 'adverse rulings on sensitive material' were anything other than correct. Those who subscribe to those points of view argue that the police have exaggerated the problem and have unduly influenced the Royal Commission and the Home Secretary as to the scale of the difficulty. Whether they are right or wrong is immaterial, though, as the principles are surely correct. The obfuscation of the real issues and unfair rulings which cause the abandonment of prosecutions properly brought have no place in a criminal justice system.

Outline of Government scheme

The proposals made by the Home Secretary involved a scheme which could be broken down into six stages:

- a duty on the investigator to preserve and retain investigation material and make it available to the prosecutor;

- a duty on the prosecutor to serve on the defence material upon which the prosecution intend to base their case;
- a duty on the prosecutor to disclose certain material upon which the prosecution intend not to rely ('primary prosecution disclosure');
- a requirement on the defence to provide before the start of the trial sufficient particulars of their case to identify the issues in dispute ('defence disclosure');
- a duty on the prosecution to identify any further material which may assist the defence in the light of information they have provided ('secondary prosecution disclosure');
- procedures for the handling of information for which PII is asserted.

The scheme also provided for sanctions for failures to carry out the requirements laid down and for disputes to be settled by the court.

The Government's proposals were very much in line with the recommendations of the Royal Commission, although there were two significant departures. The first was in relation to the test for disclosure where the Royal Commission had stated that 'the prosecution's initial duty should be to supply to the defence copies of all material relevant to the offence or to the offender or to the surrounding circumstances of the case' Runciman Commission Report, Chapter 6, para. 51). This criterion reflected the duty of disclosure in the *A-G's Guidelines* and did not, of course, take into account the more restrictive materiality test set out in *Keane*. The Government's scheme concentrated on the effect of the unused material on the prosecution's case and that of the defence, when revealed.

The second main difference concerned defence disclosure. The Runciman Commission thought that it would be sufficient for the defence to disclose the substance of their case and that this could be done, in most instances, by ticking a list of possibilities such as 'accident', self-defence', 'consent', etc. The Home Secretary's new scheme required the defence to provide more detailed information in advance of the trial which would reveal what was really in dispute. Defence disclosure is such an emotive issue that it requires separate consideration.

DEFENCE DISCLOSURE

The very notion of accused persons having to disclose anything of their defence to the prosecution is enough to raise hackles and set many pulses racing. Despite the recommendation of the majority of members of the Runciman Commission, Professor Michael Zander was so strongly opposed to the idea that his note of dissent was included at p. 221 of the Runciman Commission Report. Although, as we have seen in the previous chapter, defence disclosure is by no means uncommon in a number of continental jurisdictions, it is considered by many to be anathema to the adversarial system of criminal justice. The Government's justification for including a defence disclosure stage in their discovery package is to assist in identifying and narrowing the issues in dispute, to encourage the better preparation of cases and to improve the conduct of the trial. Are these laudable objectives to be achieved at a cost of disadvantaging the accused and risking the conviction of the innocent? The proposals contemplate that once primary disclosure has been made by the prosecution, the defence will provide sufficient particulars of their case to identify the issues in dispute.

The case against defence disclosure rests largely on the premise that in an adversarial system of criminal justice, the prosecution have to prove their case. The defendant does not have to prove innocence, so why should the defendant help the prosecution by providing information as to the nature of the defence and the witnesses that will be called in support of the defence case? It is also claimed that in the majority of cases the defence is obvious from the papers and what the accused has told the police in interview. Furthermore, if the prosecution are told of the defence before trial, they will have an unfair advantage in investigating it and preparing rebuttal evidence. It is also questioned whether time and money will really be saved as, in order to prepare sufficient particulars to identify the issues before trial, there will be a need for extra work and conferences, thus causing delay and expense. Some of these arguments are more persuasive than others, but there can be no doubting that defence disclosure represents a fundamental change to the general principles under which the criminal trial in England and Wales has traditionally taken place.

The arguments against defence disclosure are countered by assertions that a better definition of the issues in dispute will ensure that cases are better prepared and that trials will be shortened and less expensive. Defence disclosure is part and parcel of the Government's overall plans to focus more sharply on the real issues in the trial by holding pre-trial reviews and preparatory hearings where many preliminary matters can be resolved, which will represent a move away from tactical advantages gained by surprise. A requirement to give notice of the defence also prevents the prosecution being ambushed by the raising of a surprise defence at the last moment and avoids lengthy, expensive and often unnecessary pre-trial disclosure of prosecution material. It is said that disclosure of the defence will not harm those with genuine defences; and it may even assist to the extent that the prosecution can make further inquiries and, if there is substance in the information provided, discontinue the prosecution.

Some of the arguments on the general principle of the correctness of compelling accused persons to provide details of their defence were advanced in *R v Cowan* (1995) *The Times*, 13 October 1995, where the Court of Appeal issued guidance in connection with the alterations in the law concerning the right to silence. The Court rejected as misconceived the argument that s. 35, Criminal Justice and Public Order Act 1994 altered the burden of proof or watered it down, as the prosecution still had to establish a prima facie case before any question of the defendant testifying was raised. In a similar way, the contention that defence disclosure might lead to defendants incriminating themselves is fallacious, as by the time any disclosure is required, the prosecution must not only have established a prima facie case in order to institute or continue proceedings but, under the Government's proposals, will already have made primary disclosure themselves.

Clearly, there are substantial and convincing arguments for and against defence disclosure. The *Consultation Document* was unclear whether defence disclosure should be mandatory in all cases, or whether it should only be used as a trigger for secondary prosecution disclosure. In other words, if the defence are satisfied with primary disclosure, is there any need for them to disclose anything of their defence beyond that required by the current law? It is only if they want further disclosure by the prosecution that they should have to give reasons, and this would involve disclosing the nature of the defence. Such a scheme might allay some fears and suspicions of the anti-defence disclosure lobby, and it is surely not unreasonable for the prosecution — which has disclosed all that it believes to be material — to ask for details when faced with requests for more information. (This has now been addressed in the CPIA 1996 which makes defence disclosure mandatory in cases tried on indictment but voluntary in summary trials.)

In addition to the objections to defence disclosure on grounds of principle, cost and efficiency, there are two other pragmatic concerns which merit comment. First, can defence disclosure be made to work and, secondly, can the prosecution cope with it? The first question is posed in the light of the overwhelming failure of earlier voluntary schemes introduced at some courts (for example, an exchange of information scheme pioneered at the Central Criminal Court by the Criminal Bar Association in the late 1970s) and existing statutory provisions which require an element of disclosure by the defence. Although the Court of Appeal have, from time to time, had to consider the exercise of discretion by judges in excluding alibi evidence (see *R* v *Sullivan* (1970) 54 Cr App 389, *R* v *Cooper* (1979) 69 Cr App R 229, *R* v *Lewis* (1969) 53 Cr App R 76 and *R* v *Hassan* (1970) 54 Cr App R 56), the number of cases where such evidence is disallowed by trial judges is minimal. Applications out of time to adduce evidence of an alibi are a mere formality as no judge is prepared to allow the defendant to be prejudiced by a failure to comply with the provisions of s. 11, Criminal Justice Act 1967. A similar picture emerges in the case of expert evidence under the Crown Court (Advance Notice of Expert Evidence) Rules 1987, where late applications are invariably acceded to, sometimes at the expense of allowing the prosecution to seek expert advice of their own. Lastly, the comments of the Consultation Paper on Long Criminal Trials (see above) in relation to the provision of a defence statement under s. 9, Criminal Justice Act 1967 in complex fraud trials are relevant. The Consultation Paper recommends sanctions for non-compliance with the requirements for defence disclosure. It will be in the discretion of the court to decide what inferences can be drawn from a failure to comply with the rules, but the portents for a robust attitude to this make it questionable that defence disclosure will work in the way that it is hoped.

The second question relates to the ability of the prosecution to cope with a full scheme of defence disclosure in every case tried on indictment and some tried summarily. No figures are available, but it is indisputable that the common law disclosure rules have meant that the preparation time spent on cases by the police, prosecuting authority and counsel has increased dramatically. Comments to the effect that more time was spent on disclosure than on reviewing the case itself are not always made in jest, and many prosecuting counsel have stories to tell of hours and days being spent in police stations examining investigation material. There may be some reduction in this as a result of the new proposals, but disclosure is now such a vital part of case preparation that it will continue to take up a great deal of the time of all members of the prosecution team. The Government scheme anticipates that the prosecution will act upon defence disclosure by assessing whether there is anything else to be disclosed and by taking appropriate steps to investigate matters further, revising what evidence needs to be called in support of the prosecution case, etc. In the more serious cases, this will undoubtedly be achieved, but compliance in all cases where the defence carry out their part of the scheme will place a substantial burden on investigators and prosecutors alike. Savings at the primary disclosure stage may be dissipated at the defence disclosure stage.

CRIMINAL PROCEDURE AND INVESTIGATIONS BILL

The Criminal Procedure and Investigations Bill, despite a fair measure of all-party support, did not have a smooth passage through Parliament. At the report stage of the Bill in the House of Lords, Lord McIntosh of Haringey drew attention to the fact that there were almost 100 Government amendments at the committee stage of the Bill in the first Chamber (see Hansard vol. 567 HL Deb, 5th ser., col 1408) and Lord Rodgers of Quarry Bank declared 'In some 25 years of parliamentary life I can remember no occasion on which a Bill that was not urgent has come forward so ill prepared and carelessly drafted' (col. 1408). In addition, the Bill eventually departed the House of Lords after its third reading minus any provisions on the vexed subject of third party disclosure which were promised at the time the Bill was introduced.

As a result of submissions received from interested parties and organisations, the Bill showed a number of changes from the proposals advanced in the *Consultation Document*. First, the Government had proposed a scheme whereby the schedule of unused material prepared by the police should not be given to the defence. This was undoubtedly misguided. If the police did not have to prepare a schedule for the use of the prosecutor there would be an argument for not preparing one for defence use on resource grounds; but as the schedule is essential in revealing to the prosecutor what material exists, there has to be good reason for not allowing the defence a sight of it. The Government were clearly concerned that this would only enhance 'the scope for opportunistic requests' to trawl through all the investigation material in the Micawberesque hope that something might turn up. If this was the worry then there was an argument for not providing the schedule as part of primary disclosure but for making it available only at the secondary stage after the defence had provided justification for being provided with a copy. However, if the objective of the disclosure proposals was to restore faith in the prosecution's ability to deal with disclosure issues fairly and responsibly, providing the defence with a schedule of the non-sensitive material gathered as part of the investigation would go a long way to achieving that aim. (It is also the situation that in many cases the defence will not be too concerned with the schedule, and even less interested in going to the police station to examine the documents listed therein.) The willingness of the Government to listen to representations on this point and to include the disclosure of the schedule as part of primary disclosure is a major factor giving credibility to the proposals overall and an important safeguard against genuine errors of judgment and inadvertent non-disclosure of relevant information. The effect of the Bill is that material listed on the schedule will not be disclosed unless the defence justify access to the material as part of their duty of defence disclosure.

The second important change in the requirements made by the Bill was that the defence no longer had to disclose in advance of the trial the names and addresses of the witnesses they proposed to call, except where the defence was one of alibi and the information was already required by law. The controversial requirement to provide names and addresses had been the subject of censure by the Law Society, Bar Council and others, and it was recognised that there would only be marginal benefits to the trial process and little advantage in practice to the prosecution. The requirement was sensibly abandoned.

After several days of deliberations in the House of Lords, the Bill was returned to the Commons and referred to a Standing Committee. Amendments and new clauses, proposed by both the Government and Opposition, continued to flow thick and fast throughout the Committee's four sittings and during the report stage in the House of Commons. Eventually, on 4 July 1996, the Bill was given the Royal Assent.

16 Criminal Procedure and Investigations Act 1996

The CPIA 1996 is in seven parts, the first two of which only are directly related to disclosure. Part I deals with the disclosure provisions and Part II with criminal investigations and the responsibility of the Secretary of State to prepare a Code of Practice (referred to hereafter as the disclosure code). Parts III and IV are concerned with pre-trial procedures, and Parts V and VI with a number of reforms of court procedures. Lastly, Part VII contains miscellaneous and general provisions designed to improve the administration of justice. Part I is considered below, and Part II and the disclosure code are examined in detail in the following chapter.

COMMON LAW RULES AS TO DISCLOSURE

Section 21(1) of the CPIA 1996 provides that as regards things falling to be done after the relevant time in relation to an alleged offence (1 April 1997), the rules of common law relating to disclosure of material by the prosecutor, which were effective immediately before that day, do not apply as regards things falling to be done after 1 April 1997 in relation to the alleged offence. The effect of s. 21 as a whole is that in relation to offences where no criminal investigation has begun before 1 April 1997, when the accused pleads not guilty in proceedings to be heard summarily or when the proceedings are committed or transferred to the Crown Court, the rules of common law no longer apply and the disclosure provisions of the CPIA 1996 take effect. The rules of common law as to disclosure in the public interest are, however, unaffected as a result of the provisions of s. 21(2). Public interest immunity will continue to be asserted in accordance with the current common law rules. The 1996 Act will unquestionably generate a new body of case law in relation to disclosure, and much of the earlier case law which preceded the new Act will be redundant. However, the development of the earlier common law rules will undoubtedly be of relevance and assistance to the courts when attempting to interpret parts of this involved and complicated legislation.

APPLICATION OF DISCLOSURE PROVISIONS

Definition of criminal investigation

Section 1 of the CPIA 1996 is concerned with the timing of disclosure, the classes of offences to which the Act applies and the application of the disclosure rules where criminal investigations begin on or after 1 April 1997. So far as the criminal investigation is concerned, this is defined by s. 1(4) as an investigation which police officers or other persons have a duty to conduct with a view to ascertaining whether a person should be charged with an offence, or whether a person charged with an offence is guilty of it. The vast majority of investigations are carried out in circumstances where a crime has been reported and the police investigate the allegation and seek the perpetrator. The definition also includes, however, those investigations where someone has been charged and inquiries are made in order to determine whether or not they are guilty. It also embraces situations where an investigation is commenced before any offence has been committed, such as where observation is kept on persons in order to detect whether those individuals are engaged in a criminal enterprise.

The common law rules of disclosure still apply to long-running investigations commenced before the appointed day. In the short term it may be prudent for investigators specifically to inform the prosecutor of the day when the investigation commenced in order to ensure that the appropriate disclosure rules are complied with. In cases where the common law rules still apply, the transitional time limit provisions of s. 13 ensure that the prosecutor carries out disclosure requirements as soon as is reasonably practicable at specified times during the course of the proceedings.

Criminal investigations conducted by persons other than the police

The Act applies not only to police investigations, but also to investigations carried out by others with a duty to ascertain whether criminal offences have been committed, for example, Customs and Excise and DTI investigators. It excludes those investigators whose primary responsibility does not relate to the possible commission of criminal offences, such as local authorities who have a duty to investigate matters in connection with the welfare of children (see also para. 1.2 of the disclosure code). The position of non-police investigators, and the application of a disclosure code to such investigators, was the subject of considerable discussion at all stages of the Bill's passage through Parliament. The Government successfully resisted attempts to introduce a disclosure code for non-police investigators on the basis that s. 26(1) of the Act charges those investigators with a responsibility to have regard to any relevant provision of the code which applies to police officers. This follows the precedent in s. 67(9), PACE 1984 relating to codes of practice issued under that Act in relation to arrest, search, detention, etc.

Classes of cases

The new disclosure provisions apply to:

- cases committed to the Crown Court for trial, including any summary offence joined in the indictment by virtue of s. 40, Criminal Justice Act 1988;
- cases of serious or complex fraud and certain cases involving children transferred to the Crown Court;
- cases initiated by way of a voluntary bill of indictment;
- either-way offences where the accused is tried summarily or by a youth court and pleads not guilty; and
- offences tried summarily where the accused pleads not guilty.

Effectively, only cases where an accused pleads guilty at the magistrates' court are excluded from the disclosure requirements of the Act.

Disclosure before a plea of guilty?

There was much debate during the committee stages of the Bill as to whether disclosure should take place before the accused is asked to plead. The Law Society had at once stage indicated that it would instruct its members that if there was any question about the adequacy of the prosecution case, clients should be advised to plead not guilty in order to bring the disclosure provisions into play. There appear to be two separate issues. First, whether the accused has sufficient information about the case for the prosecution; and, secondly, whether the accused should have any information concerning material which does not form part of the case for prosecution. In so far as the prosecution case is concerned, the accused receives statements and/or other transfer documents in relation to a case destined for the Crown Court; all the relevant prosecution evidence where a voluntary bill has been obtained; and advance information in either-way offences in accordance with the Magistrates' Courts (Advance Information) Rules 1985. It is only in relation to purely summary offences that the accused will not always have any statement of the prosecution case. In many instances the prosecution voluntarily provide such information and there is seldom real hardship to the accused in taking a plea in those remaining cases where no advance information of the prosecution case has been provided.

The Government's objection to making primary disclosure of unused material before plea at the magistrates' court is that there is no demand for it and there would be serious repercussions for the criminal justice system as a whole if it was introduced. It would result in an enormous amount of work for investigators and prosecutors in supplying statements, documents, schedules, etc. Given the huge number of defendants disposed of at the lower court (i.e. 905,199 according to the CPS Annual Report 1995/6, of which 731,314, nearly 81 per cent, pleaded guilty) this is undoubtedly so. Thus, the CPIA 1996 makes no provision for primary disclosure of unused material before a plea is taken.

Is there any justification for the claims of unfairness that an accused person being tried at the magistrates' court does not have information which may undermine the prosecution case and a schedule of investigation material before being asked to plead guilty or not guilty? The majority of cases tried summarily are short and straightforward where the issues are plain and the law clear, and in these circumstances there is only the remotest possibility of an accused being placed at a disadvantage by the absence of any material which the prosecution do not intend to use. In many cases tried summarily there is no unused material of any significance, let alone statements or other documents which undermine the prosecution case. If any such material exists, it is more than likely that the prosecution will conclude that there is no realistic prospect of conviction to satisfy the test in the Code for Crown Prosecutors and, as a consequence, will abandon the case.

In reality, there is no difference in principle where, following charge, the prosecution learn that they *may* be unable to proceed in the event of a not guilty plea; for example, where the principal witness is going abroad or has moved address and may be difficult to trace in the event of a trial; or the witness is seriously ill and may not be able to attend court, or has even died. Does justice require that this sort of information be conveyed to an accused before he or she is asked to indicate whether he or she is guilty or not? The likelihood of miscarriages of justice where an accused admits guilt and where the prosecution have material undermining their case, which would have caused a contrary plea, is so rare that the justification for an elaborate scheme requiring disclosure in offences tried summarily prior to a plea being taken cannot be upheld on grounds of unfairness.

GENERAL INTERPRETATION PROVISIONS

Section 2 of the CPIA 1996 provides that where there is more than one accused, the disclosure provisions apply separately to each of the accused. At primary disclosure stage, this will make little difference to the prosecutor's responsibilities as the existence of any material which undermines the prosecution case will, in most instances, undermine the case equally against each accused. Complications are more likely to arise at secondary disclosure stage after each accused has made defence disclosure which will trigger the further disclosure obligations of the prosecutor. If one accused gives a full defence statement which prompts further disclosure, there is no requirement to disclose such information to a co-accused who may have provided less information and seems to be satisfied with what has been disclosed at the primary stage. That is really no different from the common law position where schedules are served on the solicitors for each accused and one may choose to inspect material at the police station while the other does not; the unused material is similarly available to both accused, although only one may have knowledge of the contents gained by taking advantage of the opportunity to inspect.

References to the prosecutor are to any person acting as prosecutor, whether an individual or a body (s. 2(3)). Private prosecutors have the same disclosure obligations as those of recognised prosecuting authorities, such as the CPS or the SFO (but they are not bound by the disclosure code — see para. 2.1). References to material includes information and objects of all descriptions (s. 2(4)). There is, therefore, a duty to disclose information received orally, although the disclosure code exhorts investigators to record the information in a durable or retrievable form. This does not require the recording of inquiries and conversations which are not relevant to the investigation and further guidance on this aspect of the investigator's duties is given in the code. The Government resisted pressure to define further, or give examples, of 'objects of all descriptions', although assurances were given that they included samples, such as blood or non-intimate specimens (see Hansard HC Standing Committee B, 4th sitting report, 21 May 1996, coll. 102–105).

PRIMARY PROSECUTION DISCLOSURE

Role of the prosecutor

Section 3 of the CPIA 1996 prescribes the first stage of the disclosure procedures. This is probably the most important part of the entire process, for if the prosecutor acts fairly and responsibly at this stage, defence disclosure will be easier and there are likely to be fewer requests for secondary disclosure. Section 3(1)(a) narrows the common law disclosure test to one where, in the opinion of the prosecutor, prosecution material exists which might undermine the prosecution case against the accused. The test is subjective and allows the prosecutor to decide what might adversely affect the case. Prosecutors are under a duty to disclose material in their possession, or that which has been revealed to them by the investigator pursuant to the disclosure code and which they have inspected. There is no duty of disclosure in relation to material held by third parties. If there is no material of the description in s. 3(1)(a) then the accused must be given a written statement of that fact in accordance with s. 3(1)(b). The scheme means that prosecutors can disclose only what the investigator has told them or brought to their notice, either at first instance or in response to requests for further information about material notified on the schedule required by the disclosure code. The code sets out the procedure for revealing material to the prosecutor by scheduling non-sensitive material, copying categories of key information and drawing to attention any material which the investigator considers may satisfy the test for primary disclosure. The duty of disclosure rests, quite properly, on prosecutors but they are hugely dependent on the competence and honesty of investigators in bringing matters to their notice.

Role of the investigator

Paragraph 44 of the Home Secretary's *Consultation Document* recognised the importance of the role of the investigator in the disclosure process:

There will be a heavy reliance on the investigator to identify material which ought to be disclosed, given that the material itself will not necessarily be scrutinised by the prosecutor. The investigator will need to ensure that a sufficiently senior and experienced officer has ultimate responsibility as the disclosure officer for the compilation of the schedule so that the prosecutor can be reassured that he has sufficient information about the material listed on the schedule. The investigator will also need to assist the prosecutor by telling him what he thinks are the issues in the case: the system demands a significant degree of liaison between the prosecutor and the investigator as a case develops and the issues in the case can change.

The return to a disclosure regime which places an emphasis on the integrity of the investigator and prosecutor is to be welcomed. The probity and honesty of the prosecution have been seriously eroded as a result of those miscarriages of justice which highlighted disclosure failings, but it is impossible to have an effective criminal justice system where the prosecution cannot be trusted and where so many checks and balances have to be introduced that the process grinds to a halt. Deliberate concealment of relevant evidence is rare, but carelessness in overlooking material information is by no means unknown and errors of judgment can never be totally removed. That is why the availability of the schedule of investigation material to both the prosecutor and the defence, by virtue of s. 4, is an essential safeguard. No disclosure regime can ever be perfect, but the prosecution must be presumed to act fairly.

The disclosure code, para. 7.2, requires the disclosure officer to draw the attention of the prosecutor to any material retained by the investigator which may fall within the test for primary disclosure, and for the disclosure officer to explain why he or she has come to that view. The explanation of the basis upon which the disclosure officer's decision has been made is important because the disclosure officer may be honestly ignorant of all that undermines the case. For example, the police may genuinely believe, as a result of what the defendant has said in interview, that the issue is a straightforward one of self-defence, or guilty knowledge or absence of dishonesty. The prosecutor may realise, however, that investigation methods or questioning may have contravened PACE 1984, which would seriously undermine the case and thus form a major plank in the defence case. Documents relevant to such issues may not have been drawn to his or her attention although they should have been listed on the schedule. The effectiveness of the scheme is dependent on the joint efforts of the investigator, in revealing full information, and the prosecutor, in making a reasonable and sensible appraisal of the information. It is hoped that this will result in informed decisions on what it is necessary to disclose at the primary stage.

The test of 'undermining the case for the prosecution'

What constitutes the undermining of the prosecution case? The test received much attention during Parliamentary discussions of the Bill, with Lord McIntosh of

234 Criminal Procedure and Investigations Act 1996

Haringey finding it 'a curious metaphor . . . from mining engineering which one might say has no particular place in legislation in the first place' (Hansard vol. 569 HL Deb, 6th ser., col. 865). The Government view was summed up by the Solicitor-General (Hansard vol. 279 HC Deb, 6th ser., col. 380, when he stated that 'generally speaking [the material] has an adverse effect on the strength of the prosecution case'. Apparently there was no dissent to the expression in the responses to the Government's *Consultation Document* although an amendment to read 'cast serious doubt on' the prosecution case was rejected during the Bill's passage.

The *Consultation Document* provided examples of what might be construed as undermining the case, but they are of limited help simply because they are all illustrations of situations where there can be no doubt that the case is undermined. In the real world, however, prosecutors will be faced with borderline situations where material exists which, while it does not advance the prosecution case, does not weaken, threaten or reduce the effectiveness of it. Some simple illustrations based on the examples given in the *Consultation Document* may serve to help.

It is said that if part of the prosecution case is a statement by a witness that he saw the accused near the scene of the crime shortly after it was committed, it will be necessary to disclose a statement from another witness that he saw a person of a different description from the accused at the same time and place. There is no difficulty with that proposition, but what of a witness who saw someone at the scene whom he is unable to describe or a witness who, at a different time, saw someone not resembling the accused? These persons do not necessarily undermine the case, but they may help the defence construct a picture of events on the day in question.

If the prosecution are in possession of a psychiatric report showing that their main witness has a history of psychiatric disorder with a tendency to fantasise, they should disclose the report since it clearly undermines the credibility of that witness. But is credibility undermined if the person concerned is a witness to a fatal traffic accident and gives an account identical to those of other independent witnesses at the scene? Or the report is five years old, since when the witness has received treatment and is now in different domestic or environmental circumstances? If credibility (and the disclosure of previous convictions) is to be determined in the future by a prosecutor's assessment of whether the information available undermines the prosecution case, this will be a major departure from the common law authorities.

The second limb of *R* v *Edwards (John)* (1991) 93 Cr App R 48 (which suggested that the prosecution must disclose details of earlier occasions when police officers had plainly been disbelieved by juries as the defendant was entitled to cross-examine the officers about those occasions) will presumably no longer have any effect as the common law has been overtaken by the CPIA 1996. However, disclosure of this type of information now falls to be decided by the prosecutor on the basis of the test of whether it undermines the prosecution case. The responsibility of the prosecution to decide on the disclosure of matters affecting credibility allows prosecutors more scope than the automatic disclosure at common law of often irrelevant details of previous convictions, but the difficulties involved (with or without any assistance by means of defence disclosure) should not be underestimated.

Some of the more difficult issues concerning the application of the test of disclosure will arise in cases where the prosecution have material which either does not emanate from the immediate investigation, or where the arrest has been the culmination of a lengthy investigation or period of observation. An example of the former is where police have been called on a number of occasions to domestic disturbances where no action was taken; a few months later the husband is accused of murdering his wife. All material arising out of the earlier visits, while not immediately relevant to the offence in question, has to be examined not only to see if there is anything admissible for the prosecution case but also to assess whether there is anything that may undermine it.

Sometimes, police operations commence before certain knowledge that a crime has been committed. Lengthy inquiries are made and long periods of observation undertaken. At the end of the day an arrest for a comparatively minor crime can result; for example, after a long investigation into possible drug importation and supplying, charges for possession or possession with intent may result. The disclosability of material from the entire operation will have to be considered to see if anything emerges which might be construed as undermining the prosecution case.

The police have complained vociferously of the hardships experienced by the enlarging of the common law rules of disclosure and prosecutors have lamented the whittling away of their discretion to decide what is relevant. The *Keane* materiality test is now replaced by a new one of undermining the prosecution case, and it will be interesting to see how the test is interpreted. Clearly, any material which is inconsistent with, or which weakens or casts doubt on the prosecution case must be disclosed; but whether it will be extended to embrace material which is neutral, or which does not advance or take the prosecution case any further remains to be seen. It is appreciated that the disclosure of information in some of the examples given above will become clearer if defence disclosure is carried out properly and the issues in dispute are clarified, but the way prosecutors exercise their discretion when applying the initial test will obviously be closely scrutinised by the courts, particularly with a view to identifying inconsistencies in approach.

Means of disclosure

Section 3(3) of the CPIA 1996 allows the prosecutor to effect disclosure either by securing that a copy of the material is given to the accused or when, in the opinion of the prosecutor, this is not practicable or not desirable, by providing facilities to inspect. The wording of s. 3(3) leaves it open whether the investigator or the prosecutor actually performs the copying task, but the responsibility of compliance lies with the prosecutor. In relation to information which has not been recorded, the prosecutor has a discretion to secure that it is recorded in any form suitable for providing a copy or for allowing inspection (s. 3(4)). If the material does not consist of information, such as a physical object, exhibit or sample, disclosure is effected by providing reasonable facilities for inspection (s. 3(5)). Sensitive material which, on an application by the prosecution, the court concludes it is not in the public interest to disclose is prohibited from disclosure by s. 3(6); and material intercepted under the Interception of Communications Act 1985 or any indication that a interception warrant has been obtained must not be disclosed by virtue of s. 3(7). Provision for time limits relating to primary disclosure is made in s. 12.

Disclosure of the prosecution schedule

Section 4 of the Act deals with the disclosure of the schedule. At the same time as the prosecutor makes primary disclosure under s. 3, the schedule of non-sensitive material prepared by the police is given to the accused. The schedule will not contain sensitive material as defined in the disclosure code, which will be notified to the prosecutor separately. Presumably, if the prosecutor disagrees with the disclosure officer's analysis of what is sensitive and what is not, the schedule of non-sensitive material will be amended to take into account the prosecutor's views.

The accused is not entitled to inspect any of the items on the schedule that have not been disclosed under s. 3 unless the defence statement provided at the next stage of the process shows that the material is likely to assist the defence case.

DEFENCE DISCLOSURE

Prosecution obligations before defence disclosure arises

Section 5 of the CPIA 1996 provides for compulsory disclosure by the accused in cases tried on indictment, while s. 6 allows for voluntary disclosure by the accused of cases tried summarily or at the youth court. Before any obligation to make defence disclosure arises, the prosecutor must comply, or purport to comply, with the primary disclosure provisions of the Act. The term 'purports to comply' appears to give prosecutors some leeway in that if they disclose all that they believe is necessary, the requirement to make defence disclosure arises. This may prove to be a troublesome term, for it could be used by an unscrupulous prosecutor to justify partial disclosure at the first stage with a view to eliciting details of the defence. When disputes inevitably arise, the courts will undoubtedly wish to examine closely the actions and reasons for such actions by prosecutors at the primary stage.

Not surprisingly, the defence disclosure provisions caused considerable debate during the passage of the Bill with the Government rejecting two principal amendments, namely the empowering of the court to waive the necessity of the accused making a defence statement when it was not in the interests of justice and a requirement on the prosecution to provide a statement of their case before the defence made their statement. It was argued that the court should be able to exercise discretion to order that a statement need not be provided in cases which are straightforward and where an accused is content with the matters disclosed at the primary stage and does not wish for any further disclosure. In such circumstances, it was maintained that the provision of a defence statement would be a meaningless and unnecessary expense. There is also the problem of unrepresented defendants who may not fully understand what is expected of them, as well as accused who are incapable (either through mental incapacity or illiteracy) of making a statement. The Government's response, to the effect that the provision is meant to ensure as far as is possible that all the issues in a Crown Court trial are identified and narrowed, enabling the prosecution to consider whether further disclosure is necessary, is not entirely convincing. There are a number of Crown Court trials on issues of such simplicity that the defence want nothing from the prosecution after primary disclosure, and advance notice of the defence is unlikely to be of great help to the prosecution. If an accused fails to provide a statement, the court may make comment on the fact and draw appropriate inferences; but it would seem that in cases where the accused could not, rather than would not, provide a statement, it is unlikely that any adverse comments or inferences would be made.

The question of the prosecution providing a statement in all cases, whether tried on indictment or summarily, so that in effect it could be used by the defence in their statement to rebut point by point, would undoubtedly have been a costly exercise. It is also an unnecessary one, as in all but summary offences the defence have the statements and/or advance disclosure comprising the prosecution case together with copy exhibits and other documents where cases have been committed or transferred to the Crown Court. There is also power under s. 31, CPIA 1996 for a judge at a preparatory hearing to order the prosecution to give the court and the accused a written statement if it is considered that the interests of justice require it. The quality of defence statements remains to be seen, but the portents are not promising judging by the observations made in the Long Trials Working Group Consultation Paper (1992), which found inadequate defence disclosure under s. 9, Criminal Justice Act 1987 one of the main problems adding to the length of trials.

Timing and content of, and means of giving, defence statement

Defence disclosure will be effected by the giving of a defence statement to the court and the prosecutor which sets out in general terms the nature of the accused's defence; indicates the matters on which the accused takes issue with the prosecution; and sets out, in the case of each matter, the reason why issue is being taken with the prosecution. In the case of an alibi, the accused must give particulars including the name and address of persons who will give evidence in support of the alibi. The definition of 'evidence in support of an alibi' is the same as that in s. 11(8), Criminal Justice Act 1967 (now repealed), which generally had been taken to contemplate the commission of an offence at a particular place rather than a continuing offence which may be spread over a period of time at more than one location.

The Criminal Procedure and Investigations Act 1996 (Defence Disclosure Time Limits) Regulations 1997 (SI 1997 No. 684) (the defence time limit regulations) prescribe that the relevant period for defence disclosure is 14 days from the date that primary disclosure is made by the prosecutor. Regulation 3 provides for the extension of that period by the court on an application by the accused before the expiry of the 14 day period. There is no limit on the time that the court may then extend the period but the court has to be satisfied that the accused cannot give, or could not reasonably have given, a defence statement within the 14 day period.

The requirement is for service on the court as well as on the prosecutor so that the court can decide whether faults in defence disclosure are apparent for the purpose of making comment or drawing adverse inferences under s. 11, CPIA 1996. There is no obligation on an accused to serve a defence statement on a co-accused. The procedures establish obligations between the Crown and an accused only, although there is nothing to prevent voluntary disclosure between co-accused. In cases involving cut-throat defences, it is anticipated that each accused will wish to reveal as little as possible to one another, while in cases involving an all-out attack on the prosecution evidence there will be advantages to the accused in mutual disclosure (see also *R* v *Adams* [1997] Crim LR 292 discussed in chapter 9).

The meaning and conditions applicable to a defence statement, which are set out in s. 5(6) to (8), apply for the purposes of voluntary as well as compulsory disclosure. It may be questioned why accused persons should volunteer to disclose their defence, but the answer appears to be that it is the only way that they are able to compel the prosecution to move on to the secondary disclosure stage. In other words, if an accused being tried summarily is not content with information disclosed at the primary stage or wishes to examine items listed on the schedule, he or she is going to have to disclose his or her defence in order to trigger further disclosure by the prosecution. A further reason for voluntary disclosure would be to attempt to persuade the prosecution to discontinue proceedings in the light of the information given.

The accused only has to set out the defence in general terms (a concession made from the original proposal in the Government's *Consulation Document*). However, when it comes to indicating matters on which the accused takes issue with the prosecution, reasons have to be given. Thus, in a case of assault, the statement of an accused that he was present at the scene but did not participate in the attack, would appear to satisfy the requirements of s. 5(6)(a). In order to satisfy s. 5(6)(b) and (c) though, the accused would have to give more detailed information, e.g., witnesses X and Y are wrong in their identification because they were not there themselves, or they could not have seen the assault, or they are mistaken, or they have a grudge against the accused or they have been put up to giving false evidence, etc.

SECONDARY PROSECUTION DISCLOSURE

Prosecution obligations

Where the accused has given a defence statement, either compulsorily or voluntarily, s. 7(2), CPIA 1996 provides that the prosecutor must disclose any prosecution material which has not previously been disclosed and which might be reasonably expected to assist the accused's defence as disclosed by the defence statement. If there is no such material, the prosecutor must give a written statement to that effect. The definition of prosecution material is the same as for primary disclosure and the prohibitions for not making disclosure of material in the public interest or that which is covered by the IOCA 1985 similarly apply (see s. 7(5) and (6)).

Primary disclosure is based on the prosecutor's opinion of what might undermine the case for the prosecution; secondary disclosure depends on a reasonable expectation of what might assist the defence case. The opinion of the prosecutor regarding primary disclosure is necessarily subjective and is governed by the limited information in the statements and background material provided by the investigator. The test for secondary disclosure is more objective and the court may be called upon under s. 8 to rule on disputes and decide whether the prosecutor has acted reasonably in disclosing (or not disclosing) information at the secondary stage. The example of secondary disclosure given in the Government's *Consultation Document* is that of a defendant who discloses a defence of involuntary intoxication which he alleges was a side-effect of medication prescribed for an illness from which he was suffering. The investigator had previously found on the premises traces of drugs, which seemed at the time to have no relevance to an issue in the case but turned out to be drugs which would be prescribed for that illness. That would need to be disclosed at the secondary stage. Not only is this a somewhat exceptional set of circumstances, but it is also arguable that the information should have been disclosed in the first place unless the defence of involuntary intoxication has come entirely out of the blue!

In reality, secondary disclosure is likely to be linked to one of two sets of circumstances. The first is where the defence know, or believe, that the prosecution have material which they have not disclosed at the first stage and which the defence are of the opinion will assist the preparation of their case. For example, in a drugs raid on a club which has resulted in the prosecution of the accused for possessing drugs, the accused had said nothing on arrest. The defence statement now makes it clear that the accused is alleging that the drugs were planted and the defence require more information about the raid as a whole, i.e. was the arresting officer involved in any other arrests, have any others arrested alleged a 'plant', which other officers were involved, etc? Provided that the defence comply with their disclosure obligations under ss. 5 or 6 of the Act and give sufficient particulars in the defence statement, the prosecution should be able to assess whether the material requested will assist the defence and act accordingly. It would not have been disclosed at the primary stage because the prosecution evidence was confined to the accused in question and the prosecutor may have been unaware that the defence would involve an attack on the veracity of police witnesses.

The second scenario is where the defence do not know whether the prosecution have anything of significance over and above that disclosed at the primary stage but they want an opportunity of finding out. This is the sort of speculative 'fishing expedition' that the Government were anxious to restrict. It is necessary, therefore, for the defence to provide sufficient information in their statement upon which the prosecution can then act, either by making further inquiries or by allowing access to the material listed on the schedule sent to the accused at the time of primary disclosure. This is little more than Lord Taylor recommended in *Keane* when he stated that 'the more full and specific the indication the defendant's lawyers give of the defence or issues they are likely to raise, the more accurately both prosecution and judge will be able to assess the value to the defence of the material'. In an allegation of a series of arsons, it is unlikely that the defence statement 'I did not set fire to this barn, someone else must have done it, therefore I want details of all fires in barns in the county for the last three years' would be acted upon. There is no reasonable expectation that the information will help the accused. A request that is more focused on the location, or unsolved arsons or whether there are any reported descriptions of perpetrators might prompt a greater response to secondary disclosure.

The practical difficulty which faces the prosecution in relation to secondary disclosure is how the inquiries are to be carried out. The accused's solicitors may indicate a line of defence and, possibly, what information they want disclosed. The prosecuting authority and counsel will have seen only the schedule and certain documents that the disclosure officer has drawn to their attention. In these circumstances, it would be dangerous to leave matters entirely to the officer in charge of the investigation or to the disclosure officer who has made the initial judgment on what material undermines the case. It will be necessary for the disclosure officer to make further inquiries prompted by the defence statement, but it is essential for disclosure at the second stage to be closely supervised by the prosecutor — no doubt under the guidance of prosecuting counsel. Depending on the nature and extent of the defence statement, it may be necessary, as was the case before the CPIA 1996, for a member of the prosecuting authority and counsel to inspect all the investigation material themselves.

Applications by accused for material

If the accused has provided a defence statement under either ss. 5 or 6 of the 1996 Act and is not satisfied with secondary disclosure made by the prosecutor, s. 8 allows for an application to be made to the court. The procedure for such applications is set out in disclosure rules (r. 7). The accused has to have reasonable cause to believe that there is prosecution material which might be reasonably expected to assist the defence and that the material has not been disclosed. As in earlier sections, material is defined in terms of material which is in the possession of the prosecutor or the investigator and which the prosecutor has inspected. The defence cannot use s. 8 to pursue applications to examine material in the possession of third parties. An application for a witness summons under s. 2(1), Criminal Procedure (Attendance of Witnesses) Act 1965 (as amended by s. 66, CPIA 1996) must be utilised to obtain access to such material.

CONTINUING DUTY OF DISCLOSURE

Section 9 of the CPIA 1996 imposes a continuing duty on the prosecutor to keep the disclosure of prosecution material under review up until the conclusion of proceedings when an accused is either acquitted or convicted, or the prosecution decide to discontinue proceedings. There is no statutory duty to keep matters under review post-conviction and convicted defendants must continue to rely on the innate sense of fairness of the prosecution in bringing to attention material which may assist in providing grounds for an appeal. If no appeal has been lodged, the prosecution are expected to take appropriate action with regard to any information which casts doubt on the correctness of a conviction. This may involve notifying convicted defendants or their legal representatives direct, or bringing the matter to the attention of the Criminal Cases Review Commission which was set up at the end of 1996.

The continuing duty is expressed in stages. First, once primary disclosure has been made, the prosecutor must keep under review the question whether at any given time there is prosecution material which has not been disclosed and which, in the opinion of the prosecutor, might undermine the case for the prosecution. In order to come to such an opinion, the prosecutor will obviously see how the case develops and how the issues emerge and are clarified. This is defined by the somewhat curiously worded s. 9(3), which states that when keeping the question under review 'by reference to any given time the state of affairs at that time (including the case for the prosecution as it stands at that time) must be taken into account'. Secondly, when any further disclosure has been made pursuant to s. 7, the prosecutor must keep under review the question whether at any given time there is prosecution material which might be reasonably expected to assist the accused's defence as disclosed by the defence statement. The methods of any further disclosure are the same as that for primary disclosure (copying or allowing inspection facilities).

FAULTS IN DISCLOSURE BY ACCUSED

Section 11 of the CPIA 1996 sets out sanctions against an accused who fails to carry out defence disclosure in prescribed circumstances. If an accused:

(a)   fails to give a defence statement when compulsorily required to do so under s. 5; or
(b)   provides a defence statement out of time; or

(c)   sets out inconsistent defences in the defence statement; or

(d)   puts forward at trial a defence which is different from that set out in the statement; or

(e)   adduces alibi evidence at trial without having given particulars as required; or

(f)   calls alibi witnesses without having complied with the requirements in s. 7(a) or (b),

the court may make such comment as appears appropriate. Alternatively, the prosecution, or a co-accused, may seek the leave of the court to make appropriate comment. The court or a jury may draw such inferences as appear proper in deciding the guilt or otherwise of the accused. Where an accused makes voluntary defence disclosure, similar sanctions apply where the disclosure is late, inconsistent, etc.

It is a matter for speculation whether the sanctions in s. 11(3) will be taken to include the prosecution putting in evidence, as part of their case, the defence statement in order to draw attention to inconsistencies in the nature of the defence, particulars of alibi, etc. The prosecution were entitled to introduce an alibi notice as part of their case as a result of the decisions in *R* v *Rossborough* (1985) 81 Cr App R 139 and *R* v *Fields and Adams* [1991] Crim LR 38. Though not without its critics (see commentaries in [1985] Crim LR 373 and [1991] Crim LR 40), the practice was firmly established and widely used under s. 11, Criminal Justice Act 1967. Section 11(4) of the 1967 Act provided for evidence tending to disprove an alibi to be introduced either before or after evidence given in support of the alibi; and s. 11(5) specifically provided that alibi notices on behalf of defendants by their solicitors should be deemed to be given with the defendants' authority unless the contrary was proved. There are no like provisions in the CPIA 1996, although the requirement on an accused to give a defence statement in circumstances where s. 5 applies is clear. Arguments rejected in *Rossborough* to the effect that to admit alibi notices would be unfair, as the notices were often given by solicitors before witnesses had been interviewed owing to pressures of time or business, would appear to carry even less weight in the light of the compulsory duty of disclosure now resting on the accused under the CPIA 1996. Whether accused persons will be additionally handicapped by having inadequate or inconsistent defence statements used against them by the prosecution is a matter for conjecture, but the threat of adverse comments or inferences is a real one.

Any substantial change in the prosecution case from that served at the committal or transfer stage will have been notified by the service of a notice of additional evidence, but if the accused has been seriously affected or disadvantaged by such an alteration in the way the prosecution put its case, s. 11(4) of the 1996 Act will undoubtedly come into play. This provides that where an accused puts forward a defence which is different from that given in the defence statement, the court shall have regard not only to the extent of the difference but whether there is any justification for it. Faults, delays and changes by the prosecution are likely to provide such justification.

A person shall not be convicted of an offence solely on an inference drawn as a result of a fault in disclosure by the accused (s. 11(5)). The prosecution must have had a realistic prospect of conviction under the Code for Crown Prosecutors in order to have commenced or continued proceedings, but if their case collapses at court they cannot rely solely on defence faults in the disclosure process to sustain the prosecution.

TIME LIMITS

Section 12 of the CPIA 1996 provides for the making of regulations to determine time limits for primary prosecution disclosure, defence disclosure and secondary prosecution disclosure. The regulations may provide for matters in connection with applications to extend the period, i.e. who may make the application, prescribed conditions for an application, by how long the period shall be extended, etc.

As we have seen above, s. 11 provides for sanctions where, *inter alia*, an accused gives a defence statement outside the relevant period. There are no sanctions against the prosecutor. The fact that the CPIA 1996 provides no sanctions against the prosecution in respect of failures or faults in their disclosure obligations has been the subject of criticism. The reason for the absence of sanctions against the Crown is that they are, by implication, catered for elsewhere. If the prosecutor does not comply with the primary disclosure obligations, an accused does not have to make defence disclosure at all, and consequently no inferences can be drawn to his or her detriment.

There was also the possibility that the court would not allow the prosecution to continue in the face of major faults in the disclosure process. The court's power in this regard has been diluted by the provisions of s. 10 in relation to the prosecutor's failure to observe time limits. Section 10(2) provides that a failure by the prosecutor to act within time limits does not on its own constitute staying the proceedings for abuse of process. Section 10(3) makes it clear, however, that a stay on grounds of abuse of process may still be appropriate if the failure to observe time limits involves such delay by the prosecutor that the accused is denied a fair trial. The law on abuse of process and its relationship with disclosure has already been commented on in chapter 12. In relation to time limits, there is authority which indicates that escaping or avoiding time limits by the prosecution may amount to a misuse of the process of the court sufficient to justify a stay of proceedings as an abuse of process. *R* v *Brentford Justices, ex parte Wong* (1981) 73 Cr App R 67, involving delay in the service of a summons, and *R* v *Great Yarmouth Magistrates, ex parte Thomas* [1992] Crim LR 116 and *R* v *Norwich Crown Court, ex parte Parker* [1992] Crim LR 500, both concerning custody time limits, illustrate that manipulation of time limits can leave the prosecution open to an argument that there has been an abuse of process.

In relation to disclosure time limits, however, the court must look further than the mere failure of prosecutors to observe their statutory duties under the CPIA 1996 in view of the provisions of s. 10(2). Often, the failure to observe time limits will be the principal cause of delay, and there is considerable legal authority on the question of delay leading to abuse of process. It would seem, however, that since *Attorney-General's Reference (No. 1 of 1990)* (1992) 95 Cr App R 296, no stay should be imposed unless the defendant can establish on a balance of probabilities that owing to delay serious prejudice will be suffered to the extent that no fair trial can be held.

PUBLIC INTEREST MATTERS

Section 21(2) of the CPIA 1996 provides that the common law rules as to whether disclosure is in the public interest are not affected by the statutory provisions relating to disclosure generally introduced by the Act. In other words, applications to assert PII in relation to sensitive material will continue as before, subject to the Government's newly announced approach following the recommendations made in the Scott Report (see chapters 9 and 10). When applications are made to the court and the court concludes that it is not in the public interest to disclose, material shall not be disclosed pursuant to ss. 3(6), 7(5), 8(5) or 9(8).

Review of public interest matters

In common with the duty to keep general disclosure issues under review, ss. 14 and 15 of the 1996 Act create a similar duty in relation to public interest material, although there is an important difference between cases tried summarily and those tried at the Crown Court. In cases tried on indictment, the court must keep the question under review without the need for an application, although there is nothing to preclude the accused from seeking a review (s. 15(4)). In the magistrates' court, however, there is no duty upon the court to keep the question of public interest material under review, although at any time the accused may still apply for a review of the question whether it is still not in the public interest to disclose material affected by the order (s. 14(2)). This is because, as a result of the decision in *R v South Worcestershire Magistrates, ex parte Lilley* (1995) *The Times*, 22 February 1995, the bench trying the case may be different from the court that decided the public interest application in the first place. Furthermore, to impose a duty on magistrates to keep the public interest under continuous review would place it at the forefront of their minds, which would increase the danger of bias when they come to make a decision on the evidence.

   If the court at any time concludes that it is in the public interest to disclose material, it shall so order and take the necessary steps to inform the prosecutor. There is no obligation to inform the accused as in the case of a small number of *ex parte* hearings the accused will be unaware that the prosecution have made an application, and to give the court a responsibility to notify the accused would nullify the effect of a secret application. Following the making of the order and notification by the court, the prosecutor must make disclosure or abandon the proceedings.

Rules of court

These have already been discussed in chapter 10.

The procedures to be adopted at hearings in connection with public interest matters are the subject of the disclosure rules, based upon the *Davis, Johnson and Rowe* procedures, which have met with general, if not universal, approval. The disclosure rules for the Crown Court and the magistrates' court are very similar, although there are some procedural differences in the making of applications to withhold material on public interest grounds. In addition, the Crown Court must keep a record of reasons for a non-disclosure order whereas there is no such requirement in the magistrates' court. There is a requirement on the clerk of the magistrates' court to make papers available to the court when reviewing a disclosure order. Unlike the position in the Crown Court, the magistrates' court has no power under r. 9 to waive requirements relating to the giving of notice. In all other significant respects, the rules applicable to trials on indictment and summary trials are the same.

Separate representation by third parties

Section 16 of the CPIA 1996 allows persons claiming an interest in the public interest material to be heard on an application as to whether the material should be disclosed. Persons claiming such an interest must show that they were involved, either directly or indirectly, in bringing the attention of the investigator or prosecutor to the material. Thus in a child abuse case, where social services have drawn to the attention of the police or prosecutor the existence of potentially relevant documents, the court will listen to any views they may have on the question of disclosure. The Scott Report was critical of the position where more than one Government department was involved in a public interest matter, prosecuting counsel representing their interests as well as those of the prosecution. The provisions of s. 16 will enable the department(s) to instruct counsel, separate from prosecuting counsel.

CONFIDENTIALITY OF DISCLOSED INFORMATION

The concerns expressed in chapter 8 in relation to the misuse of documents disclosed for the purposes of the criminal trial have been addressed by ss. 17 and 18, CPIA 1996. If the accused is given or is allowed to inspect documents, there must be no further use or disclosure of any of the information recorded in the documents. The confidentiality applies only to material which does not form part of the prosecution case. There is no restriction on use of the statements served as part of the case or on anything read out in the course of the proceedings. Sometimes, documents disclosed will be put to witnesses in cross-examination and confidentiality does not attach to answers given in open court.

The accused may use or disclose the object or information in connection with the current proceedings or with a view to taking further proceedings such as an appeal.

If the accused wishes to use the disclosed material for purposes other than those described in s. 17(2) and (3), an application may be made to the court under s. 17(4) at any time, even after conviction or acquittal. When such an application is made, the prosecution or a person claiming to have an interest in the material must be given an opportunity to be heard. The practice and procedure to be followed in relation to such applications are the subject of the Crown Court (Criminal Procedure and Investigations Act 1996) (Confidentiality) Rules 1997 (SI 1997 No. 699) and the Magistrates' Court (Criminal Procedure and Investigations Act 1996) (Confidentiality) Rules 1997 (SI 1997 No. 704) (the confidentiality rules) made pursuant to s. 19(2)(b) of the Act.

The knowing use or disclosure of information in contravention of s. 17 is a contempt of court under s. 18 of the Act, punishable summarily by a maximum of six months' imprisonment or a fine not exceeding £5,000 or both, and in the Crown Court by imprisonment not exceeding two years or a fine or both. If a person is guilty of contempt, the object concerned may be forfeited, destroyed, given to the prosecutor or made the subject of any other order that the court may specify. The alleged contemner or any person claiming an interest in the object has a right to be heard during the proceedings for contempt. The confidentiality rules made pursuant to s. 19(2) govern the practice and procedure in relation to proceedings to deal with contempt of court in respect of breaches of disclosure confidentiality.

Breaches of the implied undertaking not to use documents disclosed on discovery in civil proceedings for any purpose except the instant action, have been dealt with as contempts quite strictly. It was said in *Miller* v *Scorey* (1996) *The Times*, 2 April 1996 that the court should adopt an objective test when deciding if a breach of the undertaking has been committed. The motives for the breach, whether contumacious or not, were relevant only to punishment. If a similar approach is adopted to s. 18, CPIA 1996, it would seem that once it has been established that a person knowingly used or disclosed information which had been disclosed under the provisions of the Act, the reasons for so doing will be relevant only in relation to punishment.

RULES OF COURT RELATING TO DISCLOSURE

Section 19 of the CPIA 1996 contains the power to make rules of court dealing with:

- public interest applications;
- applications by the defence for the disclosure of further prosecution material;
- applications in relation to the confidentiality of disclosed material; and
- contempt proceedings.

The disclosure rules and the confidentiality rules referred to above are made pursuant to this provision. By virtue of s. 20 of the Act, a duty under any of the disclosure provisions is not affected by any duty arising under any other enactment with regard to material to be provided to or by the accused, subject to the requirements arising out of orders made at preparatory hearings. The provisions of the IOCA 1985 are, for example, unaffected by the new disclosure requirements. Part III of the Act relates to preparatory hearings and ss. 28–38 were implemented on 15 April 1997. Section 31 allows a judge to make a ruling as to any question on the admissibility of evidence or any question of law relating to the case. Section 20(2) in the disclosure part of the Act provides that in making an order under s. 31, the judge may take into account anything which has been done, has been required to be done or will be required to be done, in pursuance of the disclosure provisions. The Criminal Procedure and Investigations Act 1996 (Preparatory Hearings) Rules 1997 (SI 1997 No. 1052) contain provision for a judge to order disclosure of the prosecution case or the defence case when the prosecutor has complied with the obligation to supply a case statement. Rule 8 makes it clear, however, that with the exception of an alibi or expert evidence, the defence need not disclose who will give evidence. The Criminal Justice Act 1987 (Preparatory Hearings) Rules 1997 (SI 1997 No. 1051) make similar provision in relation to preparatory hearings under the Criminal Justice Act 1987. Section 20 also allows for the making of rules for the disclosure of expert evidence, and as a result the Magistrates' Courts (Advance Notice of Expert Evidence) Rules 1997 (SI 1997 No. 705) have been introduced. In addition, the Crown Court (Advance Notice of Expert Evidence) (Amendment) Rules 1997 (SI 1997 No. 700) amend the 1987 rules, with effect from 1 April 1997, in relation to proceedings for offences into which no criminal investigation has begun before that date. The provision of the 1987 rules concerning mutual disclosure of expert evidence between the parties to criminal proceedings in the Crown Court following committal or an order for retrial, are extended to apply to proceedings following a notice of transfer and the preferment of a voluntary bill.

RIGHTS AND DUTIES OF ACCUSED PERSONS

It will be readily appreciated from the above summary of the provisions of the CPIA 1996 that the legislation is complex and places onerous responsibilities on the prosecutor and accused alike. Although not a requirement of the CPIA 1996, the Government decided that in cases where Part I of the Act applies, i.e. disclosure falls to be dealt with in cases where the investigation commenced on or after 1 April 1997, the prosecutor should send to accused persons a notice setting out their rights and duties under the Act. A copy of the suggested notice is at Appendix 4. This should be sent to the accused when the prosecutor makes primary disclosure.

17 The Disclosure Code of Practice

CRIMINAL INVESTIGATIONS

Part II of the CPIA 1996 is concerned with criminal investigations, which are defined in s. 22(1) and embraced by the code of practice issued under the Act. For the purposes of the code, the meaning of a criminal investigation is the same as that set out in s. 1(4), CPIA 1996 relating to the disclosure provisions and the references to 'material' are the same as those set out in s. 2. Section 23 of the Act empowers the Home Secretary to prepare a code of practice and the content, operation, revision and effect of the code are described in ss. 23 to 26. Section 27 makes provision for the common law rules as to criminal investigations, which cease to have effect once the code is brought into operation.

The Runciman Commission Report had recommended that the detail of the supporting arrangements for disclosure should be in subordinate legislation or a code of practice. The Government preferred a code of practice, resembling those issued under PACE 1984, on the grounds that a code would be more flexible and could more easily be revised and altered in the light of developing law and practice.

PURPOSE OF CODE OF PRACTICE

Section 23(1) of the CPIA 1996 states that the Secretary of State shall prepare a code of practice containing provisions designed to secure a number of objectives set out in paras (a) to (j), namely:

(a)   where a criminal investigation is conducted, all reasonable steps are taken for the purposes of the investigation and, in particular, all reasonable lines of inquiry are pursued;

(b)   information obtained in the course of a criminal investigation, which may be relevant to the investigation, is recorded;

(c)   any record of information so obtained is retained;

(d)   any other material obtained in the course of a criminal investigation, which may be relevant to the investigation, is retained;

(e)   such information and material is revealed to a person who is involved in the prosecution of criminal proceedings arising out of the investigation;

(f)   where such a person inspects information or material and that person requests that it be disclosed to the accused, the accused is allowed to inspect or is given a copy of it;

(g)   where such a person is given a document indicating the nature of information or other material and that person requests that it be disclosed to the accused, the accused is allowed to inspect or is given a copy of it;

(h)   the person allowing disclosure decides whether inspecting or copying is appropriate;

(i)   the accused should be given a copy of material inspected unless the person allowing inspection is of the opinion that it is not practicable or desirable to give one;

(j)   the prosecutor is given a written statement that prescribed activities required by the code have been carried out.

The code provides, therefore, for the recording and retention of relevant information and material, its revelation to the prosecutor and disclosure to the accused in accordance with disclosure requirements described in Part I, CPIA. Section 23 of the Act also states that the code may include a number of provisions relating to:

(a)   the responsibilities of police officers carrying out prescribed activities in accordance with the code;

(b)   the form in which information is to be recorded;

(c)   the manner in which, and period for which, records and material are to be retained;

(d)   the time, form and manner in which material is to be revealed to the prosecutor.

A number of examples of the kinds of provisions that may be included are given in s. 24 of the Act.

OPERATION, REVISION AND EFFECT OF CODE OF PRACTICE

The bringing into operation of a disclosure code was subject to the conditions in s. 25, CPIA 1996, that the Home Secretary had to publish a draft, consider representations from interested parties and modify the draft accordingly. This process was carried out in the latter part of 1996 with the final version being approved by the House of Commons on 18 March 1997 and by the House of Lords on 20 March 1997. Section 25(4) of the Act allows for the periodic revision of the code.

Chapter 12 considered the remedies available for disclosure irregularities and the likely effect that failures by the prosecution to comply with the disclosure requirements of the Act and code would have on a prosecution. These include the exclusion of evidence as a result of breaches leading to an acquittal or a successful appeal; an application for abuse of process which finds favour with the trial judge; and additional sanctions of costs against the prosecutor or disciplinary proceedings against police officers. By virtue of s. 26(2) of the Act, a failure by the police or other investigator to comply with the code will not in itself render them liable to criminal or civil proceedings, although the failure will be taken into account during any relevant proceedings (s. 26(4)). In all criminal and civil proceedings, the code is admissible in evidence under s. 26(3).

Much time was taken up in Standing Committee with discussion of the effect of the disclosure code on investigators other than the police. The Government proposals in the Bill favoured an approach similar to that in s. 67(9), PACE 1984, that non-police investigators of criminal offences should have regard to the provisions of the code, thus allowing them to take into account their own particular circumstances. Opposition amendments to the effect that investigators from departments such as Customs and Excise and the Health and Safety Executive, should be required to observe the relevant provisions were rejected. Section 26(1) of the 1996 Act therefore follows the PACE 1984 precedent in that non-police investigators 'shall have regard to' the relevant provisions of the code. It is difficult to conceive that flagrant disregard of the code's requirements by non-police investigators would have anything other than serious, if not ruinous, consequences to any prosecution.

CONTENT OF CODE OF PRACTICE

Introduction and definitions

Paragraph 1.1 makes it clear that the disclosure code applies to criminal investigations conducted by police officers which began on or after 1 April 1997 when the code came into operation. Investigations commenced before that date are subject to the common law disclosure provisions. Persons other than police officers who are charged with the duty of conducting a criminal investigation are to have regard to the relevant provisions and should take them into account in applying their own operating procedures. Thus, where the code sets out the general responsibilities of investigators, officers in charge and disclosure officers and their duties in relation to the prosecutor, departments with their own investigation branches (such as Customs and Excise and the Department of Trade and Industry) will have to take the separate responsibilities into account when operating their own procedures.

Paragraph 1.2 confirms that the code has no application to those who are not charged with conducting a criminal investigation as defined in the 1996 Act. The code does not, therefore, apply to experts such as forensic scientists, or to investigators whose responsibilities are not to investigate crime but, for example, to ensure the welfare of children.

The non-disclosure of material intercepted in obedience to a warrant issued under s. 2, IOCA 1985 is confirmed and preserved by para. 1.3 of the code.

The definition of a criminal investigation in para. 2.1 is the same as that in s. 1(4), CPIA 1996, namely an investigation conducted by police officers with a view to it being ascertained whether a person should be charged with an offence or whether a person charged with an offence is guilty of it. Charging a person with an offence includes laying an information and issuing a summons. A criminal investigation therefore includes:

(a) investigations into crimes that have been committed;

(b) investigations the purpose of which is to ascertain whether a crime has been committed with a view to possible institution of criminal proceedings; and

(c) investigations which begin in the belief that a crime is about to be committed, e.g., when the police keep premises or individuals under observation for a period of time, with a view to the possible institution of criminal proceedings.

The investigator, the officer in charge of an investigation and the disclosure officer are separately defined in para. 2 of the code (see further in 'General responsibilities' below). The prosecutor is defined as the authority responsible for the conduct of criminal proceedings on behalf of the Crown. In s. 2(3), CPIA 1996, references to the prosecutor are to any person acting as prosecutor, whether an individual or a body. Although the disclosure provisions in the 1996 Act are applicable equally to an authority, such as the CPS, and a private prosecutor, an individual instituting a prosecution on his or her own behalf is not subject to the requirements of the disclosure code.

The code defines 'material' as material of any kind, including information and objects, which is obtained in the course of a criminal investigation and which may be relevant to the investigation. Material may be relevant to the investigation if it appears to an investigator, or to the officer in charge of any offence under investigation or to the disclosure officer, that it has some bearing on any offence under investigation or any person being investigated, or on the surrounding circumstances of the case, unless it is incapable of having any impact on the case.

The retention of material is dealt with in para. 5 of the code, which provides examples of the type of material which the police are under a duty to retain, but the definition of 'relevant to the investigation' is a wide one which incorporates words and phrases taken from the *A-G's Guidelines* and the *Guinness Ruling*. The difference, of course, is that while under the *Guidelines* and subsequent rulings the prosecution were under a duty to disclose such material to the accused, the duty under the code is to retain it in order that the prosecutor can then decide whether disclosure is necessary on the grounds that the material might undermine the prosecution case or might be reasonably expected to assist the accused's defence. Although the categories of material in para. 5 are fairly comprehensive, decisions concerning what to retain and what is incapable of having any impact on the case are necessarily subjective and are likely to be the source of contention in particular circumstances.

Sensitive material is defined as material which the police believe it is not in the public interest to disclose. Examples are given in para. 6.12 of the code and these will be examined later.

References to the disclosure of material to a person accused of an offence include references to the disclosure of material to the accused's legal representative.

General responsibilities

Paragraph 3 of the code prescribes disclosure responsibilities for those taking part in a criminal investigation. The investigator is any police officer involved in the conduct of a criminal investigation, and all investigators have a duty to abide by the requirements of the code in relation to the recording and retention of information and other material. The officer in charge (o.i.c.) is the police officer who directs the criminal investigation with responsibility for ensuring that proper procedures are in place for recording information and retaining records and other material. He or she may delegate tasks to others, but the o.i.c. remains responsible and accountable for the investigation. Paragraph 3.3 emphasises that it is an essential part of the o.i.c.'s duties to ensure that all material which may be relevant to the investigation is retained and made available either to the disclosure officer or (in exceptional circumstances) directly to the prosecutor.

The innovation in the code is the post of disclosure officer, who has responsibility for examining material retained by the police during an investigation; revealing material to the prosecutor; certifying that this has been done; and disclosing material to the accused at the request of the prosecutor. It seems from para. 3.3 that this post may be held by a civilian to whom the o.i.c. may delegate tasks. While some major investigations in the past may have involved an officer with specific disclosure responsibilities, they were the exception rather than the rule. The introduction of such a post is recognition of the importance now placed on the duty of dislosure, and it falls upon the chief officer of police for each force to put in place arrangements to ensure that in every investigation the identity of the o.i.c. and the disclosure officer is recorded.

The functions of the investigator, the o.i.c. and the disclosure officer are separate; but although the duties are distinct, the code does not preclude one officer performing all three roles. Much will depend on the nature and complexity of the case and the internal administrative arrangements of each police force. Paragraph 3.1 of the code makes it clear, however, that where the functions are undertaken by more than one person, close consultation between them is essential for the effective performance of the duties imposed by the code. In large and/or complex inquiries, the importance of such consultation cannnot be over-emphasised. Many disclosure failings in the past have been as a result of oversights and breakdowns in communication rather than of a desire deliberately to conceal or withhold information. There is also an obligation under para. 3.6 to ensure that, in the event of retirement, sickness, transfer etc., the responsibility for carrying out the various functions does not lapse. There is a duty upon supervisers to assign someone else to the task and to make sure that the new person's identity is recorded.

The Runciman Commission Report emphasised (at para. 1, p. 9) that the manner in which police investigations are conducted is of critical importance to the functioning of the criminal justice system. It is stating the obvious that miscar- riages of justice will result if the investigation is neither thorough nor conducted with care. The Report continued: 'In undertaking this search (for evidence which is both admissible and probative), it is the duty of the police to investigate fairly and thoroughly all the relevant evidence, including that which exonerates the suspect.' It is likely that in the past not all police officers have seen their investigatory duties in this light; and even if they have, they have not placed sufficient emphasis on the duty to gather and consider exculpatory evidence. Paragraph 3.4 of the disclosure code now ensures that the police are aware of their future responsibilities by stating: 'In conducting an investigation, the investigator should pursue all reason- able lines of inquiry, whether these point towards or away from the suspect. What is reasonable in each case will depend on the particular circumstances.'

The code does not change the position in relation to third-party material. The police still have no duty to trawl other persons for material which may have some possible relevance to the investigation. Paragraph 3.5 does require, however, that if there is a belief that other persons may be in possession of material that may be relevant to the investigation, those persons must be informed of the existence of the investigation by the disclosure officer and be invited to retain the material in case they receive a request for its disclosure. The disclosure officer should inform the prosecutor that they may have such material. It is stipulated, though, that the o.i.c. and the disclosure officer are not required to make speculative inquiries of other persons: there must be some reason to believe that they may have relevant material. That reason may come as a result of information given by the accused or from another source.

The effect of para. 3.5 is that, for example, in an allegation of child abuse where the victim is in care or has been the subject of local authority attention, social services should be notified of the investigation (if they are not aware of it already) in order that relevant material can be retained. Similarly, in a fraud inquiry which may touch upon a number of companies, businesses and financial institutions, it may be necessary to alert such third parties to the investigation so that potentially relevant material is preserved. It will be recalled that the Scott Report made a number of recommendations in relation to documents held by a Government department other than the investigating or prosecuting authority (see para. K5.1). It may be prudent, in some instances, for the existence of an investigation to be notified to a third party in writing so that a copy of the notification can be supplied to the defence to demonstrate compliance with the code.

Recording of information

In the course of a criminal investigation, the police gather information from a variety of sources and by an assortment of ways and means, including the physical receipt of objects, documents, audio and video tapes, as well as data received by computer and information received orally. Paragraph 4.1 of the code provides that if material which may be relevant to the investigation consists of information which is not recorded in any form, the o.i.c. must ensure that it is recorded in a durable or retrievable form (whether in writing, on video or audio tape, or on computer disk). Thus, relevant information received orally must be recorded in writing or, as is the case in an increasing number of investigations, logged on a computer.

Paragraph 4.2 allows that where it is not practicable to retain the initial record of information because it forms part of a larger record which is to be destroyed, its contents should be transferred as a true record to a durable and more easily stored form before that happens. Messages on police radios or calls to the emergency services cannot be retained forever, but as long as the relevant information is recorded and transferred accordingly to a durable and retrievable form, the original record need not be retained. Paragraph 4.4 makes it clear that the recording of information must be made as soon as practicable and cites as an example information contained in house-to-house inquiries, although the requirement to record information promptly does not require an investigator to take a statement from a potential witness where it would not otherwise be taken.

The guidance contained in para. 4 recognises the impracticality of retaining vast amounts of material where only a small part is of potential relevance. It also emphasises the need for information to be recorded to ensure its availability to an accused. Nevertheless, police officers still have a fair amount of discretion as to what should, and what need not, be recorded and, as in any situation which involves the exercise of discretion, disputes will be inevitable. Paragraph 4.3 reminds officers that negative information may be relevant to the investigation and, if it is relevant, should be recorded. The point is illustrated where a number of persons present in a particular place at a particular time state that they saw nothing unusual.

Retention of material

It is a clear that in order to have an effective disclosure scheme, there must be adequate provision for the retention and preservation of relevant material. The duty of retention is not entirely straightforward, however, as when an investigation commences there is no telling what may or may not be significant. A crime may not even have been committed; and even if it has, a suspect may never emerge. Paragraph 5.1 of the code exhorts the investigator to retain relevant material, which includes not only material coming into the possession of the investigator (such as documents seized in the course of searching premises) but also material generated during the investigation (such as interview records). Material may be retained in the form of a copy rather than the original if the original has to be returned to the owner. It may be photographed if the original is perishable. Material seized under the powers conferred by s. 22, PACE 1984 can be retained only subject to the provisions of that section (para. 5.12).

If the o.i.c. becomes aware as a result of developments in the case that material previously examined but not retained (because it was not thought at the time to be relevant) may now be relevant to the investigation, steps should be taken to ensure that it is retained for inspection or production. Such a situation could arise at any time, but is perhaps most likely to occur at secondary disclosure stage when the accused's defence has been made known.

The *Guinness Advice* issued by the DPP to chief officers of police in 1992 (see chapter 7) provided examples of categories of material which should be routinely retained in a criminal investigation. The disclosure code has drawn heavily on these when citing (in para. 5.4) categories to be retained provided that the material itself may be relevant. They are:

- crime reports (including report forms, relevant parts of incident report books or police officers' notebooks);
- custody records;
- records which are derived from tapes of telephone messages (for example, 999 calls) containing descriptions of an alleged offence or offender;
- final versions of witness statements (and draft versions where their content differs from the final version), including any exhibits mentioned (unless they have been returned to their owner on the understanding that they will be produced in court if required);
- interview records (written records, or audio or video tapes, of interviews with actual or potential witnesses or suspects);
- communications between the police and experts such as forensic scientists, reports of work carried out by experts, and schedules of scientific material prepared by the expert for the investigator, for the purposes of criminal proceedings;
- any material casting doubt on the reliability of a confession;
- any material casting doubt on the reliability of a witness;
- any other material which may fall within the test for primary prosecution disclosure in the Act.

The duty to retain material falling within these categories does not extend to items which are purely ancillary to such material and possess no independent significance. Paragraph 5.5 gives as an example, duplicate copies of records or reports.

Length of time for which material is to be retained

The draft code, which the Home Secretary circulated for observations in July 1996, required chief officers of police to develop their own policies on the length of time for which material should be retained — either in circumstances where a criminal investigation did not result in charges, or after the conclusion of any criminal proceedings if the investigation resulted in charges. In so doing they were invited to take into account various criteria such as the seriousness of the offence, the plea entered, sentence, the possibility of complaint being made, etc. Under the then existing regimes, police forces were not subject to any statutory requirements and some had retention policies while others did not (or certainly not fully developed policies).

Following the consultation process, the Home Office acceded to representations that there should be a national retention policy, with the result that the code placed before Parliament on 18 December 1996 contained provisions for a common practice. These were along the lines that all relevant material should be retained until a decision was taken whether to institute proceedings against a person for an offence. If proceedings were instituted, all material which might be relevant had to be retained until the accused was acquitted or convicted, or the prosecutor decided not to proceed. Where the accused was convicted after a not guilty plea, relevant material should be retained for at least one year in respect of convictions obtained at a summary trial, and for three years in respect of a conviction on indictment. If an appeal followed conviction, the material must be further retained until the appeal had been determined. No provision was made for the retention of relevant material following a plea of guilty.

In the clamour of publicity that accompanied the decision not to contest the appeals of the Bridgewater Three on 21 February 1997, concerns were expressed that the code's provisions were insufficient to ensure the availablity of the papers in cases like that of the Three, Judith Ward and other notorious miscarriages. The Home Secretary therefore placed an amended code before Parliament which changed the minimum retention periods to a scheme based on the length of sentence imposed. Paragraphs 5.6–5.10 of the approved code now deal with retention periods where the accused has been convicted. All material which may be relevant must be retained at least until he or she is released from custody or discharged from hospital in those cases where the court imposes a custodial sentence or hospital order. In all other cases, material must be retained for six months from the date of conviction. If the accused is released from the custodial sentence or discharged from hospital earlier than six months from the date of conviction, the material must nevertheless be retained for at least six months from the date of conviction. If an appeal is in progress at the end of one of these periods, or an application is being considered by the Criminal Cases Review Commission, the period is extended until the appeal is concluded, or the Commission decide not to refer the application to the Court of Appeal, or the Court determines the appeal resulting from the reference. By virtue of para. 5.10 of the code, material need not be retained by the police if it was seized and is to be returned to its owner.

The requirements of the code should now ensure that papers are not destroyed after a minimum of three years, thus preventing the sort of re-examination of evidence which has brought to notice miscarriages of justice. It is the case, however, that under the pre-code informal arrangements operated by most forces, the papers in high profile cases were kept, allowing matters to be reopened and reviewed.

Preparation of material for prosecutor

The DPP's *Guinness Advice* introduced for the first time the concept of a schedule maintained by the police which would list all the material coming into their possession. Maintaining a schedule from the outset of an investigation was not mandatory, but in cases destined for committal or summary trial the CPS would insist upon one. In so far as sensitive material was concerned, the police were advised to bring such material to the notice of the CPS in order that the material could be given due and proper protection. Paragraph 6 of the disclosure code has built on and developed this practice.

Relevance is the key factor in the disclosure process and para. 6.1 of the code provides for the police to seek advice from the prosecutor about whether any particular item of material may be relevant to the investigation. Material which may be relevant to the investigation, which has been retained in accordance with the code, and which the disclosure officer believes will not form part of the case for the prosecution, must be listed on a schedule (para. 6.2). If the disclosure officer is satisfied that this material is not sensitive, the schedule must include a statement to that effect (para. 6.3). Paragraph 6.4 provides that any material which is believed to be sensitive should be listed on a separate sensitive schedule or, exceptionally, revealed to the prosecutor separately. These sub-paragraphs therefore explain the manner in which investigation material is prepared, in the first instance, for the prosecutor. Once the case has been reviewed, it may be that certain scheduled material will form part of the prosecution case or, conversely, that statements which the police believed would be led by the prosecution will not be used. This is catered for in para. 8 under the heading 'Subsequent action by disclosure officer' (see below).

Paragraphs 6.6 to 6.11 of the code set out the circumstances in which a schedule is to be prepared. These are where the accused is charged with an offence triable only on indictment; where it is considered that an either-way offence is likely to be tried on indictment; or where there is likely to be a contested trial at the magistrates' court. Paragraph 6.7 allows for the fact that a schedule may not be needed if a person has admitted an either-way or summary offence, or where a police officer has witnessed such an offence and that person has not denied it. If it is believed that the accused is likely to plead guilty at summary trial, it is not necessary to prepare a schedule in advance. However, if an expected plea of guilty at the lower court does not materialise, or it is decided that the case will be tried at the Crown Court, a schedule must be prepared as soon as is reasonably practicable. These provisions are sensible and prevent time being wasted on the preparation of schedules where they are unlikely to be needed.

Paragraphs 6.9 to 6.11 set out the way in which material is to be listed on the schedule. Each item must be numbered consecutively and the description should contain sufficient detail to enable the prosecutor to decide whether the material needs to be inspected before a decision is made as to whether it needs to be disclosed. This is of importance because in a large number of cases the prosecutor will never see the material itself. Reliance must be placed on the full and accurate scheduling of material so that where items or their contents are considered likely to undermine the case for the prosecution, they can be called for and inspected in order that a decision can be made. Section 4 of the 1996 Act provides for the disclosure of the schedule to the defence, and this gives a form of protection to the accused who will know what material is in the possession of the investigator. The accused is not entitled to inspect such material routinely, however, and the giving of the schedule should not act as an escape route for a prosecutor failing to carry out the duty of considering whether material undermines the prosecution case and, as a result, should be disclosed.

Items of a similar or repetitive nature need not be listed separately but may be described by quantity and generic title in a block; but even if material is listed in a block, the disclosure officer must ensure that any items among the material which might meet the test for disclosure are listed and described individually. Thus, in a quantity of correspondence, an individual letter of significance must be drawn to attention.

The scheduling of material and the bringing to the notice of the prosecutor any information which may undermine the case is clearly a crucial stage of the disclosure process. If a witness has convictions, or has sought a reward or has any motive for giving false evidence, the prosecutor must be told. Similarly, if the investigation has at any time led in the direction of someone other than the accused or there are any doubts about the reliability of an accused's confession, such information should not be withheld by the investigator. This does not mean that an officer's speculations or theories about a crime are disclosable, but any tangible information which casts doubt on the prosecution case must be revealed in order that the prosecutor may decide whether disclosure is appropriate.

Sensitive material

Paragraph 6.12 of the code provides that the disclosure officer must list on a sensitive schedule any material which he or she believes it is not in the public interest to disclose, and the reason for that belief. The schedule must include a statement that the disclosure officer believes that the material is sensitive. In exceptional circumstances, where an investigator considers that the material is so sensitive that its revelation to the prosecutor by means of an entry on the sensitive schedule is inappropriate, para. 6.13 allows for the existence of the material to be revealed to the prosecutor separately. This will apply where compromising the material would be likely to lead directly to the loss of life, or directly threaten national security. The responsibility for informing the prosecutor lies with the investigator who knows the detail of the sensitive material, and steps must be taken to ensure that the prosecutor is able to inspect the material and assess whether an application to the court for a ruling is necessary (para. 6.14).

Sensitive material is defined in para. 2 of the disclosure code as being material which an investigator, the o.i.c. or the disclosure officer believes it is not in the public interest to disclose. In order to assist them, para. 6.12 of the code lists examples of such material and they provide an interesting amalgam of groupings, drawn from the *A-G's Guidelines*, case law, and recognised PII classes together with some new categories. The paragraph makes it clear that the examples are not exclusive and that whether disclosure is not in the public interest will depend on the circumstancès. With the future of PII class claims uncertain at the time of writing, it remains to be seen whether some of the categories will survive an application to the court not to disclose, but the list does provide investigators with some help in deciding what is sensitive and what is not.

The survivors from the *A-G's Guidelines* are the more obvious categories, which in some cases are given a more detailed description:

- material relating to national security;
- material relating to the identity or activities of informants, or undercover police officers, or other persons supplying information to the police who may be in danger if their identities are revealed;
- material revealing, either directly or indirectly, techniques and methods relied upon by a police officer in the course of a criminal investigation, for example, covert surveillance techniques, or other methods of detecting crime;
- material the disclosure of which might facilitate the commission of other offences or hinder the prevention and detection of crime.

The importance of protecting intelligence, which has been recognised by the courts, is reflected in the following categories:

- material received from the intelligence and security agencies;
- material relating to intelligence from foreign sources which reveals sensitive intelligence gathering methods;
- material which relates to the use of a telephone system and which is supplied to an investigator for intelligence purposes only.

Those who assist the police in preventing and detecting crime are protected by the categories below:

- material given in confidence;
- material revealing the location of any premises or other place used for police surveillance, or the identity of any person allowing a police officer to use them for surveillance; and
- material containing details of persons taking part in identification parades.

Material given in confidence is an all-embracing category which not only includes the receipt of intelligence and information by the police or regulators (which are categorised separately), but also extends to anyone who is willing and able to help in a criminal investigation. It may include those who provide answers in house-to-house inquiries and others who telephone information to television programmes such as 'Crimewatch' or 'Crimestoppers'. The public will be reassured that information given in confidence will be treated sensitively, but confidentiality can be guaranteed only to the extent that the information does not undermine the prosecution case or help the accused's defence. Material upon the strength of which search warrants were obtained is included in the list separately, although often this will comprise information given by members of the public in confidence.

Material supplied to an investigator during a criminal investigation which has been generated by an official of a body concerned with the regulation or supervision of bodies corporate or of persons engaged in financial activities, or which has been generated by a person retained by such a body, is recognised as amounting to sensitive material which it is not generally in the public interest to disclose. Similarly, the code acknowledges the need to protect the welfare of children in relation to material supplied to an investigator during a criminal investigation which relates to a child or young person and which has been generated by a local authority social services department or other party contacted by an investigator during the investigation.

The integrity of a criminal investigation in general is recognised by the inclusion in para. 6.12 of internal police communications such as management minutes, enabling the police to manage and direct the investigation with a certain amount of confidentiality. Interestingly, there is no specific mention of communications between the police and CPS, some of which have been held at common law to be protected by PII. It would be surprising if material relating to the seeking and receiving of legal advice is no longer to be regarded as 'sensitive'.

Once the police or other investigator have revealed the existence of sensitive information, it falls to the prosecutor to decide whether the material is in fact sensitive. If it is, the prosecutor must decide what action is then appropriate; if it is not sensitive, further action by the disclosure officer may be necessary (see below).

Revelation of material to prosecutor

The code provides that the disclosure officer must give the schedule to the prosecutor in order that disclosure may be made in accordance with s. 4, CPIA 1996. If there is a schedule of sensitive material, this too must be forwarded to the prosecutor. Wherever possible, the revelation of material should be made at the same time that the file containing the prosecution case is given. The disclosure officer should draw the attention of the prosecutor to any material that an investigator has retained (whether listed on the schedule or not) which may fall within the test for primary disclosure. An explanation should also be made as to why the disclosure officer has come to that view (para. 7.2).

Paragraph 7.3 provides that in addition to listing material on the schedule, the disclosure officer must give the prosecutor a copy of material which falls into the following categories:

- records of the first description of a suspect given to the police by a potential witness, whether or not the description differs from that of the alleged offender;
- information provided by an accused person which indicates an explanation for the offence charged;
- any material casting doubt on the reliability of a confession;
- any material casting doubt on the reliability of a witness.

Material coming within each of these categories undoubtedly undermines the prosecution case and revelation to the prosecutor will almost certainly be followed by disclosure to the accused. Paragraph 7.3 also provides that if there is any other material which the investigator believes may fall within the test for primary disclosure, this too must be revealed.

The scheme of the code, therefore, is that material which in the opinion of the investigator undermines the case must be copied and revealed to the prosecutor and any other material retained should be listed on the schedules. If the prosecutor asks to inspect material which has not already been copied, the disclosure officer must allow such inspection; and if the prosecutor requires a copy one shall be provided, unless the material is too sensitive to be copied (para. 7.4). If material consists of information which is recorded other than in writing, e.g., on audio or video tape or on computer, para. 7.5 allows for the manner of revelation to be agreed between the disclosure officer and prosecutor.

Subsequent action by disclosure officer

At the time that the schedule of non-sensitive material is initially revealed to the prosecutor, the disclosure officer will not know what material will comprise the case for the prosecution; nor will the relevance of unused material be known with any certainty, especially if advice has not been sought from the prosecutor before submission of the case papers. It is not unusual for the prosecutor to decide that certain evidence proposed by the police should not form part of the prosecution case, or that other material, not included by the police as part of the case, should in fact be adduced. When the prosecutor has further advised on the relevance of material not forming part of the case, together with the sensitivity of any items, the schedule may need amending. This is catered for in para. 8.1 of the code in that once such matters have been determined, the disclosure officer must give the prosecutor an amended schedule of non-sensitive material unless the prosecutor states in writing that disclosure will be made by the prosecutor. Thus, in order to avoid the delay involved in preparing fresh schedules, the prosecutor may make any necessary disclosures.

The duty of secondary disclosure under s. 7, CPIA 1996, and the continuing duty of disclosure imposed by s. 9 of the Act mean that investigators have a corresponding duty to keep under review the revelation of material which meets the test for disclosure. After a defence statement has been given, the disclosure officer must look again at the material which has been retained and must draw the prosecutor's attention to any material which might reasonably be expected to assist the defence disclosed by the accused (para. 8.2). No doubt the reconsideration of material will be closely supervised by the prosecutor, who is likely to offer advice and guidance on the sort of material to which the investigator should pay particular attention. It is anticipated that in certain circumstances, the prosecutor and/or prosecuting counsel may wish to involve themselves directly in this stage of the pre-trial proceedings. If a defence statement has been provided in accordance with the requirements of the CPIA 1996, there can be no excuse for the prosecution not taking all reasonable steps to ensure that everything that should be disclosed is, in fact, made available to the accused.

Certification by disclosure officer

In accordance with para. 9.1 of the code, disclosure officers must certify to the prosecutor that to the best of their knowledge all material which has been retained and made available to them has been revealed to the prosecutor in accordance with the code. This is a very important stage of the process because the certification provides the prosecutor with the necessary assurance that all has been revealed which should be revealed and, in turn, the defence and the court will have a specific indication of compliance with the requirements of the code. It will be necessary to certify not only at the time when the schedules and accompanying material are submitted to the prosecutor, but also when material which has been retained is reconsidered after the accused has provided a defence statement. Whether certification is made on the schedule itself or on a separate document to the prosecutor is not specified.

The wording of para. 9.1 indicates that the disclosure officer is certifying that material which has been retained and revealed to him or her has then been revealed to the prosecutor. The certification does not appear to embrace the requirements placed on the investigator or o.i.c., so that if relevant material has not been retained and made known to the disclosure officer it is unlikely that blame can be attached to the latter unless he or she has acted negligently. It would, indeed, be unrealistic to expect a disclosure officer in a major inquiry involving a large number of investigating police officers to certify that each had complied with individual responsibilities created by the code. Certification should be made, however, only after inquiry of the o.i.c. and satisfaction, in so far as is reasonable, that retention and revelation have been fully and properly carried out.

Disclosure of material to the accused

If the tests for disclosure set out in the CPIA 1996 are satisfied the material must be disclosed to the accused, and para. 10 of the code sets out how this should be effected. If material has not already been copied to the prosecutor (presumably because, in the opinion of the disclosure officer, it does not come into any of the categories in para. 7.3), it must nevertheless be disclosed to the accused where the prosecutor so requests on the ground that it falls within the tests for either primary or secondary disclosure; or where the court has ordered disclosure of the material after considering an application from the accused under Part I of the Act.

Whether material copied to the prosecutor is physically disclosed by the disclosure officer or the prosecutor is a matter for agreement between them (para. 10.2). Disclosure is effected by giving the accused a copy or by allowing inspection. If the accused asks for a copy of any material which has been inspected, the disclosure officer must provide one unless it is not practicable or desirable. Paragraph 10.3 provides as examples of impracticability where the material consists of an object which cannot be copied or where the volume of material is so great, and of undesirability where the statement is that of a child witness in relation to a sexual offence.

If the material inspected by the accused consists of information which is recorded in a form other than in writing, it is within the discretion of the disclosure officer to, for example, provide a copy of an audio or video tape or a transcript. If the material is transcribed, the transcript must be certified as a true record (para. 10.4).

If a court concludes that it is in the public interest for an item of sensitive material to be disclosed, disclosure must be made if the case is to proceed. Paragraph 10.5 provides, however, that such disclosure may be made with redactions; or a summary may be provided or admissions made in accordance with s. 10, Criminal Justice Act 1967.

The comprehensive provisions of the code secure the objectives set out in s. 23 of the 1996 Act, although the provision in s. 23(7) for exceptions or different requirements depending on the classification of cases has not been included. Breaches of the code's requirements may have severe consequences, not only for the outcome of the case itself but also for the individual concerned who may have to face disciplinary proceedings as a result of a failure to observe the requirements. The overall aim is to ensure that an accused has available any material which may help to show innocence. The demands of the code are substantial and onerous, but as long as the responsibility for the investigation and prosecution of crime remains in separate hands, procedures for the notification of the existence and significance of investigation material must be thorough and detailed if miscarriages of justice caused by non-disclosure are to be avoided.

18 Conclusions

At the time of concluding this treatise on the law on disclosure, the CPIA 1996 has just come into operation. The debate continues, however, as to whether the disclosure provisions in the Act were necessary, whether they are an improvement on the common law rules, whether they will be applied fairly by the prosecution, whether the interests of the accused are sufficiently safeguarded, etc. Many of the answers will emerge only after a period of time when the operation of the new scheme and its effects can be properly gauged. It is submitted, however, that once the full implications of Glidewell LJ's judgment in *Ward* had been digested, legislation was inevitable. As the 'fall out' from *Ward* descended on a bemused criminal justice system, it became increasingly clear that changes were inevitable and it was merely a question of how extensive the changes would be and how long before they came into effect.

During the Standing Committee debate on the Criminal Procedure and Investigations Bill, Chris Mullin MP opined: 'The Judith Ward case was the subject of the best judgment ever given by the Court of Appeal . . . the Appeal Court judges clearly set out where the responsibility lay for the failure to disclose large quantities of material that should have been disclosed' (see Hansard HC Standing Committee B, 21 May 1996, col. 138). While the case may have been successful in unearthing shortcomings in the disclosure rules and pointing the finger at those comprising the prosecution who applied them, the law requires more from a judgment of the Court of Appeal than the apportioning of blame and responsibility. As Lord Reid observed in *Myers* v *DPP* (1964) 48 Cr App R 348 at p. 362, in relation to the role of judges extending and developing the law, 'if we do in effect change the law, we ought in my opinion only to do that in cases where our decisions will produce some finality or certainty'. The principles of law and practice set out in *Ward* did neither.

Each Crown Court judge had his or her own opinion on what the prosecution should be disclosing and how the judgment should be interpreted, and a succession of judgments from the higher courts did nothing to ease the confusion. The disclosure rules which had come under starter's orders in the *Guinness Ruling*, had been released from the stalls by *Ward* and were soon running out of control. Attempts to restore management and direction in *Keane* came too late to retrieve the position, although Lord Taylor CJ's judgment was to prove important in determining the future legislative pattern.

The purpose of rules of disclosure is to enable an accused to have a fair trial. They should not provide an acccused with an advantage over the prosecution, neither should they allow the prosecution to manipulate the trial process by withholding or concealing information which may help the accused. The principle of 'equality of arms' should ensure that the machinery of state, with its investigative and prosecutorial strength and resources, does not prevent an accused from learning any relevant information which may assist in establishing innocence. Few would argue against the proposition that an accused is entitled to anything gathered by the prosecution that is relevant. The key issues are what is relevant, how should relevance be determined and by whom? If the problems of relevance can be solved, we are getting closer to achieving a fair and workable disclosure regime. It is true that the problems of protecting sensitive information the disclosure of which endangers the public interest still remain, but determining relevance is the cornerstone on which a disclosure regime is constructed. Enlisting the assistance of the defence to clarify and define the issues can only aid the pursuit of a fair trial.

What is perhaps surprising is how other jurisdictions have managed to survive without becoming embroiled in the plethora of disclosure issues which have overwhelmed the courts of England and Wales. The answer may lie in the fact that disclosure is more easily effected in an inquisitorial judicial system, but this does not provide a complete explanation as some adversarial criminal systems still permit disclosure to be carried out on an informal basis with a minimum of rules and virtually no legislation. As we have seen to our cost, however, it takes only one miscarriage of justice to reveal deficiencies; and is there a criminal jurisdiction in the world which can place its hand on its judicial heart and say with absolute confidence that it does not have a 'Judith Ward' lurking in its system?

It is not uncommmon — and is even fashionable — to criticise the criminal justice system of England and Wales, but comparisons with other jurisdictions often provide a timely reminder that matters are often not as black as they are painted. We looked in amazement at some of the pre-trial and courtroom procedures at the OJ Simpson trial in America. To many, the French system of criminal investigation overseen by a *juge d'instruction* is the way in which England and Wales should be progressing — until an English schoolgirl is murdered in France. The circumstances surrounding the release of the original suspect is perhaps an indication that the English police investigation process is not as flawed as is often said to be the case. Before 1996, few commentators would have considered the criminal justice system in Belgium as being a potential source of corruption and unfairness, but its credibility now lies in tatters as a result of events sparked off by one case. In short, no criminal justice system is, or can ever be, perfect and it sometimes takes only a single case to expose weaknesses and deficiences.

What is more worrying than defects in the disclosure rules which have needed to be corrected by legislation, is the view, held by some, that there is a culture of unfairness in the prosecution process in England and Wales. Such views were voiced repeatedly during the progress of the Criminal Procedure and Investigations Bill through Parliament, with allegations of police deliberately suppressing information and prosecuting authorities withholding material in order to secure convictions. These factors are seen by many as the principal obstruction to any disclosure regime, be it one comprised of common law rules or one enforced by legislation. There are very few examples to support the allegations, but as long as such accusations are made the myth will be perpetuated. What is closer to reality is that investigators and prosecutors have been confused and uncertain as to their obligations, and they have been badly let down by a judiciary which failed to appreciate the practical considerations involved.

The new legislation is far from perfect and a number of potential difficulties have been highlighted in the preceding chapters. The CPIA 1996 and disclosure code should nevertheless be welcomed as an attempt to define responsibilities with greater clarity than the common law rules. Their success will depend not only on the honesty of the investigator and the competence of the prosecutor, but also on the willingness of the defence to comply fully with the new obligations placed upon them.

Appendix 1

THE ATTORNEY-GENERAL'S GUIDELINES FOR THE DISCLOSURE
OF 'UNUSED MATERIAL' TO THE DEFENCE

1. For the purposes of these guidelines the term 'unused material' is used to
include the following:
(i)   All witness statements and documents which are not included in the
committal bundles served on the defence.
(ii)   The statements of any witnesses who are to be called to give evidence
at committal and (if not in the bundle) any documents referred to therein.
(iii)   The unedited version(s) of any edited statements or composite
statement included in the committal bundles.

2. In all cases which are due to be committed for trial, all unused material
should normally (i.e. subject to the discretionary exceptions mentioned in para. 6)
be made available to the defence solicitor if it has some bearing on the offence(s)
charged and the surrounding circumstances of the case.

3. (a)   If it will not delay the committal, disclosure should be made as soon as
possible before the date fixed. This is particularly important — and might even justify
delay — if the material might have some influence upon the course of the committal
proceedings or the charges upon which the justices might decide to commit.
(b)   If however it would or might cause delay and is unlikely to influence the
committal, it should be done at or as soon as possible after committal.

4. If the unused material does not exceed about 50 pages, disclosure should be
by way of provision of a copy — either by post, by hand, or via the police.

5. If the unused material exceeds about 50 pages or is unsuitable for copying,
the defence solicitor should be given an opportunity to inspect it at a convenient
police station or, alternatively, at the prosecuting solicitor's office, having first
taken care to remove any material of the type mentioned in para. 6. If, having
inspected it, the solicitor wishes to have a copy of any part of the material, this
request should be complied with.

6.   There is a discretion not to make disclosure — at least until counsel has considered and advised on the matter — in the following circumstances:

(i)   There are grounds for fearing that disclosing a statement might lead to an attempt being made to persuade a witness to make a statement retracting his original one, to change his story, not to appear at court or otherwise to intimidate him.

(ii)   The statement (e.g. from a relative or close friend of the accused) is believed to be wholly or partially untrue and might be of use in cross-examination if the witness should be called by the defence.

(iii)   The statement is favourable to the prosecution and believed to be substantially true but there are grounds for fearing that the witness, due to feelings of loyalty or fear, might give the defence solicitor a quite different, and false, story favourable to the defendant. If called as a defence witness upon the basis of this second account, the statement to the police can be of use in cross-examination.

(iv)   The statement is quite neutral or negative and there is no reason to doubt its truthfulness — e.g. 'I saw nothing of the fight' or 'He was not at home that afternoon'. There are however grounds to believe that the witness might change his story and give evidence for the defence — e.g. purporting to give an account of the fight, or an alibi. Here again, the statement can properly be withheld for use in cross-examination.

(NB. In cases (i) to (iv) the name and address of the witness should normally be supplied.)

(v)   The statement is, to a greater or lesser extent, 'sensitive' and for this reason it is not in the public interest to disclose it. Examples of statements containing sensitive material are as follows:

(a)   It deals with matters of national security; or it is by, or discloses the identity of, a member of the security services who would be of no further use to those services once his identity became known.

(b)   It is by, or discloses the identity of, an informant and there are reasons for fearing that disclosure of his identity would put him or his family in danger.

(c)   It is by, or discloses the identity of, a witness who might be in danger of assault or intimidation if his identity became known.

(d)   It contains details which, if they became known, might facilitate the commission of other offences or alert someone not in custody that he was a suspect; or it discloses some unusual form of surveillance or method of detecting crime.

(e)   It is supplied only on condition that the contents will not be disclosed, at least until a subpoena has been served upon the supplier — e.g. a bank official.

(f)   It relates to other offences by, or serious allegations against, someone who is not an accused, or discloses previous convictions or other matter prejudicial to him.

(g)   It contains details of private delicacy to the maker and/or might create risk of domestic strife.

7. If there is doubt as to whether unused material comes within any of the categories in para. 6, such material should be submitted to counsel for advice either before or after committal.

8. In deciding whether or not statements containing sensitive material should be disclosed, a balance should be struck between the degree of sensitivity and the extent to which the information might assist the defence. If, to take one extreme, the information is or may be true and would go some way towards establishing the innocence of the accused (or cast some significant doubt upon his guilt or upon some material part of the evidence on which the Crown is relying) there must either be full disclosure or, if the sensitivity is too great to permit this, recourse to the alternative steps set out in para. 13. If, to take the other extreme, the material supports the case for the prosecution or is neutral or for other reasons is clearly of no use to the defence, there is a discretion to withhold not merely the statement containing the sensitive material, but also the name and address of the maker.

9. Any doubt as to whether the balance is in favour of, or against, disclosure should always be resolved in favour of disclosure.

10. No unused material which might be said to come within the discretionary exceptions in para. 6 should be disclosed to the defence until (a) the investigating officer has been asked whether he has any objections, and (b) it has been the subject of advice by counsel and that advice has been considered by the prosecuting solicitor. Should it be considered that any material is so exceptionally sensitive that it should not be shown to counsel, the Director of Public Prosecutions should be consulted.

11. In all cases counsel should be fully informed as to what unused material has already been disclosed. If some has been withheld in pursuance of para. 10, he should be informed of any police views, his instructions should deal — both generally and in particular — with the question of 'balance' and he should be asked to advise in writing.

12. If the sensitive material relates to the identity of an informant, counsel's attention should be directed to the following passages from the judgments of (a) Pollock CB in *Attorney-General* v *Briant* (1846) 15 Meeson & Welsby's Reports 169 and (b) Lord Esher MR in *Marks* v *Beyfus* (1890) 25 QBD 494.

(a) 'The rule clearly established and acted on is this, that in a public prosecution a witness cannot be asked such questions as will disclose the informer, if he be a third person. This has been the settled rule for fifty years, and although it may seem hard in a particular case, private mischief must give way to public convenience . . . and we think the principle of the rule applies to the case where a witness is asked if he himself is the informer'.

(b) 'If upon the trial of a prisoner the judge should be of opinion that the disclosure of the name of the informant is necessary or right in order to show the prisoner's innocence, then one public policy is in conflict with another public policy, and that which says that an innocent man is not to be condemned when his innocence can be proved is the policy that must prevail'.

13. If it is decided that there is a duty of disclosure but the information is too sensitive to permit the statement or document to be handed over in full, it will become necessary to discuss with counsel and the investigating officer whether it would be safe to make some limited form of disclosure by means which would satisfy the legitimate interests of the defence. These means may be many and various but the following are given by way of example:

(i)   If the only sensitive part of a statement is the name and address of the maker, a copy can be supplied with these details, and any identifying particulars in the text, blanked out. This would be coupled with an undertaking to try to make the witness available for interview, if requested; and subsequently, if so desired, to arrange for his attendance at court.

(ii)   Sometimes a witness might be adequately protected if the address given was his place of work rather than his home address. This is in fact already quite a common practice with witnesses such as bank officials.

(iii)   A fresh statement can be prepared and signed, omitting the sensitive part. If this is not practicable, the sensitive part can be blanked out.

(iv)   Disclosure of all or part of a sensitive statement or document may be possible on a counsel-to-counsel basis although it must be recognised that counsel for the defence cannot give any guarantee of total confidentiality as he may feel bound to reveal the material to his instructing solicitor if he regards it as his clear and unavoidable duty to do so in the proper preparation and presentation of his case.

(v)   If the part of the statement or document which might assist the defence is factual and not in itself sensitive, the prosecution could make a formal admission in accordance with s. 10 of the Criminal Justice Act 1967, assuming that they accept the correctness of the fact.

14. An unrepresented accused should be provided with a copy of all unused material which would normally have been served on his solicitor if he were represented. Special consideration, however, would have to be given to sensitive material and it might sometimes be desirable for counsel, if in doubt, to consult the trial judge.

15. If, either before or during a trial, it becomes apparent that there is a clear duty to disclose some unused material but it is so sensitive that it would not be in the public interest to do so, it will probably be necessary to offer no, or no further, evidence. Should such a situation arise or seem likely to arise then, if time permits, prosecuting solicitors are advised to consult the Director of Public Prosecutions.

16. The practice outlined above should be adopted with immediate effect in relation to all cases submitted to the prosecuting solicitor on receipt of these guidelines. It should also be adopted as regards cases already submitted, so far as is practicable.

Appendix 2

CRIMINAL PROCEDURE AND INVESTIGATIONS ACT 1996

1996 CHAPTER 25

An Act to make provision about criminal procedure and criminal investigations.

[4th July 1996]

BE IT ENACTED by the Queen's most Excellent Majesty, by and with the advice and consent of the Lords Spiritual and Temporal, and Commons, in this present Parliament assembled, and by the authority of the same, as follows:—

PART I
DISCLOSURE

Introduction

1. Application of this Part

(1) This Part applies where—

(a) a person is charged with a summary offence in respect of which a court proceeds to summary trial and in respect of which he pleads not guilty,

(b) a person who has attained the age of 18 is charged with an offence which is triable either way, in respect of which a court proceeds to summary trial and in respect of which he pleads not guilty, or

(c) a person under the age of 18 is charged with an indictable offence in respect of which a court proceeds to summary trial and in respect of which he pleads not guilty.

(2) This Part also applies where—

(a) a person is charged with an indictable offence and he is committed for trial for the offence concerned,

(b) a person is charged with an indictable offence and proceedings for the trial of the person on the charge concerned are transferred to the Crown Court by virtue of a notice of transfer given under section 4 of the Criminal Justice Act 1987 (serious or complex fraud),

(c)   a person is charged with an indictable offence and proceedings for the trial of the person on the charge concerned are transferred to the Crown Court by virtue of a notice of transfer served on a magistrates' court under section 53 of the Criminal Justice Act 1991 (certain cases involving children),

(d)   a count charging a person with a summary offence is included in an indictment under the authority of section 40 of the Criminal Justice Act 1988 (common assault etc.), or

(e)   a bill of indictment charging a person with an indictable offence is preferred under the authority of section 2(2)(b) of the Administration of Justice (Miscellaneous Provisions) Act 1933 (bill preferred by direction of Court of Appeal, or by direction or with consent of a judge).

(3)   This Part applies in relation to alleged offences into which no criminal investigation has begun before the appointed day.

(4)   For the purposes of this section a criminal investigation is an investigation which police officers or other persons have a duty to conduct with a view to it being ascertained—

(a)   whether a person should be charged with an offence, or

(b)   whether a person charged with an offence is guilty of it.

(5)   The reference in subsection (3) to the appointed day is to such day as is appointed for the purposes of this Part by the Secretary of State by order.

2.   General interpretation

(1)   References to the accused are to the person mentioned in section 1(1) or (2).

(2)   Where there is more than one accused in any proceedings this Part applies separately in relation to each of the accused.

(3)   References to the prosecutor are to any person acting as prosecutor, whether an individual or a body.

(4)   References to material are to material of all kinds, and in particular include references to—

(a)   information, and

(b)   objects of all descriptions.

(5)   References to recording information are to putting it in a durable or retrievable form (such as writing or tape).

(6)   This section applies for the purposes of this Part.

The main provisions

3.   Primary disclosure by prosecutor

(1)   The prosecutor must—

(a)   disclose to the accused any prosecution material which has not previously been disclosed to the accused and which in the prosecutor's opinion might undermine the case for the prosecution against the accused, or

(b)   give to the accused a written statement that there is no material of a description mentioned in paragraph (a).

(2)   For the purposes of this section prosecution material is material—

(a)   which is in the prosecutor's possession, and came into his possession in connection with the case for the prosecution against the accused, or

(b)   which, in pursuance of a code operative under Part II, he has inspected in connection with the case for the prosecution against the accused.

(3)   Where material consists of information which has been recorded in any form the prosecutor discloses it for the purposes of this section—

(a)   by securing that a copy is made of it and that the copy is given to the accused, or

(b)   if in the prosecutor's opinion that is not practicable or not desirable, by allowing the accused to inspect it at a reasonable time and a reasonable place or by taking steps to secure that he is allowed to do so;

and a copy may be in such form as the prosecutor thinks fit and need not be in the same form as that in which the information has already been recorded.

(4)   Where material consists of information which has not been recorded the prosecutor discloses it for the purposes of this section by securing that it is recorded in such form as he thinks fit and—

(a)   by securing that a copy is made of it and that the copy is given to the accused, or

(b)   if in the prosecutor's opinion that is not practicable or not desirable, by allowing the accused to inspect it at a reasonable time and a reasonable place or by taking steps to secure that he is allowed to do so.

(5)   Where material does not consist of information the prosecutor discloses it for the purposes of this section by allowing the accused to inspect it at a reasonable time and a reasonable place or by taking steps to secure that he is allowed to do so.

(6)   Material must not be disclosed under this section to the extent that the court, on an application by the prosecutor, concludes it is not in the public interest to disclose it and orders accordingly.

(7)   Material must not be disclosed under this section to the extent that—

(a)   it has been intercepted in obedience to a warrant issued under section 2 of the Interception of Communications Act 1985, or

(b)   it indicates that such a warrant has been issued or that material has been intercepted in obedience to such a warrant.

(8)   The prosecutor must act under this section during the period which, by virtue of section 12, is the relevant period for this section.

4.   Primary disclosure: further provisions

(1)   This section applies where—

(a)   the prosecutor acts under section 3, and

(b)   before so doing he was given a document in pursuance of provision included, by virtue of section 24(3), in a code operative under Part II.

(2)   In such a case the prosecutor must give the document to the accused at the same time as the prosecutor acts under section 3.

5.   Compulsory disclosure by accused

(1)   Subject to subsections (2) to (4), this section applies where—

(a)   this Part applies by virtue of section 1(2), and

(b)   the prosecutor complies with section 3 or purports to comply with it.

(2)   Where this Part applies by virtue of section 1(2)(b), this section does not apply unless—

(a)   a copy of the notice of transfer, and

(b)   copies of the documents containing the evidence,

have been given to the accused under regulations made under section 5(9) of the Criminal Justice Act 1987.

(3)   Where this Part applies by virtue of section 1(2)(c), this section does not apply unless—

(a)   a copy of the notice of transfer, and

(b)   copies of the documents containing the evidence,

have been given to the accused under regulations made under paragraph 4 of Schedule 6 to the Criminal Justice Act 1991.

(4)   Where this Part applies by virtue of section 1(2)(e), this section does not apply unless the prosecutor has served on the accused a copy of the indictment and a copy of the set of documents containing the evidence which is the basis of the charge.

(5)   Where this section applies, the accused must give a defence statement to the court and the prosecutor.

(6)   For the purposes of this section a defence statement is a written statement—

(a)   setting out in general terms the nature of the accused's defence,

(b)   indicating the matters on which he takes issue with the prosecution, and

(c)   setting out, in the case of each such matter, the reason why he takes issue with the prosecution.

(7)   If the defence statement discloses an alibi the accused must give particulars of the alibi in the statement, including—

(a)   the name and address of any witness the accused believes is able to give evidence in support of the alibi, if the name and address are known to the accused when the statement is given;

(b)   any information in the accused's possession which might be of material assistance in finding any such witness, if his name or address is not known to the accused when the statement is given.

(8)   For the purposes of this section evidence in support of an alibi is evidence tending to show that by reason of the presence of the accused at a particular place or in a particular area at a particular time he was not, or was unlikely to have been, at the place where the offence is alleged to have been committed at the time of its alleged commission.

(9) The accused must give a defence statement under this section during the period which, by virtue of section 12, is the relevant period for this section.

6. Voluntary disclosure by accused

(1) This section applies where—

    (a) this Part applies by virtue of section 1(1), and

    (b) the prosecutor complies with section 3 or purports to comply with it.

(2) The accused—

    (a) may give a defence statement to the prosecutor, and

    (b) if he does so, must also give such a statement to the court.

(3) Subsections (6) to (8) of section 5 apply for the purposes of this section as they apply for the purposes of that.

(4) If the accused gives a defence statement under this section he must give it during the period which, by virtue of section 12, is the relevant period for this section.

7. Secondary disclosure by prosecutor

(1) This section applies where the accused gives a defence statement under section 5 or 6.

(2) The prosecutor must—

    (a) disclose to the accused any prosecution material which has not previously been disclosed to the accused and which might be reasonably expected to assist the accused's defence as disclosed by the defence statement given under section 5 or 6, or

    (b) give to the accused a written statement that there is no material of a description mentioned in paragraph (a).

(3) For the purposes of this section prosecution material is material—

    (a) which is in the prosecutor's possession and came into his possession in connection with the case for the prosecution against the accused, or

    (b) which, in pursuance of a code operative under Part II, he has inspected in connection with the case for the prosecution against the accused.

(4) Subsections (3) to (5) of section 3 (method by which prosecutor discloses) apply for the purposes of this section as they apply for the purposes of that.

(5) Material must not be disclosed under this section to the extent that the court, on an application by the prosecutor, concludes it is not in the public interest to disclose it and orders accordingly.

(6) Material must not be disclosed under this section to the extent that—

    (a) it has been intercepted in obedience to a warrant issued under section 2 of the Interception of Communications Act 1985, or

    (b) it indicates that such a warrant has been issued or that material has been intercepted in obedience to such a warrant.

(7) The prosecutor must act under this section during the period which, by virtue of section 12, is the relevant period for this section.

8. Application by accused for disclosure

(1) This section applies where the accused gives a defence statement under section 5 or 6 and the prosecutor complies with section 7 or purports to comply with it or fails to comply with it.

(2) If the accused has at any time reasonable cause to believe that—

(a) there is prosecution material which might be reasonably expected to assist the accused's defence as disclosed by the defence statement given under section 5 or 6, and

(b) the material has not been disclosed to the accused,

the accused may apply to the court for an order requiring the prosecutor to disclose such material to the accused.

(3) For the purposes of this section prosecution material is material—

(a) which is in the prosecutor's possession and came into his possession in connection with the case for the prosecution against the accused,

(b) which, in pursuance of a code operative under Part II, he has inspected in connection with the case for the prosecution against the accused, or

(c) which falls within subsection (4).

(4) Material falls within this subsection if in pursuance of a code operative under Part II the prosecutor must, if he asks for the material, be given a copy of it or be allowed to inspect it in connection with the case for the prosecution against the accused.

(5) Material must not be disclosed under this section to the extent that the court, on an application by the prosecutor, concludes it is not in the public interest to disclose it and orders accordingly.

(6) Material must not be disclosed under this section to the extent that—

(a) it has been intercepted in obedience to a warrant issued under section 2 of the Interception of Communications Act 1985, or

(b) it indicates that such a warrant has been issued or that material has been intercepted in obedience to such a warrant.

9. Continuing duty of prosecutor to disclose

(1) Subsection (2) applies at all times—

(a) after the prosecutor complies with section 3 or purports to comply with it, and

(b) before the accused is acquitted or convicted or the prosecutor decides not to proceed with the case concerned.

(2) The prosecutor must keep under review the question whether at any given time there is prosecution material which—

(a) in his opinion might undermine the case for the prosecution against the accused, and

(b) has not been disclosed to the accused;

and if there is such material at any time the prosecutor must disclose it to the accused as soon as is reasonably practicable.

(3) In applying subsection (2) by reference to any given time the state of affairs at that time (including the case for the prosecution as it stands at that time) must be taken into account.

(4)   Subsection (5) applies at all times—

(a)   after the prosecutor complies with section 7 or purports to comply with it, and

(b)   before the accused is acquitted or convicted or the prosecutor decides not to proceed with the case concerned.

(5)   The prosecutor must keep under review the question whether at any given time there is prosecution material which—

(a)   might be reasonably expected to assist the accused's defence as disclosed by the defence statement given under section 5 or 6, and

(b)   has not been disclosed to the accused;

and if there is such material at any time the prosecutor must disclose it to the accused as soon as is reasonably practicable.

(6)   For the purposes of this section prosecution material is material—

(a)   which is in the prosecutor's possession and came into his possession in connection with the case for the prosecution against the accused, or

(b)   which, in pursuance of a code operative under Part II, he has inspected in connection with the case for the prosecution against the accused.

(7)   Subsections (3) to (5) of section 3 (method by which prosecutor discloses) apply for the purposes of this section as they apply for the purposes of that.

(8)   Material must not be disclosed under this section to the extent that the court, on an application by the prosecutor, concludes it is not in the public interest to disclose it and orders accordingly.

(9)   Material must not be disclosed under this section to the extent that—

(a)   it has been intercepted in obedience to a warrant issued under section 2 of the Interception of Communications Act 1985, or

(b)   it indicates that such a warrant has been issued or that material has been intercepted in obedience to such a warrant.

10.   Prosecutor's failure to observe time limits

(1)   This section applies if the prosecutor—

(a)   purports to act under section 3 after the end of the period which, by virtue of section 12, is the relevant period for section 3, or

(b)   purports to act under section 7 after the end of the period which, by virtue of section 12, is the relevant period for section 7.

(2)   Subject to subsection (3), the failure to act during the period concerned does not on its own constitute grounds for staying the proceedings for abuse of process.

(3)   Subsection (2) does not prevent the failure constituting such grounds if it involves such delay by the prosecutor that the accused is denied a fair trial.

11.   Faults in disclosure by accused

(1)   This section applies where section 5 applies and the accused—

(a)   fails to give a defence statement under that section,

(b)   gives a defence statement under that section but does so after the end of the period which, by virtue of section 12, is the relevant period for section 5,

(c) sets out inconsistent defences in a defence statement given under section 5,

(d) at his trial puts forward a defence which is different from any defence set out in a defence statement given under section 5,

(e) at his trial adduces evidence in support of an alibi without having given particulars of the alibi in a defence statement given under section 5, or

(f) at his trial calls a witness to give evidence in support of an alibi without having complied with subsection (7)(a) or (b) of section 5 as regards the witness in giving a defence statement under that section.

(2) This section also applies where section 6 applies, the accused gives a defence statement under that section, and the accused—

(a) gives the statement after the end of the period which, by virtue of section 12, is the relevant period for section 6,

(b) sets out inconsistent defences in the statement,

(c) at his trial puts forward a defence which is different from any defence set out in the statement,

(d) at his trial adduces evidence in support of an alibi without having given particulars of the alibi in the statement, or

(e) at his trial calls a witness to give evidence in support of an alibi without having complied with subsection (7)(a) or (b) of section 5 (as applied by section 6) as regards the witness in giving the statement.

(3) Where this section applies—

(a) the court or, with the leave of the court, any other party may make such comment as appears appropriate;

(b) the court or jury may draw such inferences as appear proper in deciding whether the accused is guilty of the offence concerned.

(4) Where the accused puts forward a defence which is different from any defence set out in a defence statement given under section 5 or 6, in doing anything under subsection (3) or in deciding whether to do anything under it the court shall have regard—

(a) to the extent of the difference in the defences, and

(b) to whether there is any justification for it.

(5) A person shall not be convicted of an offence solely on an inference drawn under subsection (3).

(6) Any reference in this section to evidence in support of an alibi shall be construed in accordance with section 5.

Time limits

12. Time limits

(1) This section has effect for the purpose of determining the relevant period for sections 3, 5, 6 and 7.

(2) Subject to subsection (3), the relevant period is a period beginning and ending with such days as the Secretary of State prescribes by regulations for the purposes of the section concerned.

(3)   The regulations may do one or more of the following—

(a)   provide that the relevant period for any section shall if the court so orders be extended (or further extended) by so many days as the court specifies;

(b)   provide that the court may only make such an order if an application is made by a prescribed person and if any other prescribed conditions are fulfilled;

(c)   provide that an application may only be made if prescribed conditions are fulfilled;

(d)   provide that the number of days by which a period may be extended shall be entirely at the court's discretion;

(e)   provide that the number of days by which a period may be extended shall not exceed a prescribed number;

(f)   provide that there shall be no limit on the number of applications that may be made to extend a period;

(g)   provide that no more than a prescribed number of applications may be made to extend a period;

and references to the relevant period for a section shall be construed accordingly.

(4)   Conditions mentioned in subsection (3) may be framed by reference to such factors as the Secretary of State thinks fit.

(5)   Without prejudice to the generality of subsection (4), so far as the relevant period for section 3 or 7 is concerned—

(a)   conditions may be framed by reference to the nature or volume of the material concerned;

(b)   the nature of material may be defined by reference to the prosecutor's belief that the question of non-disclosure on grounds of public interest may arise.

(6)   In subsection (3) 'prescribed' means prescribed by regulations under this section.

13.   Time limits: transitional

(1)   As regards a case in relation to which no regulations under section 12 have come into force for the purposes of section 3, section 3(8) shall have effect as if it read—

'(8)   The prosecutor must act under this section as soon as is reasonably practicable after—

(a)   the accused pleads not guilty (where this Part applies by virtue of section 1(1)),

(b)   the accused is committed for trial (where this Part applies by virtue of section 1(2)(a)),

(c)   the proceedings are transferred (where this Part applies by virtue of section 1(2)(b) or (c)),

(d)   the count is included in the indictment (where this Part applies by virtue of section 1(2)(d)), or

(e)   the bill of indictment is preferred (where this Part applies by virtue of section 1(2)(e)).'

(2)   As regards a case in relation to which no regulations under section 12 have come into force for the purposes of section 7, section 7(7) shall have effect as if it read—

'(7)   The prosecutor must act under this section as soon as is reasonably practicable after the accused gives a defence statement under section 5 or 6.'

Public interest

14.   Public interest: review for summary trials

(1)   This section applies where this Part applies by virtue of section 1(1).

(2)   At any time—

(a)   after a court makes an order under section 3(6), 7(5), 8(5) or 9(8), and

(b)   before the accused is acquitted or convicted or the prosecutor decides not to proceed with the case concerned,

the accused may apply to the court for a review of the question whether it is still not in the public interest to disclose material affected by its order.

(3)   In such a case the court must review that question, and if it concludes that it is in the public interest to disclose material to any extent—

(a)   it shall so order, and

(b)   it shall take such steps as are reasonable to inform the prosecutor of its order.

(4)   Where the prosecutor is informed of an order made under subsection (3) he must act accordingly having regard to the provisions of this Part (unless he decides not to proceed with the case concerned).

15.   Public interest: review in other cases

(1)   This section applies where this Part applies by virtue of section 1(2).

(2)   This section applies at all times—

(a)   after a court makes an order under section 3(6), 7(5), 8(5) or 9(8), and

(b)   before the accused is acquitted or convicted or the prosecutor decides not to proceed with the case concerned.

(3)   The court must keep under review the question whether at any given time it is still not in the public interest to disclose material affected by its order.

(4)   The court must keep the question mentioned in subsection (3) under review without the need for an application; but the accused may apply to the court for a review of that question.

(5)   If the court at any time concludes that it is in the public interest to disclose material to any extent—

(a)   it shall so order, and

(b)   it shall take such steps as are reasonable to inform the prosecutor of its order.

(6)   Where the prosecutor is informed of an order made under subsection (5) he must act accordingly having regard to the provisions of this Part (unless he decides not to proceed with the case concerned).

16.   Applications: opportunity to be heard
Where—

(a)   an application is made under section 3(6), 7(5), 8(5), 9(8), 14(2) or 15(4),

(b)   a person claiming to have an interest in the material applies to be heard by the court, and

(c)   he shows that he was involved (whether alone or with others and whether directly or indirectly) in the prosecutor's attention being brought to the material, the court must not make an order under section 3(6), 7(5), 8(5), 9(8), 14(3) or 15(5) (as the case may be) unless the person applying under paragraph (b) has been given an opportunity to be heard.

Confidentiality

17.   Confidentiality of disclosed information

(1)   If the accused is given or allowed to inspect a document or other object under—

(a)   section 3, 4, 7, 9, 14 or 15, or

(b)   an order under section 8,

then, subject to subsections (2) to (4), he must not use or disclose it or any information recorded in it.

(2)   The accused may use or disclose the object or information—

(a)   in connection with the proceedings for whose purposes he was given the object or allowed to inspect it,

(b)   with a view to the taking of further criminal proceedings (for instance, by way of appeal) with regard to the matter giving rise to the proceedings mentioned in paragraph (a), or

(c)   in connection with the proceedings first mentioned in paragraph (b).

(3)   The accused may use or disclose—

(a)   the object to the extent that it has been displayed to the public in open court, or

(b)   the information to the extent that it has been communicated to the public in open court;

but the preceding provisions of this subsection do not apply if the object is displayed or the information is communicated in proceedings to deal with a contempt of court under section 18.

(4)   If—

(a)   the accused applies to the court for an order granting permission to use or disclose the object or information, and

(b)   the court makes such an order,

the accused may use or disclose the object or information for the purpose and to the extent specified by the court.

(5)   An application under subsection (4) may be made and dealt with at any time, and in particular after the accused has been acquitted or convicted or the prosecutor has decided not to proceed with the case concerned; but this is subject to rules made by virtue of section 19(2).

(6)   Where—

(a)   an application is made under subsection (4), and

(b)   the prosecutor or a person claiming to have an interest in the object or information applies to be heard by the court,

the court must not make an order granting permission unless the person applying under paragraph (b) has been given an opportunity to be heard.

(7) References in this section to the court are to—

(a) a magistrates' court, where this Part applies by virtue of section 1(1);

(b) the Crown Court, where this Part applies by virtue of section 1(2).

(8) Nothing in this section affects any other restriction or prohibition on the use or disclosure of an object or information, whether the restriction or prohibition arises under an enactment (whenever passed) or otherwise.

18. Confidentiality: contravention

(1) It is a contempt of court for a person knowingly to use or disclose an object or information recorded in it if the use or disclosure is in contravention of section 17.

(2) The following courts have jurisdiction to deal with a person who is guilty of a contempt under this section—

(a) a magistrates' court, where this Part applies by virtue of section 1(1);

(b) the Crown Court, where this Part applies by virtue of section 1(2).

(3) A person who is guilty of a contempt under this section may be dealt with as follows—

(a) a magistrates' court may commit him to custody for a specified period not exceeding six months or impose on him a fine not exceeding £5,000 or both;

(b) the Crown Court may commit him to custody for a specified period not exceeding two years or impose a fine on him or both.

(4) If—

(a) a person is guilty of a contempt under this section, and

(b) the object concerned is in his possession,

the court finding him guilty may order that the object shall be forfeited and dealt with in such manner as the court may order.

(5) The power of the court under subsection (4) includes power to order the object to be destroyed or to be given to the prosecutor or to be placed in his custody for such period as the court may specify.

(6) If—

(a) the court proposes to make an order under subsection (4), and

(b) the person found guilty, or any other person claiming to have an interest in the object, applies to be heard by the court,

the court must not make the order unless the applicant has been given an opportunity to be heard.

(7) If—

(a) a person is guilty of a contempt under this section, and

(b) a copy of the object concerned is in his possession,

the court finding him guilty may order that the copy shall be forfeited and dealt with in such manner as the court may order.

(8) Subsections (5) and (6) apply for the purposes of subsection (7) as they apply for the purposes of subsection (4), but as if references to the object were references to the copy.

(9) An object or information shall be inadmissible as evidence in civil proceedings if to adduce it would in the opinion of the court be likely to constitute a contempt under this section; and 'the court' here means the court before which the civil proceedings are being taken.

(10) The powers of a magistrates' court under this section may be exercised either of the court's own motion or by order on complaint.

Other provisions

19. Rules of court

(1) Without prejudice to the generality of subsection (1) of—

(a) section 144 of the Magistrates' Courts Act 1980 (magistrates' court rules), and

(b) section 84 of the Supreme Court Act 1981 (rules of court),

the power to make rules under each of those sections includes power to make provision mentioned in subsection (2).

(2) The provision is provision as to the practice and procedure to be followed in relation to—

(a) proceedings to deal with a contempt of court under section 18;

(b) an application under section 3(6), 7(5), 8(2) or (5), 9(8), 14(2), 15(4), 16(b), 17(4) or (6)(b) or 18(6);

(c) an application under regulations made under section 12;

(d) an order under section 3(6), 7(5), 8(2) or (5), 9(8), 14(3), 17(4) or 18(4) or (7);

(e) an order under section 15(5) (whether or not an application is made under section 15(4));

(f) an order under regulations made under section 12.

(3) Rules made under section 144 of the Magistrates' Courts Act 1980 by virtue of subsection (2)(a) above may contain or include provision equivalent to Schedule 3 to the Contempt of Court Act 1981 (proceedings for disobeying magistrates' court order) with any modifications which the Lord Chancellor considers appropriate on the advice of or after consultation with the rule committee for magistrates' courts.

(4) Rules made by virtue of subsection (2)(b) in relation to an application under section 17(4) may include provision—

(a) that an application to a magistrates' court must be made to a particular magistrates' court;

(b) that an application to the Crown Court must be made to the Crown Court sitting at a particular place;

(c) requiring persons to be notified of an application.

(5) Rules made by virtue of this section may make different provision for different cases or classes of case.

20. Other statutory rules as to disclosure

(1) A duty under any of the disclosure provisions shall not affect or be affected by any duty arising under any other enactment with regard to material to be

provided to or by the accused or a person representing him; but this is subject to subsection (2).

(2)   In making an order under section 9 of the Criminal Justice Act 1987 or section 31 of this Act (preparatory hearings) the judge may take account of anything which—

    (a)   has been done,

    (b)   has been required to be done, or

    (c)   will be required to be done,

in pursuance of any of the disclosure provisions.

(3)   Without prejudice to the generality of section 144(1) of the Magistrates' Courts Act 1980 (magistrates' court rules) the power to make rules under that section includes power to make, with regard to any proceedings before a magistrates' court which relate to an alleged offence, provision for—

    (a)   requiring any party to the proceedings to disclose to the other party or parties any expert evidence which he proposes to adduce in the proceedings;

    (b)   prohibiting a party who fails to comply in respect of any evidence with any requirement imposed by virtue of paragraph (a) from adducing that evidence without the leave of the court.

(4)   Rules made by virtue of subsection (3)—

    (a)   may specify the kinds of expert evidence to which they apply;

    (b)   may exempt facts or matters of any description specified in the rules.

(5)   For the purposes of this section—

    (a)   the disclosure provisions are sections 3 to 9;

    (b)   'enactment' includes an enactment comprised in subordinate legislation (which here has the same meaning as in the Interpretation Act 1978).

21.   Common law rules as to disclosure

(1)   Where this Part applies as regards things falling to be done after the relevant time in relation to an alleged offence, the rules of common law which—

    (a)   were effective immediately before the appointed day, and

    (b)   relate to the disclosure of material by the prosecutor,

do not apply as regards things falling to be done after that time in relation to the alleged offence.

(2)   Subsection (1) does not affect the rules of common law as to whether disclosure is in the public interest.

(3)   References in subsection (1) to the relevant time are to the time when—

    (a)   the accused pleads not guilty (where this Part applies by virtue of section 1(1)),

    (b)   the accused is committed for trial (where this Part applies by virtue of section 1(2)(a)),

    (c)   the proceedings are transferred (where this Part applies by virtue of section 1(2)(b) or (c)),

    (d)   the count is included in the indictment (where this Part applies by virtue of section 1(2)(d)), or

(e) the bill of indictment is preferred (where this Part applies by virtue of section 1(2)(e)).

(4) The reference in subsection (1) to the appointed day is to the day appointed under section 1(5).

PART II
CRIMINAL INVESTIGATIONS

22. Introduction

(1) For the purposes of this Part a criminal investigation is an investigation conducted by police officers with a view to it being ascertained—

(a) whether a person should be charged with an offence, or

(b) whether a person charged with offence is guilty of it.

(2) In this Part references to material are to material of all kinds, and in particular include references to—

(a) information, and

(b) objects of all descriptions.

(3) In this Part references to recording information are to putting it in a durable or retrievable form (such as writing or tape).

23. Code of practice

(1) The Secretary of State shall prepare a code of practice containing provisions designed to secure—

(a) that where a criminal investigation is conducted all reasonable steps are taken for the purposes of the investigation and, in particular, all reasonable lines of inquiry are pursued;

(b) that information which is obtained in the course of a criminal investigation and may be relevant to the investigation is recorded;

(c) that any record of such information is retained;

(d) that any other material which is obtained in the course of a criminal investigation and may be relevant to the investigation is retained;

(e) that information falling within paragraph (b) and material falling within paragraph (d) is revealed to a person who is involved in the prosecution of criminal proceedings arising out of or relating to the investigation and who is identified in accordance with prescribed provisions;

(f) that where such a person inspects information or other material in pursuance of a requirement that it be revealed to him, and he requests that it be disclosed to the accused, the accused is allowed to inspect it or is given a copy of it;

(g) that where such a person is given a document indicating the nature of information or other material in pursuance of a requirement that it be revealed to him, and he requests that it be disclosed to the accused, the accused is allowed to inspect it or is given a copy of it;

(h) that the person who is to allow the accused to inspect information or other material or to give him a copy of it shall decide which of those (inspecting or giving a copy) is appropriate;

(i)   that where the accused is allowed to inspect material as mentioned in paragraph (f) or (g) and he requests a copy, he is given one unless the person allowing the inspection is of opinion that it is not practicable or not desirable to give him one;

(j)   that a person mentioned in paragraph (e) is given a written statement that prescribed activities which the code requires have been carried out.

(2)   The code may include provision—

(a)   that a police officer identified in accordance with prescribed provisions must carry out a prescribed activity which the code requires;

(b)   that a police officer so identified must take steps to secure the carrying out by a person (whether or not a police officer) of a prescribed activity which the code requires;

(c)   that a duty must be discharged by different people in succession in prescribed circumstances (as where a person dies or retires).

(3)   The code may include provision about the form in which information is to be recorded.

(4)   The code may include provision about the manner in which and the period for which—

(a)   a record of information is to be retained, and

(b)   any other material is to be retained;

and if a person is charged with an offence the period may extend beyond a conviction or an acquittal.

(5)   The code may include provision about the time when, the form in which, the way in which, and the extent to which, information or any other material is to be revealed to the person mentioned in subsection (1)(e).

(6)   The code must be so framed that it does not apply to material intercepted in obedience to a warrant issued under section 2 of the Interception of Communications Act 1985.

(7)   The code may—

(a)   make different provision in relation to different cases or descriptions of case;

(b)   contain exceptions as regards prescribed cases or descriptions of case.

(8)   In this section 'prescribed' means prescribed by the code.

24.   Examples of disclosure provisions

(1)   This section gives examples of the kinds of provision that may be included in the code by virtue of section 23(5).

(2)   The code may provide that if the person required to reveal material has possession of material which he believes is sensitive he must give a document which—

(a)   indicates the nature of that material, and

(b)   states that he so believes.

(3)   The code may provide that if the person required to reveal material has possession of material which is of a description prescribed under this subsection and which he does not believe is sensitive he must give a document which—

(a)   indicates the nature of that material, and

(b)   states that he does not so believe.

(4)   The code may provide that if—

(a)   a document is given in pursuance of provision contained in the code by virtue of subsection (2), and

(b)   a person identified in accordance with prescribed provisions asks for any of the material,

the person giving the document must give a copy of the material asked for to the person asking for it or (depending on the circumstances) must allow him to inspect it.

(5)   The code may provide that if—

(a)   a document is given in pursuance of provision contained in the code by virtue of subsection (3),

(b)   all or any of the material is of a description prescribed under this subsection, and

(c)   a person is identified in accordance with prescribed provisions as entitled to material of that description,

the person giving the document must give a copy of the material of that description to the person so identified or (depending on the circumstances) must allow him to inspect it.

(6)   The code may provide that if—

(a)   a document is given in pursuance of provision contained in the code by virtue of subsection (3),

(b)   all or any of the material is not of a description prescribed under subsection (5), and

(c)   a person identified in accordance with prescribed provisions asks for any of the material not of that description,

the person giving the document must give a copy of the material asked for to the person asking for it or (depending on the circumstances) must allow him to inspect it.

(7)   The code may provide that if the person required to reveal material has possession of material which he believes is sensitive and of such a nature that provision contained in the code by virtue of subsection (2) should not apply with regard to it—

(a)   that provision shall not apply with regard to the material,

(b)   he must notify a person identified in accordance with prescribed provisions of the existence of the material, and

(c)   he must allow the person so notified to inspect the material.

(8)   For the purposes of this section material is sensitive to the extent that its disclosure under Part I would be contrary to the public interest.

(9)   In this section 'prescribed' means prescribed by the code.

25.   Operation and revision of code

(1)   When the Secretary of State has prepared a code under section 23—

(a)   he shall publish it in the form of a draft,

(b)   he shall consider any representations made to him about the draft, and

(c)   he may modify the draft accordingly.

(2)   When the Secretary of State has acted under subsection (1) he shall lay the code before each House of Parliament, and when he has done so he may bring it into operation on such day as he may appoint by order.

(3)   A code brought into operation under this section shall apply in relation to suspected or alleged offences into which no criminal investigation has begun before the day so appointed.

(4)   The Secretary of State may from time to time revise a code previously brought into operation under this section; and the preceding provisions of this section shall apply to a revised code as they apply to the code as first prepared.

26.   Effect of code

(1)   A person other than a police officer who is charged with the duty of conducting an investigation with a view to it being ascertained—

(a)   whether a person should be charged with an offence, or

(b)   whether a person charged with an offence is guilty of it,

shall in discharging that duty have regard to any relevant provision of a code which would apply if the investigation were conducted by police officers.

(2)   A failure—

(a)   by a police officer to comply with any provision of a code for the time being in operation by virtue of an order under section 25, or

(b)   by a person to comply with subsection (1),

shall not in itself render him liable to any criminal or civil proceedings.

(3)   In all criminal and civil proceedings a code in operation at any time by virtue of an order under section 25 shall be admissible in evidence.

(4)   If it appears to a court or tribunal conducting criminal or civil proceedings that—

(a)   any provision of a code in operation at any time by virtue of an order under section 25, or

(b)   any failure mentioned in subsection (2)(a) or (b),

is relevant to any question arising in the proceedings, the provision or failure shall be taken into account in deciding the question.

27.   Common law rules as to criminal investigations

(1)   Where a code prepared under section 23 and brought into operation under section 25 applies in relation to a suspected or alleged offence, the rules of common law which—

(a)   were effective immediately before the appointed day, and

(b)   relate to the matter mentioned in subsection (2),

shall not apply in relation to the suspected or alleged offence.

(2)   The matter is the revealing of material—

(a)   by a police officer or other person charged with the duty of conducting an investigation with a view to it being ascertained whether a person should be charged with an offence or whether a person charged with an offence is guilty of it;

(b)   to a person involved in the prosecution of criminal proceedings.

(3) In subsection (1) 'the appointed day' means the day appointed under section 25 with regard to the code as first prepared.

Appendix 3

CRIMINAL PROCEDURE AND INVESTIGATIONS ACT 1996
CODE OF PRACTICE UNDER PART II

Introduction

1.1   This code of practice is issued under Part II of the Criminal Procedure and Investigations Act 1996 ('the Act'). It applies in respect of criminal investigations conducted by police officers which begin on or after the day on which this code comes into effect. Persons other than police officers who are charged with the duty of conducting an investigation as defined in the Act are to have regard to the relevant provisions of the code, and should take these into account in applying their own operating procedures.

1.2   This code does not apply to persons who are not charged with the duty of conducting an investigation as defined in the Act.

1.3   Nothing in this code applies to material intercepted in obedience to a warrant issued under section 2 of the Interception of Communications Act 1985, or to any copy of that material as defined in section 10 of that Act.

Definitions

2.1   In this code:
— a *criminal investigation* is an investigation conducted by police officers with a view to it being ascertained whether a person should be charged with an offence, or whether a person charged with an offence is guilty of it. This will include
— investigations into crimes that have been committed;
— investigations whose purpose is to ascertain whether a crime has been committed, with a view to the possible institution of criminal proceedings; and
— investigations which begin in the belief that a crime may be committed, for example when the police keep premises or individuals under observation for a period of time, with a view to the possible institution of criminal proceedings;

— charging a person with an offence includes prosecution by way of summons;

— an *investigator* is any police officer involved in the conduct of a criminal investigation. All investigators have a responsibility for carrying out the duties imposed on them under this code, including in particular recording information, and retaining records of information and other material;

— the *officer in charge of an investigation* is the police officer responsible for directing a criminal investigation. He is also responsible for ensuring that proper procedures are in place for recording information, and retaining records of information and other material, in the investigation;

— the *disclosure officer* is the person responsible for examining material retained by the police during the investigation; revealing material to the prosecutor during the investigation and any criminal proceedings resulting from it, and certifying that he has done this; and disclosing material to the accused at the request of the prosecutor;

— the *prosecutor* is the authority responsible for the conduct of criminal proceedings on behalf of the Crown. Particular duties may in practice fall to individuals acting on behalf of the prosecuting authority;

— *material* is material of any kind, including information and objects, which is obtained in the course of a criminal investigation and which may be relevant to the investigation;

— material may be *relevant to an investigation* if it appears to an investigator, or to the officer in charge of an investigation, or to the disclosure officer, that it has some bearing on any offence under investigation or any person being investigated, or on the surrounding circumstances of the case, unless it is incapable of having any impact on the case;

— *sensitive material* is material which the disclosure officer believes, after consulting the officer in charge of the investigation, it is not in the public interest to disclose;

— references to *primary prosecution disclosure* are to the duty of the prosecutor under section 3 of the Act to disclose material which is in his possession or which he has inspected in pursuance of this code, and which in his opinion might undermine the case against the accused;

— references to *secondary prosecution disclosure* are to the duty of the prosecutor under section 7 of the Act to disclose material which is in his possession or which he has inspected in pursuance of this code, and which might reasonably be expected to assist the defence disclosed by the accused in a defence statement given under the Act;

— references to the disclosure of material to a person accused of an offence include references to the disclosure of material to his legal representative;

— references to police officers and to the chief officer of police include those employed in a police force as defined in section 3(3) of the Prosecution of Offences Act 1985.

General responsibilities

3.1   The functions of the investigator, the officer in charge of an investigation and the disclosure officer are separate. Whether they are undertaken by one, two or more persons will depend on the complexity of the case and the administrative arrangements within each police force. Where they are undertaken by more than one person, close consultation between them is essential to the effective performance of the duties imposed by this code.

3.2   The chief officer of police for each police force is responsible for putting in place arrangements to ensure that in every investigation the identity of the officer in charge of an investigation and the disclosure officer is recorded.

3.3   The officer in charge of an investigation may delegate tasks to another investigator or to civilians employed by the police force, but he remains responsible for ensuring that these have been carried out and for accounting for any general policies followed in the investigation. In particular, it is an essential part of his duties to ensure that all material which may be relevant to an investigation is retained, and either made available to the disclosure officer or (in exceptional circumstances) revealed directly to the prosecutor.

3.4   In conducting an investigation, the investigator should pursue all reasonable lines of inquiry, whether these point towards or away from the suspect. What is reasonable in each case will depend on the particular circumstances.

3.5   If the officer in charge of an investigation believes that other persons may be in possession of material that may be relevant to the investigation, and if this has not been obtained under paragraph 3.4 above, he should ask the disclosure officer to inform them of the existence of the investigation and to invite them to retain the material in case they receive a request for its disclosure. The disclosure officer should inform the prosecutor that they may have such material. However, the officer in charge of an investigation is not required to make speculative enquiries of other persons: there must be some reason to believe that they may have relevant material. That reason may come from information provided to the police by the accused or from other inquiries made or from some other source.

3.6   If, during a criminal investigation, the officer in charge of an investigation or disclosure officer for any reason no longer has responsibility for the functions falling to him, either his supervisor or the police officer in charge of criminal investigations for the police force concerned must assign someone else to assume that responsibility. That person's identity must be recorded, as with those initially responsible for these functions in each investigation.

Recording of information

4.1   If material which may be relevant to the investigation consists of information which is not recorded in any form, the officer in charge of an investigation must ensure that it is recorded in a durable or retrievable form (whether in writing, on video or audio tape, or on computer disk).

4.2   Where it is not practicable to retain the initial record of information because it forms part of a larger record which is to be destroyed, its contents should be transferred as a true record to a durable and more easily-stored form before that happens.

4.3   Negative information is often relevant to an investigation. If it may be relevant it must be recorded. An example might be a number of people present in a particular place at a particular time who state that they saw nothing unusual.

4.4   Where information which may be relevant is obtained, it must be recorded at the time it is obtained or as soon as practicable after that time. This includes, for example, information obtained in house-to-house enquiries, although the requirement to record information promptly does not require an investigator to take a statement from a potential witness where it would not otherwise be taken.

Retention of material

(a)   Duty to retain material

5.1   The investigator must retain material obtained in a criminal investigation which may be relevant to the investigation. This includes not only material coming into the possession of the investigator (such as documents seized in the course of searching premises) but also material generated by him (such as interview records). Material may be photographed, or retained in the form of a copy rather than the original, if the original is perishable, or was supplied to the investigator rather than generated by him and is to be returned to its owner.

5.2   Where material has been seized in the exercise of the powers of seizure conferred by the Police and Criminal Evidence Act 1984, the duty to retain it under this code is subject to the provisions on the retention of seized material in section 22 of that Act.

5.3   If the officer in charge of an investigation becomes aware as a result of developments in the case that material previously examined but not retained (because it was not thought to be relevant) may now be relevant to the investigation, he should, wherever practicable, take steps to obtain it or ensure that it is retained for further inspection or for production in court if required.

5.4   The duty to retain material includes in particular the duty to retain material falling into the following categories, where it may be relevant to the investigation:

—   crime reports (including crime report forms, relevant parts of incident report books or police officers' notebooks);

—   custody records;

—   records which are derived from tapes of telephone messages (for example, 999 calls) containing descriptions of an alleged offence or offender;

—   final versions of witness statements (and draft versions where their content differs from the final version), including any exhibits mentioned (unless these have been returned to their owner on the understanding that they will be produced in court if required);

—   interview records (written records, or audio or video tapes, of interviews with actual or potential witnesses or suspects);

—   communications between the police and experts such as forensic scientists, reports of work carried out by experts, and schedules of scientific

material prepared by the expert for the investigator, for the purposes of criminal proceedings;
— any material casting doubt on the reliability of a confession;
— any material casting doubt on the reliability of a witness;
— any other material which may fall within the test for primary prosecution disclosure in the Act.

5.5   The duty to retain material falling into these categories does not extend to items which are purely ancillary to such material and possess no independent significance (for example, duplicate copies of records or reports).

(b)   Length of time for which material is to be retained

5.6   All material which may be relevant to the investigation must be retained until a decision is taken whether to institute proceedings against a person for an offence.

5.7   If a criminal investigation results in proceedings being instituted, all material which may be relevant must be retained at least until the accused is acquitted or convicted or the prosecutor decides not to proceed with the case.

5.8   Where the accused is convicted, all material which may be relevant must be retained at least until:
— the convicted person is released from custody, or discharged from hospital, in cases where the court imposes a custodial sentence or a hospital order;
— six months from the date of conviction, in all other cases.

If the court imposes a custodial sentence or hospital order and the convicted person is released from custody or discharged from hospital earlier than six months from the date of conviction, all material which may be relevant must be retained at least until six months from the date of conviction.

5.9   If an appeal against conviction is in progress when the release or discharge occurs, or at the end of the period of six months specified in paragraph 5.8, all material which may be relevant must be retained until the appeal is determined. Similarly, if the Criminal Cases Review Commission is considering an application at that point in time, all material which may be relevant must be retained at least until the Commission decides not to refer the case to the Court of Appeal, or until the Court determines the appeal resulting from the reference by the Commission.

5.10   Material need not be retained by the police as required in paragraph 5.8 if it was seized and is to be returned to its owner.

Preparation of material for prosecutor

(a)   Introduction

6.1   The officer in charge of the investigation, the disclosure officer or an investigator may seek advice from the prosecutor about whether any particular item of material may be relevant to the investigation.

6.2   Material which may be relevant to an investigation, which has been retained in accordance with this code, and which the disclosure officer believes will not form part of the prosecution case, must be listed on a schedule.

6.3   Material which the disclosure officer does not believe is sensitive must be listed on a schedule of non-sensitive material. The schedule must include a statement that the disclosure officer does not believe the material is sensitive.

6.4   Any material which is believed to be sensitive must be either listed on a schedule of sensitive material or, in exceptional circumstances, revealed to the prosecutor separately.

6.5   Paragraphs 6.6 to 6.11 below apply to both sensitive and non-sensitive material. Paragraphs 6.12 to 6.14 apply to sensitive material only.

(b)   Circumstances in which a schedule is to be prepared

6.6   The disclosure officer must ensure that a schedule is prepared in the following circumstances:

— the accused is charged with an offence which is triable only on indictment;

— the accused is charged with an offence which is triable either way, and it is considered either that the case is likely to be tried on indictment or that the accused is likely to plead not guilty at a summary trial;

— the accused is charged with a summary offence, and it is considered that he is likely to plead not guilty.

6.7   In respect of either way and summary offences, a schedule may not be needed if a person has admitted the offence, or if a police officer witnessed the offence and that person has not denied it.

6.8   If it is believed that the accused is likely to plead guilty at a summary trial, it is not necessary to prepare a schedule in advance. If, contrary to this belief, the accused pleads not guilty at a summary trial, or the offence is to be tried on indictment, the disclosure officer must ensure that a schedule is prepared as soon as is reasonably practicable after that happens.

(c)   Way in which material is to be listed on schedule

6.9   The disclosure officer should ensure that each item of material is listed separately on the schedule, and is numbered consecutively. The description of each item should make clear the nature of the item and should contain sufficient detail to enable the prosecutor to decide whether he needs to inspect the material before deciding whether or not it should be disclosed.

6.10   In some enquiries it may not be practicable to list each item of material separately. For example, there may be many items of a similar or repetitive nature. These may be listed in a block and described by quantity and generic title.

6.11   Even if some material is listed in a block, the disclosure officer must ensure that any items among that material which might meet the test for primary prosecution disclosure are listed and described individually.

(d)   Treatment of sensitive material

6.12   Subject to paragraph 6.13 below, the disclosure officer must list on a sensitive schedule any material which he believes it is not in the public interest to disclose, and the reason for that belief. The schedule must include a statement that the disclosure officer believes the material is sensitive. Depending on the circum-stances, examples of such material may include the following among others:

— material relating to national security;
— material received from the intelligence and security agencies;
— material relating to intelligence from foreign sources which reveals sensitive intelligence gathering methods;
— material given in confidence;
— material which relates to the use of a telephone system and which is supplied to an investigator for intelligence purposes only;
— material relating to the identity or activities of informants, or under-cover police officers, or other persons supplying information to the police who may be in danger if their identities are revealed;
— material revealing the location of any premises or other place used for police surveillance, or the identity of any person allowing a police officer to use them for surveillance;
— material revealing, either directly or indirectly, techniques and methods relied upon by a police officer in the course of a criminal investigation, for example covert surveillance techniques, or other methods of detecting crime;
— material whose disclosure might facilitate the commission of other offences or hinder the prevention and detection of crime;
— internal police communications such as management minutes;
— material upon the strength of which search warrants were obtained;
— material containing details of persons taking part in identification parades;
— material supplied to an investigator during a criminal investigation which has been generated by an official of a body concerned with the regulation or supervision of bodies corporate or of persons engaged in financial activities, or which has been generated by a person retained by such a body;
— material supplied to an investigator during a criminal investigation which relates to a child or young person and which has been generated by a local authority social services department, an Area Child Protection Committee or other party contacted by an investigator during the investigation.

6.13 In exceptional circumstances, where an investigator considers that ma-terial is so sensitive that its revelation to the prosecutor by means of an entry on the sensitive schedule is inappropriate, the existence of the material must be revealed to the prosecutor separately. This will apply where compromising the material would be likely to lead directly to the loss of life, or directly threaten national security.

6.14 In such circumstances, the responsibility for informing the prosecutor lies with the investigator who knows the detail of the sensitive material. The investiga-tor should act as soon as is reasonably practicable after the file containing the prosecution case is sent to the prosecutor. The investigator must also ensure that the prosecutor is able to inspect the material so that he can assess whether it needs to be brought before a court for a ruling on disclosure.

Revelation of material to prosecutor

7.1   The disclosure officer must give the schedules to the prosecutor. Wherever practicable this should be at the same time as he gives him the file containing the material for the prosecution case (or as soon as is reasonably practicable after the decision on mode of trial or the plea, in cases to which paragraph 6.8 applies).

7.2   The disclosure officer should draw the attention of the prosecutor to any material an investigator has retained (whether or not listed on a schedule) which may fall within the test for primary prosecution disclosure in the Act, and should explain why he has come to that view.

7.3   At the same time as complying with the duties in paragraphs 7.1 and 7.2, the disclosure officer must give the prosecutor a copy of any material which falls into the following categories (unless such material has already been given to the prosecutor as part of the file containing the material for the prosecution case):

— records of the first description of a suspect given to the police by a potential witness, whether or not the description differs from that of the alleged offender;

— information provided by an accused person which indicates an explanation for the offence with which he has been charged;

— any material casting doubt on the reliability of a confession;

— any material casting doubt on the reliability of a witness;

— any other material which the investigator believes may fall within the test for primary prosecution disclosure in the Act.

7.4   If the prosecutor asks to inspect material which has not already been copied to him, the disclosure officer must allow him to inspect it. If the prosecutor asks for a copy of material which has not already been copied to him, the disclosure officer must give him a copy. However, this does not apply where the disclosure officer believes, having consulted the officer in charge of the investigation, that the material is too sensitive to be copied and can only be inspected.

7.5   If material consists of information which is recorded other than in writing, whether it should be given to the prosecutor in its original form as a whole, or by way of relevant extracts recorded in the same form, or in the form of a transcript, is a matter for agreement between the disclosure officer and the prosecutor.

Subsequent action by disclosure officer

8.1   At the time a schedule of non-sensitive material is prepared, the disclosure officer may not know exactly what material will form the case against the accused, and the prosecutor may not have given advice about the likely relevance of particular items of material. Once these matters have been determined, the disclosure officer must give the prosecutor, where necessary, an amended schedule listing any additional material:

— which may be relevant to the investigation,

—   which does not form part of the case against the accused,
—   which is not already listed on the schedule, and
—   which he believes is not sensitive,

unless he is informed in writing by the prosecutor that the prosecutor intends to disclose the material to the defence.

8.2   After a defence statement has been given, the disclosure officer must look again at the material which has been retained and must draw the attention of the prosecutor to any material which might reasonably be expected to assist the defence disclosed by the accused; and he must reveal it to him in accordance with paragraphs 7.4 and 7.5 above.

8.3   Section 9 of the Act imposes a continuing duty on the prosecutor, for the duration of criminal proceedings against the accused, to disclose material which meets the tests for disclosure (subject to public interest considerations). To enable him to do this, any new material coming to light should be treated in the same way as the earlier material.

Certification by disclosure officer

9.1   The disclosure officer must certify to the prosecutor that, to the best of his knowledge and belief, all material which has been retained and made available to him has been revealed to the prosecutor in accordance with this code. He must sign and date the certificate. It will be necessary to certify not only at the time when the schedule and accompanying material is submitted to the prosecutor, but also when material which has been retained is reconsidered after the accused has given a defence statement.

Disclosure of material to accused

10.1   If material has not already been copied to the prosecutor, and he requests its disclosure to the accused on the ground that:

—   it falls within the test for primary or secondary prosecution disclosure, or
—   the court has ordered its disclosure after considering an application from the accused,

the disclosure officer must disclose it to the accused.

10.2   If material has been copied to the prosecutor, and it is to be disclosed, whether it is disclosed by the prosecutor or the disclosure officer is a matter for agreement between the two of them.

10.3   The disclosure officer must disclose material to the accused either by giving him a copy or by allowing him to inspect it. If the accused person asks for a copy of any material which he has been allowed to inspect, the disclosure officer must give it to him, unless in the opinion of the disclosure officer that is either not practicable (for example because the material consists of an object which cannot be copied, or because the volume of material is so great), or not desirable (for example because the material is a statement by a child witness in relation to a sexual offence).

10.4   If material which the accused has been allowed to inspect consists of information which is recorded other than in writing, whether it should be given to the accused in its original form or in the form of a transcript is a matter for the discretion of the disclosure officer. If the material is transcribed, the disclosure officer must ensure that the transcript is certified to the accused as a true record of the material which has been transcribed.

10.5   If a court concludes that it is in the public interest that an item of sensitive material must be disclosed to the accused, it will be necessary to disclose the material if the case is to proceed. This does not mean that sensitive documents must always be disclosed in their original form: for example, the court may agree that sensitive details still requiring protection should be blocked out, or that documents may be summarised, or that the prosecutor may make an admission about the substance of the material under section 10 of the Criminal Justice Act 1967.

Appendix 4

CRIMINAL PROCEDURE AND INVESTIGATIONS ACT 1996
PART I: DISCLOSURE
RIGHTS AND DUTIES OF ACCUSED PERSONS

1. The Criminal Procedure and Investigations Act 1996 makes important changes to the law on prosecution and defence disclosure in criminal cases. This notice sets out your rights and duties under the relevant provisions. Please read it carefully and show it to your solicitor if you have one.

2. Although this notice is sent to you by the prosecutor, he cannot advise you on its contents and you should not approach him for advice.

Disclosure by the accused

3. Before the trial begins, the prosecutor must disclose to you prosecution material which he thinks might undermine the case against you. If there is no such material, he must write to you to say so. In either case, he must also send you a schedule of non-sensitive material at the same time.

4. *If your case is to be tried in the Crown Court,* you must give the prosecutor and the court a 'defence statement' containing certain information about your defence. This must—

(a)   set out in general terms the nature of your defence, i.e. the reasons for your intention to plead not guilty,

(b)   state the matters on which you disagree with the prosecution, and

(c)   state in each case the reason why you disagree.

5. If you have an alibi, you must give details of the alibi in the defence statement, including—

(a)   if you know it, the name and address of any witness you believe is able to give evidence in support of the alibi, or

(b)   any information you have which might be useful in finding any such witness.

'Evidence in support of an alibi' means 'evidence tending to show that by reason of the presence of the accused at a particular place or in a particular area at a particular time he was not, or was unlikely, to have been at the place where the offence is alleged to have been committed at the time of its alleged commission'.

6. You must give the defence statement within **14 days** of the prosecutor making disclosure to you. The 14-day period starts on the date when the prosecutor writes to you, not the date when you receive his letter. If you cannot give a defence statement within 14 days, you may ask the court for more time. The court will want to know why you cannot do so, and how much more time you need. If you apply for more time, you must—

(a) do so before the 14 days are up, and

(b) give the prosecutor a copy of your application.

7. Section 11 of the Act says that if you fail to comply with these requirements, certain consequences follow. You fail to comply with the requirements if you:

(a) do not give a defence statement, or

(b) give a defence statement after the end of the 14-day period, or after the end of any longer period of time allowed by the court, or

(c) set out inconsistent defences in the defence statement, or

(d) put forward a defence at trial which is different from any defence set out in the defence statement, or

(e) put forward evidence in support of an alibi at trial, without giving details of the alibi in the defence statement, or

(f) call a witness in support of an alibi at trial without giving details of the witness in the defence statement.

8. If you fail to comply with these requirements, the court (or, if the court allows, any other party) may comment on the failure to comply, and the jury may draw such inferences as appear proper in deciding whether you are guilty.

9. If you put forward a defence at trial which is different from any defence set out in the defence statement, then (when deciding whether to comment on the failure to comply) the court must consider the extent of the difference in the defences, and whether there is any justification for it.

10. You cannot be convicted solely on the basis of an inference drawn from a failure to comply with these requirements.

11. *If your case is to be tried in a magistrates' court*, you may give a defence statement if you wish (for example, to get further prosecution disclosure) but you are not required to do so. If you do not give a defence statement, no inference may be drawn. If you do give a defence statement, the same procedures apply as if your case was being tried in the Crown Court (paragraphs 4–10 above), except that there is no jury but the court may draw inferences from a failure to comply with the relevant requirements.

12. If you decide not to give a defence statement, your case may come to court more quickly if you tell the court and the prosecutor before the end of the 14-day period.

Right of accused person to apply for additional prosecution disclosure

13. If you give a defence statement, the prosecutor must then disclose to you any additional prosecution material which might reasonably be expected to assist

the defence which you disclosed in your defence statement. If there is no such material, he must write to you to say so.

14.   After this, if you have reason to believe that there is more prosecution material which has not been disclosed to you and which might reasonably be expected to assist the defence which you disclosed in your defence statement, you may apply to the court for an order to disclose it. You must—

(a)   identify the material you need, and

(b)   tell the court why you think it might assist your defence.

If you apply to the court, you must give the prosecutor a copy of your application. If you contact the prosecutor first, you may be able to obtain the material you need without having to apply to the court.

Right of accused person to apply for review of a non-disclosure ruling

15.   If the prosecutor has material which he ought to disclose to you, but which is sensitive for some reason, he may apply to the court for a ruling that on balance it is not in the public interest to disclose it.

16.   If the court rules against disclosure, you may ask the court to review its ruling. If you do so, you must—

(a)   say why you think the ruling should be reviewed, and

(b)   give the prosecutor a copy of your application.

Duty to treat disclosed material in confidence

17.   You may use material disclosed to you for the purposes of your trial, or (if you are convicted) in connection with any appeal. If you want to use the material for any other purpose, you must first apply to the court for permission to do so, and say why you want to use it. Your must also give a copy of your application to the prosecutor.

18.   If you use the material for any other purpose without getting the permission of the court, you may be liable to proceedings for contempt of court. If the court finds you guilty of contempt, it may commit you to custody for a specified period or fine you or both.

Bibliography

Allan, T.R.S., 'Public Interest Immunity and Minister's Responsibilities' [1993] Crim LR 660

Archbold, *Criminal Pleading, Evidence and Practice*, Mitchell, Stephen (ed.), 40th edn, London: Sweet and Maxwell, 1979

Archbold, *Criminal Pleading, Evidence and Practice*, Richardson, P.J. (ed.), 1993 edn, London: Sweet and Maxwell

Baldwin, John, 'Advance Disclosure: Problems Arising' (1988) 152 JP 259

Baldwin, John, and Mulvaney, Adele, 'Advance Disclosure in Magistrates' Courts' (1987) 151 JP 409

Bentil, J. Kodwo, 'Exclusion of evidence in criminal trial on ground of public policy' (1989) 153 JP 590, 608

Blackstone's Criminal Practice, 7th edn, London: Blackstone Press, 1997

Bowes, Michael, 'The supremacy of legal professional privilege: the Derby Magistrates Case' (1996) 4 *Archbold News* 5

Chitty, *A Practical Treatise on the Criminal Law*, London: Butterworths, 1816

Choo, Andrew L-T, *Abuse of Process and Judicial Stays of Criminal Proceedings*, Oxford: Clarendon Press, 1993

Code for Crown Prosecutors, London: Crown Prosecution Service, 1994

Code of Conduct of the Bar of England and Wales, London: General Council of the Bar, 1990

Conlon, Gerard, *Proved Innocent*, Harmondsworth: Penguin Books, 1990

Criminal Law Review, Editorial 'Disclosure and Disequilibrium' [1995] Crim LR 585

Criminal Procedure and Investigations Act 1996, Code of Practice, London: HMSO, 1997

Cross on Evidence, 7th edn, London: Butterworths, 1990

Crown Prosecution Service, Annual Report 1995/6, HC 425, London: HMSO, 1996

Denning Lord, *The Road to Justice*, London: Stevens, 1955

Devlin, Lord, *Report on the Evidence of Identification in Criminal Cases*, HC 338, London: HMSO, 1976

Devlin, Lord, *Trial by Jury*, London: Stevens, 1956

Diplock, Lord, *The Interception of Communications in Great Britain*, Cmnd 8191, London: HMSO, 1981

Director of Public Prosecutions, 'Justice for all – all for Justice', Tom Sargant Memorial Lecture, 28 November 1994

Duke-Cohan, David, 'In the Public Interest' (1994) LS Gaz 17

Dyer, Clare, 'Fishing for real abuses', *The Guardian*, 15 November 1994

Farquharson, The Hon Mr Justice, *Report on the Role of Prosecution Counsel*, May 1986

Feeney, Floyd, 'Advance Disclosure of the Prosecution Case', *Managing Criminal Justice*, Home Office Research and Planning Unit, 1985

Fennel, Phil, Harding, Christopher, Jorg, Nico and Swart, Bert (eds.), *Criminal Justice in Europe*, Oxford: Clarendon Press, 1995

Field, Stewart, and Young, James, 'Disclosure, Appeals and Procedural Traditions: *Edwards v United Kingdom*' [1994] Crim LR 264

Findlay, Mark, Odgers, Stephen, and Yeo, Stanley, *Australian Criminal Justice*, Melbourne, Australia: Oxford University Press, 1994

Fisher, Sir Henry, *Report into the circumstances leading to the trial of three persons arising out of the death of Maxwell Confait*, HC 90, London: HMSO, 1977

Foot, Paul, *Murder at the Farm*, London: Penguin Books, 1988

Foster, Charles, Wynn, Toby, and Ainley, Nicholas, *Disclosure and Confidentiality, A Practitioner's Guide*, London: FT Law and Tax, 1996

General Council of the Bar, *The Efficient Disposal of Business in the Crown Court*, 1992

Glynn, Joanna, 'Disclosure' [1993] Crim LR 841

Home Office, *Disclosure: Consultation Document*, Cm 2864, London: HMSO, 1995

Humphreys, Christmas, 'Address to Inns of Court Students Union' [1955] Crim LR 739–48

James, Rt Hon. Lord Justice, *Report of the Interdepartmental Committee on the Distribution of Criminal Business between the Crown Court and Magistrates' Courts*, Cmd 6323, London: HMSO, 1975

Jerrard, Rob R., 'The Police Officer's Notebook' (1993) 157 JP 6

Jones, Alun, QC, 'The Decline and Fall of the Preparatory Hearing' [1996] Crim LR 460

JUSTICE, *Miscarriages of Justice*, London: Justice, 1989

JUSTICE, *Science and the Administration of Justice*, London: Justice, 1991

Justice of the Peace, 'Notes of the Week – Disclosing the evidence' (1995) 159 JP 277

Kennedy, Ludovic, *Truth to Tell*, London: Bantam Press, 1991

Kenney's Outlines of Criminal Law, J.W. Cecil Turner (ed.), London: Cambridge University Press, 1962

Law Reform Committee of the Bar Council, *Disclosure – Home Office Consultation Document*, 1995

Legal Action Group, *Preventing Miscarriages of Justice*, London: LAG, 1993

Leng, Roger, 'Losing Sight of the Defendant: The Government's Proposals on Pretrial Disclosure' [1995] Crim LR 704

London Criminal Courts Solicitors Association, *Disclosure, A Response to the Home Office Consultation Paper*, 1995

Lord Chancellor's Department, Home Office, Legal Secretariat to the Law Officers, Consultation Paper on Long Criminal Trials, 1992

McLean, J.D., 'Informers and Agents Provocateurs' [1969] Crim LR 527

Mansfield, G. and Peay, J., *The Director of Public Prosecutions (Principles and Practices for the Crown Prosecutor)*, London: Tavistock Publications, 1987

Mansfield, Michael, QC, *Presumed Guilty*, London: Mandarin, 1994

Martin, The Hon. G. Arthur, *The Attorney General's Advisory Committee on Charge Screening, Disclosure and Resolution Discussions*, Ontario, 1993

May, Sir John, *Interim Report on Bomb Attacks in Guildford and Woolwich*, HC 556, London: HMSO, 1990

May, Sir John, *Report on the Bomb Attacks in Guildford and Woolwich*, HC 449, London: HMSO, 1994

Miller, Frank W., *Prosecution – The Decision to Charge a Suspect with a Crime*, Little, Brown & Co (Canada) Ltd, 1969

Mitchell, Andrew, 'Disclosure – whose responsibility?' (1993) 137 SJ 854

Morton, James, 'Advance Disclosure Rules – A Bugbear' (1988) 152 JP 104

Morton, James, *Bent Coppers*, London: Warner Books, 1994

O'Connor, Patrick, 'Prosecution Disclosure: Principle, Practice and Justice' [1992] Crim LR 464

Pannick, David, QC, 'When immunity is not in the public interest', *The Times*, 15 March 1994

Plotnikoff, Joyce, and Woolfson, Richard, *Prosecuting Child Abuse*, London: Blackstone Press, 1995

Police and Criminal Evidence Act 1984, Codes of Practice, London: HMSO, 1984

Pollard, Charles, 'A case for disclosure' [1994] Crim LR 42

Report of the Committee of Privy Councillors Appointed to Inquire into the Interception of Communications, Cmnd 283, London: HMSO, 1957

Report of the International Criminal Justice Seminar held at the London School of Economics, *The Role of the Prosecutor*, Prof. Hall-Williams, J.E. (ed.), London: Avebury, 1987

Report of the Working Party on Disclosure of Information to the Defence, Home Office, January 1978

Roberts, Paul, 'Remedies for Non-Disclosure after Ward' (1994) 9 *Archbold News* 5

Rose, David, *In the Name of the Law*, London: Jonathan Cape, 1996

Royal Commission on Criminal Justice, Cm 2263, London: HMSO, 1993

Royal Commission on Criminal Justice, *Research Study on the Role of Forensic Science Evidence in Criminal Proceeedings*, London: HMSO, 1993

Royal Commission on Criminal Procedure, Cmnd 8092-1, London: HMSO, 1981

Royal Commission on Police Powers and Criminal Procedure, Cmnd 3297, London: HMSO, 16 March 1929

Rozenberg, J., *The Search for Justice*, London: Hodder & Stoughton, 1994

Sharpe, Sybil, 'Covert Police Operations and the Discretionary Exclusion of Evidence' [1994] Crim LR 793

Smith, Prof. J.C., 'Criminal Appeals and the Criminal Cases Review Commission' (1995) 145 New LJ 533 and 572

Spencer, J.N., 'Advance Disclosure, The Effect of the Provisions' (1986) 150 JP 356

Spencer, Prof. J.R., 'The Criminal Appeal Act' (1995) 9 *Archbold News* 3

Stockdale, Eric, and Castle, Sylvia (eds.), *Criminal Justice under Stress*, London: Blackstone Press, 1992

Trow, M.J., *'Let Him Have It, Chris'*, London: Constable & Co., 1992

UNAFEI, *Criminal Justice Profiles in Asia*: United Nations Asia and Far East Institute, Tokyo, Japan, 1995

UNAFEI, *Resource Material Series Nos 39 to 46*: United Nations Asia and Far East Institute, Tokyo, Japan, 1990 to 1995

Walker, Clive, and Starmer, Keir (eds.), *Justice in Error*, London: Blackstone Press, 1993

Webb, Robert C., 'Public Interest Immunity: The Demise of the Duty to Assert' [1995] Crim LR 556

Zander, Michael, *A Matter of Justice*, Oxford: Oxford University Press, 1988

Index